Unsettling Beliefs

Teaching Theory to Teachers

A volume in
International Social Studies Forum: The Series
Richard Diem and Jeff Passe, *Series Editors*

Unsettling Beliefs

Teaching Theory to Teachers

Edited by

Josh Diem
University of Miami (FL)

and

Robert J. Helfenbein
Indiana University–Indianapolis

INFORMATION AGE PUBLISHING, INC.
Charlotte, NC • www.infoagepub.com

Library of Congress Cataloging-in-Publication Data

Unsettling beliefs : teaching theory to teachers / edited by Josh Diem and Robert J. Helfenbein.
    p. cm. – (International social studies forum the series)
   Includes bibliographical references.
   ISBN 978-1-59311-670-5 (pbk.) – ISBN 978-1-59311-671-2 (hardcover)
1. Teachers–Training of–United States. 2. Social sciences–Philosophy. I. Diem, Josh.
II. Helfenbein, Robert J.
  LB1715.U58 2007
  370.71'1–dc22   2007033619

Printed in the United States of America

*To the three people who mean everything to me—Erin, Max Levi,
and Rose Eden. Your unwavering love and support keeps me going
and serves as both a reminder and a source of strength to do my part
and embrace the responsibility we all have to make our world
a better place, and to write really long sentences.*
—Josh Diem

*To all the teachers—past, present, and becoming—that have inspired
and reminded me how this work matters. To my wife, Kellie for unending
support and an ability to challenge me like no other. And to my father,
who always wanted my/our name on the spine of a book.*
—Rob Helfenbein

CONTENTS

ACKNOWLEDGMENTS

We would like to express our deepest thanks to the contributors of this volume who made the daunting task of putting this book together so pleasurable. We would also like to thank the series editors, Rich Diem and Jeff Passe, for the opportunity to do this work which we all view as so important. Additionally, we would like to state a heartfelt thank you to all the folks at Information Age Publishing who made this book a reality. In particular, we are eternally grateful to George Johnson, Founder and Publisher, who gave us our first stab at putting together a book. Last, but certainly not least, we would like to thank our mutual mentor George Noblit. This book serves as a testament to the lessons we learned while lucky enough to receive your guidance and tutelage as we embarked on our academic careers.

—**Josh Diem and Rob Helfenbein**

FOREWORD

It is a matter of public record that economic, social, and educational inequalities in the United States are deep, persistent, and in many ways widening with each passing decade. The rich get richer and the poor get poorer not only in terms of economic wealth, but in the cultural capital that opens doors of opportunity and fulfillment of individual aspirations.

Public and private schools have long been implicated in this process that in the 1970s came to be called, somewhat benignly, the "social reproduction" of a stratified, racist, and sexist society that is structured to protect vested interests. For over 30 years, it has been clear to a great many students of national culture that, while education may serve some individuals well as a route to social mobility, state and local school systems in the U.S. do very little to disrupt the overall maldistribution of opportunity. On the one hand, the public supports its schools because they are believed to be important institutions in a democratic society. On the other, there seems very little reason to challenge the mature John Dewey's assertion, in "Education and Social Change," that schools are weak agents for leading social change; that schools are by their nature "conserving" institutions, and at best they can be *allies* of social changes that are already afoot (Dewey, 1937).

It is difficult for schools even to be meaningful allies of change, as many have argued from the right as well as the left, if teachers themselves are not capable agents of change. Whether the desired change is closing the achievement differences between different racial/ethnic groups; or helping students recognize and resist racism, sexism and homophobia in their daily lives; or developing in children and youth the capacity and commitment to become advocates for social justice in an oppressive culture, teachers matter. And here lies the challenge that is taken up by the editors and authors of this volume. Given that the hegemonic effects of socialization into an inequitable society have had their way with all of us to one degree

Unsettling Beliefs: Teaching Theory to Teachers, pages xi–xvi
Copyright © 2008 by Information Age Publishing
All rights of reproduction in any form reserved.

or another, and given that the schools have historically played a largely supportive role in that hegemony, where and how do teachers learn what it might mean for them to do anything other than serve established power? How can teachers, who are themselves products of the conserving institution called school, become critically thinking authors of institutional change who are able to serve the best interests of their students rather than the interests of the status quo? What kind of professional preparation and development of teachers would this call for, and what does it look like, in practice?

Teacher educators throughout the nation struggle with these questions, and Social Foundations teacher educators in particular feel their urgency. Since its origins in the 1930s, the field of Social Foundations of Education has explicitly targeted the need to engage prospective and practicing teachers and administrators in new ways of understanding a world they thought they already understood. The problem is much older, of course, as Plato's *Republic* tries to illustrate with its parables and allegories of the ship's captain, the cave, and the divided line, among others. But this first became salient as an essential problem in the field of Social Foundations of Education the moment the self-conscious effort to create such a field took shape.

What this book recognizes, in essay after essay, is that helping people learn new ways of seeing a familiar world is no easy task. The editors tell us in the introduction, for example:

> What we intend to do in this book is to provide the reader with a diverse array of perspectives on exactly what goes on when you teach social theory to a group of pre-service teachers who upon entering teacher education programs think that teacher education is learning about lesson plans and classroom management, and instead they get a discussion on Neo-liberalism and its impact on the discourse of accountability and testing. We will include pieces where professionals reflect on their experiences teaching various strains of social theory, as well as offer advice on pedagogical practices that have been effective.

Of course, the discussion of Neo-liberalism is just an illustration of the many different theoretical perspectives that are brought to bear in the volume. The array of perspectives is diverse as promised, the professional reflections are as advertised, and the advice on pedagogical practices is instructive. This volume makes a distinctively valuable contribution to a decades-old conversation about how social theory should be taught in teacher preparation programs. That is, these chapters have something new to say about the unsettling of beliefs that were once settled—helping educators and prospective educators learn to examine beliefs that are otherwise unexamined.

This conversation about how to unsettle teachers' beliefs began in more than one place and time, but certainly one seminal influence was George Counts's volume, *The Social Foundations of Education* (1934). Like the present volume, which is sponsored by the International Social Studies Forum, the Counts book had a social studies connection. It was commissioned by the American Historical Association as volume IX of their study of social studies in the nation's schools. As a professor at Teachers College Columbia, Counts was part of the (William Heard) Kilpatrick study group that met for a number of years in the 1930s and 40s and led to the deliberate founding of a new pedagogical enterprise, which the group called the Social Foundations of Education (Butts, 1993).

Counts's book makes a strong case for the importance of the teacher education institution becoming "a place for the study of American culture in its historic and world connections," where "the most profound questions of national policy should be debated and understood." He concludes that if teachers understood the significance of the school in an imperfectly democratic society, they would learn to "champion the cause of the masses of people" (p. 558). At the same time, he is not optimistic about this happening, given the preponderance of social and economic institutions that socialize people against democratic values. He concluded his discussion of the need for a new approach to teacher preparation as follows: "Any completely satisfactory solution to the problem of education therefore would seem to involve fairly radical social reconstruction" (p. 560).

In over 560 pages of text about the political, economic, and social underpinnings of education in the United States, Counts neglected to address *how* teachers should be taught to become champions of the masse. Since that time, with a few notable exceptions, this has largely been true of the history of the field; hence, this new volume. Its editors and authors, apparently not content to wait for a "radical social reconstruction," are tackling the question of how teachers can be taught in ways that will best disrupt power and privilege, best serve democratic ideals, in the schools.

This volume devotes little space to the question of *whether* teacher preparation in general, and social foundations coursework in particular, should serve social forces tending toward a more democratic society. Rather, the democratic ethic of the public school is taken largely as a given and these chapters address what that means and how it can be accomplished. More pointedly, these chapters ask, how can current and prospective teachers and administrators learn to think in more disciplined ways about the gap between democratic ideals and their practice as educators? How do we get people to *change their minds*, in effect, about ideas and taken-for-granteds so deeply held that their very identities may depend on them? What are the necessary pedagogies?

As a member of the Kilpatrick discussion group at Teachers College, Counts contributed to shaping the pedagogy of the first required course in social foundations of education, ED200F (Butts, 1993, Rugg, 1941). Sections of ED200F were team-taught by the likes of Counts, R. Freeman Butts, Kenneth Benne, and occasionally advanced doctoral students such as the young Lawrence Cremin. The idea of teaming was partly to create a multi-theoretical discourse that would engage student in thinking critically about the extent to which society and its schools were living up to democratic ideals. But what taken-for-granteds were confronted in these classes, and how were they confronted? To what extent did social theory enable these classes to challenge racism, whiteness, patriarchy, and heteronormativity, for example, and what were the details of the pedagogy? And if the students resisted new ways of thinking, then what?

While it is clearly beyond the scope of this Foreword to comment on all those who have contributed to the conversation since Counts in the 1930s and ED200F in the 1940s (see Rugg, 1941), it is worth noting that every decade since then has brought new contributions to this discussion. In the 1950s, for example, the Social Foundations division at University of Illinois produced an ambitious volume of original readings in social theory and critique by such authors as Malinowski, Margaret Mead, the Lynds, Gunnar Myrdal, and C. Wright Mills, in which the editors argued the need for teachers to "overcome the tendency to take for granted, as somehow 'natural,' existing educational polices and practices" (Stanley, Smith, Benne, and Anderson, 1955, p. 6.). But the pedagogy envisioned by the authors was not well articulated. In the 1960s, Charles Brauner; in the 1970s, Maxine Greene (1976) and the first edition of the *Standards for Academic and Professional Instruction in Foundations of Education, Educational Studies, and Educational Policy Studies* (1978) repeatedly addressed the aims and methods of social foundations instruction. The *Standards* were re-published and then revised in 1986 and 1996, respectively. Also in the 1980s and 1990s, with Stuart McAninch (1986), Bonnie Armbruster and others (1994), I tried to explore the role of social foundations in the professional preparation of teachers. And more recently, in 2005, Dan Butin's edited volume, *Teaching Social Foundations of Education*, not only explored some of the contemporary challenges of teaching the foundations, but it also reproduced several syllabi to allow readers to see what different scholars do in the foundations classroom.

But this volume is different from all of those; it goes deeper than any of them into the praxis, that nexus of theory and practice, of teaching teachers to think in unaccustomed ways. Part of its newness lies in bringing together so many different approaches, in content and method, and part of it lies in the authors' reflective depth and detail in describing the pedagogical challenges of trying to pull people from the cave, in Plato's image.

Conceptual approaches range from human rights education to prophetic pragmatism to the theory and practice of teacher learning-teams in schools. Pedagogical approaches range from the use of media portrayals of educators and schools, to virtual field experiences, to engaging students in social theorizing, and finally to addressing student resistance to new theoretical perspectives. All of these conceptual and pedagogical approaches are illuminating not just for social foundations teachers, but for teacher educators in general.

Like those earlier efforts, this volume stands squarely within an approach to teacher education that values social critique. And like those who founded the field of social foundations of education, it portrays not only a multitheoretical field of study but a professional pedagogical enterprise—an approach to preparing professionals for particular roles in an inadequately democratic culture. But more than those earlier volumes, this book invites the reader to struggle with the *pedagogy* of preparing teachers in particular institutional contexts in a specific historical moment. It does not solve the problem of how to get people to see more critically and how to become agents of democratic change in the conserving atmosphere of the school. But it gives us reason to believe that these goals are now being achieved by different scholars, in different ways, in different settings. This book therefore offers not simply a language of critique, or a language of possibility, but a language of demonstration. It moves the conversation forward.

Steve Tozer

Past President, American Educational Studies Association (AESA)
Professor of Policy Studies
College of Education
University of Illinois at Chicago

REFERENCES

Brauner, C. J. (1964). *American educational theory*. Englewood Cliffs: Prenctice-Hall.

Butin, D. W. (2005) *Teaching Social Foundations of Education*. Mahwah, NJ: Erlbaum.

Butts, R. F. (1993) *In the first person singular: The foundations of education*. San Francisco: Caddo Gap Press.

Council of Learned Societies in Education. (1996). *Standards for academic and professional instruction in foundations of education, educational studies, and educational policy studies* (2nd ed.). San Francisco: Author.

Counts, G. S. (1934). *The social foundations of education*. New York: Scribner.

Dewey, J. (1937). Education and social change, in *The Social Frontier, 3*(May), 235–237.

Greene, M (1976). Challenging mysticiation: Educational foundations in dark times. *Educational Studies, 7*(1), 9–29.

Rugg, H., & Division I, (1941) In Foundations of Education, Teachers College, Columbia University (Eds.), *Readings in the Foundations of Education.* New York: Teachers College Press.

Stanley, W. O., Smith, B. O., Benne, K. D., & Anderson, A. W. (1955). *Social foundations of education.* New York: Holt, Rinehart and Winston.

Tozer, S., & McAninch, S. (1986). Social foundations of education in historical perspective. *Educational Foundations, 1*(1), 5–32.

Tozer, S., Armbruster, B., & Anderson, T. (1994). *Foundational studies in teacher education: A Re-examination.* New York: Teachers College Press.

INTRODUCTION

Joshua Diem and Robert Helfenbein

In the summer of 2004 we were completing our PhDs and teaching a Master of Arts in Teaching (MAT) level course titled "Introduction to Schools". We taught the course to students who were just beginning the MAT program, and they were taking this course concurrently with a course titled "Introduction to Teaching". These courses served not only as an introduction to graduate school for most of these students, but also as an introduction to education as a field of study. The program, as many MAT programs are, was comprised of people from a diverse array of educational, professional, and personal backgrounds. A vast majority of the students had little or no educational background in the field of education. Though diverse in terms of age and life experiences, the group was fairly homogeneous in terms of race, ethnicity, and sexuality. That is to say that most of the students were young, white, heterosexual middle class women.

The stated purpose of the course was to provide an introduction to the study of schools and schooling as historically/politically/culturally-rooted social institutions. Essentially, the course was an introduction to the social foundations of education. Given the broad stated scope of the course, our own orientations as scholars, and the fact that we were graduate students about to leave the institution we were teaching in, we decided to take a somewhat bold move and teach the course almost exclusively as a social theory course. We used Peter McLaren's seminal text, *Life in Schools*, as our primary text, added in some articles and book chapters from authors that ranged from the right to the left of the political spectrum, and led the students down a path of examining the practices of schooling and the institution of schools through various theoretical lenses. This was an interesting experience to say the least.

Unsettling Beliefs: Teaching Theory to Teachers, pages xvii–xx
Copyright © 2008 by Information Age Publishing
All rights of reproduction in any form reserved.

We say that we made a bold move by deciding to teach the course as a social theory course, but that move was not necessarily explicitly planned out ahead of time. It just happened. We approached the course as our chance to design our very own graduate level course on the social foundations of education from scratch, as the course had been taught for many years by the same professor who had begun to phase out of teaching summer school. One isolated decision after another, along with where the students wanted the course to go, led us down the road of exploring the role of schools in American society through the various theoretical orientations we employed. We did this while stressing the importance of understanding schools as a social institution that can and should be examined using various perspectives and how issues like race, gender, class, and sexuality can attempted to be explained and understood using these perspectives. As we continued down this road we kept saying to each other that we needed to read about the experiences other instructors had with the issues we were dealing with. What pedagogical approaches were others using? What theoretical viewpoints were other people teaching? What were the students' reactions? These were the questions that we felt we needed to answer.

What we found was that there is a glaring hole in the literature regarding precisely these issues. More directly, though social foundations professors across the country are engaged in the practice of teaching social theory to pre-service teachers in their social foundations courses, there does not seem to be a body of literature that addresses the multitude of issues associated with this practice. Those who make the claim of teaching social foundations are writing about social foundations, and those who make the claim of teaching teacher education courses are writing about issues associated with teacher education, but not explicitly about the connection of the two. This is the case even though many of the same people are engaged in the teaching social foundations and training pre-service teachers, many times by training teachers exclusively in social foundations courses. Additionally, after examining the literature that we did find, we were left with an overwhelming feeling that the literature we were reading was talking to and people, and with people. This seemingly obvious lack of communication seemed ripe for scholarly study and is precisely the literary hole we believe that this book can begin to fill.

We began to discuss various ideas of how we could tackle this issue, and then broadened our conversation to friends and colleagues across the country who we knew were engaged in the exact practice we were engaged in. We were not surprised to find that our colleagues agreed with our assessment that this is an issue that is practiced but not studied or written about enough. What we also found was that this phenomenon is happening across the country in public and private universities, in college towns and major urban areas, and the pedagogical approaches employed and theoretical perspectives explored are incredibly diverse. This screamed "EDITED BOOK!" to us.

What we intend to do in this book is to provide the reader with a diverse array of perspectives on exactly what goes on when you teach social theory to a group of pre-service teachers who upon entering teacher education programs think that teacher education is learning about lesson plans and classroom management, and instead they get a discussion on Neo-liberalism and its impact on the discourse of accountability and testing. We will include pieces where professionals reflect on their experiences teaching various strains of social theory, as well as offer advice on pedagogical practices that have been effective.

The intended audience for this book is students and faculty members in Schools/Colleges of Education that seek to learn more about the process and role of social foundations courses in teacher education programs. While the text, or parts thereof, can be used for virtually any level, the two primary audiences are social foundation courses in teacher education programs and courses dealing with pedagogical aspects involved in the teaching of social theory. In addition, we believe that many faculty members will be interested in reading about the issues faced by their peers across the country when engaged in the practice of teaching social theory in teacher education programs. Furthermore, we believe that the contributing authors will have a great deal to offer not only in terms of reflections on experiences, but also in terms of pedagogical approaches that seem to work well in this practice.

The contributors we assembled represent a diverse and wide-ranging group of scholars that offer diversity in terms of race, gender, age, sexuality, geography, pedagogical orientation, and theoretical interests. The book includes chapters that have a variety of foci, including the following: different pedagogies employed in the exploration of social theory in teacher education and how they have/can succeed and fail; scholars' reflections on the process of teaching social theory to a sometimes unreceptive audience; scholars' reflections on the various institutional ideologies about the role of social theory in teacher education programs; and how different students resist the idea of the importance of learning social theory in a teacher education program.

Again, the purpose of this book is to begin dialogues about the issues that the various contributors address. We have all presented our work here because we want to have conversations and exchange ideas about the issues that we care about and that drive our professional lives. Our traditional means of producing artifacts that we present as representations of our ideas and work (articles, books, etc.) are not the best means for exchange, nor do we believe are they intended to be such. Understanding that, we include the email addresses of each contributor at the end of each chapter.

We hope that you see these chapters as the first step in a long procession of exchanges that can ultimately lead to a better understanding of the issues presented here.

CHAPTER 1

UNSETTLING BELIEFS

A Cultural Studies Approach
to Teacher Education

Robert J. Helfenbein
Indiana University–Indianapolis

ABSTRACT

This chapter deals with how people become teachers, how they take up that new identity of *teacher*. By using examples from student work in teacher education courses in urban settings, the chapter argues that students doing cultural studies work themselves on the representations of teachers and education in general leads to critical and reflective identity work. In this way, the hope is to both deal with unsettling beliefs that we all bring to new situations and to explicitly unsettle beliefs as we pursue teacher education in the transformative tradition.

"First of all," he said, "If you can learn a simple trick, Scout, you'll get along a lot better with all kinds of folks. You never really understand a person until you consider things from his point of view..."
"Sir?"
"...until you climb into his skin and walk around in it

—Lee (1988, p. 33)

Unsettling Beliefs: Teaching Theory to Teachers, pages 1–14
Copyright © 2008 by Information Age Publishing

This chapter begins with reflections on teaching social foundations courses at two universities and attempts to introduce cultural studies as a methodology for understanding school and society and as a pedagogical approach to teacher education. Specifically, this study examines preservice teachers' views of the representations of school and schooling in forms of popular culture (i.e. Young Adolescent Literature or TV/film). These reflections begin in the position that popular culture phenomena hold rich possibilities for educational researchers. Stated simply: Representations of teachers and schooling matter. But, that being said, it is also important to clearly lay out what this paper is not. Cultural Studies as a field of inquiry has taken many forms and directions over the four decades it has existed with many attendant debates as to what is and what is not cultural studies (Gaztambide-Fernandez, Harding, & Sorde-Marti, 2004; Hytten 1998a; Johnson 1986/87). This paper will not take that project up. Cultural studies also often argues that popular culture forms and media literacy projects should become aspects of both curriculum and pedagogy as they are sites of meaning making in our contemporary world (Giroux 2004/1994/1981; Storey 1998) and, while I might agree, this too is not the project of this chapter. I will leave my position on those arguments as again stated simply: representations of school and schooling matter. Instead of taking up these debates, I come back to an essential question of cultural studies inquiry: what is at stake? What is at stake when preservice teachers take the representations of education in popular culture as an object of inquiry? What types of meaning do they make in such a project? And does it matter?

METHODOLOGY

This chapter explores the cultural studies work of preservice teachers *themselves* in the hopes of gleaning insight into the ever changing role/s of teacher in contemporary American society. How preservice teachers *themselves* interpret the representations of school and schooling in popular texts may also inform the work of teacher educators, opening a window into our students' thoughts as they begin the process of becoming teachers and try to connect the broader social context with the world of classrooms. It may, in effect, be another way to think about how one teaches theory to teachers.

This project involved an emergent qualitative research design that used student work from preservice education classes at a Midwestern university. The initial questions that led to this chapter came from experiences teaching undergraduate and Master of Arts in Teaching (MAT) level preservice education classes at another university and an interest in popular culture forms. Questions arose for me onhow one might use popular culture in the work of teaching teachers, both analytically and pedagogically. Participants included 40 undergraduate education majors, both elementary and secondary, from an urban Midwestern university recruited from two courses currently offered in the School of Education: Teaching and Learning in Middle School and Education and American Culture. Participation was voluntary and students were free to exclude themselves from the project at anytime during and after the semester. Analysis of student work took place after grades were turned in for the semester and, of course, there was no connection between grades for the course and participation in the research project.

Using qualitative research methods, themes generated from the student responses to class assignments in relation to teacher representations in popular culture illuminated both consistent and contested threads of meaning. As cultural studies inquiry is premised on the notion that meaning is never guaranteed and that often individuals hold multiple and contradictory positions in relation to texts (Hytten, 1998a), these conclusions were not disturbing but rather served to reinforce both findings and method.

Also appropriate in a cultural studies inquiry is the explicit positioning of myself as researcher—and in this case instructor—within the scope of the research project. Without question, part of the pedagogy used in these two classes was an argument that popular culture forms do indeed matter and student work would naturally reflect (or cautiously reject) that central premise. In large part, the realities of the student/instructor relationship preclude any reliable findings as to cultural studies as an instructional tool (but, again: not the project). Thus, the pedagogical choice is considered a given and the research questions revolve around what students *did* with these assignments. It should also be noted that I, as instructor, was largely disappointed with the ways in which my students analyzed and/or read these texts. In my view, students were engaging with the representations in their chosen texts in shallow and cursory ways, not thinking very hard. Besides reflecting standard teacher frustration, this too reflects the lack of guarantee in the meaning making of students and *might* prove my central premise wrong. However, as the rest of the paper lays out, I don't think it does.

A CULTURAL STUDIES APPROACH

Cultural studies is an expressly left intellectual project that is political, interventionist, socially committed, ethically charged and critical. Its aims are both to interpret cultural phenomenon and to intervene in the world in transformative an empowering ways. (Hytten, 1998a, n.p.)

The acknowledgement that cultural studies as an approach is both intellectual and interventionist seems particularly relevant to the work of teacher education. Indeed, what we try to do in teacher education is to introduce those who would teach to both the realities of school and schooling in contemporary society but also to instill some degree of empowerment, a sense that they as effective teachers can work towards a more progressive future. Perhaps these two goals not only reflect a fundamental tension in the work of teacher education but help explain some of the forbidden appeal of cultural studies; its own rejection of the dichotomy and willing embrace of the inherent contradictions cut too close to home. But to push the point further, Hytten (1998b) suggests that cultural studies work includes an ethical imperative—one that should not be lost here. She writes: "The ethical point is that academic work is not simply a commodity for other intellectuals, but should help individuals to better understand their lives and conditions so that they can then work towards positively altering them." (p. 253)

But, of course, herein lies the rub as we can run the risk of pursuing academic work both in terms of personal research and curriculum in our courses that effectively ignores the needs of our students. This often, too, comes down to the job we do of communicating to our preservice teachers the intentions of our efforts.

Culture, as a process, involves the ways in which meaning is made of self, society, and the interactions that inform social practices (Fiske 1989; Grossberg, Nelson, & Treichler 1992; Storey 1998). Therefore, the ways in which the institution of schooling is represented in a popular text reflect, at least to some degree, popular conceptions of governmental institutions, schooling, teachers and the ways in which they interact. It is important to note that the texts these students engaged are indeed of *popular culture*—a troubling term at best and the subject of extensive debate amongst cultural studies scholars (for examples see Storey 1998). Further, to bring in the popular is not to say that ideologies are not at work in these texts (i.e. market, patriarchal, or even neoconservative politics), but rather that because it is dependent on the pleasure of the reader, popular culture must necessarily be *popular*—resonating with readers in ways that are not guaranteed, that perhaps provide a possibility for resistance.[1] As Fiske (1989) states, "there is always an element of popular culture that lies outside social control, that escapes or opposes hegemonic forces" (p. 2). In this way, popular culture always operates on the level of the semiotic and reflects the tension between ideological forces in its production and the unpredictable possibilities in the reading of texts. It is precisely those spaces of escape or opposition in relation to larger structural forces—that pedagogical possibility to unsettle beliefs—in teacher education that this chapter explores.

I suggest that popular culture forms can prove to be beneficial teaching tools in the educational foundations training of future teachers and that this study may enlighten such work. This qualitative project expands on the cultural studies work of preservice teachers themselves in the hopes of gleaning insight into the ever changing role of the teacher in contemporary society. How preservice teachers themselves interpret the representations of school and schooling in popular texts may also inform the work of teacher educators (Trier 2004), opening a window into our students' thoughts as they begin the process of becoming teachers and try to connect the broader social context with the world of classrooms.

The ultimate object of cultural studies is not, in my view, the text,
but the social life of subjective forms at each moment of their circulation,
including their textual embodiments.

—Johnson, 1986/87, p. 62

To take up a cultural studies approach then—for both this chapter and the tasks given to preservice teachers—is not to analyze these texts *per se* but rather to think of them as embodied in particular, complex social interactions. As Giroux reminds us in a discussion on Stuart Hall, "Culture is the social field where power repeatedly mutates; identities are constantly in transit; and agency is often located where it is least acknowledged (2000, p. 141). For the students in my courses of teacher education, these interactions revolve primarily in the work of *becoming teachers*. Returning to the point of intentionality, this term, *becoming teachers*, was repeatedly used in these courses referring to the preservice teachers in the hopes that they would see themselves as actively within a fluid process. Necessarily, the students in these classes are reading these texts in ways they haven't or wouldn't have before; they are reading, or at least beginning to read, as teachers.

Cultural studies is politically driven…is committed to producing knowledge
that both helps people understand that the world is changeable and
that offers some direction for how to change it.

—Grossberg, 1997, p. 264

The work of teacher education is not only engaging in the project of becoming but also in the disruption of already-held views, the creation of intellectual dissonance around issues of learning, teaching and the social world of school; here is where we wish to unsettle beliefs. But certainly, those of us engaged in this complex project have intentional aims and our visions of the world that we would like educators to work toward. Herein lies some troubled ground as most scholars in education embrace a constructivist view of learning and interaction with children. Perhaps with some level of contradiction then, we turn to our preservice teachers and encourage particular views of the world and the ways in which they interact with the lived experience of schools—our views. How does one combine a "forceful political history of the present" (McRobbie, 2000, p. 214) with the acknowledgement that classrooms should be spaces in which students are allowed/encouraged to make meaning in their own ways? Again appears the conundrum that serves as the impetus for this book. My answer, at least in part, is that one possibility might be for teacher educators to validate the cultural studies work of the preservice teachers themselves, to provide the theory (or perhaps more colloquially, "some language") to help with understanding the things they have experienced in schools and are increasingly turning their attention to.

This way of thinking describes this author's own experience with Cultural Studies. As a young doctoral student fresh out of a high school social studies position, my struggles with inferiority in relation to peers fresh from scholarly master's level work in educational theory were balanced by an excitement with theory as precisely "some language" to get at what I long felt as an inadequacy of understanding what was happening in the classrooms I had inhabited. What this author found in Cultural Studies was a lively home for scholars and students interested in theory—typically contemporary social theory and its application to some discipline that does not necessarily welcome such pursuits.

Why Pay Attention?

A portion of the qualitative data represented here comes from a capstone course in Educational Foundations for those studying to be elementary school teachers. Not a field known for an explicit engagement with theory, elementary level teacher education suffers from its own set of stereotypes that do not need to be perpetuated here; but, it might be fair to say that the course syllabus for this course was seen as burdensome. The fact that these students had completed one 8-week portion of the required student teaching experience is not without note. These students had already taken a first stab at teaching children and this final capstone course was a brief hiatus before they ventured yet again into an unknown classroom environment with new children to meet and attempt to teach. Common authors were present (Dewey, Tyack & Cuban, Giroux, Grumet) but perhaps what differed was the requirement to write critical book reviews that showed engagement with the theoretical material of the course in relation to texts that included some representation of youth, teachers, teaching, or school. These students took not only their own personal experiences with schooling into this exercise but also beginning experiences with teaching; it mattered.

Initial responses to questions about popular culture and its import to educators tended to revolve around the notions of "student-centered" pedagogy. The preservice teachers felt that as popular culture forms were such an important part of the mediated lives of today's children—as in "this is the stuff children pay attention to"—teachers needed to pay attention in order to be able to effectively interact with their students. One response reflected in a way that tied this "connection with children" to a relevance between school and home life:

> I think our purpose for making the connection with children is to let them know that we hear and see the same things they do, and that we are not ignoring outside influences just because we are in school. It all ties into incorporating their lives outside of school with what we do in school.

These reactions reflect an appreciation for understanding the lives of children and the positive effects that effort might have on learning but fail to center their own involvement in these cultural forces. Later responses start to get at something a little more interesting; two students point to why preservice teachers might be uneasy when dealing with these representations of teachers and school They write:

> I think it is essential that we pay close attention to the perceptions that are made by popular culture of school and schooling. I think we separate ourselves from the image of the teacher/school that is portrayed through popular culture because that is the one thing we strive not to become. I know that I pay close attention to the images of schools and teachers that I read about...because typically that is on the other side of the spectrum from the place I wish to be.

> What is portrayed is the exact opposite of what we are all working so hard to achieve in our future classrooms. We need to focus some of our attention on pop culture to help us get a better understanding on how schools and us as educators are being portrayed to children. Hopefully by making ourselves aware we can help to change some of the negative stereotypes that are out there and coming into classrooms with our students.

In these two reactions, the preservice teachers speak in terms of knowing resistance to the images of school and schooling in popular forms; they are very aware of the ways in which the work they have decided to embark on is portrayed and are struggling against what are termed "stereotypes." These students are negotiating a teacher identity, a teacher self that, in and of itself, is a negotiation with larger cultural forces. It is here where I suggest that what these preservice teachers are doing is, as defined in this chapter, the beginning of a cultural studies project.

The process of becoming often begins with some determinations of what one does *not* want to become. Although, whether or not these views constitute rebellion as these interactions also reflect the views of the larger School of Education would be questionable, this naming and placing of oneself in an oppositional position represents an important move. Indeed, this type of positioning is precisely what we wish our students to do and it is often lamented that the frustration of our graduates lies in the seeing practice in "real-world" schools that contradicts much if not all they were taught by teacher educators. While I am hesitant to suggest that this is some revelatory answer, could it be that this intentional cognizance of teacher self as oppositional might be fruitful? Could it be that teacher representations in popular culture more accurately reflect the lived experiences of schools than we like to admit? If this is so, then perhaps calling this out, naming it, and placing ourselves in oppositional stances provides a more coherent logic in which students can place themselves.

Over the course of the semester, student comments on popular culture and education continued on this reflective path. Where I might characterize the opening forays into this discussion as rather cursory—perhaps even saying what they thought I wanted to hear—as time passed and the conversation continued, students began to put themselves into an analysis of how young people interact with larger cultural forces. One student makes the call explicit by asking the class on the online discussion forum, "has talking about pop culture made you think about the pop culture in your school days? Did it have any impact on your education or the way you viewed school?" Another student stated something even more compelling,

> I think everyone is a product of cultural pedagogy, whether it is positive or negative. Our families, friends, experience have shaped our cultural attitudes. Therefore, as teachers, we need to think about the critical pedagogy that Giroux is known for. We can help students think about their cultural pedagogy and society's attitudes about race and class and work towards making them better.

This preservice teacher has expanded her view of both culture and pedagogy—in fact even defining a term for herself, cultural pedagogy—beyond both the static views of education and culture and even the more critical reaction to popular culture to include the notion that culture itself teaches and, as teachers, we are only part of a larger process. This student proposes an interchange between what she calls "cultural pedagogy" and critical pedagogy that begins with teachers encouraging an introspective look that, as Grossberg says, is politically driven.

Another student, in response to the prompt "Why pay attention to popular culture?" responds with an complex view of the operation of schools. In it, she cites the textbook of another class (Elementary Social Studies Methods) but presents a remarkably "cultural studies" view of how society and institutions intertwine. She states:

> Popular culture often humorously portrays traditional teachers as didactic and wielding power. In contrast, children now have a voice in the classroom and teachers are listening. Learner and society interactions, along with experiences students bring to school, reflect society at large. "Culture...serves as a guide for human behavior in any given society" (Parker, W.C., 2005, p. 145). Students and teachers are greatly influenced by popular culture evolving from global connections, technological advances, the media, and diverse family structures. As in the past, competition between and stereotypes of teachers, students, and schools remains a driving force in how schools operate.

This student, in pointing to the "competition between and stereotypes of" cogently points to the complex interplay of forces that act upon the lived experience of schools for both teachers and students. Indeed, this future educator already sees herself as a producer and *product of* classroom relations that include a wide variety of factors (technology, the media, popular culture, and student voices and listening teachers); she is doing cultural studies. Teachers entering classrooms with this type of understanding hold the potential for creating the "extraordinary conversations" that "provoke ripples of resistance inside schools, communities, faculties, and indeed the student body" (Weis & Fine, 2003, p. 121). In my view, this complex sense of the processes of schooling opens the door to challenging asymmetrical relations of power and privilege in education. Again, this type of "cultural pedagogy" welcomes not only the inclusion of popular culture into classrooms but sees culture itself as the field in which the political struggles of education take place.

I remind the reader at this point that this chapter represents a research project—one informed by the theoretical underpinnings of cultural studies. But, who is the researcher here? In part, the effort to get at what teacher representations in popular culture might mean becomes a collaborative identity project, an exploration of selves as teachers. I'm told by students that one of the most appreciated parts of my classes is my frequent reference to my school teaching (and schooling) days and particular students, teachers, administrators, and incidents from my own autobiography; I tell them stories. One might argue that this is simply more enjoyable form of class time or less rigorous for students—some of which is probably true—but I might offer that this practice serves another purpose. Lather (2004/1986) reminds us of the "need for reciprocity" in critical approaches to research and how "mutual negotiation of meaning and power" not only challenges the borders between researcher and researcher; but, offers a means to test the usefulness of theory (pp. 46–49). This reciprocal component (i.e. I'll tell you a story if you tell me one) is relationship work. So then, I offer that it is not only through the sharing of stories that one might get at theory in education; but, that through the sharing of stories—in reciprocal ways open to critique—we might be able to build relationships with students in these classes that vivify those mutual negotiations of meaning.

Casey's Story

As part of the assignment to produce a critical book review of a text that includes representation of teachers and/or school or schooling, one student chose *To Kill a Mockingbird* by Harper Lee. In a class that at first was resistant to discuss race and racism as related to education, this student found the fictional account to be a way to relate to the experiences of students and their relationship to identity.

The achievement of *To Kill a Mockingbird* places racial prejudice in perspective, which allows us to see it as an aspect of a larger thing. This book and narrative shows how people are influenced by their societies, and that a child's identity becomes shaped by the society they are raised in. The true learning experience of the novel is that to judge a person, one must try to see things from that person's point of view, learn to walk around in his skin, and only then can one truly understand better why a person acts or believes as he or she does.

Racial prejudice as "an aspect of a larger thing" seems pregnant with meaning in this part of her reflection. Does she mean here to excuse the racism of a particular time? Or, does this imply that she places prejudice with a larger social context? My reading is that in her experience with this text, bounded by her experiences in our class, this student was able to come to think about identity in complicated, contested ways. This complication of identity and culture takes the idea of student-centered teaching to another level as her choice of the hesitant syntax (although clunky grammar) of coming to "truly understand better" shows this work as a process, necessarily incomplete. Her analysis however, does not end there.

The student also recounted how a reading of *To Kill a Mockingbird* brought back memories of a racial incident in her own past. Casey, a pseudonym, seemed troubled by the memories that her experience with the book brought back. Confused as to whether this might be part of what she could express in her review, we settled on an autobiographical style to her paper. She writes:

In a real life situation, a high school student in public education received a phone call from a friend saying that, "it's happened." Confused, the student asked her friend what she was talking about. She said some seniors had just burnt down a barn and hung a noose on a tree where a couple of African Americans lived. A white couple had just adopted two little African American children who attended the elementary school. Although she knew it was very wrong for them to do that, she had to hide her true feeling to be cool in the eyes of her peers. At school the next day she wondered how the teacher was going to approach the topic. This should have been a real teachable moment, but instead this teacher stated, "Some people belong here and some people don't." That was it; nothing else was said and nobody really ever mentioned it again.

A major part of this capstone course for preservice teachers involves asking the hard questions of education and the perpetuation of social injustice. Students, typically resistant to both the topic of social reproduction and theory itself, were presented with the pressing issues of race, gender, class, and sexuality and education's role in ameliorating or perpetuating related social problems. Casey, in this case, wrote of *To Kill a Mockingbird* as a study in "moral education" and how schools prove woefully inadequate to the task. Her anecdotal story of contemporary racism in a Midwestern town—which should be recognized as racial terrorism—only validates her view. The difference of course is that Casey recognizes now the power of the teacher in her remembered classroom—this was a "teachable moment" that could have been capitalized on, that could have disrupted the conventional discourse around race. In this way, Casey takes up the work of cultural studies and, in particular the challenge of Stuart Hall. She has joined the struggle by taking up a new set of questions around what type of teacher she might become. For Hall (1996), that project involves

> Using the resources of history, language and culture in the process of becoming rather than being: not "who we are" or "where we came from" so much as what we might become, how we have been represented and how that bears on how we might represent ourselves. (p. 3)

CONCLUSIONS

Again I return to what this paper is not; it is not a call to using cultural studies as a new paradigm in teacher education, indeed a contradiction of terms. Here I echo the cautionary tone of Carlson and Dimitriadis (2003) in thinking through what cultural studies might offer us in the project of teaching theory to teachers. Their position is that:

> It is best approached, we believe, as an intersection, a space where people working in all of these areas [curriculum, foundations, and teacher education] can find some shared language and overlapping interests. It is, at best, a borderlands space, constructed and maintained through dialogue among border crossers. (p. 31)

We too, as teacher educators interested in how theory might affect our practice, are border crossers. We too operate within a "field of struggle" that includes the broader forces at work in society from globalization to popular culture. Representations of school and schooling do matter, but they matter most importantly in how we take them on and take them up within a cultural studies frame, in "political, interventionist, socially committed, ethically charged and critical" ways (Hytten, 1998b, n.p.). This chapter (and indeed this collection of chapters) began in the "dialogue among border crossers" and it is hoped that this conversation is, as it must perpetually be, only beginning.

This chapter suggests that these encounters with the representations of teachers and schools are indicative of the larger negotiations that preservice teachers have to engage in as they go through the process of finding their "teacher self." What we do in foundations of education courses specifically and in schools of education in general is present preservice teachers with the brutal realities of American education and how it plays out in the lived experience of our children. In no way do I think we should back away from this charge but perhaps using a cultural studies approach helps our students in this process. These students want to work with and help children and yet, what we often present them with is the hard truth that often teachers are irrelevant in the face of larger social inequity and, even worse, complicit in the process of oppressing those very children. As the education students in this study show however, they must go through the process of complicated identity work. As one student quoted a class reading in her reflection, "identities are always in transit, mutate, change, and often become more complicated as a result of chance encounters, traumatic events, or unexpected collisions" (Giroux, 1998, p. 149). Or, stated another way, "isn't it amazing how now that we are 'educated' about education, that we are reflecting on everything we see and hear?" While perhaps this is overstated for effect, I would offer that it is precisely the goal in a preservice foundations course: to provide a collision with something unexpected, to create reflective teachers that actively work against those 'stereotypes' of bad education. The question, in my view, should not be "does theory matter?" but rather, "how will theory matter to you as a classroom teacher? How will it inform your practice as you become this teacher you want to be?"

This chapter offers up the way a cultural studies approach to teacher education might work through the age-old disconnect between theory and practice. Students exposed to some of the theoretical commitments of critical pedagogy and cultural studies through foundations and methods courses came to complicate their own sense of self as teacher and school as component of a larger, more complicated world. Students began with questions around the culture of their students—an Othering of sorts—but ended with a deeper critique of themselves as teachers and the teachers they might become. By engaging critically with popular culture texts and the representations of schooling therein these students started "doing" cultural studies work that included their own positionality and "identity in transit." I'm not sure what else we could hope for.

To return the epigraph that begins this paper I remind the reader of Atticus Finch and his call to "climb into his skin and walk around in it." Although it could be argued that Casey through an interaction with a text climbed into a skin and walked around in issues of race that she hadn't before, I suggest that of equal significance is that this young woman walked around in the skin of a teacher—a teacher with an obligation to confront issues of race and class with her students, a teacher she is hoping to become.

NOTE

1.   The quick example here being the "flop" or in more colloquial terms, "jumping the shark" where large corporate machinations fail to reach the public in any compelling or profitable way.

REFERENCES

Brown, S. K., & Helfenbein, R. (2004). *Conjuring curriculum, conjuring control: A reading of resistance in* Harry Potter and the Order of the Phoenix. Unpublished manuscript.

Carlson, D. & Dimitriadis, G. (2003).Introduction. In G. Dimitriadis & D. Carlson (Eds.), *Promises to keep: Cultural studies, democratic education, and public life* (pp. 1–35). New York: RoutledgeFalmer.

Fiske, J. (1989). *Reading the popular.* Boston: Unwin Hyman.

Gaztambide-Fernandez, R. A., Harding, H. A., & Sorde-Marti, T. (2004). *Cultural studies and education: Perspectives on theory, methodology, and practice.* Cambridge, MA: Harvard Educational Review.

Giroux, H. (1981). *Ideology, culture, and the process of schooling.* Philadelphia: Temple University Press.

Giroux, H. (1998). Critical pedagogy as performative practice: Memories of white-ness. In C. A. Torres & T. R. Mitchell (Eds.),. *Sociology of education: Emerging perspectives* (pp. 143–153). Albany, NY: State University of New York Press.

Giroux, H. (2000). Public pedagogy as cultural politics: Stuart Hall and the 'Crisis' of culture. In Gilroy, P., Grossberg, L., & A. McRobbie (Eds.) *Without guarantees: In honour of Stuart Hall* (pp. 134–147). New York: Verso.

Giroux, H. (2004/1994). Doing cultural studies: Youth and the challenge of pedagogy. In R.A. Gaztambide-Fernandez, H.A Harding, & T. Sorde-Marti (Eds.). *Cultural studies and education: Perspectives on theory, methodology, and practice* (pp. 233–260). Cambridge, MA: Harvard Educational Review.

Grossberg, L. (1997). *Bringing it all back home: Essays in cultural studies.* Durham, NC: Duke University Press.

Grossberg, L., Nelson, C., & P. Treichler (Eds.) (1992). *Cultural Studies.* New York: Routledge.

Hall, S. (1996). Introduction: Who needs identity? In S. Hall & P. du Gay (Eds.), *Questions of cultural identity.* Thousand Oaks, CA: Sage Publishers.

Hytten, K. (1998a). Cultural studies in education: What's the point? *Philosophy of Education.* Retrieved October 31, 2005, from http://www.ed.uiuc.edu/EPS/PES-Yearbook/1998/hytten.html

Hytten, K. (1998b). The ethics of cultural studies. *Educational Studies* 29(3), 247–265.

Johnson, R. (1986/87). What is cultural studies anyway? *Social Text* 16, 38–80.

Lather, P. (2004/1986). Research as praxis. In R. A. Gaztambide-Fernandez, H. A. Harding, & T. Sorde-Marti (Eds.). *Cultural studies and education: Perspectives on theory, methodology, and practice* (pp. 41–60). Cambridge, MA: Harvard Educational Review.

Lee, H. (1988). *To kill a mockingbird, Thirty-Fifth Anniversary Edition.* New York: HarperCollins.

McRobbie, A. (2000). Stuart Hall: The universities and the 'hurly burly'. In P. Gilroy, L. Grossberg, & A. McRobbie (Eds.) *Without guarantees: In honour of Stuart Hall* (pp. 212–224). New York: Verso.

Parker, W. C. (2005). *Social studies in elementary education, 12th edition.* New York: Prentice Hall.

Storey, J. (1998). *An introduction to cultural theory and popular culture.* Athens, GA: University of Georgia Press.

Trier, J. (Spring 2004). School film "videocompilations" as pedagogical texts in pre-service education. *Journal of Curriculum Theorizing 19* (1), pp. 124–148.

Weis, L., & Fine, M. (2003). Extraordinary conversations in public schools. In G. Dimitriadis & D. Carlson (Eds.), *Promises to keep: Cultural studies, democratic education, and public life* (pp. 95–123). New York: RoutledgeFalmer.

CHAPTER 2

WHY TEACHING CRITICAL SOCIAL THEORY AS "THEORY" MIGHT NOT BE ENOUGH[1]

Avner Segall
Michigan State University

Critical social theory's primary contribution to education is the crisis it helps create in disrupting education's discourses of the obvious and investigating education as a humanly constructed political and cultural practice. As such, critical social theory questions the given and the taken for granted in education by examining the relationship among culture, knowledge, power, discourse, and subject-formation, exploring how knowledge, texts, cultural practices and products are produced, circulated, and used, as well as what (and who) they produce, circulate and use in that process. That is, critical social theory disrupts the current organization of knowledge and creates procedures by which traditions, discourses, and practices are analyzed for how they function to include or exclude certain meanings, produce or prevent particular ways of being, behaving, and imagining (Giroux, 1996). Still, while critical theory—as a body of literature that examines the world in critical ways—is able to do the above, my experience, as a teacher educator, has pointed out that as a body of literature in and of itself it is not always able to help student teachers do the same.

Unsettling Beliefs: Teaching Theory to Teachers, pages 15–30
Copyright © 2008 by Information Age Publishing

Critical social theory—any theory—can mean a variety things: as a *noun* it can entail little more than an accumulation of knowledge found in books, chapters, and journal articles to be consumed by the learner. As a *verb*, however, critical social theory—again, any theory—can become a way of knowing. No longer simply a body of work to be consumed, it becomes an activity—a form of critically theorizing or theorizing critically. Thinking about the difference between critical social theory as a noun and a verb is important for while s/he who authors critical social theory has surely undergone critical social theorizing in the process of producing that theory, reading critical social theory doesn't necessarily lead to the reader doing his/her own theorizing as a result of such reading. The difference, then, between using critical social theory as a noun or a verb has little to do with the substance of critical social theory itself but, rather, with the ways in which it is incorporated and used in education. It is this "use" that I wish to address in this chapter. Specifically, and following Giroux (1996), I wish to argue that merely teaching critical social theory to teachers often does not result in emergence of the very issues critical social theory attempts to promote. In fact, as I will illustrate from my own experiences of engaging critical social theory with prospective teachers, critical social theory as a body of knowledge can do little to engage students in critically theorizing the (and, more importantly, in the case of preservice education, their own) world of teaching and learning. What I wish to engage in this chapter, then, is not the promise of critical social theory itself in teacher education. Rather, I want to focus on the *teaching* of critical social theory to teachers and how, in the process—often *because* of the process—much of the promise of critical theory is diminished, it's potential for creating a "crisis" in students' learning that could generate change, subverted. My point of departure in this chapter is not the idea, often heard in teacher education, that theory is "only" theory and thus, is useless, in and of, itself. Nor does this come from the idea, that in order for theory to become meaningful, it has to be practical. In fact, I believe that theorizing is an important form of "doing" and that theory does not precede "doing" but is an important element of one's doing (and undoing) and ultimately underlies our doing all along.

This, however, is not how I always felt about this issue. Like many teacher educators, I began my career by designing tightly-knit syllabi with pre-designed topics and activities accompanied by a long list of journal articles and book chapters that I hoped would help students explore education the way I thought it ought to be explored—that is, from a critical perspective that strives to make education and, as a consequence, society in general more democratic, open, equitable, and just. While students tended to enjoy the course (evaluations were high), I felt a sense of artificiality in what took place. It seemed that in spite of what students were reading and discussing, of what they were writing in their assignments, we were all merely participating in the perpetuation of the obvious, not addressing real issues of significance and educative ideas (Popkewitz, Tabachnink, & Wehlage, 1981). While students were writing papers and journals that called for a critical exploration of schooling and engaged a variety of readings from the school of critical theory/pedagogy and cultural studies to help them re-think the taken for granted in the educative process and connect it to broader social issues, what most often took place was a "performance of learning" rather than learning. Or, put otherwise, there was learning that did not get implicated and students who did not implicate themselves or their practicum environments in that learning.

Three issues, I found, combined to eliminate the "crisis" critical social theory intends, and prevented students from doing what critical theory asks of them—that is, to implicate theory and theorize practice in its broader social, political, and economic spheres. The first of those issues is that students had learned how to read texts without writing them. The second, is what Britzman (2003), using Felman (1982), refers to as the desire to ignore theory and its implication. The third is the nature of reflection promoted in teacher education and the way it is structured within schooling. I will briefly address each in turn.

READING WITHOUT WRITING

Reading without writing is something born out of habit. By the time students enroll in my course—the last one in their teacher preparation program—they have acquired the skill to read a text without writing it. That is, avoiding implicating themselves and the world in the text and vice versa. Instead, readings become a way to externalize issues, a shield from them; issues get addresses vicariously as they pertain to other places, other teachers, other contexts. This way to externalize readings helps students disengage from the text even as they purportedly engage it. I refer to that as the avoidance of theorizing through the use of theory. These "sanitized" readings are both a symptom of a system and the perpetuators of (another) system. The cycle works this way: University classes utilize what Giroux (1996) calls a "pedagogy of theory" whereby students are required to learn (and in the case of teacher education, implement) theories generated by others (mostly from the academy). This not only perpetuates the problematic distinction that theory resides at the university but also that much of the purpose of university courses is to consume rather than generate theories. Not surprisingly, then, student teachers don't tend to think of themselves as theorists but as practitioners who are merely required to implement theories generated by others.

Much of this has to do with the kind of texts students are invited to read in teacher education courses. To use terms coined by Barthes (1974), too often students are asked to read *readerly* rather than *writerly* texts and do so in readerly rather than writerly ways. A readerly text or a readerly way of reading it, are predictable and, according to Fiske (1989), invite an essentially passive, receptive, disciplined reader who tends to accept its meaning as already made. It is a relatively closed text (or process of reading), easy to read and undemanding of the reader. These texts, or forms of reading, conform to ordinary expectations of meaning and meaning-making and are often processed passively and automatically. It is precisely that "predictable structure," write Sumara and Luce-Kapler (1993), "that makes the reader [or reading] feel comfortable, so that once the reading is finished there is a sense that the experience with the [text] has been complete" (pp. 389–390). Opposed to a readerly text is a writerly text which "challenges the reader constantly to rewrite it, to make sense out of it. In the case of the *writerly*, I did not relate the term to a text and a form of reading (as I did while using the term *readerly*) because a writerly text inherently invites a writerly reading of it for it's foregrounds its own textual constructedness invites the reader to participate in the construction of meaning" (Fiske, 1989, p. 103). "Within the reading experience with a writerly text," Sumara and Luce-Kapler (1993) add, "the reader is not meant to feel comfortable." Indeed, it is those feelings of estrangement and discomfort that lead to a deeper understanding of the text and of one's self as a reader (p. 390). As Szuberla (1997) points out, dissatisfaction "admits the existence of a problem, and in the perception of a problem, reflective thinking finds its origins." (p. 384; see also Dewey, 1933). Instead of becoming the product of unthinking customs, writerly texts/ readings invite students to wonder about practice, to mull over alternatives, question motives, and critically reassess values and purposes (Knoblauch & Brannon, 1993, p. 8). No longer fitting into and onto the structures of teaching and learning student teachers already know so well and therefore no longer question, these latter modes open a deliberate gap between students and their expected environment (Daloz, 1986), a gap whose closure requires that students become more critically conscious of their own experiences learning to teach.

Ignorance

Ignorance, according to Felman (1982), is not a passive state of absence—a simple lack of information: it is an active dynamic of negation, an active refusal of information... the incapacity—or the refusal—to acknowledge *one's own implication* in the information" (p. 26). Anyone working in teacher education has, no doubt, experienced this notion of ignorance, whereby students either actively avoid issues and/or avoid implicating themselves and their teaching contexts in issues that are discussed, especially when the latter are issues raised by critical social theory that require students to implicate education, and themselves as educators, in broader societal contexts. What critical social theory calls for is creating a gap between students' current understandings of education and how it might be considered otherwise and use that gap to have students re-consider education differently. But fundamental to that notion is not only troubling students' existing understandings about education. It also requires allowing this new knowledge to survive students' desire to ignore it and to use their refusal as the grounds for learning rather than to avoid learning (Britzman, 2003). To that end, Britzman is instrumental in helping us understand some of the mechanisms teachers use not only to reject knowledge but also to furiously embrace it in order to avoid its implications. When students consider theory, Britzman suggests, they often view it as a dismissal of real experience, a profound idealization, or a useless fantasy. To render theory and practice dichotomous—to split theory and practice...however, can work as a defense against not knowing. If the theory is viewed as 'not working,' and usually learning a theory begins with breaking it before it has a chance to break the learner, then the problems that one confronts can somehow be attributed to the fault of theory. (Britzman, 2003, p. 86)

The learner, Britzman adds, has a variety of methods for defending against knowledge generated by theory. As she explains, from her own experience as a teacher educator attempting to engage her student teachers in psychoanalytic theoretical discussions about education, students actively defend themselves against such theory, attempting to break it before it has an opportunity to break them or the comfort with what they believe they already know as true:

> Comments such as 'It is nice in theory but not in the real world,' or 'I don't have the time to think slowly,' or 'I can't see how such an idea can be implemented' may well represent unfinished symptoms that defend against the more difficult question of what happens when our pedagogy is caught somewhere between ignorance and knowledge, between not knowing what to do but still having to act, and between not seeing and seeing too much. (Britzman, 2003, p. 74)

Reflection

A third aspect involved in students not implicating critical social theory, in not theorizing it, relates to the nature of reflection advocated in many teacher education programs that tends to exclude discussions of the social, political, and economic spheres that give rise and meaning to education. This aspect relates not to the "what"—the theory of knowledge advocated—but, to the "how"—the ways in which theory is considered, used, reflected upon. While commonly considered a process of learning (or relearning, unlearning) through questioning and investigation that will "lead to a development of understanding" (Loughran, 2002, p. 34), current prevailing practices regarding reflection within teacher education have been challenged on various grounds (e.g., Calderhead, 1992; Fendler, 2003; Goodman, 1992). Much of the criticism pertains to the existing emphasis on casting reflection as a personal endeavor whereby, as Zeichner (1996) points out: individual teachers are encouraged to reflect inwardly, by themselves, about their own teaching. Such reflection not only positions teachers to "see their problems as their own [and as their own failures], unrelated to those of other teachers" but it also diminishes the possibility of any consideration of the social conditions of schooling and their implication in broader political, social, and economic discourses that influence the teacher's work within the classroom.

The promotion of reflection as an individual rather than collective process and restricting the substance of reflection within the boundaries of the individual classroom, Zeichner adds, makes it less likely that teachers will be able, not to mention inclined, to act beyond the classroom and collectively "confront and transform those structural aspects of their work that hinder the accomplishment of their educational goals" (pp. 204–205; see also, Zeichner 1992, 1995). Typical reflection, then, not only positions teachers to "see their problems as their own [and as their own failures], unrelated to those of other teachers" (Zeichner, 1996, p. 205) but also diminishes the possibility of any consideration of the social conditions of schooling and their implication in broader political, social, and economic discourses that influence the teacher's work within the classroom.

ENGAGING A PEDAGOGY OF THEORIZING
IN A SOCIAL STUDIES METHODS COURSE

While it is impossible to eliminate the effects of the three issues discussed above in student teachers' learning (or not learning), I have, in the last five years of teaching my social studies methods course at Michigan State University, come to some pedagogical understandings that attempt to address students' inclination to not implicate critical social theory in their lived experiences as teachers of others and their desire to actively ignore its implications. These pedagogical strategies have helped my students engage in what Giroux (1996) refers to as a "pedagogy of theorizing" rather than a "pedagogy of theory." To reiterate, what differentiates between the two is that a "pedagogy of theory" asks students to consume theories articulated by others while a "pedagogy of theorizing" is an activity to be practiced in the lived world of the educational experience (p. 50). In that context, theory, to borrow from Barthes, does not mean abstract. Instead, "it means *reflexive*, something which turns back on itself: a discourse [or practice] which turns back on itself is by virtue of this very fact theoretical" (cf. Young, 1981, p. 1). Theory, Zavarzadeh and Morton (1994) add, is not "an abstract apparatus of mastery, but an inquiry into the grids of social intelligibilities produced by the discursive activities of a culture. Theory is a critique of intelligibility" (p. 53).

How does this form of theorizing tie into my goals as a teacher educator? Contrary to the premise of much of the discourse in education which constantly requires a movement forward by attempting to "improve" education, move it forward, make it somehow better, I asks my students to pause and spend some time *with* education, to, in a sense, live with it, exploring its regressions, its moments of frustration, its intricate, simultaneous movement forward, backward, and sideways. This focus allows us to ponder reflexively on the experiences of education and those made in it rather than lose sight of their significance by rushing, too quickly, to move on. In defining education as difficult, Britzman (2003) poses it as the other of the dream of progress, mastery, and absolute knowledge—a desire for which, Britzman argues, "domesticates curiosity and our capacity to be surprised" (p. 21). What we need instead, Britzman suggests, is to "acknowledge that our knowledge is made not from solutions but from our capacity to face dilemmas, uncertainty, and unexpected replies to our work" (p. 85).

My main goal in the methods course is to prepare interns to critically reflect on the purposes and processes of teaching social studies and relate those both to broader societal issues and to the day-to-day practices in the school contexts in which they teach, with the purpose of exploring the relationship between them. Or, to use Britzman (2003), I ask students to consider how education, in its current forms, affects its own imaginary. To do so I need to ensure my students engage a process of theorizing, one that implicates education, at all levels, in its social context. What I (as I'm sure other teacher educators do) try to establish in my class, then, are spaces that allow for two things: first, I wish to create opportunities that require students to implicate their own education and the one they are now providing others in the critical social theory readings we discuss. Second, and in order to further enable the above, I try to construct my course as an oppositional space, one that creates a disjuncture between students' past experiences in education and the ones I provide them in my class. The purpose of this disjuncture, similar to my earlier discussion about readerly and writerly texts, is to create a degree of discomfort, of strangeness, of disequilibrium among learners that will (hopefully) lead them to question what we are doing in this class and, as a result, to compare—and thus question and theorize—it to other educational environments with which they are by now accustomed, helping dislodge the natural, trouble the taken for granted in educational environments.

This is where pedagogy comes into play. More than critical theory as content (issues, topics), what underlies my course is critical theory as pedagogy. My intent is to draw students' attention to the process through which knowledge, meaning, voice, identity, and experience are produced by addressing the 'how' and 'why' questions of their production. Examining them critically enables learners to connect the processes through which they 'come to learn' with how they learn and, ultimately, with what they learn (Lusted, 1986, p. 7). To arrive at this, however, I need to abandon practices that maintain "the politics of the usual" and establish my class as an oppositional space (Alvarado, 1983), a space that actively works in opposition, to borrow, as van Reijen and Veerman (1988) do, from Lyotard (1984), "to established thought, to what has already been done, to what everyone thinks, to what is well-known, to what is widely recognized, to what is [easily] readable" (p. 302. cf. Peters & Lankshear, 1996, p. 11; see also Greene, 1978, pp. 53–73). In making a pedagogical shift from the expected to the unexpected, (Britzman & Pitt, 1996, p. 119), I strive to avoid that which, to borrow from Lather (1996), "maps easily onto [students'] taken-for-granted regimes of meaning" (p. 528). Rather than simply cater to my students' existing systems of meaning making, I strive to help them undo meanings, "displacing the . . . satisfaction of easy intelligibility with the disruptive dis-ease of . . . critique" (Fish, 1994, p. 236).

While this pedagogical approach provides the course its epistemological direction, the day-to-day pedagogical strategies I use are not in any way monumental—indeed, they may seem to others quite subtle to generate the change I hope for—but they have worked in my class. For example, while my university requires that I provide students with a syllabus on the first day of class, the syllabus I hand out is merely a sketch, an overview of the general goals of the course and the assignments for the course; it does not comprise a day-by-day schedule of topics, reading, and activities for the entire semester. There is a pedagogical reason behind this: One of the things I do in this course is help students design meaningful units of instruction. In doing so, I emphasize that, as social studies teachers, they teach students rather than content and that their curriculum ought to, as much as possible, begin with where their students are and reflect their interests, concerns, and desires. In other words, to design a curriculum *with* rather than only *for* their students, a curriculum that is organic and that grows out of students' interests and concerns, and that, to some extent, allows them to be authors not simply in but also *of* their learning. Simply suggesting to my students that they ought to take that route in their own classroom while presenting my students with a curriculum that was fully designed even before I met them does not make much sense in that regard (though I am certain none of my students would question such a practice since it is what they have been presented with in every other university course they have taken). My intent then is two fold: to trouble their expectations and to provide an example. In troubling their expectations (and, as the course proceeds through their experiences of co-authoring the curriculum with me), we have the opportunity to discuss what a curriculum means, who it is for, how it is enacted, what pedagogical ends it serves, etc. Such conversations inevitably address issues of knowledge, power, and representation as well as questions as to who has the power to determine learning, who learning is for, whose voices are included, whose are not, etc. While my students can (and do) read critical curriculum theory about these issues, such issues become lived and implicated in the very construction of our own curriculum and, consequently, in students' considerations regarding the curriculum they construct for their own students. Little of this, I believe, could happen without the class, as a community, exploring for themselves the process of creating an organic curriculum.

To promote reflection that is social—collective and focuses on the social underlying the "educational"—I divide my three-hour class in two. The second part of each class is devoted to an examination of a particular issue/topic using assigned readings or materials. This engagement is normally followed by an in-class activity around one of those particular topics/issues, often resulting in interns designing a mini-lesson for their own students (I will return to this part of class later on). The first part of class, the one I will focus on here, is devoted to collective discussions, the topics for which are generated from students' journals (which they email me in advance), from their assignments or (and mostly) by students spontaneously sharing experiences from/about their practicum experiences or ones that pertain to our own course. While I sometimes begin class by asking a student to share his/her journal (one that usually focuses on an issue that ran across several of the students' journals for that week), much of the ensuing discussion is generated by students. That is, they raise issues to be discussed and, in many ways, other than my own probing of issues, determine the *curriculum* for that part of class. This does not mean I am not involved in the conversation or do not push it in directions I deem necessary, often posing difficult question that turn the conversation around; that, I feel is my responsibility as instructor. But what this first half of class allows, is for students to engage in a curriculum for which they are, for the most part, its designers rather than one that is fully pre-planned by others for them.

The idea of public, critical reflection, however, also has another purpose, beyond that of allowing students to author their own curriculum. It is also, and probably more importantly, intended to allow students to speak from and about their own experiences and, in the process, theorize those experience, examine the theories that structure them and students' meaning making of (and in) them and, hopefully, through questioning by others, reexamine those theories for what they yield and/or conceal, for what they make im/possible. It is through such a process that students become "theorists" and participate in what Giroux (1996) called a pedagogy of theorizing. As students' initial theories about education and its relation (or lack thereof) to the world get articulated and troubled, students not only learn that they already have theories about the world but that those theories provide a framework for their practice (and for discussing practice), and that in order to learn further one needs to extended, deepen, often trouble those theories by articulating them to oneself as well as by opening them up to the scrutiny of others.

While I have been using this approach for some time now, the process of enacting critical, public reflection in a classroom is never easy. Students have gone through many years of schooling in which they were mostly passive, where knowledge was considered to be held by the teacher and/or in readings and students are expected to access, decipher, and then return that knowledge to the teacher. While they might not have liked this kind of learning as students, it has become habit and habits are hard to break, especially for those, like the majority of my students, who tended to succeed in the existing system. These habits are especially hard to break when that which is being broken pertains not only to how students learn but also to how they will teach others. This *breaking* is thus not simply an academic exercise for them as students; it also is implicated in their thinking about their own future practice and the various fears of it. As such, they are inclined to see critical reflection on teaching and learning, particularly on their own teaching and learning, as a burden more so than for the freedoms it allows. That is because, in their eyes, student teaching is a time to primarily gain confidence in teaching, not a time in which one's existing confidence about teaching gets troubled (Segall, 2002). This, Britzman (2003) suggests, operates as "a defense against experience or...a defense against learning from experience" and the "anxiety that interpretation might ruin the goodness of knowledge (p. 100). It is thus often difficult to get the kind of critical collective reflection discussed in this chapter going, to have students publicly critique each others' assertions, to question, challenge, and dispute. (It is much easier to do this to an author who is not present, who cannot talk back). It also, naturally, has to do with the fact that my students have had very few prior opportunities to analyze the assumptions and interests that structure teaching and learning in schools (or, for that matter, in schools of education). As McLaren (2003) points out:

> students come to believe and accept that the rules, regulations, systems of moral scruples, and social practices that under gird and inform everyday life in (educational institutions) are necessary if learning is to be successfully accomplished. They fail to recognize that tradition has provided this condition, not because it is based on some 'metaphysical truth' or wisdom but because these regulations have been 'discursively won' through a long series of historical and cultural struggles over whose knowledge counts, what knowledge is most worthwhile, and who is to benefit most from things remaining the way they are. (p. 237)

Much of my focus in the discussions conducted in the first part of class is to expose students to the tacit assumptions in the conventions of everyday educational practice thereby making them aware of the fact that as teachers they too will (as I do in my own course) be propagating particular ideologies in their own classrooms (Kincheloe, 1993, p. 30). I will use several examples from what takes place in the first and second parts of my class—in a sense, connecting those examples—to illustrate how a pedagogy of theorizing is not only useful in and of itself in order to invite students to implicate the teaching and learning in which they are partaking but also to highlight how it can be generated by implicating students in the readings from the school of critical social theory they read in my course.

When I first taught the methods class I had students read a series of articles and chapters from the school of critical social theory. Yet, as mentioned earlier, students, more often than not, refused to implicate themselves or the schools in which they teach in that theory, maintaining it at arms-length, and avoiding its implications. One of those readings was Terrie Epstein's piece (1996) in which she highlights how African-American and Euro-American students think and believe differently about history. Having asked participants (secondary social studies students) to rank the most important people and events in American history, Epstein demonstrates how while Euro-American students chose the traditional white, "national" figures and events, their African-American colleagues included African American figures and events pertaining to their history (or "national" events seen from an African-American perspective) in their lists. Another of Epstein's findings was that while white students tended to trust the teachers and the textbook for historical information, African American students tended to trust outside sources such as families, churches, the media, more than they did the textbook. I chose to use this piece because, I believed, it would help my mostly white students re-think what, how, and whose history is taught and how it tends to position the other as "Other" and, in the process of that re-thinking, perhaps as an impetus for it, to consider their own location as white students in the equation Epstein pointed to and thus consider how they might structure their own teaching (often to students of color) differently. Yet none of this happened. Instead, having read Epstein's piece, all my students claimed that, having gone through our teacher education program, none of this was new to them: that is, they, in no way, think like the white students in Epstein's study or act to perpetuate the divide noted in her piece. When students are not ready to implicate themselves, to consider their unproblematized positionality as problematic when attempting to teach *all* students, there is little an instructor can do and the conversation is basically over (as it was the first time I taught Epstein's piece in the methods course).

Having learned from this experience, I now have my students respond to the same questions Epstein posed to her participants *before* they read her piece. When we begin discussing her piece and my students begin making claims similar to those expressed by students in my first year of teaching, I simply take out the tabulation of this class' answers to Epstein's questions and put it on an overhead. I then ask them to compare those to the answers given by the white students in Epstein's study. There is always (I have been doing this for four years now) a few seconds of silence and distress before students, somewhat surprisingly, acknowledge how similar the responses are (and how different they are from those given by the African American students in Epstein's study and, as we discuss, probably from the responses given by the African American students in the very classes they are currently teaching).[2] Having collected this kind of data in the last four years, I share responses from students in previous classes. While, on the one hand, my students are relieved to see that former students responded similarly, the gravity of the similarity soon settles in—that is, they realize how systemic, widespread, and deeply-rooted the issue is. No longer able to ignore their own implication in Epstein's piece, the discussion takes on a very different turn, exploring the why issues—why do my students think the way they do, what has structured such thinking, how do power and discourse (and whose power, whose discourse) play in the degree to which students embrace and/or reject knowledge in school, and what might they need to do in order to allow African American students to "own" the curriculum and, at the same time, to help white students who think of the teacher and textbook as providers of truth to begin to critically examine and question the relationship between power, discourse and truth.

Addressing such issues inevitably spills into a discussion of the incorporation of multiple perspectives in social studies education. This idea is not new to my students; they have discussed this more than once in their previous courses. Indeed, by the time they come to my class, they all believe in and advocate the inclusion of multiple perspectives in the curriculum. Naturally, I do little to dissuade them of this notion. What I attempt to trouble, however, in our discussions are the assumptions underlying their descriptions of these newly incorporated perspectives—most often referring to them as *other* perspectives. That is, I invite them to *pause* and consider that by referring to them as *other* perspectives they are not only othering these perspectives but are also placing the dominant white, middle-class, male perspectives at the center (and thus as central). More, by relegating some perspectives as *other* (other than what?) they are defining the traditional curriculum as an extraterritorial space outside of history and agency, beyond positionality and its own location in a cultural struggle to dominate meaning.

Embedded in the idea of multiple perspectives is the notion that nonmainstream lenses often provide renditions of the past that tend not to paint the U.S. history in as favorable a light as that of the traditional curriculum. So while my students understand the need to show multiple versions of history, they are disturbed by the ability of what they often terms as *bad* stories to portray a negative side of the U.S., troubling students' existing sense of pride in their country. Thus, as we consider issues of balance and audience and debate the purpose of social studies education (is it to reproduce the existing social order or to challenge it?), we also focus on the very use of the terms *good* and *bad* stories and what that might indicate about my students' own location within the politics of knowledge production in schools. This inevitably leads to a discussion about what stories tend to dominate the curriculum, what such stories promote, who benefits from them and who does not, who has the power to put them there and what forces conjure to invite us to consider some stories as *good* and others as *bad*?

Trying to help my students see the role of, for example, the implicit and null curriculum and how they relate to and or contradict the explicit curriculum as they all work together to educate, can be done by having students read Eisner (1985) or Giroux (1983). But as I have found, these terms can remain abstract, even empty, if only explored that way. My aim then is, throughout the course, to connect their own teaching to these issues, to help them examine the relationship between the explicit, implicit, and null curriculum in their own classrooms and schools (as well as in the one we share at the university). An illustration of this is when students in my class discuss their government unit on Congress, one in which they divide students into members of the House of Representatives and the Senate according to party lines, have them select a piece of legislation that is relevant to their own lives (normally about school rules) and pass it through an imagined Congress. It is easy to see why my students are proud of these units: their students are involved in hands-on learning, they engage an issue that is relevant to their lives, they are interested, active, and learn collaboratively while, at the same time, actually learning the curriculum. But as we discuss the benefits of this kind of learning and how it could be applied to other units, I invite students to consider what else their students might be learning from this unit. For, as all of my interns explain when describing how their units end, the bill their students were attempting to pass—normally allowing them to wear baseball caps or chew gum in class—are inevitably vetoed by the school principal or the teacher acting as the U.S. President during that unit. That students are not afforded the opportunity given the congress to override a presidential veto is not only problematic when learning how a bill gets passed; it also further entrenches the already existing cynicism among youth against government. If the purpose of social studies, as my interns often state, is to create an active, critical, and engaged citizenry, I invite students to question how might demonstrating to their students the futility of that which they hope to instill in them might help in that regard? How might this encourage them to become active in changing the world if what they ultimately learn is that such efforts are futile? In other words, I invite students to examine what larger goals of social studies, or of teaching in general, might be lost in what might otherwise be considered "good" social studies teaching. As we address these questions—as we theorize about them and that which underlies the practices that help both form and inform my students' practice, we connect their teaching to broader school practices and to those of the larger society that structure them. In the process we (often through my input) invoke critical social theory. That critical social theory, however, is used as a verb, to raise questions, to theorize, rather than as a body of theory to be mastered in itself.

CONCLUSION

In *After Education*, Britzman (2003) asks: what becomes of theory when it cannot become itself, that is, when it's cannot become the means for thinking? The examples provided in this chapter attempted to address Britzman's question by exploring the possibilities opened up by a pedagogy of theorizing that uses critical social theory as a means for thinking in, with, and about such theory in one's practice as a teacher. This form of theorizing cannot be automatically expected when only reading critical social theory; for such theorizing to take place, students need to be asked to implicate their own teaching with/in theory, to examine the theories they already hold about education, teaching, and learning, and to theorize (or, in light of critical social theory, to re-theorize) their teaching and their practicum environments. It is in this dialectic—between theory and theorizing—that students can critically examine what teaching is, and as a result, imagine what it can be otherwise.

NOTES

1. Some of the ideas discussed in this chapter have been addressed in Segall, A., and Gaudelli, W. "Reflecting socially on social issues in a social studies methods course," *Teaching Education* (in press)
2. I usually have 25–30 students in this class. In the six years I've taught this course, there were only four persons of color, and never more than one student of color in each class.

REFERENCES

Alvarado, M. (1983). The question of media studies. In M. Alvarado & O. Boyd-Barrett (Eds.). (1992). *Media education: An introduction* (pp. 94–96). London: The British Film Institute.

Barthes, R. (1974). *S/Z* (trans. R. Miller). New York: Hill & Wang.

Britzman, D. P. (2003). *After-Education: Anna Freud, Melanie Klein, and psychoanalytic histories of learning.* Albany, NY: SUNY Press.

Britzman, D. P., & Pitt, A. J. (1996). Pedagogy and transference: Casting the past of learning into the present of teaching. *Theory into Practice, 35*(2), 117–123.

Calderhead, J. (1992) The role of reflection in learning to teach. In L. Valli (Ed), *Reflective teacher education: Cases and critiques* (pp. 139–146). Albany: State University of New York Press.

Daloz, L. (1986). *Effective teaching and mentoring.* San Francisco, CA: Jossey-Bass.

Eisner, E. (1985). *The educational imagination: On the design and evaluation of school programs* (2nd. Ed.). New York: Macmillan.

Epstein, T. (1996). *African American and European American adolescents' perspectives on United States history.* Unpublished manuscript.

Felman, S. (1982). Psychoanalysis and education: Teaching terminable and interminable. In B. Johnson (Ed.), *The pedagogical imperative. Yale French Studies, 63,* 21–44.

Fendler, L. (2003). Teacher reflection in a hall of mirrors: Historical influences and political reverberations. *Educational Researcher, 32* (3), 16–25.

Fish, S. (1994). *There's no such thing as free speech and it's a good thing too.* New York: Oxford University Press.

Fiske, J. (1989). *Understanding popular culture.* London: Routledge.

Giroux, H. (1996). *Counternarratives: cultural studies and critical pedagogies in postmodern spaces.* New York: Routledge.

Giroux, H. A. (1983). *Theory and resistance in education: A pedagogy for the opposition.* South Hadley, MA: Bergin & Garvey.

Goodman, J. (1992). Feminist pedagogy as a foundation for reflective teacher education programs. In L. Valli (Ed), *Reflective teacher education: Cases and critiques* (pp. 174–186). Albany: State University of New York Press.

Greene, M. (1978). *Landscapes of learning.* New York: Teachers College Press.

Kincheloe, J. L. (1993). *Towards a critical politics of teacher thinking: Mapping the postmodern.* Westport, CT: Bergin and Garvey.

Knoblauch, C. H., & Brannon, L. (1993). *Critical teaching and the idea of literacy.* Portsmouth, NH: Boynton/Cook Publishers.

Lather, P. (1996). Troubling clarity: The politics of accessible language. *Harvard Educational Review, 66*(3), 525–545.

Loughran, J. J. (2002). Effective reflective practice. *Journal of Teacher Education, 53* (1), 33–43.

Lusted, D. (1986). Why pedagogy? *Screen, 27*(5), 7–10.

Lyotard, J. F. (1984). *The postmodern condition: A report on knowledge.* Minneapolis: University of Minnesota Press.

McLaren, P. (2003). *Life in schools (4th Edition).* Boston: Pearson.

Peters, M., & Lankshear, C. (1996). Postmodern counternarratives. In H. A. Giroux, C. Lankshear, P. McLaren, & M. Peters (Eds.), *Counternarratives: Cultural studies and critical pedagogies in postmodern spaces* (pp. 1–39). New York & London: Routledge.

Popkewitz, T. S., Tabachnink, B. R. and Wehlage, G. (1981). *The myth of educational reform.* Madison: University of Wisconsin Press.

Segall, A. (2002). *Disturbing practice: Reading teacher education as text.* New York: Peter Lang.

Segall, A., & Gaudelli, W. (in press). Reflecting socially on social issues in a social studies methods course. *Teaching Education.*

Sumara, D. J., & Luce-Kapler, R. (1993). Action research as a writerly text: Locating co-labouring in collaboration. *Educational Action Research, 1*(3), 387–395.

Szuberla, C. A. L. (1997). Learning theory and the preservice teacher. *Education, 117*(3), 381–385.

van Reijen, W., & Veerman, D. (1988). An interview with Jean-Francois Lyotard. *Theory, Culture and Society, 7,* 302.

Young, R. (1981). *Poststructuralism: An introduction.* In R. Young (Ed), *Untying the text: A post-structuralist reader* (pp. 1–28). London: Routledge.

Zavarzadeh, M., & Morton, D. (1994). *Theory as resistance: Politics and culture after (post) structuralism.* New York and London: Guilford Press.

Zeichner, K. (1992). Conceptions of reflective teaching in contemporary U.S. teacher education program reforms. In L. Valli (Ed), *Reflective teacher education: Cases and critiques* (pp. 161–173). Albany: State University of New York Press.

Zeichner, K. (1995). Reflections of a teacher educator working for social change. In T. Russell & F. Korthagen (Eds.), *Teachers who teach teachers: Reflections on teacher education* (pp. 11–24). London & Washington, D.C.: Falmer Press.

Zeichner, K. (1996) Teachers as reflective practitioners and the democratization of school reform. In K. Zeichner, S. Melnick, & M. L. Gomez (Eds), *Currents of reform in preservice teacher education* (pp. 199–214). New York: Teachers College Press.

CHAPTER 3

TEACHING THEORY THROUGH PERFORMANCE

Role Playing Cultural Capital in the Classroom

Beth Hatt
Illinois State University

"Theory" can be a fuzzy concept that is difficult for many educators to grasp and understand completely. So, why teach it to teachers? In order to explain why I teach it, I need to first explain what theory means to me as an instructor working to raise the consciousness of pre-service teachers regarding issues of race, class, and gender. To me, theory is not truth nor is it the measure of a "true" scholar. In academia, we have a tendency to place theory on a pedestal along with those who claim to be theorists. Theory often works as a smartness card used to assign status. We use it to claim legitimacy. In essence, theories about power can even be about power themselves. Theory can be very useful but only when we humble it.

Theories are ideas or stories about how the world works. In regards to education, theories can relate to how people learn, why some students fail vs. others succeed, or even what the purpose of schooling should be. Hence, all teachers theorize even when we do not realize that is what we are doing. Mohanty (2003) states, "The best theory makes personal experience and individual stories communicable...This kind of theoretical,

Unsettling Beliefs: Teaching Theory to Teachers, pages 31–38
Copyright © 2008 by Information Age Publishing

analytical thinking allows us to mediate between different histories and understandings of the personal." (p. 191). I agree with Mohanty and attempt to use theory in the classroom to encourage pre-service teachers to not just understand but question as well their own personal experiences and to learn from the contradictory stories of other pre-service teachers and from their students as well. I want them to learn and interpret how others have experienced the world differently than themselves, especially the pre-service teachers who come from privileged economic and racial backgrounds. Schrader (2004) states, "We might use theories as stories to explore certain communicative events, and how these communicative events can in turn be viewed as lived, told, and unfolding stories." (p. 208). In sum, I introduce theory as story and as a way to bring pre-service teachers' personal experiences or stories into the classroom to be discussed, challenged, and better understood as a beginning into critical, reflective practice.

Secondly, I use theory to encourage my pre-service teachers to more actively *theorize* themselves about the ways society and schools work rather than simply abiding by dominant discourse or spoon fed assumptions from others. For example, I encourage them to rethink dominant discourse around pregnant teens (Luttrell, 2003) and to begin theorizing through their own questions and experiences. Noblit (1999) states, "Theorizing is thinking through the conclusions I draw from different sets of information so that I may try to understand how things go together or do not. Theorizing is a process of trying out ideas," (p. 12). Theory can be used to disrupt dominant discourse and to encourage pre-service teachers to "try out ideas" as they attempt to make sense of what they are learning about what it means to teach. Theorizing encourages pre-service teachers to question and to continue questioning the world around them in struggling to understand why the world operates as it does and how their individual identities fit into it. In the end, this allows them to have better judgment in the classroom because they are able to rethink dominant ideology and to be more thoughtful in their practice.

TEACHING THEORY THROUGH PERFORMANCE

As mentioned previously, theory can be "fuzzy" and difficult to connect back to personal experiences and our everyday lives. Consequently, it can be a bit tricky to teach. One strategy that I have found particularly helpful is teaching theory through performance. Alexander (2005) states the following regarding pedagogy as performance:

It acknowledges that detached reflection can not be upheld as knowing. It has to be a deeply penetrating critical reflexivity that is engaged both after the act (of teaching and learning), as well as in the moment of the engagement. (p. 60).

Learning and teaching about theory can often end up being about "detached reflection" but as Alexander states, this, "can not be upheld as knowing." Teaching theory through performance can lead to "critical reflexivity" within the moment but also beyond the classroom. We want critically reflexive teachers and theory provides us an avenue to work towards this. Denzin (2003) states that performance shows how: "In concrete situations, persons produce history and culture, 'even as history and culture produce them.'" (Denzin, 2003, p. 263; Glass, 2001, p. 17). Performance places theory into concrete terms and identities. It shows how culture and history move through us as spoken discourse and behavior. Alexander (2005) in discussing Turner's (1982) work on performative reflexivity states:

> The most insightful members of particular communities turn backwards and inwards, to engage the double-lensed act of looking at themselves *look at themselves*. This is in order to gain insight to the nature of their own performance practices, and how they are implicated in the effects of their own labor. (p. 43)

Through observing the performance of theory, pre-service teachers can begin to understand how they perform culture themselves. Their own identities become implicated. Ideally, they begin to become the "insightful members of particular communities" through being able to critically reflect not just on their teaching but also how their own pedagogy is filtered through their identities.

Finally, performance allows for a greater sense of agency as well. Giroux and Shannon (1997) state that: "The pedagogical as performative does not merely provide a set of representation/texts that imparts knowledge to others; it also becomes a form of cultural production in which one's own identity is constantly being rewritten." (p. 6). The pre-service teachers begin to rethink how they can alter their performance in the ways they are implicated. "They realize how to make and perform changes in their own lives, to become active agents in shaping the history that shapes them." (Denzin, 2003, p. 264). Performance allows pre-service teachers to have a concrete image of such abstract concepts as theory, culture, and power. They begin to see how they are a part of it and to theorize how they might change it through their teaching.

PERFORMING CULTURAL CAPITAL

Many pre-service teachers focus on teaching as being solely about content, method, and assessment. They often do not understand how teaching is a cultural act, and that everything they do in the classroom is filtered through culture. I have found Pierre Bourdieu's (1977) theory regarding cultural capital especially helpful in guiding pre-service teachers' understanding of cultural practices in schools. Bourdieu claims that it is through cultural practices that social inequality is shaped, determined, and reproduced through schooling. Bourdieu perceives inequalities as being reproduced through the unequal distribution and exchange of capital. He frames capital within three main categories: economic, cultural, and symbolic. Economic capital relates to possessing money and expensive material goods. Cultural capital is associated with valued ways of looking, behaving, thinking, and forms of knowledge. Symbolic capital is connected with being publicly perceived as having status and authority. Students entering school with valued cultural and symbolic capital are more likely to be perceived as "smart" and possessing valuable knowledge. Additionally, someone must have economic capital in order to have access to valued cultural and symbolic capital.

Originally when I had pre-service teachers simply read some of Bourdieu's work, they found it difficult and seemed disengaged with the overall theory. I realized I had to find a way to make the theory come alive for them. Consequently, I decided I needed to find a way to "perform" cultural capital in the classroom. As a performance, I chose the "scene" of wine presentation at a formal dinner.

Coming from a working class background, I did not grow up exposed to wine or the form of etiquette expected in formal dinner settings. I learned about the expected etiquette and proper presentation of wine through working as a server at a fine dining establishment during graduate school. Before beginning the job, I had never opened a bottle of wine myself. Hence, I experienced a steep learning curve during my training. What amazed me the most was how seriously the forms of etiquette were regarded. We were even taught how to recognize in the words of my supervisor, "A person with class." For example, my supervisor would often state: "A person with class will..." and provide an example of how that person would respond. This was especially made apparent regarding the presentation of wine. The clientele were clearly schooled in the forms of etiquette and immediately knew, and were often offended, if I missed a step in the process. As a part of the performance, I share some of these experiences with the students.

I never begin the lesson with the performance. Instead, I begin discussing the idea of cultural capital through the notion of smartness. Through my own research, I have studied the ways the concept of smartness operates as a cultural construct in schools and is used to reproduce social inequality in the classroom (Hatt, 2007; Hatt-Echeverria, 2004). Additionally, my work shows how smartness is a performance that people who choose that identity enact. Consequently, I ask students to tell me what a "smart" person looks, talks, and acts like. I encourage them to even use stereotypes. I want them to see how we assign "smartness" to people through behaviors and artifacts such as clothing, books, or eye glasses, which are all part of performing smartness. Overwhelmingly, the students typically describe the person as wearing glasses, dressing in a suit, reading the Wall Street Journal, and listening to classical music. Additionally, the person almost always speaks in "proper" English and uses "big" words. We then discuss how race/ethnicity, gender, and class play into these descriptions. The pre-service teachers begin to see how smartness is overwhelmingly framed in the image of a White, middle-to-dominant class, male. We then move to discussing how these assumptions play into teacher expectations for students and are connected to valued cultural capital.

Next, it is time for the performance. I set up a table in the middle of the room with four chairs and ask for four volunteers. I tell the volunteers that they are eating at a fine dining establishment and I will be their server. I provide four wine glasses and ask which one of them would like to be the person who orders the wine. I typically use bottled water or soda as the wine. I present the "wine" to the person who "ordered" it and ask the volunteer if they know how they are supposed to respond. Typically, people respond that they are supposed to check the bottle to make sure it is what they ordered. This is true but there is one more step and as my supervisor stated, "A person with class will place their hand on the bottle to check for temperature." Red wine should be room temperature while white wine should be chilled. Next, I present the cork. The students usually state that they are supposed to smell the cork but, as I was trained, the person "who has class" will check for moisture and ensure the cork has not cracked. Finally, I state that the wine should be served beginning to the left of the person who ordered wine with women being served first. The person who ordered the wine must be served last, taste the wine, and acknowledge to the server whether the wine is acceptable. We then move on and discuss wine tasting.

I usually begin discussion by sharing how I learned the ritual as a server. I then ask if any of the pre-service teachers were already familiar with the ritual of wine presentation. Generally, there is one person who either learned the ritual through being a server themselves or by having regularly seen their parents order wine while growing up. The discussion typically shifts to formal dining etiquette as a whole. We begin discussing how and where people learn these formal rules and how they can be used to denote "outsiders" or those "without class." At this point, I share one of my embarrassing moments of showing myself as being "without class," such as the first time I encountered shrimp with the shell on and tried to eat it *with* the shell while on a first date! Additionally, we discuss serving size and how working class expectations at restaurants are typically framed as having a large enough serving to be full while dominant class expectations are framed around presentation of the food rather than serving size. I then invite the pre-service teachers to share their own stories.

It becomes a wonderful intersection of laughter and stories along with a deepening of understanding regarding their own identities and how we embody culture and perform it. Of course, I cannot promise that *every* person in the class finds the performance particularly meaningful but I do feel that the majority of the pre-service teachers learn a lot from it. For the people who grew up learning the rituals, they can at times be a bit embarrassed that they do know the rituals. They especially feel themselves being implicated in the performance. I am not always sure if I handle their feelings of being implicated appropriately. I partly frame their cultural knowledge as a product of the family they were born into, which we do not choose. However, I do state clearly that we do have choice in how we continue to perform once we become aware of the performance.

In connecting the performance back to education, we discuss how cultural capital shapes the experiences of students within school walls. For example, we read about tracking and the ways the decision as to which track a child belongs is often connected to whether children possess valued cultural capital, which reproduces racial, class, and gender inequalities (Oakes, 1985; Sapon-Shevin, 1999). Furthermore, I encourage them to begin theorizing why working-class students of color are overwhelmingly framed as "not caring" about education and how these perceptions may be connected to cultural capital (Valenzuela, 1999). We theorize about social norms in general, where they come from, and whom they benefit the most. The pre-service teachers do not always remember the term "cultural capital" or Pierre Bourdieu's name but they do remember the performance of wine tasting, the ways they were personally implicated, and their own theorizing through the issues which, to me, are the most important things.

CONCLUSIONS

As mentioned above, theory is most useful when we humble it. When it becomes framed as "truth," received knowledge, or a claim to status, we can lose the opportunity to see the personal stories within theory and the chance for our pre-service teachers to become theorists. To work towards equity in schools, we need teachers that can see and question the ways power, privilege, and oppression operate in everyday practices within school walls along with how they are personally implicated. Bringing theory into the classroom is a wonderful way to introduce future educators to these concepts. Yet, it is for nothing, if they cannot understand it in concrete terms or connect it to practice.

For me, performing theory in the classroom has been a valuable tool in connecting theory to practice. Through performing theory, pre-service teachers can literally see how their individual identities are implicated within structures of power, privilege, and oppression in everyday practices within school walls. By better understanding their own identities, they will be better equipped at getting their essential work done as teachers (Lampert, 1985). Additionally, pre-service teachers can begin to theorize about issues in their own classrooms along with imagining alternative performances.

I do not offer my example in this chapter as the best example of teaching theory through performance. I am constantly refining the performance, thinking of additional ways to perform other theories, and ways to make it more meaningful to my students. Rather, I see this chapter as more of an invitation to you, as the reader, to humble theory and to try performing it in your own classroom. Perhaps then, together, we can encourage future teachers to better understand how who they are shapes their teaching and to ask, in the words of Parker Palmer (1998), "How does the quality of my selfhood form—or deform—the way I relate to my students, my subject, my colleagues, my world?" (p. 4). Teachers must understand not only how their own identities determine the ways they choose to perform in the classroom but also how the same applies for their students, who perform identity as well. In sum, performance as a tool is but one of many possibilities in "teaching theory to teachers" as a way to ensure we have educators that are critically reflexive and self-aware in their teaching.

REFERENCES

Alexander, B. (2005). Critically analyzing pedagogical interactions as performance. In B. Alexander, G. Anderson, & B. Gallegos (Eds.), *Performance theories in education* (pp. 41–62). Mahwah, NJ: Erlbaum.

Bourdieu, P. & Passeron, J. C. (1977). *Reproduction in education, society, and culture.* (Trans. Richard Nice). London: Sage.

Denzin, N. (2003). Performing [auto]ethnography politically. *The Review of Education, Pedagogy, and Cultural Studies, 25,* 257–278.

Glass, R. D. (2001). On Paulo Freire's philosophy of praxis and the foundations of liberation education. *Educational Researcher, 30,* 15–25.

Giroux, H., & Shannon, P. (1997). (Eds). *Education and cultural studies.* New York: Routledge.

Hatt, B. (2007). Street smarts vs. book smarts: The figured world of smartness in the lives of marginalized youth. *The Urban Review, 39*(2), 145–166.

Hatt-Echeverria, B. (2004). *"Make good choices": Social positioning, control, and silencing through the cultural producting of "being smart."* Unpublished doctoral dissertation, University of North Carolina, Chapel Hill, NC.

Lampert, M. (1985). How do teachers manage to teach? Perspectives on problems in practice. *Harvard Educational Review,* 55(2), 178–194.

Luttrell, W. (2003). *Pregnant bodies, fertile minds: Gender, race, and the schooling of pregnant teens.* New York: Routledge.

Mohanty, C. T. (2003). *Feminism without borders: Decolonizing theory, practicing solidarity.* Durham, NC: Duke University Press.

Noblit, G. (1999). *Particularities: Collected essays on ethnography and education.* New York: Peter Lang.

Oakes, J. (1985). *Keeping track: How schools structure inequality.* New Haven: Yale University Press.

Palmer, P. (1998). *The courage to teach.* San Francisco: Jossey-Bass.

Sapon-Shevin (1999). Gifted education. In D. Gabbard (Ed.), *Knowledge and Power in the Global Economy: Politics and the Rhetoric of School Reform* (pp. 121–129). Mahwah, NJ: Erlbaum.

Schrader, S. (2004). Performing narratives: Telling the story of theory. *Teaching Education, 15(2),* 203–214.

Turner, V. (1982). *From ritual to theatre: The human seriousness of play.* New York: Performing Arts Journal.

Valenzuela, A. (1999). *Subtractive schooling: U.S. Mexican youth and the politics of schooling.* Albany, NY: State University of New York Press.

CHAPTER 4

A STORY OF "ACCOUNTABLE" TALK

Unsettling the Normalization of a Culture of Performance at Márquez Elementary

William R. Black
University of South Florida

ABSTRACT

In this chapter, I draw from fieldwork conducted for my dissertation and in order to provide a reflexive examination of the normalization of a culture of performance at Márquez Elementary, a high-performing, high-minority school located in a performance-oriented school district in Texas. Additionally, I seek to provide readers with theoretically informed reflections on the conflicts, complications and possibilities I experienced as a former administrator conducting a year-long qualitative study of the school. I struggled with issues of researcher power, standpoint, and subjectivity (Denzin & Lincoln, 1998; Dewalt, Dewalt, & Wayland, 1998; Foley, 2002; Hatch, 2003) and felt conflicted over how to engage the effects of high-stakes testing and the resulting culture of performance while "in the field" a "field" where two years before, I had been an administrator in a similarly populated school within the same district. I conclude with implications for guiding former administrators

Unsettling Beliefs: Teaching Theory to Teachers, pages 39–73
Copyright © 2008 by Information Age Publishing

in school-based qualitative research projects and a discussion about teaching through explicitly engaging theoretically-informed critical perspectives within educational field(s) powerfully informed by functionalist "results-based" or "performance-oriented" discourses and practices.

PEPPIN' FOR THE TAKS: DECONSTRUCTING SPECTACLE/MANAGING SPECTACLE

On Monday, February 23rd, I arrived at Márquez Elementary,[1] my research site, at 7:40 a.m. and walked by the marquee announcing the morning's TAKS (Texas Assessment of Knowledge and Skills) pep rally. The following day, the fourth graders were to take the first high-stakes examination of the year, the 4th grade writing TAKS. Smilingly, the principals had told me the previous week that they were going to spend part of their weekend dying their hair and rewriting the lyrics to the tune, YMCA, substituting "Y-M-C-A" with a new chanted chorus, "T-A-K-S." I could not help but reflect on the irony of appropriating a song that homosexual performers used to queer institutional heteronormalcy 25 years ago to inspire and motivate elementary school children to perform on a high-stakes test.

Some students were eating breakfast as I cruised by the cafeteria. Walking down the hall towards the gym, I heard music and rattling noises. I made my way through several parents, respectfully listening to the TAKS rally in the hallway outside of the gym. As I entered the edge of the pep rally, I saw four or five teachers smiling and clapping, moving around groups of students. The fifth grade sat in three lines at the front of the cafeteria with students in descending grade levels seated in lines behind them—all facing forward. Ms. Smith, an African-American early grade teacher was at the front of the crowd, exuberantly leading chants. "Beat the TAKS!' she shouted into the microphone in rhythm with the bass lines of the music, alternating with "Get a 4!",[2] as students were exhorted to chant along.

As students and their parents arrived and moved into the gym, each were given blue and white pom-poms. One parent who happened to be in my ESL class[3] told me that a group of parents had been working on making butcher paper cut-out blue and white pom-poms for three days. The PTA president approached me and told me that they did a rally every year. This year, however, they made new pom-poms because the old ones looked bad. The music and chanting continued and then Ms. Soriano, the parent training specialist, saw me, smiled, and quickly provided me a set of pom-poms as I became a participant observer waving and gyrating my pom-pom with the parents, teachers, students, and administrators. I noticed the area superintendent, Mr. Lions, pom-pom calibrated to the beat, at the back of the gym.

Ms. Gamez, the Principal, and Ms. Largo, the Assistant Principal, then appeared at the front of the crowd and students gasped, laughed, and giggled at their blue tinted hair. They immediately joined in the "Beat the TAKS" and "Get a 4" chants still being led by an even more animated Ms. Brown, who in turn introduced the main attraction, Ms. Gamez, with great zeal. Throughout the assembly 5th graders appeared less enthused, cooler and less likely to participate in the arm pumping and singing than the younger students. Maria introduced Mr. Lions as a celebrity guest. The students turned and clapped for him. He responded with a smile and a couple of waves of his blue and white pom-pom. Within a minute, he walked out of the gym, made a phone call in the hall, walked back and forth in the hall for thirty seconds, then put down his pom-pom and scurried out of the building.

Music still pumping, albeit softer, Ms. Gamez started out stating that she and Ms. Largo had worked over Saturday, that yes they work on Saturdays, and that they had made up their own words to a song. "Who here knows that YMCA song?" About a third of the students raised their hands. "Well we are all going to sing along, using T-A-K-S instead of Y-M-C-A and Ms. Largo will show you how to do the movements." Standing at the front of the gym, Ms Largo then demonstrated to the students the movements to accompany each letter of the new choral refrain. The students were taught to do a little T so that they would not hit each other, then the A, K, and S movements. A staff member then turned on the tape and the administrators started singing and reading their own newly minted, motivational test-centered lyrics, having the kids move and sing "T-A-K-S" for the chorus. The teachers and many students were smiling, singing along with the chorus, and moving their pom-poms in a streaking blue and white pulse. I unenthusiastically fluttered my pom-poms up and down as well.

After they finished singing, the second, third and then first grade classes got up and read "cheers" that were a few sentences long and placed on large pieces of butcher paper hanging on the gym walls. The second graders had to repeat their cheer a couple of times, as they had not practiced and the recitation consisted of the teachers reading words from a student held strip of butcher paper. After each cheer, students would clap and shake their "cowbells," which were used plastic soft drink bottles with beans in them—homemade shakers that the parents had put together along with the pom-poms. Ms. Smith then returned with a booming version of "Beat the TAKS" and we all moved our pom-poms and shook our cowbells.

With great energy, Maria Gamez stated that last year the 4th graders had scored 100%! "You did such a great job and you can do it again 4th grade!" I know we can do it again, she pronounced. She reminded them that they had test-taking strategies that they could use tomorrow and to remember those. She urged them to eat well and to get a good night's sleep. She said that she believed in and cared about them. Then they were reminded to be serious in their efforts: "You need to do it with care," Ms. Gamez told them, a serious gaze emanating from underneath the blue-tinted hair.

At the end of the rally, the community's gaze focused on the 4th grade students. Ms. Gamez and Ms. Largo told them that they could leave first and lead the entire school community out of the assembly. Students, parents, and faculty clapped as the smallish bodies rose and started to parade out of the gym. Some fourth graders smiled, but many did not. The fourth graders returned their pom-poms into large, empty cardboard boxes, and with serious, flat expressions, they marched out between those of us located at the exit, with each fourth grade student carrying a distinguishing set of beads around their neck (they were taking the test on Fat Tuesday). During the rally and the "T-A-K-S" chorus, a Central Texas School District Police officer was standing behind me and walking around the school. Talking to him before and after the rally with blue-tined hair, Ms. Gamez and Ms. Largo had discussed with the officer the details of a reported domestic violence incident in the home of a student. Rosa Lopez, a reading teacher at the school, originally thought the morning assemblies were a waste of time, but then she came around to support them because they help reach a common focus and set the environment for the day. She asked me:

> Have you been to the morning assemblies? Then you see that everyone cheers for one another and pats each other on the back. Like for the TAKS, everybody creates a poster and banner. It's like cheering for our team. That is something beneficial and there is a build up from first grade on.

Contradictions and Tensions from the Inside/Out

When I discussed this episode with my doctoral-level administration students, one principal enthusiastically and unreflexively stated: "Oh, those pep rallies really work—the students really do perform better." As a researcher engaged with poststructuralist notions, how do I deconstruct the spectacle of performativity and meanings evident in "Peppin for the TAKS" in a theoretically informed manner that engages teachers and helps them decouple micro-political spectacle from what may be considered authentic engagement (Anderson & Gallegos, 2005)? As a former administrator and a professor who now prepares future administrators, how do I begin to help students critically reflect on new outcome-based discourses of effectiveness, and their relationship to the efficiency discourses deeply embedded within the foundations of educational administration (Calla-han, 1962; Gunter, 1995) and the subsequent effective schools movement (Sloan, 2004)? Effectiveness discourse is now tightly-linked to high-stakes performance, and its powerful position within the broader educational field is symbolized by the U.S. Department of Education' Institute of Education Science's *What Works Clearinghouse* (www.w-w-c.org). School effectiveness studies and concerns are certainly worthy of pedagogical focus, and effectiveness is a concept that I engage with my students. Yet, it is effectiveness discourse and its tightly related concern, performance, where several theoretical engagements can help students to trouble and mediate overly consumptive notions of outcome-obsessed effectiveness discourses and practices that are particularly evident in "urgent" discourses resounding through urban educational environments in which teachers and administrators [re]turn to neo-Tayloristic top-down logics of control (Maxcy & Nguyen, 2006; Valenzuela, 2005) in order to respond "effectively" to performance orientations (McNeil, 2005).

The analysis of the Márquez Elementary culture of performance presented in this chapter should provide not only a grounded context for reflection on pedagogical engagements with school performance discourses and practices, but also provide some reflection on how to guide school-based inquiry processes within such environments. As a novice ethnographically-oriented researcher, I struggled with how to provide a complex description that fairly, yet critically represents (interprets) the webs of significance around a culture of performance at Márquez Elementary: a high-performing, primarily Latino school (Emerson, Fretz & Shaw, 1995; Foley, 2002; Spradley, 1980; Wolcott, 1994). As a former administrator in the district of study-a partial insider with access to the school administration and Central Texas Independent District norms and policies, how do I engage in fieldwork reflexively, paying particular attention to subjectivity, standpoint, and power in a highly anxious, performance-oriented environment which is becoming much more commonplace in schools (Hirsh, 2005; Lipman, 2004)? As a professor of Educational Leadership and Policy Studies, how might I lead my students through conflicts, complications, and possibilities of conducting critical policy analysis-framed ethnographic work in educational contexts in which they have some form of insider status? In a turn of a phrase, how might I come to use social theory, in particular critical policy analysis, in an "accountable fashion"; that is in a way that leads to students to agendic, mediatory, reflective, moral, and purposeful teacher and administrator practice around educational policies. How might students come to conceptualize policies as lived, cultural notions, rather than unreflectively accepting policy as fiats "from above"?

This chapter is an initial attempt at such work. It draws from dissertation research that aimed to provide a critical policy analysis (Apple, 2001; Ball,

1994; Lipman, 2004; Taylor, et. al, 1997) of how high-stakes accountability and bilingual education policies intersected in the lived experience of four 3rd and 5th grade students at one particular elementary school. It provides a thick description (Geertz, 1973) of the accountability sensitive, performance-oriented school culture that circulated through the social body of Márquez Elementary. Given the shadowing role high-stakes accountability policies play in the administration of schools and in the training of educational leaders and teachers, a contemporary critical policy analysis, which aims to provide an "account of how educational policies are received and articulated in schools" and to illuminate "how the political economy and cultural practices of schools are linked" (Taylor, et. al, 1997, p.viii), can be a valuable framework to engage how multiple aspects of high-stakes accountability policies are lived within discourse and practice in specific school settings.

I also engage methodological tensions I experienced as a former administrator conducting eight months of fieldwork at Márquez Elementary, a high-performing, high-minority school located in a performance-oriented school district in Texas. As a former "insider" (administrator at a school in the same southwestern, urban district) I felt it was useful to maintain a sense of interpretivist distance in order to attain descriptive validity (Wolcott, 1994), develop explicit awareness, and deliberately search for disconfirming evidence (Spradley, 1980), yet I had become engaged with critical policy perspectives around educational accountability systems in Texas (McNeil, 2000; Valenzuela, 2005), which urged a more activist stance in my research, thus producing contradictions and tensions that were uniquely informed by my own insider/outsider research standpoint. Issues of researcher power and subjectivity (Denzin & Lincoln, 1998; Dewalt et al., 1998; Foley, 2002; Hatch, 2003), related to my positionality as a former administrator in the district, informed and related to my conflict over how to engage the effects of high-stakes testing and the resulting culture of performance with multiply positioned participants—teachers, parents, and administrators. Few studies have engaged issues specific to ethnographically oriented research in schools where the participants themselves clearly identify the researcher as a former administrator (Blase & Anderson, 1995; Hatch, 2003), and there has been scant focus on the implication of former administrators engaging critical policy ethnographies in a stress-filled, high-stakes educational accountability environment (Lipman, 2004; Murthada-Watts, 2002; Shore & Wright, 1997 Valenzuela, 2005), and the contradictions and tensions such work implies.

STUDY CONTEXT AND METHODS

The research site, Márquez Elementary, is located in an urban setting in Texas and was geographically and personally accessible to the researcher. During the 2003–2004 school year, the school had approximately 370 students enrolled, 19.6% of whom were classified as African-American, 78.7% as Latino, and 1.7% as White. Sixty-eight percent of the students are officially demarcated as "at-risk," 91.6% as economically disadvantaged, and 30.8% as "Limited English Proficient." The school had been labeled "Recognized" in the Texas Accountability System rating system for the previous two years and manifested multi-year upward performance trends on the high-stakes Texas Assessment of Knowledge and Skills (TAKS) (TEA, 2005). Information was collected over a period of eight months in the 2003–2004 school year through semi-structured and informal interviews, observations, non-obtrusive data, reflective journaling, and District and State policy text analysis (Denzin & Lincoln, 1998; Emerson, Fretz, & Shaw, 1995; Fontana & Frey, 2003; Glesne, 1999; Hatch, 2003). Initial themes were elicited through categorization (Miles & Huberman, 1984; Strauss & Corbin, 1990; Wolcott, 1994) and used to develop analytic themes, which were theorized and explored throughout the data collection process through the use of analytic memos. This ongoing analysis linked local understanding to broader policies and informed further observation and interviews in an iterative cycle of description, analysis, and reflexive inquiry (Denzin, 1989; Emerson et al., 1995; Mirriam, 1998). Thematic analysis was further expanded through close, critical readings of the text of interviews and fieldnotes. This study did not attempt to compare the discourse and practices at this particular school site with other school sites, other than for triangulation of data and further contextualization of school-based analysis within a performance-oriented school district. A primary concern of the research was to understand how selected testing and accountability policies intersected with bilingual education policy and came to influence and shape the lives of immigrant students in a particular school context.

In the next section of the chapter, I describe a major theme that emerged from my school-based critical policy inquiry, informed as it was by my previous administrative positionality: the normalization of a performance culture at Márquez Elementary. Subsequently I reflect on my particular ethnographic engagement within a performance-oriented district that centers performance discourses around students and schools. It is within these particular kind of contexts that dominant accountability discourse and performance orientations will reveal themselves as "reality" or "practical" to our students. I then begin to answer what do we do about that—how do we unsettle these practices, while still remaining materially accountable to diverse school communities and the multiple values come to layer around schools (Furman, 2003)? I engage/construct implications for teaching and unsettling future teachers and administrators, as well as guiding the development critical policy inquiry lenses through this case study of a school culture likely to be framed in accountability performance victory tropes as effective and progressive.

THE STORY OF ACCOUNTABLE TALK:
NORMALIZING A CULTURE OF PERFORMANCE

High-Stakes Accountability Policies Lived and Led at Márquez Elementary

As is often the case with any educational policy, accountability policies are mediated and transformed in the complexity and profusion of practice at the school level (Ball, 1994; Levinson & Sutton, 2001). Often traditional policy analyses "dramatically underestimate the considerable discretion exercised by state and local agencies when implementing federal law" (Sabatier & Mazmanian, 1995, p. 2). At Márquez Elementary, school administrators and staff made great efforts to leverage the accountability system to professionalize teaching, to tightly couple instructional and managerial systems, to maintain high expectations for students in a variety of domains, to know each student's strengths and weaknesses, and to maximize instructional time. Additionally, experienced, highly competent teachers who were native speakers of Spanish taught immigrant students.

I argue that these practices are, in effect, localized policy responses to what is an increasingly high-stakes, test-driven educational macro-political environment that provides sustenance to an ethic of profession (accountable educators) agendicly pursuing performance orientations through symbols and political spectacle, such as test pep rallies (Edelman, 1988; Smith, 2004). At Márquez, a school culture developed in which test preparation and performance rituals were incorporated into assemblies (where rewards and consequences for student effort and attention to TAKS questions were prominently noted), parent preparation of pre-TAKS breakfasts, public display of practice test results, and other public practices. The school based administrators embraced systematic management of relaxation exercises for students in order to help them feel better, but also to produce performance validity, i.e. maximum student test performance. In this culture of performance, a sense of performance for the collective benefit of the school becomes normalized, and students came to have a sense of performance agency (Black, 2004).

Member-checking my analysis and perspectives with participants and former administrators, during my time at Márquez, I came to view how resources were coordinated to maximize passage of the test. I saw how students were explicitly taught test-taking strategies and disciplined to maximize effort on assessment and comprehension tasks. Within efforts to maximize time on the delivery of the curriculum, I interrogated how student bodies were disciplined to provide a relatively quiet and orderly school where classroom doors were locked, recess was limited, and students read books while they are constantly told to be quiet during lunch in the cafeteria. From my standpoint as a researcher and former administrator, I accessed and saw these types of events and discourses as creating webs of significance (a story of accountable talk) that I described as a culture of performance.

Normalizing Collective Performance

The pep rally is not only a public ritual that exposes meaning and values of the Márquez Elementary school culture, but it also helps to construct and annually reinvigorate important elements of that school culture that maximize performance. It does so by borrowing symbols and rituals from secondary schools embedded in the pep rally. It served to mark the beginning of the TAKS season, and soon all the other test-taking grades will be involved. The assembly served to ritually end it and carried rewards and sanctions for effort. The performance rallies and assemblies also served as an initiation ritual for the early grade students, who learn the importance of performing well on the TAKS. The younger students participate in ways that teach them that the school's performance is important to their lives. As they read the "text" of the events, the third through fifth grade students are prepared to take the tests seriously, and are being disciplined to perform, as maximum effort and comprehensive use of strategies is normalized. Internally, students know that they need to prepare, and that they also will hold the reputation of the school in their collective hands and pencils. The younger students have time to participate in the construction of a cultural memory that emphasizes test performance. They now possess the knowledge that they too will need to perform individually in order to bring future fame or malady to the school.

In peppin' for the TAKS, the fourth graders were symbolically anointed as small TAKS warriors, who through their TAKS performance the following day, would defend the culture and honor of the school. As the students left I projected some weight on the slight shoulders of the students, who now wore Mardi Gras beads like warrior plates. Students' high performance has brought honor and glory to the school in the past, and it is expected that these students now continue the tradition, as well enhance their own individual possibilities.

The previous week had brought the adulation of the highest district staff, and this researcher was here partially based on the construction of Márquez as a successful school because of the bilingual students' test scores. In the current policy environment, schools with immigrant and low SES-populations are most likely to perform poorly on high-stakes tests (TEA, 2004; Valencia & Villareal, 2004). Student performance in these schools is indelibly linked to protecting the lifeworld of the school (Maxcy, 2004). High performance means that the school fortress holds— it does not become subject to District or State intervention, which could dramatically alter the school culture and ways of making meaning. The students' continued strong performance means that the state or district does not invade or penetrate with focused interventions such as closely monitored curriculum delivery and weekly assessments. Already racialized students and schools are less likely to be symbolically marked as deficient, and more likely to be labeled positively, which translates into material benefits and opportunities. High performance translates into the relative protection of the school culture, and the further expansion of the reputation of the school, which definitely benefits the adults working in the school, the leadership most of all.

So, the 4th graders, who are given the metaphorically warlike "beat the TAKS" message, are ritually sent out to battle. During the rally and assembly, the whole school was behind the test-taking students, and their performance was not simply about individual merit or competence, but also about the collective. The high-stakes penalties were averted metaphorically by preparing students for battle. At Márquez, the TAKS is not only a high-stakes assessment, but the most public performance of a broad, underlying culture of performance. As districts play a significant role in school-level reform (Rorrer, 2002), this emphasis on performance was congruent with my administrative experience in the district, yet it seemed wildly exaggerated in this particular school environment.

For instance, the end of the high-stakes testing season arrived in late April. I entered the school the day the third through fifth grade students were to take the Math TAKS. Students in Pre-K through 2nd grade wore their Márquez t-shirts to school in order to show solidarity with the tasks of their elder brethren. Posters hanging outside of classrooms exhorted students to do their best and Ms. Woods, the fifth grade teacher, wore a white T-shirt exclaiming "Pass the TAKS". I walked into a relatively calmer morning assembly, where Maria Gamez, the principal, took 20 minutes to exhort and cheer on the test-taking students. She went over strategies with students, as she and the students reminded each other of things to do that day: drink water, "push their thinking button" (a type of physical relaxation response), brain gym activities and other triggers for comprehension. Maria attempted to be as comprehensive as she could, a bit to the chagrin of a couple of teachers who seemed to just want to get on with testing. A counselor spotted one student who seemed to be sleepy, noting that she needed to check up on him. Scanning over the rest of the student bodies, the counselors were ready to intervene to make sure all would be as effort-ful as possible.

Maria told the students that she loved them. She mentioned how there was a Friday sleepover planned for the girls and a field trip planned for the boys. She then reminded them that she would be visiting the classes during the day and how sad it would be for the boys to not concentrate or do their best, because they would then be in the office while the others were having fun. Maria does not monitor performance, over which she has little control over at this point, but effort, and uses threats and rewards to further her students' efforts. At the end of the assembly, Maria reminded them: "you need to do well not just for yourself, but for the school."

Pushing, supporting, and excoriating the students through a rally at the beginning of the testing season and an assembly before the last tests, the collective focus on TAKS performance served multiple purposes-both material and symbolic. They sought to motivate student effort and thus maximize individual and collective performance on each specific TAKS test. These young students had been receiving content knowledge instruction focused around the TEKS (standards) as well as explicitly articulated test-taking strategies for the high-stakes TAKS (such as consistently reading passages several times to insure complete comprehension). The rally sought to add excitement and motivation that would last throughout the season, while in the assembly sought careful, comprehensive effort at the end of a lengthy preparation cycle. If the students are motivated and concentrate to the best of their ability, then the test results with be made maximally valid—the students will show all that they know and concurrently the test will show the truest and most valid levels of performance of the students.

Extending this line of thought, it becomes irresponsible, perhaps even an ethical lapse of professional practice, to not give students the greatest opportunities to succeed in life because their test score was not maximized, and the test score serves as the most concrete measure of learning and thus human capital development, which in turn opens up future opportunities for the students. Maria worked very hard and she felt enormous responsibility to maximize classroom instructional time so that students would learn and produce high performance on TAKS. She believed the test was a relatively valid measure, and that student success on the test meant creating greater opportunities to succeed later in life. Thus, high rates of student success on the TAKS are normalized as a moral leadership imperative.

Is this a get-real moment? One that should not be deconstructed, I asked myself. I knew as a former administrator that the test had some minimal validity and the performance on the test labeled a student and shaped his/her educational experience—those with lower scores did tend to get more skills-based remediation (McNeil, 2005).

On another occasion, Ms. Gamez told the District personnel during a monitoring visit that one of the exceptional aspects of the school is that the staff works hard to have students take assessments seriously. They really work to make sure they get maximum effort on the benchmarks and the release TAKS so that they instill discipline in the young test takers as well as provide reliable indicators for predicting student performance on the "real" TAKS. The district personnel applauded her for this and spoke about how this is a concern on other campuses—students are not taking non-TAKS assessments seriously enough and so school managers cannot accurately gauge what they know and adjust the delivery of curriculum accordingly. This concern is also echoed in Texas Education Agency guides that stress the importance of appropriately timing the testing of bilingual students so as to not bias the test results (TEA, 2002, 2004). I did not want to map and monitor student test efforts to maximize validity as an administrator—is that linked to moral purpose of schooling (Starratt, 2004), but that is a constraint of practice in a performance oriented district. As I analyzed these types of practices, I met once with the Associate Superintendent of Elementary schools—she urged me to figure out and write about what worked in the school and then come back to the work in the district to implement my findings as an administrator. Such research actually made administrative work less appealing, a collateral effect for those of us that now head to the academy.

Maximizing Time and Disciplining Bodies

Melissa Woods, the fifth grade teacher, felt that there were great teachers at the school and believed that they "work really, really hard here." Yet, she felt that the atmosphere could be much more positive. Melissa, along with several parents expressed negative connotations of the school being run as a business-cold, run around numbers. This relates to the creation of a new public sphere, where student test scores are commodified and high-stakes accountability systems are linked to globalizing processes (Hursh, 2005). The reading teacher noted how worrisome it was when a high-performing student, a valuable commodity in the performance economy, transfers out of the school. In this case we discussed, the loss was most severe because the student was in the 5th grade, the grade that was the most behind academically. A few thought the school was so oriented toward market-like efficiencies, that less than appropriate emphasis was placed on socialization, human development, and joy. Melissa put it this way: "sometimes you walk in and I don't feel that um, this is an elementary school…I just feel that walking into an elementary school it should feel happy and you know, not so businessy [laughs]." Efficiency was reflected in multiple ways time was maximized and academic productivity was embodied within the governance of students' bodies (disciplinarity). I focus on three marginal[4] social spaces where such efficiency and discipline are reflected: the cafeteria, recess, and in the production of a quiet school.

Cafeteria

In my first visit to the cafeteria in October, I was struck by how different it was from my own experience as a principal in a 1,000 student Elementary School. Two activities struck me as particular: some students were spaced apart and quietly reading books, and alternately by choice and coercion of an imposing monitor, others were simply sitting quietly. The teacher who monitored the cafeteria occasionally grabbed the microphone and stated forcefully that students were too loud, demanding one minute of silence. Even I felt the need to obey, to quiet my body, and the three adults I was with stayed quiet. A few minutes later, I was going to ask a student a question, but curtailed that impulse, as I felt watched by the judging eye of the monitor. About a fourth of the students who had finished eating had picked up books they had brought with them and were reading quietly.

On several more occasions while I was speaking to the third and fifth graders at lunch I felt the gaze of the monitor and even I felt I needed to regulated myself to keep quiet or I else I would "get in trouble" and be evicted from the cafeteria. I even told the students that I was not going to speak either, while they laughed about it. Isaac, a fifth grader, told me that the cafeteria was his least favorite place in the school, a space where once he told me with a wry smile to watch what will happen—the students are going to talk, it will get louder and then they will not be able to talk, which is exactly what occurred. The Márquez Elementary cafeteria is a space where my observations as well as comments of participants reveal a seriousness of purpose and the curtailment of socialization as a meritorious activity in and of itself. The cafeteria was not a space to release or fully socialize—it was efficiently used as a space to continue to incorporate discipline management (and the control of bodies) and to extend the academic curriculum as many students contentedly read books and created math problems amongst themselves. In this way, students pushed themselves beyond their compatriots in other schools and reflected productive self discipline in a potentially chaotic social space—a modernist accomplishment.

However, Lori, a parent, comments:

> I disagree with them being so quiet in the lunchroom, because it is time to socialize with your peers, forget about not school, but work. Forget about the

pressures and the stress and all that and just have a little good time talking to your friends. They have them all just sitting on one side, you know, boy-girl, boy-girl and they can't talk. Even at home you socialize at dinner. You socialize not to get to, not really to vent, but to let your day out, to go out of your system and to prepare for what is later.

Here Lori comments on both the ongoing stress of the school environment, which she attributes to the way the leadership has dealt with high-stakes tests and laments the fact that this performance emphasis and stress stretch throughout the students days they can't "let their day out." [How do we let the day out as administrators and teachers?]. Knowing I had the ear of the principal as a former administrator, several parents started to come to me and relay their discomfort with the cafeteria. Several many did do not go in there when a particular monitor was there, as they felt she would unjustly hand out detention to the students who were talking. They felt this situation had been made worse, because recess and gym had been limited, and even lunch no longer qualified as any kind of undisciplined time. Their comments tested me: Could I not, as a researcher, see this? Could I not, as an administrator, change this?

Recess

At Márquez, teachers could decide their recess time, but they also knew that Maria wanted them to maximize their time teaching. On many visits to the school, I would peer out at the playground and hardly see students there. Ms. Camarillo's students (third graders) told me that they really did not do recess often and not at all before the TAKS, although they did go out and do laps on the track. I understood and admired the ability to focus on curriculum, particularly given the immense amount of tasks to be completed in any school organization and the growing emphasis on instructional leadership (Adams & Copland, 2005; Murphy, 2003). During a Superintendent's visit, Maria commented to the District staff that they do not take much time for recess, as they needed to concentrate on academic tasks. The Superintendent nodded in agreement with the policy. So, to be a professional in this atmosphere, teachers went to recess occasionally, but they did not "waste" their time on it.

Lorrie Karl, the counselor, commented that she was raised with the idea that breaks, particularly recess or physical breaks, are important in school—that school can be a stressful environment for students. She lamented the lack of consistent recess at Márquez and asked me about research around the issue. "It may be ok if they do not have recess, but I do not think that not having it necessarily increases student performance. In Kansas there was never a mention of eliminating recess—I hope there is a better way." It was clear that there was less recess at Márquez than at any of the other schools she had worked in outside the state and this was due, in her analysis, to the pressures to perform on the TAKS. A discourse of efficiency, most embedded in policy and administrative discourse, trumped notions of childhood:

> It is different here—there is not an opportunity to do parties and up until the end of the school year the students need to be learning. Here they also have their field trips scheduled at the end of the school year. Children are children and they need that exposure throughout their school time so that they will figure out where they will like to be.

Parties, field trips, and recess are all activities that become secondary and are clustered intensely around the end of the school year calendar, when the "testing season" had ended. Advocates of accountability-based systems could argue that this is a rational and productive allocation of school time oriented toward learning the foundational knowledge as represented on the TEKS and tested on the TAKS.

When I spoke with Maria about recess, she did not believe there was any problem. She felt that she felt a huge sense of responsibility to make sure students maximized their daily opportunities. They are behind and I want to give them the greatest amount of opportunities possible when we only have them for a short time. She continued:

> I can't afford, because of this situation, to have these kids take a recess, that you know 20 minutes turns into 30, 40 by the time you get back. Plus, I know that the kids play at home, so they get that.

Her position ties back to school as business and maximizing effort themes; her intention is to develop and support a school culture that counters what elementary students of color have historically encountered—excessive amounts of recess and waste of curricular time (Kozol, 1980). This statement reveals a deep sense of commitment to the children and the schools, but as applied to a larger district context leads to the segregating of recess—students in schools populated by lower income students would be bereft of recess, while the higher income schools would not only be passing TAKS, but they have fun at recess as well.

The Production of a Quiet School

From my journal I lift this October reflection:

> Laughing at myself as a white interloper, an inarticulate Joseph Conrad, I believe that the school seems Dark. People keep telling me about it being a great school, and I believe that, but the physical building seems oldish and grey/brown and the natural light does not stream in—there is no light flood-

ing into the school. Then, there seems to be a lot of effort on control. Silent students wandering the hall, quiet, be quiet, signal up to be quiet, don't talk in the cafeteria, don't talk in the assembly. Yes, control is necessary to some degree for learning, but what do they have that they have to be quieted so much—will some darkness come out of the bodies? Not many students moving about (compared to my previous job), quiet lines occasionally go to the cafeteria, there is no back up of students going places, being loud, like at [the schools where I worked before]. The playground is far, far. The cafeteria is separated. The two wings are separated. They all remain quiet. Lightness and laughter is not apparent in the cafeteria or in the halls—perhaps it springs in the classroom—I will need to see and feel.

In subsequent visits as I got to know people, I did not feel so strongly about repressed quietness, darkness, but this feeling remained for the duration of my research experience. Without an engagement with theory, I would have thought the actions I observed around the student bodies as "normal"—what educators might do at some level with children—we often just call it redirection, order, or in more expressive ways, discipline. What I became interested in was disciplining bodies, particularly around the notion of performance. On one occasion, I was walking down the hall and a frustrated teacher was talking to a student, expressing the desire for him to embody quietness: "all day long I have been telling you to stop talking. Monday, Tuesday, Wednesday, I had to tell you to stop talking. How many times do I have to tell you to stop talking and get on the ball!" The physical control of bodies is also consistently reflected in the quiet, hands-behind-the-back passage of lines of students walking through the hallways, proctored by teachers who systematically identify which student is best in line. This disciplining of bodies was productive behavior, but increasingly unpopular and a source of anger amongst some parents, who not only wanted me to see it (as the researcher), but to change it (as the administrator). I had now become a sounding board for complaints about the school from a group of parents. One parent was particularly unhappy with procedures for keeping students physically under control. She stated:

> They have the children walking in line like they are in TYC [Texas Youth Commission—incarcerated as juvenile offenders] or something. Their hands are folded behind their backs like they have handcuffs on, walking in a line, you know. Kids, they hate coming to school and it is not supposed to be that way. You have seen that happen, Bill, I know you have.

Sitting in the library after a district-level leadership had visited, Maria, the Principal asked me what I thought about the visit and the school. Positioned as a former administrator, as well as associated with the University, I became an important node for feedback that was separate from the school, but also an "equal of sorts." I complemented her on the systematic, thoughtful way she had brought the school along and how students are able to talk to each other about their learning processes. I did mention to her, that as a broad impression, the school seemed very quiet to me—I described my experience in the cafeteria, how quietly the students walked around the school, and how the "no talk zone" sign on the front door struck me as different since I had come from a much larger and much louder school. I basically asked if the kids had an opportunity to "let out" and or speak socially. She was taken aback and responded that she experienced Márquez as a loud school and pointed out that students do a lot of talking in the classrooms. While we talked, Lori, a parent, was shelving books and said "I am sorry, but I agree with Mr. Black-the kids need to be kids and have recess." Maria suggested we continue this conversation in my office.

Maria was a bit upset over what she (rightfully) interpreted as a critique, and struggled to explain to me that her desire for a quiet school is pragmatic and about building opportunity: "I want them to learn how to be quiet, how to be disciplined, how to get along." So being quiet is about holistic caring, expanding beyond the official curriculum and giving the students skills and attitudes that will serve them in the labor force, as well as in life. She continued: "If they are being inappropriate then they won't get ahead and that is what I see within my family. I don't know, but that seems to be the way to go." She feels tension over this critique, as it conflicts with some values around notions of childhood, but overarching is a professional ethic that values the idea that learning to be quiet and disciplined will help them to get ahead in life and be more productive in the future—provide them with social and cultural capital (Bourdieu, 1977). My critique in the relatively public school library, had now placed me in the position of slowing progress, interfering in the school—no longer a dispassionate observer, I had inspired some anger.

Locked Doors Disciplining Classroom Professionalism

At Márquez the production of a quiet and disciplined school included locked doors that protected classroom and school spaces from internal and external disturbances. Generally, all classroom doors remained locked throughout the day—Maria and Camila would themselves enter with keys. When I taught the ESL class to parents, I always had to get the custodian to come and open the portable. When Ms. Gamez or another staff member would arrive during the school day, a custodian would be called to open the gate to the parking lot and to then close and lock it after they drove in. Maria had told me that when she first came to the school seven years ago parents would interrupt classroom instruction by selling tamales and bringing sweets—she was originally unpopular for eliminating that practice, but did what is best for kids by returning focus on the core technology of the school-effective, maximized time on instruction. To keep instructional time sacred, classroom doors were locked— even students who went to the reading teacher had to knock on the door to get back into their classroom. As a methodological aside, this presented some significant difficulties for me gaining original and even ongoing access to classrooms, as I consistently felt like an interloper and uncomfortable interrupting classroom instruction, particularly during the stressful build up to the TAKS examination. The locked doors served to preserve and enhance the notion of the classroom as a professional, serious space, yet it also insulated them from the community around the school and as Lorena Soriano, the Parent Training Specialist noted to me on several occasions, projected a less than friendly orientation towards parents. Lorena would say in a slightly bitter tone that teachers there did not believe that parents had the right to visit the classrooms. This was made evident to her most vividly on African-American parents day.

On February 9th, I arrived at the school around 8:15 and saw one flyer announcing that today was African-American parents day, and then another one in Spanish announcing it was parents day. Ms. Soriano had coffee, juice, and cookies for parents, and invited me into her office to have coffee when I came in. The District had sent a flyer last week about making Monday black parent day, "and you know how we have problems with African-American parents coming in" and she claimed, "the district had not given us enough time."

During the course of the day, I saw no African-American parents. When I went into Ms. Camarillo's classroom, I did see two parents that were in my ESL class—their children later told me that they would get "points" if their parents came. There were no parents in Ms. Woods' fifth grade class. After observing in the classrooms, I went back down the hall and went into Ms. Soriano's parent room. When I walked into the parent room, I became an audience to disaffected employees and parents. The seven or so Latina mothers, talking in Spanish, said to me that they were taking "chismes", or gossiping about the school. Ms. Soriano then told me that a couple of teachers had told the Latina mothers that they should leave the classroom they had come to visit. Ms. Soriano claimed that teachers asked the parents to leave as they were working on important classroom material (the TAKS was within the immediate horizon). According to Ms. Soriano and the parents in the room, the teachers intimated that the parents were an instructional distraction. Upset, Ms. Soriano stated that she always told parents that it is their school and that they can go in whenever they wanted to.

Here the conflict over goals seemed to emerge: was it primarily a community-based or community-open institution or an institution focused on its primary function as a closed system: zealously maximizing and protecting instructional time of the students? Ms. Soriano was clear in her reaction: "I don't know about these teachers. I have a 7 year old daughter who goes to school [in another town] and they let me in to the classroom, *pase, pase* [come in]. That's why I had to go to Ms. Gamez and she had to get on the intercom and tell some teachers to let them in."

Spoken in front of the parents in the room, my presence lent the story of the school as unwelcoming to parents further credence. Throughout the semester, Ms. Soriano held a very conflicted stance vis-à-vis her role as the Parent Training Specialist at Márquez. As she told me later, "I tell the parents that they are always invited and it is not right that they are not let in. I know the teachers are stressed and they want order, but the parents should be able to go in at any time." To me this incident marked the beginning of the creation of her office space as one where she and certain parents participated in various critiques of the school. A month later, during cafeteria duty, she told me flatly, "the teachers here do not want parents involved" and they do not want to work with students. Over the course of two months, I listened and did not refute her critique. A consistent story of conflict between parents and their ally the Parent Training Specialist, and the professional class of educators began to emerge. From a teacher's perspective, within a performance-oriented school culture, their time is at a premium and it is a rational decision to minimize distractions to the high-stakes tasks at hand-that is a main purpose of accountability policies—to focus time on what is most important, standards-guided curriculum and learning (Hamilton, Steecher, & Klein, 2002). Parent participation is something upon which they will not be assessed. Even if parent involvement is encoded in policy texts originating from a school district department, it does not emanate from where power is dispersed, and so parent involvement, while desired, is marginalized or controlled.

Ms. Gamez knew I had been in the parent training room while critiques began. Ms. Gamez suspected some of them had stolen some school material out of the room where I taught an ESL class. As a former administrator, I listened and in some manner legitimized the parents' critiques. At the end of the study and school year, Ms. Soriano was dismissed from her duties. Did her confession and critique become more dangerous because of my presence? I have not asked Maria Gamez.

Instilling Competition

I asked myself in my journal, what does it mean to value the rising turtles? During the learning walk, the group of administrators, including the Superintendent, walked into a fourth grade classroom where they encountered a board full of small, green paper cut-outs of turtles. Each turtle had a student name and assessment score. The turtles were arranged in a hierarchy—the highest scoring students' turtles were at the top. The visiting District Curriculum Director commented that it must be a safe classroom, for the students seemed comfortable with each other. The Superintendent, on the other hand, appeared "fired up" about the turtles, commenting a couple of times that he liked the idea. I wish I had that when I was a student, he enthused, because I would have wanted mine to go higher and higher. Both the turtles and the reaction from the Superintendent reflect a belief in the progressive character of modern processes that individualize and rank, thus delineating differences that motivate students and in doing so, discipline performance. These individualizing and ranking processes are central to the dispersal of power through bureaucratic institutions and the governing of its subjects, like teachers and students (Foucault, 1977).

This form of governmentality, that aimed to manufacture and motivate focused performance, was apparent in the awareness students had of where they stood vis-à-vis other students. Students in the third grade class had seen their practice TAKS scores listed from best to worst. One student told me his scores on the practice test (mid 80's) and that made him confident that he would pass the TAKS. He also could tell me the scores of other students in his class. In Ms. Wood's fifth grade class only two students out of 11 test-taking students in the class passed all three sections of the Spring of 2004-reading, math, and science. The students were also acutely aware of who those peers might be. The students in both classes I observed displayed a type of performance literacy, and could read from the text of their practice assessments their probability of success.

Many of my current administrative students and future teacher leaders believe the form of student monitoring and performance orientations put forth in this section of the chapter can easily be constituted as effective practices. In the next major section, I turn to how teaching through reflexive stances and theory can help students "not throw the baby out with the bathwater" in terms of being accountable to their students and community. To extend the metaphor (perhaps badly), I contend that we can help students reflect on multiple aspects of the baby, the lifeworld and culture of school institutions, and critically view the societal water in which they are bathed.

**ENGAGING CONTRADICTIONS
FROM THE INSIDE/OUTSIDE: TEACHING TEACHER
LEADERS ABOUT ETHNOGRAPHIC ENGAGEMENT IN A
PERFORMANCE-ORIENTED DISTRICT**

Insider/Outsider

In my fieldnotes, I frequently reflected on what I would identify as my "administrator's impulse". As an Assistant Principal and short-term Principal, I was accustomed to making decisions, which requires quick evaluation, followed by some visible action to solve an identifiable problem—a perpetually urgent state. Yet, in my role as a participant observer partially in search of the meaning-making of others, I often had to discipline myself and limit initial judgments and actions. My administrator's impulse worked against a sense of suspension needed to produce the "explicit awareness" Spradley (1980) believes is useful for cultural analysis. This was particularly acute at the beginning of the project, when I felt impelled to discipline a student, or give a teacher another suggestion. My frustration rose when I followed my advisor's advice and would simply reply, "that's interesting" to a comment or performative behavior that I wanted to contest or as this book title suggests, unsettle. My urge to be productive—produce pedagogy, solve a problem, embrace action-to engage in "pragmatics" of administration, action[5] became muted and frustrated. Despite being a relatively full-time graduate student, my engagement was not sufficiently long or deep to ever dissipate that frustration, particularly given my inconsistent delivery of ESL classes to parents (one way I intended to "give something back" to the school) over the semester due to other responsibilities. To collaboratively create some long term action would have been consistent with critical qualitative research traditions and would have been more satisfying, but such engagements are typically not practical for Educational Administration students, particularly those practicing administrators in Ed.D programs.

As frustrating as my insider identity was, I was also often perturbed by my identification as a University researcher. I found that I categorized my school-based identity as a more "productive" identity. In the first couple of months, I also wanted to reassert that previous identity because I encountered, as others have that being an ethnographer is often uncomfortable (Foley, 1995). I desired the privileges of the administrative position, which provided referent frames for interaction. Now, like a salesman, I thought, I had to go up and introduce myself and sell my project. Not similarly protected by institutional authority, I approached people unsure if what I was doing was of use to them, when I did not even know if it was or even is. Am I selling lemons, I asked myself? Maybe not doing damage is the best that I can do—what diminished expectations from my teacher and administrator identities!

Talkin' Philosophy: The Weakness of Knowledge and the "Strength" of Action

Excerpted and written from fieldnotes from January 20, 2004:

> 8:15 A.M. I walked in to the front office at Márquez and Maria [the principal] was in her office, saw me, and invited me in to talk. After exchanging pleasantries, Maria [who speaks Spanish] told me that she is now speaking in English to the upper grade students." I know I have to prepare them for Middle School and TAKS [in English at the secondary level] and I want to help them keep their culture, but I feel guilty and feel that I am doing them a disservice if I continue to speak to them in Spanish when I know what awaits them and the parents want them to learn English. I feel really conflicted."

Maria then continued to tell me about the new immigrant student who is getting extra support in class from the reading specialist only in English and also in an after-school English class. "I speak to him in English too and he is so excited to learn English—I want to speak to him in Spanish, but I think I need to speak to him in English so as to not to do him a disservice." She then talked about how there is a group of girls in the 5th grade who really have not made the transition to English, but they were pushing them. "Are they receiving all of their instruction in English?" I asked. Yes, but then Maria added that they speak Spanish to themselves and a beautiful Spanish out on the playground to each other. Maria's voice pitched up as she said she was conflicted, but in the end she thought that English-only instruction in the upper grades of elementary school was the best thing for students. All fifth graders were scheduled to take the TAKS in English, and as well as many of the bilingual 4th graders. I asked about the writing portion of the exam, which comes earlier in the year (February instead of April). Yes, there is a group doing the writing TAKS in Spanish, "but their writing is beautiful." She knows this because Maria has all the students give her a writing sample every quarter and she takes the time to write a response back to them. The students felt connected and important to the principal through this activity.

Maria then said that the District highly discouraged the students taking the new Science TAKS in Spanish, as the vocabulary is "so high." I said that I understand, but commented that she had some teachers that were capable of using the high level Spanish. Yes, she agreed, but throughout the conversation, Maria said it was "hard," "complex," and that she felt "torn" about the working with and keeping the "culture" of the students and asked me what I thought. At this point, I felt as if I was positioned both as a former practitioner, but primarily as a researcher, someone who might possess University-based expert knowledge. I talked about language ideology and power and language and that I thought there were ideological notions embedded within the new bilingual education program, the *Elevar* program.[6] I stated that from her description it seemed to abandon some of the thesis of Krashen's work and the notions of transference. Maria asked what I thought—should you teach in English or Spanish in the upper elementary grades if they are going to the middle school. I said that there were things to consider and talked about Guerrero's (1999, 2003) work and the notion of making decisions based on whether a school or district has effectively fluent and confident teachers in Spanish—they may be certified but not competent. But that is what is so good about Márquez I offered—you have some strong teachers and you can design a bilingual, not just compensatory program (Brisk, 1998; Freeman, 2004).

What about if you don't have those teachers, she asked? I talked about delivery of content, good pedagogy and the "pragmatic reality" that I would rather have strong, experienced, and good teachers in a well articulated ESL program, than weak, inexperienced bilingually certified teachers in a school with no consistent bilingual program. Yes, this was difficult and complex, she answered. I then discussed a couple of points around power and language—language ideologies and notions of cultural subtraction that still remain important to bilingual education (drawing from, for instance, Corson, 1995; Crawford, 2001; Dueñas-Gonzalez, 2001; Stanton-Salazar, 2001; Valenzuela, 1999). [Her body language indicated that she seemed quite open to this kind of discussion].

Maria asked about what to do with the limited-English, limited-Spanish student and she said that they try to look at the parents' home environment "the age of the parents and what grade they are in schools." I acknowledged that these are the most difficult students to deal with within the resource constraints of schooling and that the IDEA test (which the district has used for years to measure Spanish and English language proficiency) is quite limited in what it tells you, so all of these factors do come into play and you need to make a case by case determination, knowing the environment of the student. Also, maybe they are not equally limited in both languages; it is just that we do not have all the information. Plus, you need to look at the resources around the child, inside and outside of school. She concurred and gave me another example of how they used information beyond the initial language proficiency examination and official student cumulative record—she used multiple sources of information to assess immigrant children's abilities, a practice that is not that common, but viewed as essential by researchers in immigrant education (Abedi, 2004). We talked about having these kind of conversations with parents and I told her I would be very excited about doing that. She said that there are coffees and she wants parents to be able to advocate for their kids and that parents who have students at Monroe (the feeder middle school) and other schools often come to her asking for advice on how to handle situations. I said I would love to have more of these conversations about bilingual education policy and practice with her and the broader Márquez community. Maria seemed genuinely enthused, and after this initial discussion about beginning a larger conversation with staff and parents, Camila Largo, the Assistant Principal walked by the office and peered in. Maria invited her in, and immediately stated: "We were just talking philosophy."

Perhaps this then becomes an is one important task in teaching ways to unsettle beliefs—we don't just talk "philosophy" (in this case meaning ideas that can be applied), we constantly disrupt the rooted notion that ideas are just about talking and that ideas are constantly placed on the weak side of the constantly constructed duality of theory versus action. In doing so, it also holds us accountable for the hard, time-consuming bridging work of relevancy that we co-construct with our students and practitioners. Maria's comment that we were talking philosophy recreates the theory (weak)/practice (strong) dichotomy that becomes further reinforced in "urgent" urban school environment as it eliminates spaces for robust, theoretically-engaged notions of practice: praxis. Her comment positioned our conversation and contents of it as incidental, when really I thought it was about things that were central to the framing and designing work of school leadership fed by urgent accountability performance discourses. Interestingly, I believe she thought such conversation and plans were important as well—she was enthused. Yet, I immediately felt that this comment seemed to end our plans—stop them in their tracks, particularly given the overarching emphasis that guides resource allocation in a culture of performance towards production on the upcoming high-stakes tests. The conversation did not become relevant, but rather was positioned as talk; while efforts around a high-stakes indicator have more power and were consistently positioned as action in discourses about the school. This reflects Marshak's (1995) critical contention that within much organizational discourse, talk is positioned as worthless, while action counts or is valued, and therefore talk must stop for action to start. As "talkin' philosophy," our conversation was implicitly demeaned.

Other organizational theorists position conversation, not just communication as vitally important to school reform and the lifeworld of schools (Sergiovanni, 2001). I thought this conversation about how to negotiate and operate within discursive regimes and institutional practices that normalize rapid transition to English was important—and yet quickly this conversation about issues and theory in practice is relegated to talking philosophy—versus pragmatic administration and common sense (in both the common parlance and Gramscian sense). This reflected my sensitivity to my outsider status as a University-based researcher, no longer an administrator making decisions at the campus level. So, I participated weakly with this subject positioning by making a joke: "oh, yes, you get someone from the University and they want to talk philosophy". The conversation fizzled to an end around about a backpack a student brought to school that had "pimp juice" as a label.

If I had been the administrator at this point, how might the conversation differed—if I had offered this research would it have been received as more "actionable" or "pragmatic"? Would my University training have provided me with the ability to see this? Yes, I believe so, to the degree that time and resources allowed. But what about my training made it so—advocate professors, content knowledge? Yes, but also curiosity and the desire to reframe practice that is possible primarily through the unsettling and resettling cycles that theoretical engagements have sent me through (and have been sent through me). Lather has argued that simple, "pragmatic" conversations are not innocent: "clear speech is part of a discursive system, a network of power that has material effects" (1996, p. 528). This, she says, is an extension of Althusser notion that "ideology always exists in an apparatus, and its practice or practices. This existence is material" (Althusser, 1971, p. 166 quoted in Lather, 1996, p. 544). She follows: "the materiality of ideology 'interpollates' or 'hails' historical subjects so that consciousness becomes an effect rather than a cause. This thesis of the materiality of language is key in poststructuralism" (Lather, 1996, p. 544). I figured we were talking about material effects and practices in our conversation, while I believe that Maria essentially invoked a theory versus practice discursive dichotomy, effectively positioning my language and intent as non-material or rhetorical, rather than pragmatic. I suspect my students, to some degree, might be doing the same in class now? In reflection, my interpretation is not about Maria, but about me. I was (and am) frustrated with my inability to translate some knowledge and effect change, in the critical/political tradition. I needed to do more during my time at the school. But my anger is also about positioning the subject of our conversation—bilingual education and language practice as secondary to the pragmatics of accountability and in this sense it was a critical and political anger.

Conflict and the Power of a "Dangerous" Administrator Identity

The day after the Superintendent and District staff had come to visit and praised the performance culture of the school, I was coming out of the ESL class I taught and one of the parents asked me, *"Mr. Black, vas a ser director, principal? Estabamos hablando entre nosotros, y queremos que Usted sea director, es que no nos gusta la que tenemos. Usted va a ser director, no?"* I was completely taken aback, then quickly responded that yes, I had been an assistant principal, but had no desire to be the principal at Márquez. I said that I was studying the school as part of my PhD dissertation work. Yes, but what are you going to do later, she asked. I said that I probably was going to become a college professor. Oh, it is just that we wanted to know what you were doing around here and we would like for you to be the new principal. Striking what seemed like a slightly evasive "neutral" position, which in retrospect I did not believe was neutral at all, I stated that I was not there to change the school. Oh, we did not know since you walked around with the Superintendent, she replied.

My previous administrative experience and my positionality as an "educated" white male contributed to my access to the Superintendent and to my ability to question and speak as an equal to the principal about both positive and concerning aspects of the school. Select parents witnessed my discussions with Maria Gamez, the principal, and several parents read my access and positionality as an opportunity to have their concerns legitimized and acted upon by someone with power—an ex-administrator in the same district.

That same day, a parent who had been in the library during my conversation with the principal, approached me and asked if we could talk in private. Her shoulders were hunched, as if tension inwardly pressed upon them. "I agree with you that there are some bad things happening. Heard you used to be a principal—you know things," she said. My identity shifted strongly from researcher to administrator in my conversations with unhappy parents. Then she stated that I agree with you about the school being too quiet and too strict (I didn't think I had said that exactly). You just need to stay in the cafeteria one whole day and see how they make the kids be quiet and they say it in a mean way, she said. She continued talking to me about how teachers were not smiling around the school. Standing outside the school, she told me, "teachers have lots of stress, sorry I am emotional…" At this point, tears had formed in her eyes. "I went to this school and it used to not be like this. The teachers are under a lot of pressure and there is nothing we can do." She added: One teacher, I heard from somebody else, said that the teacher called a child a "bad word" and then denied it when the parent called that day and then the teacher spent the entire next day calling the kid a liar. I listened and responded after a short while, I told Lori (the parent) that I could tell her who to talk to in the district, but they will tell you that you need to talk to the principal first.

Lori then asked for my card in case she needed to talk to someone. Reluctantly, I gave her my business card. I said that I was uncomfortable, because she should be talking to Maria, the current principal. Lori said that does not do any good. I did tell her that I could provide her information about the district. In struggling to find the appropriate role, I better understood the role of neutrality as a self-protective one, as I attempted to limit my role to that of an information provider, neither fully contesting Lori's notions, nor fully attempting to help her. In addition, later that same day, Ms. Soriano, the parent training specialist also asked if I had been principal before and relayed that parents had been talking about whether I was going to be the next principal. A select group of unhappy parents had positioned me as a successor principal who was sympathetic to their concerns—a dangerous space for an ethnographic researcher. I did not want to destabilize Maria's position nor compromise my access to the school-which would need to be made available through the administration. Yet, my own analysis of the culture of performance and its effects made me sympathetic to their position.

Despite my refusal to entertain select parents' notion that I wanted to be the next principal, these parents eagerly began to share counter-narratives to the construction of the school as a successful school, which is what the TAKS performance indicators narrative and upper level administration conveyed. When we met, we discussed such issues as the over-emphasis on test performance, the business-like environment in the school, the high levels of stress and anxiety for teachers and students, the excessive disciplining of student bodies, the inevitability of locally-mediated testing practices leading to dropouts, and the establishment of a type of managerial professionalism that constructed parents as "little people." My work was not simply innocent, but uncomfortable and full of potential conflict, as ethnographic work can be (Shore & Wright, 1997). But the particulars of the conflict also came from my unique position of a former administrator and in this case, I was legitimizing parent conflict with the current administration through listening and attempting to understand. My response to these was in effect to lay low for a couple of weeks, but these tensions continued to boil within the school.

During the course of the study, I encountered participants who did not want to be taped for fear of repercussions for any critical comments, particularly given my past position and access to decision makers. Others avoided me altogether, partially due to stress and a lack of time. Some teachers felt that I was another "official," and therefore another layer that evaluated their preparation of students for the tests. Then after parents witnessed me discussing the lack of recess with the principal, I became a conduit for complaints about how the school was a stressful environment, how the curriculum had become test driven, and how parents were positioned "as little people". Parents expressed desire for information about organizations in Texas that fought for accountability policy reform.

During one conversation in the parent training room, the parents and Parent Training Specialist were indicating that I should become the next principal, privileging me for listening and I believe for my own ex-administrator, white male positionality. Uncomfortable, I noted that I was in a hard position and was at the school at the invitation of Maria and I did not want to break that trust. Maria had supported me and introduced me on various occasions to visitors as a researcher from the University of Texas who was there to help them. Roma, an African-American parent and Lori, a Latina parent, then commented on my invitation from Maria and my positionality as a means to point out what bothered her from a class and race based perspectives:

> Roma: But you see, the thing about that is…the principal is smiley, smiley, ha, ha, hee, hee in front of certain people. Not to be funny, OK? But you're Caucasian, right? She likes the fact that, OK, he is on so much my level, not more on the little people's level
>
> Bill: Well that I come from the University?
>
> Roma: Right. She is more about politics and numbers and political issues and not more about children and that is a major prob-·lem. And I think that too, with the communication in our school, um, when you have people that are or were poor and they got the big head and they look down upon you.
>
> Lori: They forget where they come from.
>
> Roma: Yeah they forget where they come from and that is mostly our problem here. That is a major problem here. The parents are considered little people. And, um mainly because we don't have our doctorate in education, or we don't wear any suits.
>
> Lori: Or because we live here!

IMPLICATIONS FOR RESEARCH AND TEACHING

A prominent concern this study and reflection relates to the general field of educational administration as it implicitly privileges embedded, traditional notions of neo-Tayloristic control (what Gunter, 1995 describes as "Jurassic Management") through such practices as centralizing and tightly coupling curriculum delivery through a high-stakes results-focused discursive regime that inevitably shapes rational choice responses of leaders such as Maria Gamez toward producing performance. This is also simultaneously coupled with the use of cultural and symbolic concepts of leadership (Peterson & Deal, 2002) to influence the normalization of a culture of performance. Many aspects of the patterns of discourse and behavior that I critically problematized as the normalization of a culture of performance at Márquez Elementary in the broader dissertation study (Black, 2004) are commonly constituted as effective and progressive practices in many educational administration texts, particularly those influenced by effective schools perspectives. These include the tight coupling of curriculum standards and assessments, the constant use of data to monitor and adjust for performance, and the drive to focus on measurable outcomes-practices that may provide material benefits to students. Yet, at Marquez, these particular practices and discourses reside in conflict and tension with their performative role in the production of a discourse of progress, and their functional role as a tool for administrative control or coherence (Anderson & Gallegos, 2005; Fullan, 2001; Hessel and Holloway, 2005; Murphy, 2003; Sergiovanni, 2001; Sloan, 2005). Within the analysis of performativity, this chapter implicitly inquires as to how former and future administrators and educational leadership researchers study schools with ethnographic methods and critical policy perspectives in a manner that critically examines the naïve modernist orientation historically embedded in the field of educational administration (Anderson, 1990, Anderson & Gallegos, 2005; Donmoyer, Imber, & Scheurich, 1995; Smith, 1989) that privileges functionalist progress and effectiveness discourses aligned with high-stakes accountability policies as they come to be lived in local contexts (Furman, 2003; Hursh, 2005; Smith, 2004; Valenzuela, 2005)? The analysis similarly puzzles linear and coherent notions of policies, as "policies are always incomplete insofar as they relate to or map on the 'wild profusion' of local practice" (Ball, 1994, p. 10).

In particular, school-based qualitative researchers who have been administrators should be aware of the possibilities for particular types of conflict and tensions that might arise during their fieldwork. They will likely struggle with the impulse to evaluate and then to "do something" immediately. They should be prepared to think about scenarios and how you they will handle them based on the context and nature of the study, as well as their own proclivities. I was not sufficiently aware of how my participation in a District-led "learning walk" with the Superintendent and high level district staff might alter my relationship with parents and teachers. Former administrators may gain access to higher administration, but this will likely alter the relationships they have with participants and alter the power ascribed to them beyond that normally reserved for a researcher. This can be beneficial to students as they bring additional resources to bear, but it signals some tricky issues of retaining access to the research sight and supporting the administration that is in place. Power will probably be ascribed to students (most particularly if other gender and race priviledged positionalities are involved) and when the inevitable conflicts precipitate around a school, former administrators need to be aware that certain people might approach them as a type of broker for their position. Research actions are never completely innocent. This is particularly true for former administrators. The legitimacy provided through dialogue with those that feel unsupported and in conflict with current ways of doing things can help inspire action, but it also carries danger. Ms. Soriano, the parent training specialist who felt comfortable with me and told me on several occasions how unhappy she had become with the way things were done at the school ended up fueling discourses of parent dissatisfaction and was fired at the end of the year. Finally, the research may not be generalizable, but others will position it as such. Critical ethnographic work is not always positioned as useful.

The contradictions and severe tensions high-stakes testing policies and practices produced in this particular school context, including the production of a culture of performance is a likely phenomenon to be encountered and researched by current teachers and educational administration students doing qualitative methodological work. Results-oriented policies already infuse an educational administration and teacher leadership field that is rhetorically oriented toward action. Using the type of analysis displayed here, students can use both method and theory to take a new view of how actions, assumptions, and behaviors that are commonly seen as highly effective can also cohere in an assimilationist, authoritarian, and unaesthetic culture of performance. The ongoing challenge, reflected in this book is how to convey this inquiry so that it links to the identities of school administrators and teachers—to better learn how to keep this kind of inquiry "real" (Foley, 2002; Tierney, 2002).

Students should also know that others could portray the school vastly differently—I have no expert patent on institutional cultural analysis. At the least, however, the example of multiple discourses and practices that I have put forth here are networked in fashions that call for greater theoretical sophistication running throughout school organizations, distributing leadership (Gronn, 2003) around disrupting and unsettling beliefs around performance in such a manner that might move institutional discourses away from the essentializing, Neo-Tayloristic, and performative interpretations of accountability policy. Distributing the ability to disrupt and unsettle beliefs through our coursework, our professional development, and writing can also work off of and from the malleable concepts of accountability and practice so that disruptive and theoretically-informed work can also be strategically captured and released under discursive regularities associated with accountable and practical work. We teach theory, we unsettle, because it is also the "accountable" and "practical" thing to do.

I also hope that this chapter urges students to be aware of those contradictions and tensions and be sensitive to the role administrators, researchers, and teachers are likely to play in perpetuating performative practices through discourses of urgency, competition, and learning as performance. Students might recognize that the type of cultural policy analysis favored in this paper is likely to be attacked through frameworks of urgency, focus, and practicality that serve to limit the scope of legitimate analysis. As the current Secretary of Education, Margaret Spellings, has postulated: "by now, I don't think we have the luxury of focusing on things other than those that produce results" (NYT, 2005). As I produce this critique, I think it is also important to unsettle beliefs that might calcify around my analysis: performance and results are not bad and certainly can and in many cases should be the objects of institutional desire. Yet, do we have the modernist luxury of focusing only on those things that produce results in our institutions and in our pedagogy?

NOTES

1. Names of institutions and people are pseudonyms.
2. The fourth grade Writing TAKS has a multiple-choice section and a writing section. Students' essays are scored with a rubric, with 4 being the highest score and 1 being the lowest score.
3. I taught an English class to Spanish-speaking parents during the duration of my study at the school.
4. By marginal I refer to what is typically viewed as non-classroom, non-academic space—the spaces where often learning is seen as either not occurring, occurring marginally, or as psycho-social spaces of play or release. "Quiet school" refers to those multiple spaces between activities or in transit.
5. The professional literature within management and organizational behavior demonstrates a rhetorical bias for action (Marshak, 1998).
6. Elevar is the title of the new bilingual education program that had just been introduced to the principals on January 7th and which has been adopted for the 2004–2005 school year. The Elevar curriculum calls for the use and specific instruction of high academic language in all of the content areas, beginning in Pre-Kindergarten. As such, it is a rupture from previous District bilingual education policy which called for 45 minutes of ESL at all grade levels. I asked whether they made the link between cognates in English and Spanish, or explicitly intended to scaffold from what the kids knew in Spanish and Maria said that in the presentation there was no mention of using Spanish or the native language at all—it focused strictly on English and the use of English in content areas. I responded to Maria saying that was interesting that nothing was made in Spanish, and as such it might align with the English-only ideology. Maria vociferously agreed. However, Maria has currently been promoted to a central office position where she is now in charge of implementing this new curriculum.

REFERENCES

Abedi, J. (2004). The No Child Left Behind Act and English Language Learners: Assessment and accountabiliy issues. *Educational Researcher, 33*(1), 4–14.

Adams, J. & Copland, M. (2005). *When learning counts: Rethinking licenses for school leaders*. Seattle: Center on Reinventing Public Education.

Althusser, L. (1971). Ideology and ideological state apparatuses (B. Brewster, Trans.). In L. Altusser (Ed.), *Lenin and philosophy and other essays* (pp. 127–188). New York: Monthy Review Press.

Anderson, G. (1990). Toward a critical constructivist approach to school administration: Invisibility, legitimation, and the study of non-events. *Education Administration Quarterly, 26*(1), 38–59.

Anderson, G. (2001). Promoting educational equity in a period of growing social inequity: The silent contradictions of the Texas reform discourse. *Education and Urban Society, 33*(3), 320–332.

Anderson, G. & Gallegos, B. (Eds.). (2005). *Performance theories in Education*. New York: Routledge.

Aparicio, F. (2000). Of Spanish dispossessed. In R. Dueñas González & I. Melis (Eds.), *Language ideologies: Education and the social implications of official language* (Vol. 1, pp. 248–275). Mahwah, NJ: Earlbaum.

Ball, S. (1994). *Education reform: A critical and post-structural approach*. Buckingham, UK: Open University Press.

Ball, S. (Ed.). (1990). *Foucault and education: Disciplines and knowledge*. London: Routledge.

Black, W. (2004). *"Equal access to mandated testing": Policies, disciplinary discourse, and practices of performance in the lives of English Language Learner youth*. Unpublished doctoral dissertation, The University of Texas at Austin.

Blase, J. & Anderson, G. (1995). *The micropolitics of educational leadership*. New York: Cassell.

Bourdieu, P. (1977). *Outline of a theory of practice* (R. Nice, Trans.). Cambridge: Cambridge University Press.

Brisk, M. (1998). *Bilingual education: From compensatory to quality schooling*. Mahwah, NJ: Erlbaum.

Callahan, R. (1962). *Education and the cult of efficiency*. Chicago: University of Chicago Press.

Central Texas Independent School District, Department of Planning and Evaluation. (2003). *Bilingual Education/ESL Program Evaluation Report*. Texas.

Corson, D. (Ed.). (1995). *The discourses of administration and supervision*. Cresskill, NJ: Hampton Press.

Crawford, J. (2001). *At war with diversity: U.S. language policy in an age of anxiety*. Clevedon, UK: Multilingual Matters.

Crawford, J. (2002). *Obituary: The Bilingual Education Act: 1968–2002, Comprehensive guide to the new Title III*. Retrieved July 23, 2003, from http://ourworld.compuserve.com/homepages/jcrawford/T7obit.htm.

Denzin, N. (1989). *Interpretive interactionism*. Newbury Park, CA: Sage.

Denzin, N., & Lincoln, Y. (1998). Methods of collecting and analyzing empirical materials. In N. Denzin & Y. Lincoln (Eds.), *Collecting and interpreting qualitative materials* (2nd ed., pp. 47–60). Thousand Oaks, CA.

Dewalt, K., Dewalt, B., & Wayland, C. (1998). Participant observation. In H. R. Bernard (Ed.), *Handbook of methods in cultural anthropology* (pp. 259–300). London: Sage.

Donmoyer, R., Imber, M., Scheurich, J. (1995). *The knowledge base in educational administration.* Albany: SUNY Press.

Dueñas González, R., & Melis, I. (2001). Introduction. In R. Dueñas González (Ed.), *Language ideologies: History, theory, and policy.* Mahwah, NJ: Earlbaum.

Edelman, M. J. (1988). *Constructing the political spectacle.* Chicago, IL: University of Chicago Press.

Emerson, R. M., Fretz, R. I., & Shaw, L. L. (1995). *Writing ethnographic fieldnotes.* Chicago: University of Chicago Press.

Foley, D. E. (1995). *The heartland chronicles.* Philadelphia: University of Pennsylvania Press.

Foley, D. E. (2002). Critical ethnography: The reflexive turn. *International Journal of Qualitative Studies in Education, 15*(4), 469–490.

Fontana, A., & Frey, J. H. (2003). The interview: From structured questions to negotiated text. In N. Denzin & Y. Lincoln (Eds.), *Collecting and interpreting qualitative materials* (2nd ed., pp. 61–106). Thousand Oaks, CA: Sage publications.

Foucault, M. (1977). *Discipline and punish: The birth of the prison.* New York: Pantheon Books.

Foucault, M. (1980). *Power/knowledge: Selected interviews and other writings.* New York: Pantheon Books.

Freeman, R. (1998). *Bilingual education and social change.* Clevedon, UK: Multilingual Matters.

Freeman, R. (2004). *Promoting multilingualism through schooling.* Philadelphia: Caslon Publishing.

Fullan, M. (2001). *Leading in a culture of change.* San Francisco, CA: Jossey-Bass.

Furman, G. (2003). *UCEA Presidential Address.* XLV (1).

García, E. E. (2001). *Hispanic education in the United States: Raices y Alas.* Lanham: Rowman and Littefield.

Geertz, C. (1973). *The interpretation of cultures.* New York: Basic Books.

Glesne, C. (1999). *Become qualitative researchers* (2nd ed.). New York: Addison-Wesley.

Gronn, P. (2003). Leadership: Who needs it? *School Leadership and Management, 23*(3), 267–290.

Guerrero, M. (1999). Spanish academic language proficiency of bilingual education teachers: Is there equity? *Equity and excellence in education, 32*(1), 56–73.

Guerrero, M. (2003). We have correct English teachers: Why can't we have correct Spanish teachers? It's not acceptable. *International Journal of Qualitative Studies in Education, 16*(5), 647–668.

Gunter, H. (1995). Jurassic management: Chaos and management development in educational institutions. *Journal of Educational Administration, 33*(4), 5–20.

Hamilton, L., Steecher, B., Klein, S. (2002). *Making sense of test-based accountability in education.* Santa Monica, CA: Rand.

Haney, W., & Raczek, A. (2000). The myth of the Texas miracle in education. *Educational Policy Analysis Archives, 8*(41), Retrieved from http: //epaa.asu.edu/epaa/v8n41.

Hatch, J. A. (2003). *Doing qualitative research in educational settings.* Albany, NY: SUNY Press.

Hessel, K. & Holloway, J. (2005). *A framework for school leaders: Linking the ISLLC standards to practice.* Princeton, NJ: Educational Testing Service.

Hursh, D. (2005). The growth of high-stakes testing in the USA: Accountability, markets, and the decline in educational equality. *British Educational Research Journal, 31*(5), 605–622.

Janofsky, M. (2005, November 3). A Bush-style education school in Texas. *New York Times.*

Krashen, S. (1996). *Under attack: The case against bilingual information.* Culver City, CA: Language Education Associates.

Kozol, J. (1980). *Savage inequalities: Children in America's schools.* New York: Crown Publishing.

Lather, P. (1996). Troubling clarity: The politics of accessible language. *Harvard Educational Review, 66*(3), 525–543.

Levinson, B., & Sutton, M. (2001). Introduction: Policy as/in practice—A sociocultural approach to the study of educational policy. In M. Sutton & B. Levinson (Eds.), *Policy as practice: Toward a comparative sociocultural analysis of educational policy* (Vol. 1, pp. 1–22). Westport, CT: Ablex.

Lipman, P. (2004). *High-stakes education: Inequality, globalization, and urban school reform.* New York: Routledge Falmer.

Marshak, R. (1995). A discourse on discourse: Redeeming the meaning of talk. In Grant, D., Keenoy, T., & Oswick, C (Eds.). *Discourse & Organization.* London: Sage Publications.

Maxcy, B. D. (2004). *Emerging democracy in an urban elementary school: A Habermasian framework for examining school governance reculturing in response to systematic reform.* Unpublished doctoral dissertation, Austin: The University of Texas at Austin.

Maxcy, B. & Nguyen, T. (2006). The politics of distributing leadership: Reconsidering leadership distribution in tow Texas elementary schools. *Educational Policy, 20*(1), 163–196.

McNeil, L. M. (2000). *Contradictions of school reform: educational costs of standardized testing.* New York: Routledge.

McNeil, L. M. (2005). Faking equity: High-stakes testing and the education of Latino youth. In A. Valenzuela (Ed.), *Leaving children behind: How "Texas-style" accountability fails Latino youth.* Albany: SUNY Press.

Mertens, D. (1998). *Research methods in education and psychology: Integrating diversity with quantitative and qualitative approaches.* Thousand Oaks, CA: Sage.

Miles, M., & Huberman, A. (1994). *Qualitative data analysis: An expanded sourcebook.* Thousand Oaks, CA: Sage.

Miles, M. B., & Huberman, A. M. (1984). *Qualitative data analysis : a sourcebook of new methods.* Beverly Hills: Sage.

Mirriam, S. (1998). *Qualitative research and case study applications in education* (Second ed.). San Fransisco: Jossey-Bass.

Murphy, J. (Ed.). (2002). *The educational leadership challenge: redefining leadership for the 21st Century.* Chicago: NSSE.

Murphy, J. (2003). *Reculturing educational leadership: The ISLLC standards ten years out.* Arlington, VA: National Policy Board for Educational Administration.

Nelson, S. (2002). *Oppression, conflict, and collusion: High-stakes accountability from the perspective of three social justice principals.* Unpublished doctoral dissertation. Austin: University of Texas at Austin.

Peterson, K. & Deal, T. (2002). *The shaping school culture fieldbook.* San Fransisco: Jossey-Bass.

Rorrer, A. (2002). Educational leadership and institutional capacity for equity. *UCEA Review, 18*(3), 1–5.

Sabatier, P., & Mazmanian, D. (1995). A conceptual framework of the implementation process. In S. Theodoulour & M. Cahn (Eds.), *Public policy: The essential readings.* Englewood Cliffs, NJ: Prentice-Hall.

Sergiovanni, T. (2001). *Leadership: What's in it for the schools?* New York: Routledge-Falmer.

Spradley, J. (1980). *Participant observation.* New York: Holt, Rinehart, and Winston.

Shore, C., & Wright, S. (Eds.). (1997). *Anthropology of policy: Critical perspectives on governance and power.* New York: Routledge.

Strauss, A. L., & Corbin, J. M. (1990). *Basics of qualitative research: Grounded theory procedures and techniques.* Newbury Park, Calif.: Sage Publications.

Wolcott, H. (Ed.). (1994). *Transforming qualitative data: Description, analysis, and interpretation.* Thousand Oaks, CA: Sage.

CHAPTER 5

CRITICAL PEDAGOGY AS ALTERNATIVE CRISIS CURRICULUM

William Gaudelli
Teachers College, Columbia University

Life is necessarily uncertain as all that we have to predict the next instant is that which preceded it. A natural response to this uncertainty is to have a measure of anxiety about what is to come. Fear of the unknown makes a receptive audience for crisis talk, typically manifest as anxiety about natural disasters, terrorism, nuclear proliferation, and climate change. Though these are materially significant and merit attention, the way in which these issues fleetingly pass through the public mind is cause for alarm in its own right, as it amounts to a social psychosis of distraction (Barnhardt, 2000).

Media has typically been blamed for perpetual crisis talk, as it frames, fixates, and fractures public attention towards episodic focus and cursory awareness (Kellner, 2003). During 2005, for example, crisis talk was fueled by a series of catastrophes: tsunamis in Southeast Asia, hurricanes along the U.S. Gulf Coast, fear of a bird flu pandemic, and an earthquake in Pakistan. These were all tragic in their human toll, ecological devastation, and resulting property loss to a degree unimaginable to those directly involved. Those who watched these events on television or via the Internet were likely empathetically engaged if not directly affected. Coverage of these events in a media-saturated, rapacious 24/7 news cycle environment was

Unsettling Beliefs: Teaching Theory to Teachers, pages 75–86
Copyright © 2008 by Information Age Publishing
All rights of reproduction in any form reserved.

predictable: live reports from the field (featuring *courageous* journalists), stories of suffering and loss, coverage of life returning to normal, followed by a complete dearth of attention after the crisis.

Critical theory is also built around a language of crisis, but of a different kind with alternative aims. Karl Marx developed crisis theory, in effect arguing that capitalism would eventually create such intolerable conditions for the working class that the economic and social disparity would precipitate a crisis, indeed a revolution (Holton, 1987). Critical pedagogy, borrowing on classical crisis theory, seeks to create a crisis by interrupting normative conceptions of pedagogy and tracing current manifestations of education to their social origins. Such crisis pedagogy seeks to cause teachers and teacher candidates to rethink assumptions about education and trace those to their social attachments. Critical pedagogues purposefully expose crises so as to cause dissonance and provoke teachers into an interrogative, social, and discursive, or *critical*, examination of pedagogy.

This chapter explores the nature of critical pedagogy crisis talk in origin, processes, and aims based on my experiences as a teacher educator. I briefly argue that much popular crisis talk, like that offered in the media, incompletely frames social problems, is anti-dialogical, and ultimately serves to unproductively confuse and miseducate. Such crisis talk exacerbates anxiety since it is both parasitic and nurturant of uncertainty, compelling people to watch, to consume, to spectate in a futile effort to still their apprehension. The bewildered public is not led to an examination of what the media frames, but rather are placed in a docilely dependent relationship where their fear is sustained through *watching more* to see *what happens next.*

A critical pedagogy of crisis, rather, seeks to liberate teachers from this dehumanizing spiral—anxiety, fear, defensive action—to embrace their role as agents whose choosing shapes the events about to unfold in a classroom. While critical pedagogues do not pretend that such praxis creates fixity in the uncertain classroom, they argue that the capacity to think for oneself within a community of professionals allows teachers to simultaneously create a space of safety within uncertainty, joy amid complexity. I contend that although critical pedagogy *as* critical reflection has attributes of popular crisis talk, it differs fundamentally. Critical reflection springs from an affirmation of human capacity to think deeply and carefully, is imbued with a recursive quality that reencounters its own assumptions, and aims towards praxis that is grounded, emergent, and aesthetic. Critical reflection, thus, is a socially connected, democratic move towards uncertain ends that serves only as a brief respite for a problematic view of future aims.

THE CRISIS ETHOS OF POST 9-11 MEDIA

General claims about *the media* are difficult to sustain since what constitutes it is open to many interpretations. The major networks, public television, public radio, newspapers, and journals are often reified as news media. Such categories are increasingly challenged, however, as websites, blogs, and podcasts take a greater share of readership. A Pew Research comparative study of how voters received news about the 2000 and 2004 presidential election noted that traditional sources lost market share (newspapers –9%, national newscasts –10%) and emergent media gained (Internet +4%, cable news +4%) (Pew Research Center, 2004). As the mediascape evolves, attention must be paid to formats that are most salient in informing perspectives and those that serve to illuminate or obfuscate.

The purposeful cluttering of public issues paradoxically and concomitantly numbs and overstimulates a worried public, best illustrated by the euphemistic *war on terror.* Reports about *credible threats* have been frequently issued by the Office of Homeland Security since 9–11, though hardly at all following the 2004 election (Matsaganis & Payne, 2005, p. 387). The media's appetite for crisis creates a wave of reports, often in the form of breaking news interruptions, about the possibility of an attack. The fact that nothing has occurred, only that something might occur or never occur, is viewed as newsworthy and creates a sense that the threat is real and pervasive. Such reports typically lack any detail about the nature of the threat, only that people should be *vigilant* and report *unusual persons and events* to authorities. Uncertainty about the nature of threat then creates a climate of heightened fear where pangs of doubt become socially diffused and normative. Sandra Ball-Rokeach (1973) refers to this phenomenon as *pervasive ambiguity* wherein people lack credible information to define a given situation, leading them to attempt to reduce feelings of tension and seek information towards that end. *Pervasive ambiguity* becomes more salient when the situation of ambiguity involves a physical risk, such as terrorism. When the threat is something as potentially deadly as terrorism, people seek definition about a situation, opening space for rhetorical agents to define a situation and prescribe actions about that situation (Matsaganis & Payne, 2005). The sporadic nature of terrorist attacks heightens and deepens a culture of fear that is ever-vigilant for violent, explosive news and simultaneously powerless to do anything about it other than feel anxious.

The manufactured nature of such *crises* is self-fulfilling when the government creates a crisis message that is devoured by media, and thereby an anxious public, seeding uncertainty, even panic. In the immediate aftermath of 9-11 through 2002, a wave of panic swept the U.S. with fears of bioterrorism, specifically anthrax. The Department of Homeland Security caused a buying panic when they reported the possibility of a bioterror attack, urging citizens to purchase duct tape and plastic sheeting (Pitt, 2005). The recommendation was revoked when scientists indicated that such efforts would be futile. But the panic was intense as was the increase in revenues for home improvement stores. Most people forget these mini-crises within a week or two of their gripping presence, but the unease caused by unending crisis is debilitating to building a healthy society.

Governor Howard Dean raised the danger of contrived crises in August, 2004 during the presidential campaign. He noted the curious release of a terror alert by the Department of Homeland Security immediately following the Democratic Convention which adversely affected the bump in poll numbers for Kerry that typically follows a candidate's official nomination. Dean (MSN News, 2004) remarked, "I am concerned that every time something happens that is not good for President Bush, he plays this trump card, which is terrorism. His whole campaign is based on the notion that, 'I can keep you safe...stick with me.'" Dean's remarks became the issue, rather than the possibility of manufactured news, as Dean was vilified as a leftist conspiracy nut. In hindsight, Dean was correct, as there were no terrorist attacks in the U.S. for the remainder of the year and the plans that caused the alert was not new information but three years old. This reality, however, was not deemed newsworthy and Dean's assertion became a footnote in the maelstrom of the campaign.

Crisis talk that is miseductive, purposefully and otherwise, not only disorients the public, but also makes them dependent on doctrine and unsubstantiated assertion for fear that they might lose any sense of stability, or what little *terra firma* they have. Ron Suskind of the New York Times wrote a provocative piece about the dogmatic, anti-discursive nature of the Bush administration. At a meeting with a senior advisor to Bush, Suskind (2004) was told that:

> he was a "reality" type person, or a person, who believes that solutions emerge from judicious study of discernible reality....That's not the way the world works anymore...we're an empire now, and when we act, *we create our own reality* (italics added). And while you're studying that reality—judiciously as you will—we'll act again, creating other new realities, which you can study too, and that's how things will sort out. We're history's actors...and you, all of you, will be left to just study what we do. (p. 51)

Most striking is the notion that government creates its own reality, or read another way, establishes an atmosphere of uncertainty and anxiety that allows a free hand to deny personal liberties, defy international law and custom, and delimit dissent at home (see Boghosian, 2004).

In the atmosphere of crisis that surrounds terror talk, the reader is positioned as a helpless voyeur who is told what to know about, what to think about it, and why it is, as the government/media mélange spins and shares preferred versions of reality. Bioterrorism, heuristically, is a threat perpetrated by Middle East (*sic*, Southwest Asian and North African) terrorists who want to destroy the U.S. way of life. These fanatical, hate-filled Islamic fundamentalists terrorize innocent victims because Western life is godless, materialistic, and hedonistic. Such messages are purveyed, notably, while a U.S. flag gently furls in the upper left corner of the television screen. Such crisis assertions, however, are not provided with appropriate historical and social context, thus leaving the voyeur-positioned audience to look on in moral outrage and horror, perhaps prompting a trip to the Home Depot to stock up on duct tape and plastic.

It is too simplistic, however, to define such crisis producing events as symmetrically causal, or information created by the government, proliferated by the media, and consumed by the public. Rather, contemporary media is more asymmetrical, since all parties—government, media, and public—are all situated as producers, purveyors, and consumers of messages (Matsaganis & Payne, 2005). Journalists, for example, who raise questions about an issue or conduct investigative work about a problem, are in effect producing attention about an issue, one that is consumed by the public and responded to by government. Bloggers, or quasi-journalist citizens, can rouse interest and attention about an issue while situating the mainstream media as consumers, as blog journalists who report on the blogosphere have become a staple of cable news reporting. The government, particularly during the Bush and Clinton Administrations, has become not only the creator of and responder to messages, but their producers as well. Reports of journalists being paid as consultants by the White House (CNN, 2005) or the seeding of new stories in Iraq about positive developments there, paid for by the Pentagon, are but two examples of this reoriented messaging (Wilson, 2005). Returning to the notion of crisis, clearly the public, government, and media are all players in the asymmetrical interaction in ways that dually feed and are fed by the pervasive ambiguity characteristic of this era.

ALTERNATIVE CRISIS PEDAGOGY PRACTICE

Colleges of education have long been focused on teaching what Giroux (1996) calls a pedagogy of theory where teacher candidates are taught a series of psychological and sociological theories along with a disconnected set of practices that they are left to blend into teaching practice. This is typically done away from the lived situation of classrooms, further alienating the theory from its point of intelligibility, the context of pedagogy. I invite my students to become *theorists* through a process of collective, collaborative reflection that, to use Paulo Freire (1970/2000), connects the word to the world and the world to the word (p. 87). I designate the first two hours of class for public reflection that begins with and centers on students' experiences in and of their internship/field settings. The point is to illustrate that the micro and the technical are what they are only because they are extrapolated from their implication in the social. It's not that the social is not there—it is so much there that its existence, indeed its prevalence—is what makes teaching seem natural, neutral, normative, a-political, and asocial (Segall and Gaudelli, 2007).

I interrupt normative ideas about pedagogy by encouraging students to engage in close observation of their cooperating teacher which allows them to develop a capacity for participant-observation. They write periodic critical reflections that allow them to explicate, speculate, interrogate, and implicate their insights. The *4-ates* focus students on key questions: What do you see? What do you think is happening? Why is it happening in this way? How might others perceive this happening? What are alternative ways for this to be happening? What social ideas are implied in this happening? And, what would you do as a teacher given what you know? Why? The sociality of these readings is enhanced when they are shared and critically examined by their peers.

Part of the methodology of this approach is to create a crisis for my students by interrupting their normative conceptions about schools and learning, providing them with an opportunity to retheorize in a way that is socially connected, while setting the stage for acting on warranted beliefs in a recursive manner. I refer to this as *alternative crisis pedagogy* since it differs substantially from the media/government crises elaborated above. This approach presents crises in ways that students are generally unfamiliar, as they typically think of crisis in terms of threats to life and limb. School, thus, is generally not seen as in *crisis* as it appears *normal.* Moreover, its normalcy is anticipated to continue *ad infinitum,* unlike the lulls between terror events. When school is discussed in terms of crisis, interestingly, it is typically done with reference to violent acts and/or academic failure.

The notion of education in crisis is not done in the isolation of an event, as is typically the way in which a terrorist attack is viewed, but always in broader, social relief and connection. Thus, when students raise concerns about parental pressure regarding grades or school fixation on discipline, for example, I see my role as encouraging both a careful reading of the micro but also a thoroughgoing encounter with the macro, seeing events as manifestations of social assumptions. Parental pressure about grades, for example, can either become transfixed on that grade or become an opportunity for dialog about the nature of assessment, its ends, and policy dimensions. Just one step beyond this discussion is viewing assessment as indicating a certain type of pedagogy, privileging certain knowledge over other, and presupposing ultimate value. In short, *Why did I get this grade?* is just a few inquiries and a couple of social connections away from *What is the good life?*

Alternative crisis pedagogy aims not to end in hand wringing, moral platitudes, or feelings of helpless uncertainty, as is so often the case with the crisis talk of elevated threat levels in the post 9–11 world, but to help teachers develop warranted beliefs about their actions and do so in an inquiring manner that is never fixed and always open to recursive interrogation. Teachers engage, thus, in an earnest examination of what they would do and share those beliefs with their peers who are encouraged to critically examine those efforts in an unending discourse about pedagogy.

Obstacles to Critical, Social Reflection of Alternative Crisis

The major obstacle of engaging students in critical, social reflection is unpacking student archetypal thinking about what education *ought* to be. Students come with very fixed ideas about the nature of knowledge and knowing, few aware of their implicit theories about teaching and learning. But theories they have. Generic theories include an array of common assumptions: individual success is measured by performance on tests, standards improve the quality of learning, students learn best by listening to teachers, textbooks are a great tool for instruction, or that students need to know proscribed content to be successful in future life. As 4th year secondary education majors,[1] they also have theories about teaching social studies: history is the core of the field, history is best represented by a master narrative, social studies is a collection of disciplines, knowledge in these disciplines is fixed and known, or disciplinary expertise is central to being a teacher of social studies.

Ambiguity is another tension in this approach since it is necessarily uncertain and somewhat threatening. Since I purposefully dispose of the fixity associated with a university class (e.g., proscribed weekly topics, tightly constructed assignments, teacher-centered, didactic instruction), some teacher candidates are cast adrift by this approach and remain so through its conclusion. Part of what troubles these teachers is the recursive, critical nature of the course, as they are asked to cast doubt on what they already have come to believe about pedagogy. As we begin the course, all students write about their current theorizing as most have done in the past in the form of a philosophy of education. What is different here is that students are then asked to cast doubt on their theories along with those of their peers in a quest to uncover the reasons and warrants that support these claims. Some students have asked, "But why should I doubt what I already told you I believe?" Assertions like this lead to a frank conversation about our ability to know what we believe, on the grounds that we believe it, and account for our own experiences in the germination of those beliefs. More concisely, student capacity to know themselves metacognitively is a central concern in the course.

The aim of critical, social reflection is not to cast doubt for its own sake, but rather to help teachers see that they in fact *have* working theories and that those theories *are* socially bound. By modeling critical, social reflection in class, I contend that there is much less fixity in the art and aesthetics of teaching than is commonly thought and that my own best practice for sorting through this complexity is to rely on careful observation, critical reading of the classroom as a social world, and a discursive exchange with beginning professionals about those meanings. Some might wonder, but where are the methods? I would suggest that this *is* a method of teaching social studies, one that in my cases focuses on discourse about social studies pedagogy, but one that is relatable to the types of discourse that ought to occur in social studies classrooms.

As I encourage this dialog, some teachers are uncomfortable with the open dissent valued in the course. Many of them offer insights from their field experiences in protective ways. A teacher candidate recounted, for example, a teacher who singled out African-American students to talk about what they thought about slavery, but quickly rejoined, "but she's a good teacher." Or another whose geography teacher made students color maps throughout the semester, defending her choice with "but she's trying really hard!" Students have shared that they feel uncomfortable with being honest about their field teacher as it promotes a negative response from their peers. Yet, when I ask them to defend these pedagogical choices on behalf of their teacher, they offer little in response. Thus, they are in effect expressing their discomfort with the notion of dissent about pedagogy, many claiming a vague methodological relativism, or, "that's just their teaching style." These tensions are rarely resolved for all students by the end of the course and many strongly reject the premise of the course, seeking a return to the normalcy of pedagogy that they carried into the course.

Dissent expressed in the context of our classroom, when teacher candidate's beliefs are subject to interrogation, presents an even greater challenge. One exchange between Robert, a student whose parents were poor, Jamaican immigrants, and Janine, a white, suburban woman offered working theories about pedagogy that were explicit and conflicting. Janine complained about the use of Black English among her students, expressing profound disbelief that her students were in high school and still did not know how to use "proper English." While most of the students seemed to implicitly agree that they had experienced similar problems, Robert, an otherwise soft-spoken, quiet student asked, "What does it mean to speak proper English?" Janine responded that it was the English usage expected at a college-level. He explained that while he recognized the need for students to be conversant in *standard* English (his phrase) to achieve academically, Janine was dismissing the importance of language variation. He cautioned that she was probably being viewed as the *other* by her students, or just another white suburban woman, when she exhorted them to "write properly." This interaction redirected our conversation for a little over an hour. I thought afterwards that Robert probably would not have raised this critique in a class that was designed to *provide* pedagogical theory, but that in this dissent-rich context, the clash of perspectives was both forthright and informative.

Student discomfort and anxiety also manifests beyond the class meetings in their fieldwork as they are positioned as strangers inside, or outsiders within, during student teaching. Drawing on Maxine Greene's (1973) metaphor of teacher as stranger, I encourage students to relish the insights that this position affords. Such a stance provides opportunities to see things that their cooperating teachers, the actors, often do not see, such as the students who are ignored, disengaged, or abused by their peers. As the semester unfolds, some students revel in their outsider status while beginning to adopt a critical stance as they listen and respond to their peers, engage social reflection in their writing, and challenge other's warranted beliefs, thereby developing their own.

Teacher candidates come to see themselves as situated in a manner that they have not previously as they grow more comfortable with the role of being a stranger. Students who do not critically examine their perspective as teacher candidates will likely become teachers who ascribe to such platitudes as "I treat everyone the same," or "I am colorblind," or perhaps more disconcerting, "That's how I was taught and it worked for me." Positioned as strangers in their field experiences and as critical inquirers in the course, students can see political and social vistas that are unnoticed both by teachers and their previous selves, and in so doing, begin to reexamine their pedagogical landscapes towards defining themselves as critical teachers. But not all teacher candidates are able to fully engage this methodology, to completely think through the crises that are generated in the context of the course. Perhaps Noel made the most revealing comment when she said, "I now understand what you are trying to get us to do in this course, but I'm not there yet. The problem is I have never been asked to think this way, so I now know ways of thinking about teaching that I never encountered before, but I'm still getting used to the ideas of using them."

CONCLUSION AND CONTINUATIONS

As I attempt to create productive crises through this methodology of critical, social reflection, I am explicitly asking students to rethink the ways in which they learn in the course and my role in that learning. My primary position is to serve as goad and provocateur, and secondarily, to offer potentially rich situations wherein careful pedagogical thinking can be articulated, explored, reworked, and most significantly, publicly engaged and socially connected. I now approach teaching as a reflexive dialog that is continually turning back on itself, opening space for discourse on what many might otherwise consider *terra firma*. Firm ground is only useful and necessary, however, to the extent that it allows the recursive process to continue. Fixed theories are intellectually dead, only given life by the discourse of recursive critique. When we have reached what seem to be conclusions in the course, I encourage students to identify those working theories and interrogate them again.

I offer this course that I have co-developed with Avner Segall (see chapter 2, this volume) not as an exemplar, but as an illustration of how teachers can engage with social theory. My approach is to foster teacher theory building capacity while having them recognize that they indeed are theorizers. The most important dimension of the work is the connection to the social such that they do not see themselves, their pedagogy, and their problems as their own, but rather as part of a wider and pervasive social context. I do not assert that this work fundamentally transforms all students, though I believe that it provides many with a welcomed respite from the pedagogy of theory that is so common in their preparation. I hope that students continue to think about their pedagogy in this critical and social manner after the course ends and have some evidence of that. A student contacted me a few months after the 2005 spring term ended and attached a critical reflection that he had written. At first I thought it was a makeup assignment, but quickly realized that he had already completed the course but felt compelled to write this when one of the students with whom he worked in internship committed suicide. He shared it with me to see if I could offer additional insights, but in reality, it provided me with more insight about the ability of a pedagogy of theorizing approach to transform teacher thinking about classrooms.

As I continue developing this methodology, questions point to tensions that remain in this work. Why does critical, social reflection resonate well with some teacher candidates, and teacher educators for that matter, and not others? Ilan Gur-Ze'ev (2005) argues that critical theory and pedagogy has become too cold and mechanistic, lacking the creative and aesthetic qualities that make for a full life (p. 19). He argues that at birth humans have immense potential that is "robed, reworked, and produced by the system," thus neglecting the innate and unique potential of life. Perhaps this insight suggests why the rational move that I attempt in critical, social reflection is not embraced by all teachers, as it appears to be too intellectual without due attention to the affective, such as the teacher candidates affinity for their new professional friends, their cooperating teachers, or their loyalty to fond memories of teaching that was something less than critical.

How does this work presume an identity and discourse pattern that is universal and hegemonic? Critical, social reflection requires a willingness to look carefully, skeptically, socially, and somewhat courageously at pedagogy, and by extension, teachers themselves. Such an approach presumes a certain identity, or at least the capacities associated with an identity, and therefore, imposes that type as necessary for effective social studies teaching. All identities other than the critical self would be, to varying degrees, less capable teachers. But is that so? Elizabeth Heilman (2005) contends that critical pedagogy's Achilles heel, so to speak, is its fixation on the mythic hero, employing the revolutionary identity as and *uber*-type. Such an identity is at odds with many people including those volunteering to work in schools (utopian-type) and those who are suspicious of politics (dystopic-type). What of those? "Neither the heroic utopic identity nor the critical dystopic identity can serve as a workable model for teachers and citizens" (p. 129). Her prescription is to focus instead on the identities as they are and are becoming and seek to create space within people's identities for civic engagement rooted in validation of who they are and what their experiences have been.

Finally, I wonder about the capacity to grow a transcendent teacher identity among beginning, vulnerable teachers. Can a teacher be a transformative force within a new context where they lack the experiences of their colleagues? This question forces me to consider if the engagement in critical, social reflection so counter-socializes the beginning teacher as to make their working in a public school untenable. Again, to invoke Heilman's (2005) work, is critical, social reflection too utopist or dystopic, depending on how it is enacted, to render the beginning teacher dysfunctional? Teacher candidates rarely adopt this approach fully in their professional lives, but rather situate it as part of what they do and use it not as the only method of reaching warranted beliefs about their pedagogy, but as a method. Thus, as they negotiate their transformative identity with their will to maintain a teaching position, most find a workable ground that allows them to live in both worlds, those of stasis and transformation.

Teachers are implicitly and ironically formed by institutions of teacher education as socially disconnected technicians implementing *best practices* learned from others encountered at arms length through theoretical literature. It is my belief that teacher candidates should not be emasculated by a pedagogy of theory, but rather empowered by a pedagogy of theorizing. To engage the former is to shield them from the perplexing, intellectual, and difficult work of pedagogy while engaging the latter is to liberate them from the defensive maneuvers and normalcy that deadens pedagogy discourse. I offer my insights gained from these efforts not as a guide to best practice, but rather as grist for the mill that invites discursive engagement in the spirit of critical, social reflection.

NOTE

1.   This description refers to my work at an institution prior to joining the faculty of Teachers College.

REFERENCES

Ball-Rokeach, S. J. (1973). From pervasive ambiguity to a definition of the situation. *Sociometry, 36*(3), 378–389.

Barnhardt, K. A. (2000). Crisis. In D. Gabbard (Ed.), *Knowledge and Power in the Global Economy* (pp. 17–24). Mahwah, NJ: Erlbaum.

Boghosian, H. (2004). The assault on free speech, public assembly, and dissent. A National Lawyers Guild report on government violations of First Amendment rights in the United States. North River Press. Retrieved from http://www.nlg.org/resources/DissentBookWeb.pdf.

CNN. (2005, February 10). *White House reporter's credentials questioned.* Retrieved from http://www.cnn.com/2005/ALLPOLITICS/02/09/white.house.reporter/.

Freire, P. (1970/2000). *Pedagogy of the oppressed.* New York: Continuum.

Giroux, H. (1996) *Counternarratives: Cultural studies and critical pedagogies in postmodern spaces.* New York: Routledge.

Greene, M. (1973). *Teacher as stranger.* New York: Longfellow.

Gur-Ze'ev, I. (2005). Critical theory, critical pedagogy and diaspora today: Toward a new critical language in education. In I. Gur-Ze'ev (Ed.), *Critical theory and critical pedagogy today: Toward a new critical language in education* (pp. 7–34). Haifa, Israel: University of Haifa Faculty of Education.

Heilman, E. (2005). Escaping the bind between utopia and dystopia: Eutopic critical pedagogy of identity and embodied practice. In I. Gur-Ze'ev (Ed.), *Critical theory and critical pedagogy today: Toward a new critical language in education* (pp. 114–142). Haifa, Israel: University of Haifa Faculty of Education.

Holton, R. J. (1987). The idea of crisis in modern society. *The British Journal of Sociology, 38*(4), 502–520.

Kellner, D. (2003). *Media spectacle.* New York: Routledge.

Matsaganis, M. D., & Payne, J.G. (2005). Agenda setting in a culture of fear: The lasting effects of the September 11 on American politics and journalism. *American Behavioral Scientist, 49*(3), 379–392.

MSN News. (2004, August 4). Howard Dean on his remarks on terror warning. Retrieved from http://msnbc.msn.com/id/5595646/.

Pew Research Center. (2004, January 11). Cable and internet loom large in fragmented political news universe. Pew Research Center for People and the Press. Retrieved from http://peoplepress.org/reports/print.php3?PageID=774.

Pitt, W.R. (2005). *After Downing Street.* Retrieved on August 2, 2007 from http://www.alternet.org/waroniraq/22200/.

Segall, A. & Gaudelli, W. (2007). Reflecting socially on social issues in a social studies methods course. *Teaching Education, 18*(1), 77–92.

Suskind, D. (2004, October 17). Without a doubt. *New York Times Magazine.* Retrieved from http://select.nytimes.com/gst/abstract.html?res=F30F1EF93A5F0C748DDDA90994DC404482.

Wilson, J. (2005, December 1). *Pentagon pays Iraq newspapers to print its 'good news' stories.* Retrieved from http://www.guardian.co.uk/Iraq/Story/0,,1654661,00.html.

CHAPTER 6

THINKING BEYOND ACHIEVEMENT IN EDUCATION

Teaching Gender through a Radical Feminist Framework

Robert K. Pleasants and Matthew B. Ezzell

ABSTRACT

This chapter is the result of their reflections on teaching feminism to under-graduates, graduate students, and future teachers. Their teaching has been grounded in their experience in sexual assault and relationship violence response and prevention. In teaching feminism, they begin with the reality of women's and men's lives and then ask students to consider the pervasive and often hidden impact of gender on their lives as an introduction to feminist theory. This chapter brings a radical angle as a critique of the more common liberal version of feminism in the classroom.

The popular discourse on gender in education is often reduced to a matter of boys' and girls' achievement, ignoring the question of gender altogether

Unsettling Beliefs: Teaching Theory to Teachers, pages 87–108
Copyright © 2008 by Information Age Publishing

through an unstated assumption of innate sex roles. Thus, a central goal for teaching gender in education must be to expand the definition of gender beyond simple notions of sex roles. Students should understand the processes of gender formation and the ways in which gender itself enables and creates interpersonal and structural inequality between men and women. In the first half of this paper, we will discuss the current context of gender in education, arguing for a feminist pedagogy that engages with material conditions of gender inequality both structurally and in the life experience of students. After establishing our framework for teaching gender in education, we will discuss our experience with student resistance and some possibilities for productive engagement.

CONTEXT

Although gender is one third of the social theory trinity of race, class, and gender, feminist theory has remained marginalized in the popular discourse of gender and education. Marcus Weaver-Hightower (2003) has pointed out that while a number of popular feminist texts on education proliferated in the mid-1990s (Orenstein, 1994; Pipher, 1994; Sadker & Sadker, 1994), an equal number of "backlash blockbusters" (Mills, 2003, cited in Weaver-Hightower, 2003) were popular by the end of the same decade (Gurian, 2001; Sommers, 2000; Pollack; 1998). In the allegedly "post-feminist" present era,[1] many studies of gender in education have shifted from girls to focus on the relative underachievement of boys in schools. Weaver-Hightower calls this shift the "boy turn," playing on the double meaning of "turn" to highlight both the shift to boys and the assumption by some scholars that boys have been historically neglected in the discourse of gender and education and are now due for attention. This focus on boys is partially the result of the fact that much feminist research on gender and education has historically worked within a liberal framework,[2] focusing on ways to win rights and raise the academic achievement of girls. Within liberal feminism, the goal has been to make girls equal to boys within the current system of education. Because girls' achievement has surpassed boys in many academic fields within education, many recent studies have begun from the assumption that the feminist movement was a success and that now boys are oppressed in a system that favors girls (see Lingard & Douglas, 1999 and Weaver-Hightower, 2003 for a more in-depth analysis).

Despite the increased academic achievement of girls, however, we have seen little structural change in gender relations in the United States. Leadership in schools, churches, families, government, business, and entertainment still belongs primarily to men. Additionally, as Mickelson (2003) has noted, although girls may outstrip boys in educational achievement and attainment, these factors have not translated into higher earnings for women relative to men in the workforce. The wage gap persists, with women still earning only approximately 75% of what men earn in the workplace (Institute for Women's Policy Research, 2005; United States Census Bureau, 2005). Moreover, girls and women—much more so than boys and men—are systematically targeted for acts of sexual harassment and other forms of sexual and domestic violence, both within and outside of schools. Within schools, the American Association of University Women (2001) found that 83% of girls and 79% of boys had experienced sexual harassment in schools. Although these numbers seem comparable, girls were twice as likely to experience a decline in self-confidence and three times as likely to report feeling scared at school. Because of sexual harassment, girls were also three times more likely to report having trouble paying attention in class.

Further, the increase in girls' scholastic achievement has done little to curb the pervasive violence suffered by girls and women at the hands of boys and men. Approximately one out of every six women in the United States has reported victimization by attempted or completed rape in her lifetime, compared to fewer than 3% of men (Tjaden & Thoennes, 1998). Additionally, approximately 75–85% of victims in relationship abuse are female (U.S. Department of Justice, 2005). Of course, boys and men are victims, too. In fact, males are victims in the majority of non-sexual violent crimes. It is important to note, however, that men are also the perpetrators in the majority of all forms of violence. Although the current focus on boys in post-Columbine America does include a conversation about school violence, many conversations fail to consider the ways in which violence is a gendered phenomenon (Katz & Jhally, 1999).

Considering the continued imbalance between women and men in the United States, teachers and researchers need to move beyond liberal analyses of boys' and girls' achievement to understand the ways in which gender serves as a factor in violence as well as an organizing principle in the lives of individual students and in the structure of schools themselves. When the discourse on gender and education works within a liberal framework and limits its focus to academic achievement, researchers only engage with gender on a surface level, ignoring the many ways gender affects students personally, socially, economically, and historically (Connell, 1987; Lorber, 1994).

In the remainder of this chapter we will argue for a feminist pedagogy that that is grounded in the material conditions of gender inequality in the life experiences of students. We will highlight the importance of modeling this approach and discuss patterns of, and ways to deal with, student resistance. We will conclude with a discussion of hope for social change. This chapter is 'autoethnographic' (see Reed-Danahay 1997) in the sense that we are speaking from our own experiences as instructors (and students) in Education, Sociology, and Women's Studies classes, in addition to drawing on our experiences as educators and advocates within the rape crisis and family violence prevention movements. The examples that we use to highlight each section should be seen as just that: exemplar cases of the patterns we have identified, from our own experiences. We write, teach, and advocate from our positions as white, educated, middle-class men, understanding that these positions each afford us privilege in relation to our students. We strive to use this conferred privilege critically and with an eye toward justice, and we see this chapter as an outgrowth of that attempt.

GROUNDING FEMINIST THEORY IN STUDENT EXPERIENCE

To best understand any social theory, students should be able to understand its practical applications. In education, social theory is irrelevant to pre-service teachers unless they can relate it to their own lives or those of their students. In part because of the aforementioned popular liberal discourse on post-feminism, many pre-service teachers do not see the relevance of feminism in their lives (Titus, 2000). Because much feminist scholarship and activism in education has been achievement-oriented, few authors have attended to the processes of genderization for students in schools (see Connell, 1996, and Thorne, 1993, for notable exceptions). Further, most research fails to examine the material conditions of inequality faced by women *outside of school* in the greater social structure of patriarchy in the United States. Therefore, the following processes are important when teaching feminist theory to pre-service teachers: a) helping teachers understand their own socially-constructed gendered identities; b) enabling awareness of the material conditions of women's oppression; and c) teaching gender as a social structure.

We argue that helping pre-service teachers understand their own identity as gendered beings is foundational to their understanding of feminist theory. Simply put, most people take their own gender for granted—they assume their gender is a given, following naturally from their biological sex. The fact that they are (and can be) active in their gender construction is often forgotten. Thus, a first step in teaching feminism to pre-service teachers is helping them understand the social construction of gender—the ways in which they have enacted and created their own gender within a social context. Theorizing gender as a social construction can help pre-service teachers understand and adopt feminist theory by offering an alternative to restrictive essentialist notions of biologically-based masculinity and femininity.

Judith Lorber's (1994) essay "'Night to His Day': The Social Construction of Gender"[3] can be an excellent starting point for initiating a feminist conversation about gender with pre-service teachers. Lorber discusses how, "As a social institution, gender is one of the major ways that human beings organize their lives" (p. 15). In this dense short essay, Lorber explains the difference between sex and gender, the pervasiveness and processes of gender, its components and manifestations (gender scripts, gender status, gender ideology, etc), and the hierarchies assigned to gender. Importantly, she also explains that gender itself is not neutral: "In a gender-stratified society, what men do is usually valued more highly than what women do because men do it, even when their activities are very similar or the same" (33). Although both males and females are rewarded for acting according to their prescribed gender, males benefit more because American culture is "male-centered" (Johnson, 2005, p. 5), defining masculine behaviors, beliefs, and institutional practices as norms. Such an understanding of gendered inequality should be foundational to a radical[4] understanding of gender.

In teaching Lorber's essay, we draw from the pedagogy of cultural studies to include a variety of popular media texts to be examined as sites where dominant ideologies are offered and sometimes contested. To illustrate Lorber's basic point about the process of genderization, we ask our students to analyze texts such as advertisements for children's toys, clothing and costume catalogs, and children's books. The use of children's books has been particularly effective in discussing gender with pre-service teachers, as these texts directly relate to the processes of schooling. Through an analysis of these texts, pre-service teachers can understand what boys and girls learn through the adoption of a masculine or feminine gender. For example, in looking at highly gendered children's toys, we ask students: what do these things tell us about what it means to be a boy or a girl? Asking students what children learn about gender also works well when looking at children's books. Pre-service teachers are often surprised that dominant gender ideologies are so blatant in popular texts—boys learning active behaviors, girls learning passivity; boys learning to be strong and smart, girls learning to be pretty. In addition to highlighting the pedagogical functions of popular media, an analysis of these texts also illustrates the early age at which the process of genderization begins. Using these texts also helps broaden the notion of pedagogy to help pre-service teachers understand the depth and frequency of learning that occurs in the context of everyday life.

After introducing our students to social construction of gender, we have often asked them to reflect on their own experiences as gendered beings. One exercise involves asking students to write a gender diary for a week of the semester.[5] In this diary, students reflect on instances in which they were aware of gender in their day to day lives. The writing of such a diary invites students to take stock of what is usually taken for granted and (re)evaluate their everyday life through a gendered lens. By making the familiar strange, this exercise can expose the many ways that people's lives revolve around gendered experiences. Most importantly, it takes the abstract concepts of gender and roots them in the lived experiences of each student.

Helping pre-service teachers reflect on gender is a necessary starting point, but this analysis of students' own lives will remain "insufficiently materialist" (Hartmann, 1997, p. 97) if not connected to gender as a hierarchical social system (Connell, 1987; Lorber, 1994). As previously stated, both non-feminist and liberal feminist work in gender and education has staked claims upon material academic achievement, ignoring the ways in which gender functions as a social structure (Connell, 1987; Lorber 1994). Indeed, because the relative underachievement of boys has been recently dominant in the popular discourse of gender and education, a feminist discussion of gender must include a larger analysis of male-female relationships, occupational statuses, comparative salaries, and the material realities of violence in our culture in order to effectively refute claims of a post-feminist era. In other words, we need to help students think beyond the simple question of whether schools favor boys or girls in matters of academic achievement. This question is of course important, but it is not important in and of itself. By itself, the question works under the assumption that achievement operates in a vacuum—that it is both the sole measure of whether or not schools are serving girls and that educational achievement is panacea for inequality. The focus on achievement is problematic for three reasons. First, it allows researchers to ignore other—and often more subtle—forms of discrimination in schools (Sadker & Sadker, 1994). Second, it valorizes achievement as the sole measure of success for girls, assuming that better grades for girls or more degrees for women can ensure success within a patriarchal workforce. Finally, a focus on achievement does not successfully work to equalize power relations and end men's violence against women.

Regarding this final point, teachers must connect achievement with a broader analysis of power between men and women, interpersonally and structurally. Both researchers and practitioners in education have largely ignored the material suffering of women at the hands of men. Men's violence against women (commonly euphemized as "sexual" and "domestic" violence) is part of the "evaded curriculum" in primary and secondary schools as well as most university schools of education (American Association of University Women, 2002). Because schools typically avoid this subject, patriarchy is enabled and supported by the threat of men's violence against women. As Tim Beneke suggests in the essay "Men on Rape" (2001), although not all women have directly experienced sexual assault, all women experience the threat of men's violence. This ever-present threat serves to limit women's freedom of movement and expression in everyday life. We have often employed a simple yet effective classroom exercise to illustrate this point. We ask students to make two lists answering the following questions: What actions do women take on a regular basis to protect themselves against sexual assault? What actions do men take for the same reason? Comparing the two lists, students are often astounded by the long list on one side of the board and the blankness on the other.

This comparative sexual assault activity is one of many that we bring into the classroom from our experience organizing for awareness of men's violence against women and teaching community anti-violence education. The exercises are useful when teaching gender within the context of education because providing students with awareness about men's violence against women gives them concrete examples of the oppression of women. Our direct experience working with female survivors of men's violence helps legitimate our advocacy for feminist theory in the classroom, much in the same way that pre-service teachers have respect for professors with extensive teaching experience in their discipline. We acknowledge that these experiences work along with our male privilege to make it less likely that students view our claims about gender as biased or self-serving. Although most professors will not share our background in anti-violence work, they can provide students with a broader analysis through discussion of men's violence against women. They can also work in conjunction with local feminist agencies to bring in guest speakers to talk about men's violence against women and its effect on students within and outside of the classroom.

In addition to discussions of the interpersonal and structural nature of men's violence, it is also important that pre-service teachers connect their personal experience and their understanding of the material inequality of gender to the idea of gendered social structures. Lorber's "Night to His Day" provides an accessible introduction to the many tiered "components" of gender, both institutionally and individually (1994, p. 30). Table 6.1 lists Lorber's breakdown of these components.

TABLE 6.1

Gender as a social institution	Individuals' experiences of gender
Gender statuses	Sex category
Gendered division of labor	Gender identity
Gendered kinship	Gendered marital and procreative status
Gendered sexual scripts	Gendered sexual orientation
Gendered personalities	Gender personality
Gendered social	Gender beliefs
Gender imagery	Gender display

In the classroom, teachers and students can begin with a discussion these components of gender and move toward an understanding of how classrooms, educational institutions, and the state itself might be gendered. R.W. Connell's *Gender and Power* (1987) provides an analysis of the ways in which gender works through three main structures: labor, power, and cathexis (emotional relations). Importantly, an understanding of the larger forms of gender in society helps shift the focus from liberal individualism towards a broader radical awareness of gender as an organizing principle in our lives.

MODELING FEMINIST PEDAGOGY

Perhaps the most practical example of feminist theory we can provide pre-service teachers is through the pedagogy we employ in the classroom. As Diem and other authors in this volume have suggested, pre-service teachers primarily want to know how social theory can improve their teaching, and feminist theory is no exception. In modeling feminist pedagogy for our students, we not only offer effective methods to enhance their teaching, but we also provide further material evidence supporting feminist theory. In addition to seeing how feminist theory can have practical advantages for their teaching, it is important that pre-service teachers also understand how feminist pedagogy serves students. In this section, we will discuss three pedagogical methods we employ from a feminist perspective in our teaching: collaborative work, inquiry-based learning, and self-reflection. In discussing each of these methods, we will also discuss the potential advantages of these methods.

Although critical pedagogues also advocate collaborative work, we want to consider the ways in which collaboration can be viewed specifically as a feminist educational practice. In positioning ourselves as facilitators and fellow learners in the classroom, teachers can attempt to relinquish the authoritative (and often authoritarian) aspects traditionally assigned to the teacher role. In conjunction with competitive models which have historically underserved girls and women, we argue that these teaching models are traditionally masculine in nature. Competitive models of education and achievement also counteract attempts to create community within the classroom. For these reasons, we argue that employing collaborative methods in the classroom is a feminist practice.

Perhaps the most common and traditional forms of classroom collaboration are small-group projects and small- and large-group discussions. In addition to these collaborative methods, we can also model collaboration through allowing pre-service teachers (as students) to take a leadership role within the classroom through their facilitation of class sessions. Again, such a move de-centers the teacher as the authority and gives students the ability to shape the dynamics of the classroom community. Students can also affect classroom dynamics when teachers invite them to collectively construct guidelines for classroom interaction. In doing so, students create the conditions in which classroom discussions will be facilitated.

Students may also guide the direction of the course when teachers allow students to contribute to the syllabus. If students are invited to set the goals for the course, they can feel a sense of ownership in relation to the curriculum and are accountable to themselves and each other. This collaborative curriculum development can aid in facilitating a sense of community and interconnectivity. In asking students to contribute to course goals, feminist pedagogy may include inquiry-based learning practices in the classroom. Again, rather than assuming the role as the authority in the classroom, teachers can join students in asking questions and working together to find answers. Madeleine Grumet's (1995) conception of curriculum is influential here:

> What is basic is not a certain set of texts, or principles or algorithms, but the conversation that makes sense of these things. Curriculum is that conversation. It is the process of making sense *with a group of people* of the systems that shape and organize the world that we can think about together (p. 19, our emphasis).

As Grumet stresses, curriculum should be more of a process of collectively understanding the ways in which the world interacts with our lives. Such collective understanding does not, of course, always mean agreement. While students may not agree on what should be taught, they should understand the ways in which all texts and curricula are value-laden. According to Gaby Weiner's description of feminist pedagogy, "texts need to be analyzed as constructions of experience and knowledge rather than 'neutral' transmitters of common-sense professional ideas and practices" (1994, p. 117).

Finally, feminist pedagogy should include self-reflexivity for both students and teachers. Reflective learning helps students personalize knowledge and find ways to make it relevant to their own praxis as teachers. One of the ways in which gender is personalized in our classrooms is through the aforementioned gender diary assignment, which helps students reflect upon the ways in which gender works in and through their lives. Additionally, we have also worked with students on a meta-level, asking them at various points in the semester: What have you learned so far? Why do you think we want you to think about these things? In one course, Robert asked students to write what they had learned in each section of the course in lieu of a final exam. After compiling their answers into a single document, he offered students a parting gift containing the knowledge they collectively created during the course. We ask students to reflect, but we also employ a self-reflexive praxis and often talk through our own classroom practices with students, giving students options in class and openly discussing our own dilemmas as teachers. We also ask students for intermittent feedback about our courses to help us change curricula to better serve students. Because gender itself is a process, such self-reflexive practices help to achieve and sustain an awareness of gender in our lives.

WORKING WITH STUDENT RESISTANCE[6]

Because pre-service teachers have so much invested in their gendered identities, they may ignore or resist discussions of gender inequality.[7] A radical analysis of gender has disarming implications, and some pre-services teachers may acknowledge inequality but feel so overwhelmed that they shut down because they feel more comfortable without gender awareness. In our classes, we have found smaller patterns within these two broad categories of resistance: denial of inequality and helpless acknowledgement. Within the category of students who deny inequality, two trends emerge. First, students tend to universalize problems with gender, equating the ways in which men and women are affected by gender. Second, students resist acknowledging inequality because they do not want to see themselves as victims or oppressors. Two trends also are notable within the category of students who acknowledge inequality but feel helpless to create change. First, students rely on biological essentialism to explain gender inequality, asserting that such inequality is inevitable. Second, students become overwhelmed by their awareness and give up. In the following section, we will describe these forms of resistance and suggest strategies to deal with them.

There Is No Problem... It's a Human Thing

In discussions of gender inequality, some students make comparisons to other examples of discrimination, suggesting that various forms of discrimination and suffering are part of the human condition. While this shift may be a form of active resistance, it may also be an attempt to connect with the experiences of others. However, as Hytten and Warren have noted, this strategy runs the risk of the "relativizing of all differences and putting them on some sort of equal footing" (2003, p. 71). For example, in a discussion about the impossible standards of beauty constructed for American women and connections to issues of self-esteem, eating disorders, and educational achievement, students (both male and female) will sometimes suggest that men are held to a standard of beauty as well. They may point out the physique of male models in fashion advertising, and point out the focus on chiseled male bodies in movies such as *Troy* (Peterson, Rathburn, & Wilson 2004). Judgment of our bodies, they suggest, is a human thing.

One striking example occurred in a class discussion of the emotional maintenance of intimate relationships between men and women, when a female student suggested that men are conditioned to be emotionally inexpressive and women are stereotyped as overly emotional. Because of these stereotypes, she said, it is commonly felt that the job of taking care of emotional aspects of a relationship is "women's work." She said that many women had to "pull teeth" to get men to open up to them. A man in the class suggested that this was exactly comparable to men having to be the sexual initiator in relationships. He said that when women "force" men to share their feelings, it was equivalent to men forcing women to engage in sexual acts. In doing this, he problematically suggested that when women try to get men to open up emotionally it is equivalent to rape, even using the language of "sexual and verbal intercourse" to highlight the connection.[8]

Such statements reflect what sociologists Michael Schwalbe (2005) and Allan Johnson (2005) call *false parallels* (see, also, Kleinman, Copp, & Sandstrum, 2006, for more on responding to false parallels). They appear true on the surface—for example, any body (male or female) *can* be judged based on its physique—but this type of resistance masks underlying inequality by taking the example out of its social and historical context. Images of women and men saturate our cultural landscape, but the consequences of these images are not the same. Whereas women (or women's bodies) are disproportionately portrayed as sexual objects, thin, silly, and/or submissive, men and men's bodies are most often portrayed, even if sexualized, as projections of (physical/economic/political) power. Moreover, women are taking up less and less symbolic cultural space as the bodies we consume in media get smaller and smaller, and men have been taking up more and more space with larger muscles and more threatening postures.[9] With students, we analyze these representations in cultural texts (ads, toys, games, etc., see above) that students bring into class for critical analysis as we promote media literacy. Moreover, we compare and connect the objectification of women to the systematic targeting of women and girls for violence by men and boys that occurs in our culture, something else that we are able to ground in the everyday experiences of students in the class. It is in the context of that violence, and the students' lived experiences, that such statements equating the physical violation of women's bodies with the 'violation' of a man's feelings start to fall apart.

Why might students turn to these strategies of resistance? For many, this resistance is an understandable echo of the liberal scholarship and individualist and anti-feminist backlash that have dominated cultural airwaves (and educational discourse) over the last decade. Students are reflecting and repeating the arguments and talking points that they have consumed through mainstream cultural outlets. But for many, it is more than a simple parroting of arguments they have heard elsewhere. These arguments wouldn't gain traction, after all, if they didn't connect with students in some ways. The man equating emotional equality to rape in Matthew's class engaged in similar acts of resistance throughout the course. In his writing and his statements in class, he was quite angry. Although the reasons for his anger were sometimes hard to pinpoint, it was clear that the target of his anger was women, particularly feminist women.

As his teacher, Matthew felt that this student—who was not physically powerful or wealthy—had, like so many other men in a patriarchal culture, felt slighted by not receiving his full patriarchal dividend (Connell 1995). As a male growing up within a patriarchal culture, he felt entitled to feelings of power and prestige. Yet, he didn't feel powerful. Instead of turning his critical gaze to patriarchal constructions of hegemonic masculinity, arguably the root causes of his suffering, he instead blamed women for challenging traditional male power and privilege. His writings made clear that he felt targeted by feminism simply by virtue of his being a man. The so-called 'men's rights movement' was there to support his misguided analysis (see Schwalbe 1996). Of course, this specific student is not reflective of all students who make use of false parallels. Most students, arguably, are not driven by such specific feelings of anger. As previously stated, many even have the positive intention of making connections across lines of difference. Because traditional pedagogies perpetuate the achievement ideology instead of encouraging students to think critically, it is not surprising that students do not push beyond surface similarities, neglecting social and historic context.

A variation on this type of resistance is a focus on personal choices, an appeal to individualism and liberalism. Students might suggest that individual actions are simply personal choices and assert that everyone has a right to live their life in the manner of their choosing. Again, such a belief is not surprising within the current socio-historic context of liberal individualism. For example, in a class discussion about the sexual objectification of women, a student raised the issue of stripping. She made the argument that stripping, as an aspect of the sex-exploitation industry, perpetuates the sexual objectification of women, highlighting how this industry values women for their appearance above all else and commodifies women's sexuality. She went further to argue that stripping was, thus, related to things like eating disorders, women's self-esteem, and men's violence against women. In reaction, a second female student responded by saying, "Well, it's her personal decision to strip if she wants to. She's making money, more power to her." As Schwalbe (2005) notes, people make an argument for personal choice with countless issues, but the consequences of such an argument are always the same: relying on individual choices denies our interconnectedness as human beings. It falsely suggests that the consequences of our actions end with us and do not impact others.

As a resistance to acknowledging women's oppression, the argument for personal choice ignores that not all choices are open to all women. It ignores the economic coercion that forces so many women into the sex-exploitation industry (Stark & Whisnant, 2005). Framing the issue as a personal choice also shifts the unit of analysis away from systemic oppression and on to the individual. In the example above, the original student's critique was aimed at the sex-exploitation industry, while the second student ignored the social, economic, and historical context and focused instead on the individual. In teaching about gender and oppression, discussions should always keep in mind the socio-historic context in which women's choices are constrained.

...I'm Not a Victim/Oppressor

Although some students falsely equate men's and women's experience, others resist seeing any inequality in their lives. In keeping with the popular discourse on post-feminism, they often argue that discrimination and oppression were very real *in the past*, but that in the present day we have achieved gender equality. As noted above, while such thinking is common, it is not supported by even a casual glance at current indicators of inequality between men and women. This type of resistance can often be addressed by talking honestly and critically about the state of our social world. This is particularly useful, again as noted above, when done in ways that connect to the students' lived experiences of gender.

Other students may have more than ignorance of social patterns as the impetus driving their resistance. For example, many girls and women may not want to see themselves as victims. There is comfort in the achievement ideology of meritocracy that suggests that if you work hard enough, you can do whatever you want. This ideology not only fosters a victim-blaming mentality in relation to problems such as poverty or racism, but it can also enable such thinking in regards to men's violence against women. Some women and girls may baldly assert that a woman who dresses a certain way/has too much to drink/goes to a man's room/is walking by herself is "asking for it." In this way, the students shift the target of violence from the broad category *women* to individual women who make bad decisions. Because victim-blaming is consistent with the dominant discourse on rape, it provides a sense of security for women in our classes. They want to believe that if they do not engage in certain careless actions, they will not be attacked. Such thinking is understandable, but the feeling of safety it engenders is a false one. The majority of female sexual assault victims have not engaged in careless behaviors—in fact, the majority of victims were actually minors at the time of their assault (Tjaden & Thoennes, 1998).

The concurrent effect of blaming victims is that such thinking not only (re)locates the focus of our attention on the women who are attacked, but it offers no hope for change, ignoring the perpetrators of these crimes. Men and boys, too, sometimes offer victim-blaming justifications for violence. Generally, they are not seeking to promote a sense of their own safety from violence with this strategy; but, they may be distancing themselves from responsibility or blame for such acts. As a related rhetorical strategy, it is common for men and boys to perpetuate the myths of rampant false reporting.

There is great disagreement about the statistics surrounding false reports of rape. Susan Brownmiller (1975) famously noted only 2% of reported rapes turn out to be false, the same rate as occurs for all violent crime. 'Men's rights' groups have attacked this statistic vociferously, with one group, Fathers For Life (2005), even suggesting that as many as 98.1% of all reported rapes are false. The truth of the matter, of course, is likely somewhere in between (but it is arguably much closer to 2 than 98%). Because rape victims continue to be blamed in dominant cultural discourses, there is little incentive for women to make false reports of this nature. Instead, many women are intimidated to report at all. Robin Warshaw (1994) found that of women whose experiences met the legal definition of rape, only 5% reported the crime to the police, and 42% did not tell anyone at all about the assault(s). Even more disturbing, Warshaw found that only 27% of women whose assault met their state's legal definition of rape identified themselves as rape victims, and a full 84% of men in the study who admitted to behaviors that legally are defined as rape were adamant that what they did was *not* rape. So whether or not false reporting may occur, we argue that that is the wrong subject for closer scrutiny. Instead, we try to shift the focus to why so many women and girls who experience these crimes keep it to themselves, or don't even name their experiences as rape in the first place. How are so many men who admit to behaviors that legally constitute rape able to maintain a belief in their innocence? What about the men whose behavior falls into the 'gray' areas in the law? How confused must we be in this culture about what constitutes sex and rape for this to occur?

Two additional points are worth noting when responding to victim-blaming in class discussions: a) it is an echo of popularly held myths, and thus not surprising when it comes up in the classroom; and b) it is anti-male. This second point often catches students off guard, particularly if they happen to be male-identified. We ask the students what view of men is underlying the idea that rape happens because of what a woman wears/has drunk/etc. They usually can see that it is a view of men as essentially beasts who cannot control themselves. We point out that, as men, such an appraisal is offensive and that we have much more faith in our own humanity. Indeed, through a radical feminist analysis, we have found a male-positive understanding of rape and our social world in general. Such an analysis can head off a related form of basic anti-feminist resistance in which students claim feminism is anti-male. In short, the analysis that we employ does not see rape as an act of innate male aggression. Such an analysis offers no hope for change because it makes sexual assault seem inevitable. Instead, we look at rape as a gendered social phenomenon. We point out that although the overwhelming majority of rapists are men, the majority of men are not rapists. This is an important distinction. It can head off a related form of resistance to the women who do not want to see themselves as victims: men who do not want to see themselves as oppressors.

As noted, many men and boys will react defensively in discussions of men's violence against women. Such resistance is not surprising given the popular anti-male view of rape as a 'boys will be boys' phenomenon. It also makes sense given the scared-straight approach to anti-rape education that many boys and men have experienced on athletic teams and other venues, in which men are collectively viewed as potential offenders. As an alternative, our approach follows the important work of groups like Mentors in Violence Prevention (MVP) and Men Can Stop Rape[10]—we see men and boys as potential leaders and as allies to women in the efforts to end men's violence against women. We note that although the majority of men are not rapists, the majority of men are silent about these issues. We highlight that silence among men is part of the problem, but that men and boys can be a big part of the solution as well.

The *I'm not a rapist* tactic of resistance is just one form of the larger *I'm not an oppressor* strategy. Any discussion of privilege can elicit such responses, and this, too, makes sense. We all want to feel like we are good people and promote a sense of ourselves as such. Moreover, students who have bought into the achievement ideology likely feel like they, and their families, have earned everything that they have. Discussions of inequality, oppression, and privilege can feel like they are challenging that hard-working, good-person status. Indeed, for students who believe in meritocracy, these discussions can promote paradigmatic changes in their worldviews, which can be frightening and uncomfortable. Of course, the unsettling experience of people with privileged identities having their unearned advantage exposed is in no way equal to the experience of oppression. Still, resistance in the face of such a shifting worldview is not surprising.

In discussions of male privilege and gender inequality, the sexual assault exercise described above can be an effective tool for exposing what should be a basic right: the freedom to live life without being targeted for sexual violation. When students realize that the fear of sexual assault offers men and women differing realities, their notions of neutral gender differences begin to break down. Other resources that we use in these situations are articles such as Peggy McIntosh's (2004) now-famous "White Privilege: Unpacking the Invisible Knapsack," and Devon Carbado's excellent epilogue to the book *Black Men on Race, Gender, and Sexuality: A Critical Reader* (1999) in which he, following McIntosh's lead, catalogues a list of male and heterosexual privileges that he is afforded, detailing how these aspects of his identity intersect with his racial identity. Videos are also helpful in fostering awareness, notably Sut Jhally's *Tough Guise* (1999) and hidden-camera comparisons like Prime Time Live's "True Colors" (Lukasiewicz & Harvey, 1992) and "The Fairer Sex" (Nelson, 1993).

There is a Problem, But... It's Always Been This Way

Students are deeply invested in their gender identities and often conceive of them as an innate part of their identity. This experience can enable the thinking that gendered inequality is also natural or biologically determined and isn't going to change. Often, this type of resistance will emerge in statements like, "There's inequality because women can get pregnant. Women are naturally better caregivers and nurturers because of that, and that's why men are in positions of power. If men could get pregnant, women would be on top. But they can't, and there's no way for us to change that." In some ways, these students are right: (most) women can get pregnant, and men cannot. However, rationalizing social organization on the basis of biological propensity ignores issues of power. Dominant groups maintain their power through a variety of ways. As Barbara Reskin (1993) and Stanley Lieberson (1982) have pointed out, one of the reasons dominant groups maintain power is that they are able to write rules and set standards; they do so, of course, in ways that justify and maintain their dominance. It is not a given, then, that if men could get pregnant women would emerge on top of the social order.

A useful tool in these discussions is Gloria Steinem's (1993) "If Men Could Menstruate." In this short piece, Steinem guides the reader through a thought-experiment in which men, not women, menstruate. She asks, "What would happen, for instance, if suddenly, magically, men could menstruate and women could not? The answer is clear—menstruation would become an enviable, boast-worthy, masculine event..." (p. 332). She then catalogues the justifications men might offer for their dominance, including the amount of bleeding being a sign of manliness, the need to "give blood to take blood" (p. 332) in the armed forces, the importance of a natural cycle of menstruation in understanding mathematical principles and theorems, and so on and so forth. Stemming off of this piece, as documented in Kleinman et al.'s (2006) article, "Making Sexism Visible: Birdcages, Martians, and Pregnant Men," we sometimes ask students how men might justify dominance if they could get pregnant. Students usually come up with a broad range of answers, including: the importance of bearing the next generation in order to lead that generation, the balance of women doing housework and childcare after men have carried the fetus for nine months, the need to pay men higher wages to compensate them for their social gift of children, etc. The point is that the same biological propensity that is used to justify a group's subordinate status could be used to justify another group's dominance. As Steinem (1993, p. 332) says: "Male human beings have built whole cultures around the idea that penis-envy is 'natural' to women—though having such an unprotected organ might be said to make men vulnerable, and the power to give birth makes womb-envy at least as logical." At issue is not the biological possibility of a particular group, but the relative dominance of that group.

Even when students understand that inequality is not biologically determined, they may still feel as if it is inevitable. It is not uncommon for students to state that "things have always been this way, and they're not going to change." Patriarchal societies have been around for thousands of years, so it is understandable that students sometimes believe this. As Allan Johnson (2005, p. 224) notes, "Even thousands of years, however, are a far cry from what 'always' implies..." Patriarchal social organization is not the only model that has existed in human life, and even within the same patriarchal culture, we can see variation over time in what constitutes 'real' manliness/womanliness. The curves of women in Rubenesque paintings stand in sharp contrast to the women walking on runways today, but both sets of women mark the standards of beauty for their times. This contrast is possible because social systems are constantly in flux, continually being created and recreated through human interaction. Systems appear stable, often, because our choices are constrained in ways that tend to recreate the status quo. But, such constraints are not inevitable. Social changes come about because human agents organize to demand that they do. In classes, teachers can illustrate other possibilities by including examples of other cultural models of gender and sexuality, social movements in our own and other cultures, and discussions of hope.

...We Might As Well Give Up

Discussions of hope are sometimes sorely needed. For students who take discussions of inequality seriously, coming to see the inequality all around them can be overwhelming. Many students, particularly toward the end of a semester or course, express feelings of despair. "The problems are too big," they tell us, "and my friends don't listen to me. Nothing's going to work." This is understandable, particularly in a culture of quick fixes and action, because quick fixes are not easy to come by. Like feelings of guilt, despair can stop students from acting at all. Allan Johnson (2005, p. 227) notes: "If we look at patriarchy as a whole, it's true that we aren't going to make it go away in our lifetime. But if changing the entire system through our own efforts is the standard against which we measure the ability to do something, then we've set ourselves up to fail." Instead of focusing on social revolution as the yardstick against which our efforts are measured, social change can be viewed as a process of complex and collective action over time. Johnson encourages us to consider Gandhi's insight that what we do as individuals will be insignificant, but it is vital that we do it.

CONCLUSION: HOPE FOR CHANGE

The relationship between individuals and systems highlights the complex nature of gender as a social system—although no single individual can change an entire system, social systems exist only because groups of individuals engage in patterned interaction. Consequently, it is through the collection of individual and collective acts that we create social change. Many students may feel that change occurs through the efforts of dynamic individuals—heroes—in history, perhaps because of the stories they have seen reflected in history classes, books, and movies. But the singular focus on the work of individuals erases the countless little actions required to enable those bigger events, along with the countless others who laid that foundation. In other words, the despair some students experience in feeling insignificant can provide a moment to reintroduce the intereconnectedness and interdependence of human agents, as well as the real reasons to be hopeful. When we, as individuals, take the path not taken, we show that alternative models of existence are possible. When we challenge a sexist joke or myth, we create the possibility of different patterns of interaction. The revolution, in this sense, need not be the overthrow of a regime or the collapse of traditional modes of thinking. It can be seen, instead, as the process of how we live out our lives.

In order to see the pervasiveness of gender in everyday lives, teachers and students should begin with an awareness of their own gender as a socially constructed process. Through further analysis of the material inequalities that exist through gendered behaviors and gendered institutions, teachers can move beyond liberal ideologies of achievement towards a more critical understanding of feminism as a relevant social theory. Reframing the discourse of gender in education to include a radical feminist approach will help students and teachers work more critically towards gender equity in our classrooms, our schools, our communities, and our world.

NOTES

1. The term "post-feminist" suggests that men and women have achieved gender equality, thus feminism is no longer necessary or relevant.

2. Liberalism, broadly defined, holds the individual as the key to social change through freedom of choice and equality of opportunity. In other words, a liberal framework seeks means to broaden access to existing social institutions as they are currently constructed, instead of changing those institutions or creating new ones.

3. Because the essay is abridged in some edited volumes, we recommend teaching the full essay as included in Lorber's (1994) *Paradoxes of Gender.*

4. As Schwalbe (2005) points out, the word "radical" comes from the Latin word for "root." As such, a radical analysis is one which seeks to get at root causes. Students are often wary of the word because of its usage in dominant cultural discourse to marginalize an idea or individual(s) as fringe, exaggerated, or dangerous. A discussion of this issue can be a useful resource early on in class interactions.

5. We thank Natalia Deeb-Sossa for sharing this exercise with us.

6. In our thinking in this section, we are indebted to Sherryl Kleinman for her mentorship, guidance, and leadership by example. Many of the strategies we describe come from her pedagogical toolkit.

7. These forms of student resistance are not unique to pre-service teachers. In remainder of this essay, we will discuss resistance from students we have taught in Education, Sociology, and Women's Studies courses.

8. In this argument, the student was influenced by the work of Jack Kammer, specifically his 2002 book, *If Men Have All the Power, How Come Women Make All the Rules: and Other Radical Thoughts for Men Who Want More Fairness From Women.* Halethorpe, MD: published by Jack Kammer. This work fits into the tide of backlash texts that emerged in the late '90s and beyond, and is grounded firmly in the 'men's rights' literature.

9. Even a casual glance at the cultural depcitions of 'maleness' over the last few decades reveals bigger, more muscular and threatening men today compared to those from the recent past. Students pick up on this with comparisons between actors like Humphrey Bogart and Jimmy Stewart to Sylvester Stallone and Vin Diesel. Depictions of 'femaleness,' however, have changed toward the other extreme. Women in mainstream media today are thinner, less curvy, and less threatening than in the past. The exception to this is female athletes, who, although generally thin, are also strong and physically capable. Depictions of female athletes, though, disproportionately focus on their desirability to a heterosexual male gaze and their performance of normative gender and sexual scripts (conventional femininity, heterosexuality, etc.) Comparisons can be drawn between women of the past like Jane Mansfield and Marilyn Monroe and women today like Halle Berry, Paris Hilton, and Anna Kournikova (see Jhally 1999 for more on this).

10.   Visit http://www.sportinsociety.org/mvp/mvphome.html and http://www
.mencanstoprape.org/ for more information about these groups.

REFERENCES

American Association of University Women. (2001). *Hostile hallways: Bullying, teasing, and sexual harassment in school.* Retrieved December 12, 2005, from http:// www.aauw.org/member_center/publications/HostileHallways/hostilehallways.pdf

American Association of University Women. (2002). The evaded curriculum. In *The jossey-bass reader on gender in education.* San Francisco: Jossey-Bass.

Beneke, T. (2001). Men on rape. In M. S. Kimmel & M. A. Messner (Eds.), *Men's lives* (5th ed., pp. 384–389). Boston: Allyn and Bacon.

Brownmiller, S. (1975). *Against our will: Women, men, and rape.* New York: Ballantine Publishing Group.

Carbado, D. (Ed.). (1999). *Black men on race, gender, and sexuality: A critical reader.* New York: New York University Press.

Connell, R. W. (1987). *Gender and power.* Cambridge, UK: Polity Press.

Connell, R. W. (1995). *Masculinities.* Berkeley: University of California Press.

Connell, R. W. (1996). Teaching the boys: New research on masculinity, and gender strategies for schools. *Teachers College Record, 98*(2), 206–235.

Fathers for Life. (2005). False abuse allegations. Retrieved December 14, 2005, from http://www.fathersforlife.org/fv/false_abuse_allegations.htm

Gurian, M. (2001). *Boys and girls learn differently: A guide for teachers and parents.* San Francisco: Jossey-Bass.

Grumet, M. (1995). The curriculum: What are the basics and are we teaching them? In J. L. Kincheloe, & S. R Steinberg (Eds.), *Thirteen questions: Reframing education's conversations* (2nd ed., pp. 15–21). New York: Peter Lang.

Hartmann, H. (1997). The unhappy marriage of Marxism and feminism: Towards a more progressive union. In L. Nicholson (Ed.), *The second wave: A reader in feminist theory* (pp. 97–122). New York: Routledge.

Hytten, K., & Warren J. (2003). Engaging whiteness: how racial power gets reified in education. *Qualitative Studies in Education, 16*(1), 65–89.

Institute for Women's Policy Research. (2005). The gender wage ratio: Women's and men's earnings. Retrieved November 12, 2005, from http://www.iwpr .org/pdf/C350.pdf

Jhally, S. (Producer and Director). (1999). *Tough guise: Violence, media and the crisis in masculinity* [Motion picture]. (Available from the Media Education Foundation, 60.)

Johnson, A. G. (2005). *The gender knot: Unraveling our patriarchal legacy* (2nd ed.). Philadelphia, PA: Temple University Press.

Katz, J. & Jhally, S. (1999, May 2). The national conversation in the wake of Littleton is missing the mark. *The Boston Globe.* p. E1.

Kleinman, S., Copp, M., & Sandstrum, K. (2006). Making sexism visible: Birdcages, Martians, and pregnant men. *Teaching Sociology, 34*(2), 126–142.

Lieberson, S. (1982). *A piece of the pie.* Berkeley: University of California Press.

Lingard, B., & Douglas, P. (1999). *Men engaging feminisms: Pro-feminism, backlashes and schooling*. Buckingham England ; Philadelphia: Open University Press.

Lorber, J. (1994). *Paradoxes of gender*. New Haven: Yale University Press.

Lukasiewicz, M. & Harvey E. (Producers). (1992). *True colors*. ABC News/CorVISION.

McIntosh, P. (2004) White privilege: Unpacking the invisible knapsack. In Rothenberg P. (Ed.) *Race, class, and gender in the united states* (6th ed., pp. 188–207). New York: Worth Publishers.

Mickelson, R. A. (2003). Gender, Bordieu, and the anomaly of women's achievement redux. *Sociology of Education, 76,* 373–375.

Nelson R. (Producer). (1993). *The fairer sex*. ABC News/CorVISION.

Mills, M. (2003). Shaping the boys' agenda: The backlash blockbusters. *International Journal of Inclusive Education, 7*(1), 57–73.

Orenstein, P. (1994). *Schoolgirls: Young women, self-esteem, and the confidence gap* (1st ed.). New York: Doubleday.

Peterson, W. (Producer/Director), Rathburn, D., & Wilson C. (Producers). (2004). *Troy* [Motion Picture] United States: Warner Bros. Pictures.

Pipher, M. B. (1994). *Reviving ophelia: Saving the selves of adolescent girls*. New York: Putnam.

Pollack, W. S. (1998). *Real boys: Rescuing our sons from the myths of boyhood*. New York: Random House.

Reed-Danahay, D. E. (Ed.). (1997). *Auto/ethnography: Rewriting the self and the social*. Oxford: Berg

Reskin, B. F. (1993). Bringing the men back in: Sex differentiation and the devaluation of women's work. In L. Richardson & V. Taylor (Eds.), *Feminist frontiers* (3rd ed., pp. 198–210). New York: McGraw Hill.

Sadker, M., & Sadker, D. M. (1994). *Failing at fairness: How America's schools cheat girls*. New York: Touchstone.

Schwalbe, M. (2005). *The sociologically examined life: Pieces of the conversation*. Boston: McGraw Hill.

Schwalbe, M. (1996). *Unlocking the iron cage: The men's movement, gender politics, and American culture*. New York: Oxford University Press.

Sommers, C. H. (2000). *The war against boys: How misguided feminism is harming our young men*. New York: Simon & Schuster.

Stark, C. & Whisnant R. (Eds.). (2005). *Not for sale: Feminists resisting prostitution and pornography*. Victoria, Australia: Spinifex Press.

Steinem, G. (1993). If men could menstruate. In L. Richardson & V. Taylor (Eds.), *Feminist frontiers* (3rd ed., pp. 332–333). New York: McGraw Hill.

Thorne, B. (1993). *Gender play: Girls and boys in school*. New Brunswick, NJ: Rutgers University Press.

Titus, J. J. (2000). Engaging student resistance to feminism: "How is this stuff going to make us better teachers?" *Gender and Education, 12*(1), 21–37.

Tjaden, P., & Thoennes, N. (1998). *Prevalence, incidence, and consequences of violence against women: Findings from the national violence against women survey*. (Report for the National Institute of Justice and the Centers for Disease Control and Prevention). Retrieved November 12, 2005, from http://www.ncjrs.org/pdf-files/172837.pdf

United States Census Bureau. (2005). *Historical income tables—people.* Retrieved December 12, 2005, from http://www.census.gov/hhes/income/histinc/p40.html

United States Department of Justice. (2005). Family violence statistics including statistics on strangers and acquaintances. Retrieved November 12, 2005, from http://www.ojp. usdoj.gov/bjs/pub/pdf/fvs02.pdf

Warshaw, R. (1994). *I Never Called it Rape: The Ms. report on recognizing, fighting, and surviving date and acquaintance rape.* New York: HarperCollins Publishers, Inc.

Weaver-Hightower, M. (2003). The "boy turn" in research on gender and education. *Review of Educational Research, 73*(4), 471–498.

Weiner, G. (1994). *Feminism in education: An introduction.* Buckingham, UK: Open University Press.

CHAPTER 7

"BUT THAT'S IN THE PAST, RIGHT?"

Using Theories of Whiteness to Challenge Meritocracy and Disrupt the Racist Narrative of Racism

Joshua Diem
University of Miami (FL)

The body of literature on the powerful and pervasive force that whiteness plays in every element of American culture, including schooling, deservedly seems to grow by the minute. In the field of education, this expanding area of study touches on virtually every conceivable element of educational research including examinations of the historical legacy of whiteness in contemporary schooling practices, examinations of the powerful manners by which whiteness manifests in language and discourse, how whiteness plays an instrumental role in the manner by which administrators and teachers construct classroom arrangements and practices, and how to incorporate critical examinations of whiteness in the professional

Unsettling Beliefs: Teaching Theory to Teachers, pages 109–135
Copyright © 2008 by Information Age Publishing
All rights of reproduction in any form reserved.

development of practicing teachers (Diangelo, 2006; Giroux, 1997; Maher & Tetreault, 1997; Rich & Cargile, 2004). In writing this chapter I seek to add to one area that doesn't seem to get enough attention. This is the area of how we engage undergraduate pre-service teachers in examinations of the manifestations of whiteness on structural and personal levels, and how whiteness has structured the very system they have successfully navigated by ending up in our classrooms. What is further lacking in the literature, though not entirely absent, are articulations of particular examples of how professors have engaged in this practice in their particular spaces (Marx, 2004; Solomona et al, 2004). Sharing this information will not result in any data that one might call generalizable. However, there is great potential for generating information that can be helpful and useful across various settings.

In the following chapter I discuss why I teach about issues related to power, privilege, and racism in American public schools, using whiteness as the centerpiece of these discussions. I discuss how I employ examinations of whiteness in a semester-long undergraduate course in the social foundations, and how events typically unfold when students engage (or don't) in critical examinations of power, privilege, and racism using this lens. I do not provide a detailed step-by-step recipe of pedagogical techniques, though I include some discussion of the general methods I employ in this endeavor. Rather, I focus my energy on articulating an argument of why it is imperative to explicitly name the presence and overwhelming power of whiteness in educational settings, and why it is particularly vital to teach future teachers theories of whiteness. I argue that there is a logical fit of examining and critiquing whiteness in a larger framework of critical pedagogy, particularly one that emphasizes challenging the concept of schools as meritocratic systems. This larger context serves as the framework to which everything in my course connects. I supply this argument with illustrations of what occurs in my courses when I engage in this practice. My primary purpose for engaging students in this examination is to disrupt, or to use the title of this book unsettle, the narrative my students use when discussing racism.

What I write about here and what I engage in when I teach is built primarily around my adaptation of work put forth by Kathy Hytten and Amee Adkins (2002). Their work is one of the most useful and informative pieces on the applications of theories of whiteness in the formation of a pedagogy for the education of pre-service teachers. In this piece the authors state it is necessary to use literature on whiteness, as well as a critique of the ways in which whiteness works, to shape our own pedagogy of whiteness. This then allows us to teach our students in a manner that models the critique of whiteness, promoting students' own development of a pedagogy of whiteness. The critique of whiteness includes, though is not limited to, the recognition that it is the existence of whiteness that even allows for white people like me to believe that we know what we speak of when it comes to race and racism. The critique is further demonstrated by the manner students do or do not accept what we say and engage (or not) with the ideas we present them about race and racism. As a white heterosexual male from a middle class background, I benefit from white privilege as well as privileges related to my gender, sexual identity, and social class and accompanying social and cultural capital. I teach about whiteness as a person who benefits almost more than anyone else from its existence. This must be part of an explicit critique that students see and hear in my teaching. This interaction of my positionality, my pedagogy of whiteness, and the level of effectiveness I achieve in getting my students to engage in this material will be discussed in detail later.

The primary function of using literature on whiteness and modeling a pedagogy embracing a critique of whiteness is to answer an important question put forth by Hytten and Adkins when they ask, "First, how can we disrupt the normativity of whiteness...?" (2002, p. 434). The "normativity of whitenss" is reflected in the narrative my students use to discuss racism in contemporary America. Providing students with literature, data, oral histories, studies, policy analyses, and voices that are usually marginalized and left absent from conversations on race and racism affords an opportunity for this disruption (Anderson, 1988; Blight, 2002; Carlson, 2004; Dingus, 2006; Kerr, 2006; King, 2006; Lipsitz, 1998). In most cases, though certainly not all, students are willing to at least listen for a moment to these ideas that are not the norm. It is in these moments, these brief ruptures of a somewhat closed mind shape by limited life experiences and the primacy of parental belief systems that we must pounce and make a difference. For while most students will listen, they usually fall back on the authoritative nature of that which they have been taught by parents, family, school, and popular culture to dismiss these new ideas. It is vital to capitalize on this temporary opening and insert something, an idea or thought, that will keep that tiny opening present or at least make it a little easier to open. By disrupting this narrative, I hope to reshape the perspective my students use to view racism and move them towards a more critical understanding of power, privilege, and racism in schooling. I want this critical understanding caused by a disruption in the dominant narrative to eventually lead to a change in behavior and classroom practices. I want my students to practice an anti-racist pedagogy that is informed by their own pedagogy of whiteness. But in the particular venue I speak of in this chapter, I confined by time to concern myself primarily with changing perspectives that I hope will later lead to a change in actions.

WHY WHITENESS?

I engage in the practices I describe here in an undergraduate social foundations course. However, I argue that the unmasking of American public schooling as an institution merely disguised as a meritocratic system is needed in all undergraduate and graduate courses that comprise teacher education programs. Critical analyses of racism in schools through the identification of the power of whiteness, studying theories of whiteness, and practices aimed at purposeful disruption of the dominant narrative of racism in American culture must be at the center of all discussions related to race and racism in American schools (Trainor, 2002).

Our current national discourse about racism, inside as well as outside the academy, lacks any semblance of a genuine, critical examination of the complexities of many of the elements that maintain and reproduce this ideology and the unjust social structure that stems from it. The history we teach about African Americans is done so in a manner that distorts with a filter of whiteness. (Carlson, 2004; Giroux, 1997; Ignatiev, 2006; Lawrence & Tatum, 2004). We use schools as sites to reify our racist social order (Hytten, & Warren, 2003). What I see and hear from my students in no different than what I see and hear in the communities I inhabit and the cultural forces, particularly media, I witness and feel. We refuse to engage in a meaningful and critical examination of the issues, appeasing ourselves with a false sense of what we see as the diminished roles racism plays in contemporary society. We make ourselves feel better by stating, almost dogmatically, how much better things are now and that change takes time. While no one can deny that progress has indeed been made, we can not be satisfied with the current state of affairs. Additionally, this view falls short of asking basic questions such as how and why, given our purported societal rejection, racism persists. Even when viewed through the lens of things being better and social change taking time, there is an acknowledgement that racism still does exist. So why then are we appeased by a simple rationale that merely explains that the racism of today are remnants of a once much more powerful and overtly visible force in America? These are the very questions that many students state as entering their mind at some point of their lives, but left unaddressed let alone unanswered, they were simply fleeting. And these are the very questions that need to be asked, and can be interrogated in much more meaningful manner using a pedagogy of whiteness.

We have come to accept the existence of racism as a natural by-product of a multicultural society. We have come to believe that while there are many benefits to a society comprised of individuals who don't all share the same racial, ethnic, religious, and national origin, there are also inherent problems in this social arrangement (Guess, 2006; Keating, 1995). Chief among these problems is that differences will manifest in a dislike among some for others with difference as the sole basis for this dislike. By naming and placing racism in the domains of individuals and small groups, we deflect attention away from issues such as institutionalized racism. We label individuals ignorant and subpopulations backward, and then move on from the issue. We discuss racism using a discourse that is far too benign and timid in its depiction of the violent and oppressive impacts this destructive ideology continues to have on our country and our institutions. This has all become part of the "normativity" of whiteness that must be disrupted (Hytten & Adkins, 2001). The classrooms we use to train our future teachers is a perfect venue to cause disruption, change these practices, and halt what at times seems like an inevitable reproductive force that continues to perpetuate these dangerous problems

If we sincerely wish to eliminate the impacts of racism in the process of schooling, we must change the discourse and engage in a conversation that addresses the issues in a more honest and direct manner that will be uncomfortable for most, and impossible for some. This conversation will be uncomfortable for many reasons, including the fact that by changing the discourse we reframe the issue (Williams & Land, 2006; Giroux, 1991). Reframing the issue forces individuals to look at racism in an entirely different manner, including a reflection and examination of what they have been taught and why. For some, the conclusions reached will be difficult to accept, to the point of being so intimidating that refusing to engage will be seen as the only viable option. While this is not exactly what many would devise as an advertisement for classroom activity, this is indeed what will occur. But this expected resistance would occur in any space. While students may opt for a behavioral pattern that reflects a refusal to engage, we can not accept this choice and must devise means by which they want to engage. Disturbing as it may be for many of our students, we must demonstrate the urgency of the issue and foster the creation of environmental conditions that get them engaged. This can be navigated and negotiated by the very nature of the dynamics of a university classroom that is successfully constructed in a manner that reflects the mandate that one of the fundamental purposes of learning is supposed to be actively engaging with new ideas that conflict with those held upon entering the classroom. Offering theories of whiteness as a framework for viewing race and racism, with the goal of producing teachers that will live and practice an anti-racist pedagogy is a difficult but necessary challenge that we must present our students.

The current public narrative of color-blindness in matters related to race is constructed in an intentional effort to paint a picture of racism that minimizes its impacts on and in our contemporary culture, thus reproducing race-based marginalization and oppression (Williams, 2006). It is in lockstep with the American desire to believe in meritocracy and the Great School Legend. I see this play out in my undergraduate course semester after semester, as I know it does in others across the country. A vast majority of my non-minority students, as well as a number of their minority peers, relegate the impacts of racism to the realm of the personal and to a distant past far removed from their lived experiences. The first part of my chapter's title comes from a common refrain that I have heard many times from my students. They think racism impacted individuals and groups of individuals in the past, and was all but ended by the legal abolition of segregation and other legally sanctioned discriminatory practices. These students do not see or understand any means by which racism was/is structural or institutionalized. The narrative of racism they have been taught states that today only a small number of ignorant people remain racist. In fact it is almost always people who are referred to as racist. An individual's beliefs or actions may be racist, but social systems or institutions are rarely referred to in this manner. And as far as schooling is concerned, my students have been taught all children, regardless of race, now have equal opportunities to succeed, as long as they work hard.

By teaching theories of whiteness and challenging the notion of schooling as a meritocratic system that solely rewards hard work and individual achievement, we equip students with the tools necessary to question and challenge the legitimacy of the existing public narrative about race and racism. This is needed to change pre-service teachers' ideas about racism as merely existing in the past, and more importantly their future practices as classroom teachers. While all this may be true, it is still understandable to question why whiteness is the ideal lens with which we should engage in examinations of racism in schooling.

WHY NOT JUST SAY RACISM?

As I began working on this chapter, I took a trip to Iowa and Illinois to collect data for an evaluation I was completing. While in Iowa I stayed with a married couple who are both sociologists, Jerry and Adriana. As academics who study social issues related to race, ethnicity, gender, and social class in the United States, they are familiar with academic literature on race and racism. In the course of a conversation about what we were all engaged in professionally, I brought up this book and my chapter. Jerry asked me why it was necessary to use the term whiteness. He said that it sounded like yet another academic term that essentially means racism but is used as a means of not having to explicitly say racism. Jerry said that while he wasn't familiar with the dominant discourse or literature in education, he feels that sociologists use terms like whiteness in place of simply saying racism because they are scared to name people, social practices, and institutions as racist. He believes that terms like whiteness are used because they are safer and a lot less powerful. He felt that by using terms less powerful than racism we implicitly state that it isn't racism; it may be a result of racism, a manifestation of racism, a means of implementing racism, but in the end the message that gets conveyed is that it isn't itself racism. Our fear to name that which is racist as racist leads our students to the conclusion that it must not be racist; if it was, we would simply name it as such.

I am closer with Adriana than I am Jerry. Adriana is my friend of many years, and this visit was actually the first time I had really talked at any length with Jerrry. Because of that, I initially shrugged off Jerry's criticisms as not warranting much thought. While he was qualified to speak about the issue in a broad sense, I tried convincing myself he didn't know what he was talking about in this instance because he didn't know me and where I was coming from, and that was reflected in his comments. If he knew me he would know that I am not afraid to call anybody or anything racist if I think it's an accurate description. But after my attempt to just simply dismiss him, I realized that Jerry is an incredibly intelligent and critical thinker who is just as concerned with social justice and equity as I am. His point about lightly treading around the issue of racism, instead of simply addressing it directly cut to the core of the issues I thought I would be raising, but in a manner that stood my whole argument on its head. I found myself questioning whether I am in fact afraid to name people, practices, and institutions as racist. Maybe repeatedly telling myself that I am not afraid is merely a self-justifying means of making my white liberal ideas seem more radical and on the side of the struggle for social justice than they actually are. Then I depersonalized the issue and questioned whether this whole area of study was essentially working in reverse of its stated goals. I discussed the issue a bit more with Jerry and Adriana but left Iowa feeling unsure of my claim that whiteness needs to be positioned at the forefront of discussions of racism and schooling.

Upon returning from my trip, getting back to the classroom, and continuing to question the importance of using whiteness with my students, I realized that Jerry's points and my belief in the value of teaching about racism through the lens of whiteness are not mutually exclusive. Jerry's made me realize that I need to make certain that I always incorporate his major thesis into how I teach whiteness. Jerry's central point was that academics, as well as all individuals in society, often appear to be afraid to explicitly name a person, institution, organization, or practice as racist. Instead we use a discourse that includes much of the sentiments of claiming something as racist, but we don't use the word "racist". While I couldn't agree more with Jerry, I don't think the move to use whiteness as a means of analyzing and critiquing the racist arrangement of our social structure and schools is a tactic born out of fear. Rather, it is almost the opposite. White-ness points the finger directly at not just the unjust social order, but specif-ically spotlights those in power and how this unjust order benefits them. It directly attributes the unjust quality of the social order to racism. It is essen-tial to explicitly state to pre-service teachers that American schools engage in racist practices; but teaching about how and why racism and racist prac-tices exist through the lens of whiteness is vital in gaining any type of com-prehensive and critical understanding of the issues, as it reconstitutes what these are and what they mean.

Furthermore, in these superficial discussions on race and racism that my students have been a part of, racialized minority groups are constructed as problematic. It is not racism that is the problem; it is the racialized indi-viduals and groups they comprise. These students have been taught through explicit and implicit means that virtually every social problem involves race, and these problems are caused by the existence of racialized groups of people (Sleeter, 1993). Through these processes my students have been taught that the behaviors, and some might even say mere exist-ence, of racialized groups are in fact the problem. Teaching theories of whiteness helps to provide students with a perspective on race and racism that is not only new, but also challenges the ways in which they have been taught to construct all issues surrounding race and racism. These issues include, but are not limited to, schooling and education. The vast majority of my students have had race and racism constructed in ways that make minority groups (African Americans primarily, and to a lesser extent Lati-nos) racialized, while leaving the dominant group (whites) without race (Carter, 1997; Perry, 2002). This division of people along racial lines with some having race and some not has been constructed in manners that clearly depict marginalized and oppressed minority groups as being nega-tively impacted by discrimination and prejudice, but there is rarely a men-tion of how the dominant groups partake in, and benefit from, said constructions and the resulting prejudice and discrimination. This does not even begin to address the fact that the students' exposure to issues related to racism is still limited in its discourse to the words "prejudice" and "discrimination". Words such as oppression, injustice, marginalization, and demonization are simply absent. With regards to learning about racism, what my students have taken part in can be described as a limited trope of addressing these issues, acted out in a superficial manner to pacify and appease the seemingly obligatory educational mandate to merely address the issues, no matter how they are actually addressed.

Teaching students about theories of whiteness and providing them with alternative perspectives on race and racism may act as an extremely effec-tive means of initiating change in the manner that students view racism is schools. Not all students are open to these perspectives and success does not mean that every student leaves my class with a more critical view on how racism manifests in American schools. But once those students who are open to hearing and reading about new ideas regarding race and racism begin to understand the ideas that are used to explain theories of whiteness, a light seems goes off in their heads. It is as if they always knew that the manners in which they were taught about race and racism were a bit simplistic and incomplete. Yes, there are white people who are open about their racist beliefs, but the majority are not. Theories of whiteness help students understand how racism is still a powerful force, present everyday in American educational systems. This is of particular importance when it comes to the students who comprise the classes I teach coming to a better understanding of racism, and hopefully embracing an anti-racist pedagogy. This is due in large part to the fact that studying whiteness moves away from a simplified black/white dichotomous view of race and racism. This is important for everyone teaching in an institution of higher learning in the United States, as our demographics shift and we become a more diverse culture, in the truest sense of the word. As someone teaching classes with large numbers of Latino students, this is a particularly important aspect that examinations of inequality and injustice using a pedagogy of whiteness affords.

GOALS: WHERE/WHAT DOES THIS GET US?

My goal in writing this chapter and in my teaching is not necessarily to enhance or expand the literature on whiteness as it relates to theoretical underpinnings or how whiteness manifests in the lived experiences and daily lives of individuals in the United States. Though it is important to note that the ways my students talk about race and racism, and the need I feel to write this chapter, are in and of themselves, examples of how whiteness manifests in our schools. My aim in writing this chapter is solely to emphasize why it is imperative to present future teachers with a perspective about race and racism in American educational systems that articulates a narrative counter to the hegemonic narrative about racism they have been forced to endure. By exposing our students to the ideas embedded in theories of whiteness we provide the necessary tools that allow for racism to be viewed as a dynamic and powerful set of complicated practices resulting from historically rooted and entrenched processes perpetuated today because of the benefits and privileges racism affords whites. This construction of racism is in stark contrast to the manner in which these students have been taught, and thus viewed, race and racism as irrational and illogical, resulting from fear and ignorance of the unknown.

It may be rightly argued that much of what I present here in terms of the construction of race in American culture and the subsequent racism and narratives on race and racism that follow is not novel. However, I feel it is necessary to explicitly state these ideas to describe the framework I use when discussing the issues with my students. I claim no authoritative position in staking out new areas of knowledge related to power and privilege and the construction of race and racism in American culture. I simply present how I lead my students through a series of readings and discussions over the course of a semester in an effort to have them see a direct connection between the construction of race and the racist nature of the narrative of racism in American culture. I have had success in this endeavor, as I have seen and heard the changing nature of my students' thoughts and narratives about race and racism. I see them struggle and embrace the difficult process entailed in this examination of racism, power, and privilege.

There are others who engage in similar processes in colleges and universities across the country, and, again, I do not mean to make any claims of proprietary exclusivity in this endeavor. But I think we all engage in this practice a bit differently and should always want to learn from each other. While there are others who embrace the idea that whiteness must be a focus of conversations surrounding racism in American schools, it should not be assumed that all students are exposed to such teachers. Furthermore, many students who do receive this type of education do so in one isolated course. The ideas I speak of in this chapter must be woven into the fabric of the entire teacher education curriculum, as we see the visible manifestations of white privilege in virtually every element of schooling and school life. There are various routes leading to the destination of disrupting racist beliefs and practices, but using theories of whiteness is vital to any attempts at success in this endeavor.

STUDENT POSITIONALITY, MINE, AND THE INTERPLAY OF THE TWO

The students I speak of in this chapter are undergraduates attending a small private university in South Florida. The course is a social foundations of education course required of all students enrolled in a teacher education program (elementary, secondary, and specialists), as well as those who will receive a minor in education. Students may also take the course as an elective. The students who take the course as an elective are usually toward the end of their undergraduate degree program, though there are a small number who take the course as an elective in their first two years. The majority of the students enrolled in the course are in one of the teacher education programs; and, as this course is the first education course they are required to take, most are in the first or second year of their undergraduate studies. The fact that the education students are usually in their first or second year of undergraduate studies is vital in how I shape the course. Additionally, the presence of older undergraduates taking the course as an elective complicates the manner by which I design the course. Course enrollment is limited to 25 which significantly aids in the ability to have class sessions with dialogue and not lectures.

As I write I am concluding my third year teaching at this institution, and my descriptions and depictions of the students taking the course are drawn from this experience. The vast majority of the students who take this course are white or Latino. The percentage fluctuates slightly from semester to semester, with the two demographic groups comprising approximately 85–90% of the total class population. The split between these two groups is usually somewhere around 60/40, with Latino students comprising 40% of the 85–90% of the total class makeup, and whites comprising the other 60%. A large number of the Latino students are from geographic areas in South Florida and the Northeast where their identity as Latino may put them in the demographic majority. This majority is even more dramatic in the public school systems in many of these students' hometowns. For example, in the 2005-06 school year, 60% of students attending Miami-Dade County Public Schools identified as Hispanic, 28% as Black Non-Hispanic, 10% as White Non-Hispanic, and 2% identified themselves as belonging to the Asian/Indian/Multiracial category (Miami-Dade County Public Schools, 2006). The white students represent a slightly more diverse geographic swath of the United States. On average, there are two or three African American students in each section of the course, and in my time teaching the course there have only been a few Asian and Asian American students take the class. A handful of international students have taken the course as well.

In addition to often growing up in areas where they are in the demographic majority, most Latino students in my class come from middle class and upper class families. With few exceptions, these students do not believe that they have been oppressed or victimized (the word that many students like to use when speaking about these issues) by racial or ethnic discrimination based on power and privilege. These students have bought into the normativity of whiteness (Hytten & Adkins, 2001; Rochmes, 2007). Many of the Latino students attended private school and though not always the case, often these schools are often overwhelmingly, sometimes near exclusively, Latino. Though they have arrived at their conclusions based on different experiences, the white and Latino students in my class believe that racism in schools is a problem of the past that was effectively eliminated with the abolition of legally segregated schools. These students, by in large, genuinely believe that the desegregation of American public schools has resulted in every child since having the same access to opportunities.

This sentiment of racism in schools effectively being eliminated by the abolition of legal segregation in 1954 was echoed by the students I taught while a graduate student in the South. Unaware that desegregation was not even enforced until the 1970s in many parts of the South, and generally unable to conceptualize historical events in a meaningful framework, these students conceptualized segregated schooling as historically arcane as the plague. Many of these sons and daughters of the South grew up in the same towns where their parents were raised and experienced the process of school desegregation first hand. But whether they grew up in Latino household in Florida or a white household in New York, many non-Black students hold true the idea that with the passage of one court decision, the presence of racism in American schooling virtually vanished. They believe this because it is what they have been taught.

It is important to understand that according to what they state in class, the majority of Latino students in my class can rarely personally relate to their ethnic identity being constructed as a deficit. Though there have been exceptions, the overwhelming majority state that they simply cannot draw on personal experiences that come close to relating to those depicted in works like Angela Valenzuela's *Subtractive Schooling*, which we read a selection from in class (1999). To hear my students tell it, their social context is nowhere near that which constructs being Latino and/or speaking Spanish as a deficiency. Again, class plays a major factor in this dynamic. *Subtractive Schooling* takes place in Houston, which shares the characteristic of many of my students' hometowns of being cities with significant Latino populations. However, the students in Valenzuela's work do not have the economic resources my students do, nor do they possess the cultural capital my students do.

Just as it is important to describe the general composition of the students I teach, it is equally important to briefly describe my own positionality. The interplay of the two has a profound impact on how everything plays out in class, particularly discussions of race and racism (Johnson-Bailey, 2002). This interplay results in an odd and problematic dynamic where my positionality plays an instrumental role in my ability to successfully engage my students in discussions of racism. This will be discussed in further detail later.

I am a white Jewish heterosexual male in my early 30s. I grew up in a fairly generic suburban environment, raised by a teacher and an education professor. When I was growing up my parents were planted firmly in the middle-class, as there was such a thing during this time. I have never personally felt any form of oppression or known what it is like to experience the brunt of social injustice. Anti-Semitism is still alive and well but my experiences are limited to name-calling and overhearing a joke not intended for my ears. The structural and systemic inequalities that manifest in an unequal distribution of power and wealth determined by race and ethnicity simply do not impact American Jews as they do African Americans and Latinos. This is something I discuss with my students and it serves as a valuable source from which to draw comparisons of racial/ethnic/religious minorities groups' varying experiences in gaining (or not) greater opportunities to succeed over time.

It is fairly well documented that as far as access to educational, vocational, and economic opportunities, Jews in the United States do not currently experience the institutionalized forms of marginalization and oppression that African Americans, Latinos, and now Muslims, individuals from the Middle East who may or not practice Islam, and virtually all other dark-skinned immigrant groups experience. We have gone through a historical process that has resulted, in all practicalities related to social structures, in our becoming white (Brodkin, 1998). This manifests in educational and occupational success that is due, in large part, to access and not ability. As an example of contrasting Jews and African Americans historical experiences related to access to opportunities, I use the membership figures for our nation's most exclusive club—the U.S. Senate.

I tell the students that while Jews currently comprise approximately 2.2% of the U.S. population, and13% of the Senate, African Americans comprise 12.7% of the total population and 1% of the Senate. Furthermore, only five African Americans have ever served in the U.S. Senate (Sheskin & Dashefsky, 2006; United States Census Bureau, 2004; United States Senate, n.d.). While I recognize where I come from and the brutality my people have experienced, I also realize that as a young white Jew in the United States today, I have virtually unlimited unearned privileges and am the prototypical portrait of who benefits from the unjust and inequitable American social arrangements that are structured by racism, sexism, homophobia, heterosexism, xenophobia, and classism. I recognize and explicitly address this with my students and explain that this belief does not mean that I also believe that I am not qualified for my job or that I haven't had to work for anything. I stress to them that it does recognize that I did not have to work as hard, nor did I encounter as many obstacles, as my peers who came out on the other side of this structural arrangement. This is but one of the many ways I connect the examination of racism to the concept of schools as meritocracy.

COURSE BACKGROUND AND FRAMEWORK

The overarching framework I use to teach my course, including discussions about power, privilege, and racism, is a critical examination of the institution of schooling as a meritocracy. This is a vital component in the construction of how I introduce a way of viewing race and racism that is new for most students. I immediately introduce this framework when the first class session begins. After introducing the overall framework for the course I summarize the course content and tell a little about myself. I explain to the students that one of the primary reasons I teach social foundations is that schools are social institutions controlled by people, and we have the ability to change that which we find problematic and I want to be a part of the process of change. The road to change is often difficult and filled with many obstacles, but it is possible. I tell the students that I assume no matter how much they liked or disliked school, there are certainly things, large and small, that they would like to be different. I explain that many of their apprehensive feelings about change are rooted in their belief that school simply is the way it is and it may not be changed. I explain that from that moment forward they will be asked to participate in a class that will require them to question things they have previously assumed as truths about education that cannot be questioned. Central to this process of questioning is critically examining the idea of schools as meritocracies that afford mobility and success to anyone who simply works hard. I do this while engaging in the time-honored first day of class routine of going through the syllabus.

After the introduction and syllabus overview I engage the students in an activity where I pose the question, "Why do we do school"? I first did this with my co-editor, Robert Helfenbein, when we taught the graduate course that was the genesis for this book. We did this then, and I do this now, to gauge where the students are when they begin the course in terms of their ideas about the role that schooling plays in American society.

We read a bit of Dewey in my course and throughout the course of the semester I attempt to model the belief that it is vital for an instructor to understand the mindset of their students, where their students are, before beginning an examination of an area of inquiry (Dewey, 1997). This is particularly important in a course on schooling because though many of the students believe that they don't know that much about schooling, they all have a great deal of personal experience with and subsequent knowledge about the institution of school. They simply don't possess the academic discourse that they believe is so important to demonstrating an understanding of any subject.

As the students provide answers for why we do school, a similar pattern emerges semester after semester. The students' answers almost always fall into one of two binary categories of school-as-good and school-as-bad. The more optimistic and bright-eyed students think that schooling provides a level playing field for people to pursue their dreams and is a place that exposes children to an array of ideas and perspectives and pushes them to think. The more critical students (some might say cynical – particularly their bright-eyed counterparts) articulate that they believe school is a place to teach children their roles in society as pre-determined by factors such as class, race, and gender. These students do not buy into the idea that school places all students on equal footing and allows them all equal access to opportunity. The more optimistic students comprise the vast majority of the class, while the more critical students are an extremely small minority. The group that enters the class with a critical lens on schooling is an interesting bunch that essentially can be broken down into two subgroups.

I try my best to simply write down the students' responses to why we do school until the end of the activity, though I occasionally fail and add a little critique now and then. When the students are exhausted of answers, we discuss the answers they gave and what they thought about their peers' responses. This usually evolves into an examination of the very pattern I just described. The students who only saw/see schooling as a positive institution and process that affords access to opportunity are somewhat amazed at the critique provided by their peers. They can't believe that their peers would view schooling in this manner. Again it is vital to remember the students' ages, as most adults, let alone undergraduate students, do not possess much skill in seeing the world outside of their own experiences. A bit of polite of arguing, discussion emerges, but the exchange is too polite to have any significant meaning. On the first day of class most students are too hesitant to say anything that they feel may be a bit controversial. But enough back-and-forth goes on for the students to recognize that though there is a clear majority that believes schools are places that provide all the opportunity to succeed, not everyone does. This is when I begin to discuss the concept of meritocracy and how we believe it works on systemic and individualistic levels. Most of the critical students believe they have, at least in one way, overcome the inequality structured into schooling. These students are almost always a racial or ethnic minority, female, GLBT, come from significantly less money than their peers, have some sort of disability, or a combination of two or more of these. While they do not see it this way, they believe that they live in a society that has constructed their identity as a deficit. In addition to their individual identity they see how their membership in a group defined by a characteristic constructed as a deficit has often placed them at a disadvantage in terms of access to opportunity. These students make it clear on the first day of class that they have lived the experience of schooling as an institution that assumes a great deal about students' abilities and lives, and sorts them accordingly. There are a few white students who claim to see schooling through a critical lens. They do see the disadvantages that many minority and/or poor students face, but they rarely see how they personally benefit from this structural arrangement. These students seem to understand the politics of schooling in the abstract, but fail to see how they, and others like them, benefit from the very critique they provide. They clearly see how others are hurt by the political and structural arrangements of schooling, but they don't see how others benefit from this inequality. This does, however, often serve as a foundation for the development of a pedagogy of whiteness as these students do explicitly state that they see and believe that schooling is not simply a meritocracy, and certain groups of people face difficulties through discriminatory and racist practices that others do not. The next step with these students is moving them to recognize the privileges this affords to others and how this unjust system is socially constructed to be just that—unjust.

CHALLENGING MERITOCRACY

After engaging in the "Why do we do school?" activity I describe my teaching philosophy and the overall structure that the course will take in a little more detail than when going over the syllabus. Though I cannot discuss every nuance in detail in one class turned off, I do discuss the concepts of meritocracy and critical pedagogy in some detail. These are the two main components of the course that are present in virtually all that we study.

The primary component I want the students to understand in the first several class meetings of the semester is that much of what we do and think is a result of commonly held beliefs that are viewed as objective, inevitable, and true. We accept these truths and our thinking of what is and what should be is based on our assumptions that these are in fact truths (McLaren, 1988; McLaren, 2006). Additionally, these ideas have a historical basis and context which is important to understand. To illustrate this point in the context of schooling, the students and I discuss the fact that they have constructed a picture of what school looks like, and much of this picture has been constructed for them. This includes, but is not limited to, the physical characteristics of schools and school buildings; but perhaps more important is the fact that this idea of what school looks like includes things that we don't literally see. For example, schools should be comprised of grades (i.e., 1st grade, 2nd grade, and so on) that have clear boundaries that separate them, and students should progress from one grade to the next after demonstrating the defined proficiency for each grade. Learning takes place when teachers lecture students and when students read their texts. Both of these sources of information are authoritative and right; they are not questioned.

After introducing the concept and the importance of questioning these beliefs and not simply believing them on face-value, we return to the answers the students provided during our "Why do we do school?" activity as points of reference. I draw the students' attention back to the apparent dichotomy of their answers and draw out of them that responses that fall in the school-as-good category can also be viewed as part of the articulated argument we, as a culture, provide for the need for and maintenance of schooling as it currently looks. When viewing these responses it becomes clear that central to the rationale of all of the individual items is the notion that American schooling is a meritocracy. It is the thread that holds all of the individual responses together.

"BUT *I* WORKED HARD FOR EVERYTHING"

One of the topics I have found my students to be most interested in is an examination of their existing beliefs about how we construct what it means to be a successful student and the subsequent practices of how and to whom we then apply that label. This seems to work for several reasons. Number one, as students who have grown up in the context of high stakes testing, accountability, and schools being assigned letter grades for the entire world to see, they are consumed with the idea of always needing to define success in the various incarnations it takes in the realm of schooling. But the primary reason this discussion topic works is because the students in my class have all come up winners in the game of schooling. They attend a private university where admittance has become extremely competitive. My students know how to effectively navigate the system, work it to their advantage, and "do school" (Pope, 2001).

We use the topic of school success as a starting point for the critical examinations of all issues related to schooling that we will engage in throughout the course of the semester. I believe it is important to let students know from the beginning how the course will proceed throughout the semester, by having them participate in a discussion that forces them to question underlying assumptions about American schooling and what it means to be successful in school. In explaining the foundational themes of the course, I explain to the students that in order to effectively engage with the readings and subject matter covered in the course, they will have to understand that assumptions without critical analysis will not be accepted. I tell the students throughout the semester that in the context of the course I don't care *what* they think. The conclusions that they reach, in the context of the bounds of the course, are not what I deem important. Rather, I care that the students have a critical understanding of *why* they think what they think, and they can articulate that rationale and it can withstand scrutiny and critique. I tell the students that they are not allowed to say, "it's just my opinion" or "I might be wrong, but..." Rather, I want the students to embrace having a viewpoint, but their viewpoints must come from some level of thought, personal experience, reading of the course material, and analysis and synthesis of all of these. I tell the students that they don't have to agree with me because that is not the point. From the moment the students walk in the door and the semester begins, they understand that they will have to think and, for most of them, this will be a dramatic departure from what they are accustomed to doing in school.

DOMINANT NARRATIVES

Throughout this chapter I've used the term "narrative" to refer to how my students talk about racism. Though some argue that the way(s) by which we talk about racism are captured by Scott's work on public and hidden transcripts, I feel there is something else at work (1990). I agree that many people, particularly minorities, must negotiate and navigate the discourse they use to talk about race and racism in a racist society that denies the profound presence of racism. There are many who, as Scott tells us, talk about race and racism differently depending on the space they occupy. However, I believe that if you listen to how my students, or anyone else in our culture, talk about racism, it is done in a manner akin to storytelling. There is a story about race and racism and its historical devolution that we use to describe the improving status of race relations in the United States. The story is filled with characters (Abraham Lincoln, Jackie Robinson, Rosa Parks, and Dr. King) and settings (the march on Washington, the Montgomery bus boycott, and the Emancipation Proclamation). This story that has been adopted to help make sense of the racism that exists and contextualize it as normal. We use stories to help us make sense of the world, and stories offer telling glimpses into how we view racism (Bell, 2003). And while there is more than one story, there is a dominant narrative that is privileged above others.

As I noted previously, my students have been taught to view racism as residing in individuals and groups who are racist because they don't know any better. All my students have been taught this view, but the white students, as well as many of the Latino students, completely digest and believe in this perspective. Minority students often have a lived experience and additional narrative that provides disruption to this view, but as noted previously, geography and class impact the views of many my Latino students. In the discourse that dominates our nation's discussions on racism, the words "ignorance," "fear," and "irrational" are used to frame the causes of racism. We are taught to view racism as existing solely within and among individuals and groups that are fearful of minorities and don't understand them. This dictum tells us that an individual is racist primarily because they have never lived, worked, or associated with minorities. Racism is simply the result of not knowing any individuals of color. If you don't know a member of minority group about which you have racist ideas, it is impossible to come to understand that your ideas are wrong. If racist individuals simply came into contact with people of color they would realize the error of their ways and change their thinking, or so goes the dominant narrative.

The dominant narrative of the effects of racism in contemporary American society is one that comes nowhere near capturing the scope of the violent and oppressive element racism is in our contemporary cultural landscape, or the omnipresent, day-to-day influence racism has in our culture. This narrative is comprised of a discourse free of explicit naming of violence (symbolic, physical, emotional, and otherwise), oppression, injustice, exclusion from access to opportunities, and the reproduction of a stratified socioeconomic hierarchy that currently exists in our culture as a result of the racist manner by which we structure our social institutions. Unfortunately, this culturally dominant narrative extends its reach to the more specific narrative of racism and public schooling, and we see this reflected in the manner we teach about race and racism in school. This is rather predictable as there is nothing more institutional and part of the day-to-day fabric of American culture than the contemporary construction and practice of schooling. The presence of this problematic narrative is not only seen in primary and secondary schooling, but it is also woven into the fabric of institutions of higher learning.

I use to believe that it was universally understood and accepted that one of the central concerns of colleges and universities was to serve as a venue for critically engaging, analyzing, and deconstructing problematic social issues. This was the narrative about higher education that I was fed, and is the narrative I so desperately want to be true. But as social institutions themselves, I have come to believe that these centers of learning play a vital role in the reproductive nature of institutionalizing and reifying the racist nature of the current narrative of race and racism, as well as the discourse utilized in the promotion of this narrative. The impact of this narrative culminates in the classroom where instructors armed with credentials and institutional and peer-sanctioned expertise pass on this narrative and teach a construction of race and racism that does not come anywhere near what may intelligently be called thorough or comprehensive. Through the promulgation of this narrative, deemed as truth by the nature of the professor/student dynamic, many university students are learning a narrative about race and racism that itself is racist. This is particularly problematic for our students, future teachers, because of the venues they will be given to teach and regurgitate this narrative.

Because this narrative dominates how race and racism are talked about in our culture, most students enter their years in higher educational settings already having been force-fed the same narrative they will hear repeated on campus. They take it for granted as being true when they enter the university and it is reinforced throughout their time on campus. We must dissect and critique this narrative and provide our students with perspectives that call into question that which they have been taught before entering our classrooms. The difficulty of pushing against that which they have already been taught id compounded by the fact that in many cases our students are simultaneously enrolled in other courses where this narrative dominates any explicit discussion of race and racism. Additionally, this narrative plays out in students' daily lives as it influences any and all social interactions between and among students and faculty. Again, this is not surprising as we do not teach in a vacuum and are merely relegated to one place, a marked space, in the world in which this narrative lives and breathes.

COUNTERING THE NARRATIVE

I have used many books, articles, and book chapters when teaching about race, power, and privilege. The pieces I have consistently found to be the most effective and approachable when attempting to initially engage undergraduate students in discussions of whiteness, schooling, and privilege are George Lipsitz's *The posessive investment in whiteness* (1998) and Christine Sleeter's *How white teachers construct race* (1993). I use these pieces every semester as foundational works to serve as introductions to whiteness and then use additional materials, changing what I use from semester to semester. Sleeter clearly and concisely describes the dominant narrative on racism as the psychological view of race, while providing a description of the view on racism I push my students towards seeing, the structural perspective. By accepting the psychological view of race, we accept the fact that racism is constructed as a problem that exists in people's minds and hearts. Racism is accepted as a flaw of ignorance, and an irrational fear of people who are different. This view of race encompasses essentially all of what I have previously stated my students believe about racism, and it is used as the basis for the narrative they are taught and reproduce.

Using the psychological perspective to teach about racism, we engage in a conversation that focuses exclusively on how racism is detrimental to minorities. Nowhere in the dominant explanations of racism that the students have received are there discussions of how racism persists not because it hurts minorities, but because it serves the interests and benefits (in real, tangible ways) of the dominant group (Lipsitz, 1998; McIntosh,

1990). These interests include the perpetuation of economic and political power of the dominant over the disenfranchised. By talking about oppressive relations in a manner that only describes the conditions of the oppressed, while simultaneously ignoring the fact that the oppressors benefit from these oppressive relations ,a discussion of these oppressive relations that moves anywhere towards liberation is not possible. The absence of such a discussion in an examination of racism, or any oppressive relation, is desired and constructed that way by the oppressors. This itself is a benefit of the existing oppressive relations and makes the push for a reconstitution of the terms of the discussion extremely difficult.

The problematic construction of racialized minority groups as the reason for problems involving race lends itself quite favorably to the exclusion of any discussion of how white people benefit from racism in their day-today lives. This includes, but is not limited to, issues related to economic and political power. Central to understanding how racism operates in today's American culture, and in particular public schools, is an exploration of unearned privilege. These two issues, the structural manifestation of racism and the ensuing unearned privilege it affords those in the dominant group, are the central components of racism that I believe are best examined and explained using theories of whiteness as a guide. Lipsitz's work helps students understand one of the many unearned privileges they have been afforded – where they attended school.

Lipsitz's work details the Federal Housing Act of 1934 and how residential and school attendance patterns emerged from its passage (1998). Students are amazed to learn that the federal government engaged in practices like redlining that determined that minorities (mainly African Americans at this time) would have access to housing in cities while whites would populate the burgeoning suburban development of the United States. While whites were fleeing cities to move to the suburbs, so was the financial capital needed to maintain adequate living conditions and public services in the cities. This is the first time my students are presented with information that connects the ghettofication of the American inner-city with suburbanization. Students are appalled to learn that residential patterns, and subsequently school attendance patterns, were orchestrated by the federal government in such a clearly racist manner. They are also shocked to learn about the racist nature of seemingly neutral social events such as the development of highways, placements of toxic waste dumps sites and landfills, and access to preventive health care. I remind the students, as I do throughout the semester, that we, human beings, set the conditions for how we live and more often than not injustice results from our deliberate acts to make it so. While the idea of social construction is something students understand, the idea that residential patterns and subsequent tax bases and school funding levels are deliberately orchestrated in this manner begins to chip away at their belief in the dominant narrative.

FISSURES EMERGE DISRUPTION BEGINS

For students who are willing to critically engage with the material and wrestle with the possibility that everything they assumed about race and racism as truth may indeed be false, the initial repercussions can be quite dramatic. Many of my students state, mainly in meetings after class or during office hours, that they don't how to make sense of this new information. Though they don't want to, they believe it; but this makes it even more difficult. Their entire understanding of the world is crumbling right inside their heads. They have been fed information, often by parents and other family members who they love, that they have just learned is not only inaccurate but also serves to reproduce an unjust social order. I have had students come to me crying and the phrase, "I feel like my head is going to explode" has been uttered on more than one occasion. The first emotional state this morphs to is guilt.

Students articulate that once they have wrestled with and accepted the ideas put forth to them, they can't help but feel guilty. Though I have never had an African American student state this, several Latino students have. They feel guilty because they feel that they have done nothing to change these conditions and some of the lighter-skinned Latino students have stated that they feel their skin tone has afforded them privileges akin to whites. For the sake of time, and because it is so different from student to student, I won't focus on how individual students move past/through this. I will say that I make space and allow students to talk about the feeling of guilt and why it's there.

My students have a single and negative connotation of the word struggle. I try to explain to them that education in general is supposed to be about the struggle. The struggle should not be about achievement, grades, or other external forms of validation; rather, the struggle should be about exposing oneself to a multitude of perspectives and grappling with these conflicting and contradictory ideas in an effort to determine what makes sense to you. This is the struggle that learning about whiteness demands. I do not attempt to make my students feel good about the discomfort they express feeling. Instead, I tell them to embrace it and learn how to be comfortable being uncomfortable. This helps them along the way, but the reality is that I can not report any miraculous results in my class. I think that many students make significant strides while in my class, but, at least for now, my interaction with them ends on the last day of class. If my students can feel like their head is going to explode, then feel guilty, and then embrace the uncomfortable struggle of questioning all that they have learned about the world and their place in it in the span of three and a half months, there is not much more I can ask. Unfortunately, I also recognize it is not anywhere close to all that is required.

For every student that states s/he feels guilty, there are always at least an equal number who state that there is no reason to feel guilty. They use common refrains about their families having just arrived in the U.S. in the 20th century or even how they personally are just a young adult so they are not implicated in any of this. There is a predictable back and forth that follows, and then the students ask me what they should feel and how they should process these feelings. I turn to my roots as a social worker, as well as the literature on whiteness, and tell them they feel how they feel. There is nothing they can do about a visceral, reactionary emotion that they feel and they shouldn't question its validity. It's a common feeling, and there is nothing wrong with it; however, there is much they can do with those feelings and they should work through them to get to a place that allows them to not wallow in these feelings but act on them. There is a great deal written about whites feeling guilty when confronted with theories of whiteness (Howard, 1999; McIntyre, 1997; Warren & Hytten, 2004). In concert with the information presented in the literature I implore my students to use that guilt and do something with it. I ask that they recognize that it comes from somewhere or something inside them that clearly points to the material they are learning making sense. I understand it's hard and it goes against everything they know, but they have to go with it and use this as a first instance of embracing struggle.

LESSONS AND REFLECTIONS

What I describe in this chapter is not meant to be a universal template for teaching about power, privilege, and racism in American schools. The process I use is determined greatly by my identity, my students' identities, and the interaction that ensues. Furthermore, I cannot overstate the importance of my course being the first education course that students take. Many students in my class take the course in their first year of undergraduate study, and those taking the course in the fall semester of their first year are only two to three months removed from high school graduation. They have said goodbye to their parent(s) one or two days before walking into my class. Though I do not believe I tread lightly with the issues I raise, I am conscious about the fact that for almost every non-minority in my class, this is new information. And it is not only new information in the same manner that an Introduction to Chemistry course will be new information. What I present to my students is new information that requires them to critically examine and deconstruct the entire framework through which they have been taught to view the world. This is particularly obvious when it comes to analyzing how they see and have been taught about power, privilege, racism, and schooling. This process mandates that they not only examine these issues in a structural, systemic, and detached manner, but also that they pause and reflect on how these issues have impacted their own lives.

For most of my students, examining how power, privilege, and racism impacts their lives entails coming to recognize that they benefit from systems of oppression and are where they are because of these systems. Inherent in the very nature of an oppressive system is the presence of the oppressed and the oppressors. While these systems oppress some, they benefit others. Recognizing that you are among the oppressors and your labeled status as a "winner" in schooling is dependent on others' oppression is a necessary but difficult road to travel. This is not something that most people are willing to entertain, let alone 18–20 year-olds who have been told by those they love and trust that they have been doing the right thing.

Throughout the course of their lives my students have been told that they are special, smart, gifted, and have worked hard for everything they have achieved. In a flash I tell them that these are all lies. I ask my students to unlearn all that they have learned and examine why they have learned these things, paying particular attention to whose interests are and are not served by the existing educational system and schooling. I ask them to do all of this in the span of three and a half months, in the first course that requires them to explicitly and critically think about schooling; and for many, this is the first time they have been asked to think critically about anything.

The process I use to engage my students in an examination of the constructions of race and racism is to deconstruct the dominant narrative of racism they accept as matter-of-fact knowledge that flows directly from said constructions. I employ this process in an attempt to provide students the space and information that will facilitate their willingness to open themselves to the possibility of the existence of other perspectives and narratives. Additionally, I use these ideas in an effort to allow students to see why they have accepted the dominant narrative, by providing an examination of whose interests this narrative does and does not serve. While I see changes in my students, these are initial mental paradigm shifts that are not necessarily permanent and are by no means enough. The ultimate goal in the context of my course is for this process to lead to a paradigm shift in how students think about and approach issues related to race and racism. My intention, again, is not only to change students' perspectives, but also to help shape how they will engage with diverse student populations as classroom teachers. This is merely a step, the first step, in that long and difficult process.

REFERENCES

Anderson, J. (1988). Anderson, J. Ex-slaves and the rise of universal education in the South, 1860–1880. *The education of blacks in the South, 1860–1935.* pp. 4–32.

Bell, L. A. (2003). Telling tales: What stories can teach us about racism. *Race Ethnicity and Education, 6*(1), 3–28.

Blight, D. (2002). Race and reunion: The civil war in American memory. Cambridge, MA: Belknap Press.

Brodkin, K. (1999). How did Jews become white folks?. *How Jews became white folks and what that says about race in America* (pp. 25–52). Pascataway, NJ: Rutgers University Press.

Carlson, D. (2004). Narrating the multicultural nation: Rosa Parks and the white mythology of the civil rights movement. In M. Fine, L. Weiss, L. Pruitt, & A. Burns (Eds.) *Off white: Readings on power, privilege, and resistance.* New York: Routledge. 163–174.

Carter, R.C. (1997). Is white a race? Expressions of white racial identity. In M. Fine, L. Weis, & L.M. Wong (Eds.), *Off white: Readings on race, power, and society* (pp. 198–209). New York: Routledge.

Chubbuck, S.M. (2005). Whiteness enacted, whiteness disrupted: The complexity of personal congruence. *American Educational Research Journal, 41*(2), 301–333.

Diangelo, R. J. (2006). The production of whiteness in education: Asian international students in a college classroom. *Teachers College Record, 108*(10), 1983–2000.

Dingus, J. E. (2006). "Doing the best we could": African american teachers' counterstory on school desegregation. *Urban Review: Issues and Ideas in Public Education, 38*(3), 211–233.

Dewey, J. (1997). *Experience and education.* New York: Touchstone.

Giroux, H. (1991). Democracy and the discourse of cultural difference: Towards a politics of border pedagogy. *British Journal of the Sociology of Education, 12*(4), 501–519.

Giroux, H. (1997). Rewriting the discourse of racial identity: Towards a pedagogy and politics of whiteness. *Harvard Educational Review, 67*(2), 285–320.

Guess, T. J. (2006). The social construction of whiteness: Racism by intent, racism by consequence. *Critical Sociology, 32*(4), 649–673.

Howard, G.R. (1999). *We can't teach what we don't know: White teachers, multiracial schools.* New York: Teacher's College Press.

Hytten, K., & Adkins, A. (2001). Thinking through a pedagogy of whiteness. *Educational Theory, 51*(4), 433.

Hytten, K., & Warren, J.T. (2003). Engaging whiteness: How racial power gets reified in education. *International Journal of Qualitative Studies in Education, 16*, 65–89.

Ignatiev, N. (2006). Breaking the code of good intentions: Everyday forms of whiteness. *American Anthropologist, 108*(2), 408–409.

Johnson-Bailey, J. (2002). Race matters: the unspoken variable in the teaching-learning transaction. *New Directions for Adult and Continuing Education, 93*, 39–49.

Keating, A.L. (1995). Interrogating "whiteness", (de)constructing "race". *College English, 57*(8), 901–918.

Kerr, A. (2006). Buying whiteness: Race, culture and identity from Columbus to hip-hop. *Sixteenth Century Journal, 37*(3), 878–879.

King, D. (2006). Working toward whiteness: How America's immigrants became white; the strange journey from Ellis island to the suburbs. *American Historical Review, 111*(5), 1528–1529.

Lawrence, S. & Tatum, B. (2004). White educators as allies: Moving from awareness to action. In M. Fine, L. Weiss, L. Pruitt, & A. Burns (Eds.) *Off white: Readings on power, privilege, and resistance.* New York: Routledge. 362–372.

Lipsitz, G. (1998). The possessive investment in whiteness. *The possessive investment in whiteness: How white people profit from identity politics.* Philadelphia: Temple University Press. 1–23.

Maher, F.A., Tetreault, M.K.T. (1997). Learning in the dark: How assumptions of whiteness shape classroom knowledge. *Harvard Educational Review, 67*(2), 321–349.

Marx, S. (2004). Regarding whiteness: Exploring and intervening in the effects of white racism in teacher education. *Equity & Excellence in Education, 37*(1), 31–43.

McIntosh, P. (1990). White privilege: Unpacking the invisible knapsack. *Independent School, 49*(2), 31.

McIntyre, A. (1997). *Making meaning of whiteness: Exploring racial identity with white teachers.* New York: SUNY Press.

McLaren, P. (1988). Schooling the postmodern body: *Critical pedagogy and the politics of enfleshment. Journal of Education, 170*(3), 53–84.

McLaren, P. (2006). *Life in schools: An introduction to critical pedagogy in the foundations of education.* New York: Allyn & Bacon.

Miami-Dade County Public Schools. (2006, May). *Statistical Highlights: 2005-2006.* Miami, FL: Author.

Perry, P. (2002). *Shades of white: White kids and racial identities in high school.* Durham, NC: Duke University Press.

Pope, D.C. (2001). *Doing school: How we are creating a generation of stressed-out, materialistic, and miseducated students.* New Haven, CT: Yale University Press.

Rich, M. D., & Cargile, A. C. (2004). Beyond the breach: Transforming white identities in the classroom. *Race Ethnicity and Education, 7*(4), 351–365.

Rochmes, D. A. (2007). Blinded by the white: Latino school desegregation and the insidious allure of whiteness. *Texas Hispanic Journal of Law & Policy, 13*(1), 7–22.

Scott, J.C. (1990). *Domination and the arts of resistance.* New Haven, CT: Yale University Press.

Sheskin, I.M., & Dashefsky, A. (2006). Jewish Population of the United States, 2006. In D. Singer & L. Grossman (Eds.), *American Jewish Year Book 2006,* Vol 106. New York: American Jewish Committee.

Sleeter, C. (1993). How white teachers construct race. *Race, identity, and representation in education.* New York: Routledge. 157–170.

Sleeter, C. (2001).   Preparing teachers for culturally diverse schools: Research and the overwhelming presence of whiteness. *Journal of Teacher Education, 52*(2), 94–106.

Solomona, R. P., Portelli, J. P., Daniel, B., & Campbell, A. (2005). The discourse of denial: How white teacher candidates construct race, racism and 'white privilege'. *Race, Ethnicity & Education, 8*(2), 147–169.

Trainor, J.S. (2002). Critical pedagogy's "other": Constructions of whiteness in education for social change. *College composition and communication, 53*(4), 631–650.

United States Census Bureau. (2004, March). *Population Projections.* Retrieved November 29, 2006, from http://www.census.gov/ipc/www/usinterimproj/natprojtab01a.pdf

United States Senate. (n.d.). *Breaking New Ground—African American Senators.* Retrieved March 6, 2007, from http://www.senate.gov/pagelayout/history/h_multi_sections_and_teasers/Photo_Exhibit_African_American_Senators.htm

Valenzuela, A. (1999). *Subtractive schooling: U.S. Mexican youth and the politics of caring.* Albany, NY: State University of New York Press.

Warren, J. T., & Hytten, K. (2004). The faces of whiteness: Pitfalls and the critical democrat. *Communication Education, 53*(4), 321–339.

Williams, D.G., Land, R.R. (2006). The legitimation of black subordination: The impact of color-blind ideology on black education. *Journal of Negro Education, 75*(4), 579–588.

CHAPTER 8

POSITIONING CULTURE IN THE CURRICULUM

A Freirian Orientation Toward the "Thinking that Gets Thought" in Teacher Education

Erik Malewski
Purdue University

ABSTRACT

This chapter focuses on the increased emphasis on proving multicultural competency though documented observation and instruction in diverse settings, and how this creates new challenges for teacher education programs. Teacher educators are often faced with exposing their preservice teachers to multicultural ideas that have little bearing on or connection with their experiences in the field. One method for making multiculturalism relevant has been to revise the curriculum in preservice courses to offer experience in observation and instruction in diverse settings utilizing virtual, interactive field experiences. This chapter describes one project that used social theory, particularly a Freirian curricular and pedagogical framework, to infuse meaningful interactive field experiences in diverse settings utilizing two-way video conferencing. The virtual interactive field experiences described herein employ Freirian notions of praxis, personalization, and dialogue to

Unsettling Beliefs: Teaching Theory to Teachers, pages 137–166
Copyright © 2008 by Information Age Publishing
All rights of reproduction in any form reserved.

guide observing and instructing in diverse settings for a group of preservice teachers enrolled in a program in a predominantly white and rural area.

> *It is not a coincidence that the curriculum of most professional programs—*
> *in our case, teacher preparation—often does not include the opportunity for future*
> *professionals to engage in a serious and profound discussion about what it means*
> *o be ethical in a world that is becoming more profoundly unethical . . .*
> *and more dehumanized by the priorities of the market.*
>
> —Paulo Freire, *Mentoring the Mentor* (1997, p. 313).

It is rather mundane to assert that the curricular understandings and pedagogical styles teachers deem of most worth are intricately tied to who they are: how they are socially, economically, and politically positioned as well as how they personally identify as educational professionals and members of an academic community. These teacher personas cannot be de-linked from social relations and officially sanctioned knowledge: what gets included in lesson plans, curriculum packets, and unit assessments is in part who we are and who we are obliged to be as educators. In the midst of an auditing craze where technocratic themes, principles, and competencies are thought to be the "real stuff" of education, there is the loss of opportunities for students of teacher education programs to critically examine how they think about themselves as educators, particularly the relationship between the meaning making they engage in, the knowledge they find worth acknowledging, and the cultural, economic, and political realities that give shape to their lives.

Unfortunately, conventional teacher education programs are often so completely driven by instrumental reason and empirical evidence that they provide little if any exposure to theoretical lenses that help educators comprehend and name the forces that give rise to their sense of being, place in the world, and identities as teachers. Becoming a critically conscious educator in a world that increasingly needs teachers who can articulate the interrelationships between seemingly disparate realities requires the ability to translate across (if not collapse) the boundaries between theory and practice, pulling threads of reality from the world to illustrate, for example, the relationship between home economics courses, changes in capitalism, and the ways French fries are produced, transported, and consumed.[1] This chapter explores the potential of Freirian thought for developing deepening cultural awareness in future and current teachers through reconceptualizing preparation and explores an attempt to "walk the talk" in a teacher education program at a research intensive Midwestern university. The culture-centered approach espoused in this article seeks translations across the theory-practice gap on the way to framing more complex, justice-oriented, and thought provoking teacher preparation programs committed to public education that aims for a) a better quality of life, b) an improved understanding of the conditions of our own existence, and c) the creation of a society in which the pursuit of all this might take place.

It is difficult to summarize Freire's contributions to education. His ideas about teaching and learning were developed out of his experiences working in different communities and therefore changed often throughout his lifetime. With that in mind, what follows is a summary of key ideas and how they might impact the ways teacher educators approach preparation of future educators. While not exhaustive, this list provides a context for exploring Freirian-inspired notions of teaching and learning. Accordingly, a review of Freire's work suggests teacher education should provide opportunities to:

1. Engage in *critique* in ways that move beyond the ability to disprove or prove an argument or distinguish what is true from what is false. Freirian critique aims to engender human thoughtfulness that can be used to examine subordinate-dominate relationships and act on those findings to elevate oppression.

2. Become aware of *ideologies* that are externally imposed. With critical consciousness educators will practice everyday with the ability to decipher the beliefs that give form to their own experiences, helping them locate forces that need to be transformed.

3. Identify the *culture of silence.* Examine situations where dominate-subordinate communities and their accorded intellects exist in oppressive relationships that involve a negative double movement, those who are alienated relying upon knowledge that oppresses and serving its interests while concurrently erasing, hiding, or positioning as non-threatening their own cultural knowledge. Naming silences can help begin the process of reconfiguring oppressive relationships.

4. Engage in *conscientization,* the process of self-actualization that extends beyond awareness and empowerment toward the humanization of all people. Knowing subjects enable themselves through an increasingly *deeper awareness* of the political, economic, and social realities that shape their everyday lives. This awareness involves understanding forces that expand and constrain the ability of individuals and communities to *transform* the realities that shape their life experiences.

5. Find *vitality* in the tension between the *horizontal* and *vertical dimensions* of education. Human beings are not objects or products of the learning process but subjects who are in the process of learning to reflect upon and take action from their own positions in the web of reality. At the crossroads of Freirian-style *action* and *reflection,* literacy is engendered and educator and learner dialogue as equals. Along

with this *horizontal dimension* is the *vertical dimension* where the teacher is both the *directive partner* and *facilitator* of the learning process. In this situation the educational experience is one where teachers position themselves among both dimensions simultaneously, *blurring differentiations* and engaging in "true dialogue [that] unites subjects together in the cognition of the knowable object which mediates between them" (Freire, 1970a, p. 12).

6. Give birth to *informed action*. With technocratic rationality it is assumed that there is a linear relationship between thought and practice. Knowledgeable practice assumes the importance of engendering counter-discourses that illuminate alternative thought, new ways of practicing, and non-linear relationships.

7. Situate educational activity in the *lived experiences* of participants. Agendas for interaction among learners are negotiated between directive partners and learners and made relevant to the lives of the people for whom the educational experience is believed to empower. Educational activities should assist in developing the agendas of those coming to new awareness of the conditions under which they live.

8. Orchestrate *praxis*. Action does not exist in isolation of thought; rather, educational practices are informed by certain values regarding the pursuit of *social transformation* and *self-actualization*. Praxis originates out of a need to bring theory into relationship with practice in ways that help explain how the oppressed can act intelligently to take control of their own lives.

9. Work the *hyphen*. The ability of teachers and students to move between the positions of educator and educatee requires reconceptualization of traditional school relationships that assume students are an empty vessel to be filled by teachers identified as the beholders of truth. In place of assumptions that teachers are expected to make deposits in learners who lack knowledge, Freirian educators dissolve traditional power relations by engaging in multi-lateral translations and troubling beliefs that knowledge travels exclusively from the knower to the learner. As interchanges occur under less formal arrangements, students and teachers who are open to a Freirian orientation find they move with fluidity between positions of educator and educatee.

10. Embrace the *dialogical method*. As an extension of changes in the relationship between students and teachers, methods of curriculum and pedagogy change as well. Accordingly, this approach toward learning eschews banking methods of pedagogy and inflexible curriculum plans in favor of dialogue and open communication where teachers

and students share in the roles of curricularist, pedagogue, and learner. Emphasizing *personalization* as a method of teaching and learning provides an alternative to conventional methods in education where curriculum, as a body of facts, is delivered through pre-formed instruction methods to passive students who have little, if any, role in shaping the knowledge they receive. In place of hierarchical, fixed assumptions about curriculum and pedagogy that can lead to the subjugation of students' ideas and experiences, the dialogical method emphasizes exchanges where, in the synergy between students and teachers, new approaches to teaching and learning are formulated and new forms knowledge are produced.

BACK TO THE FUTURE: GETTING BEYOND TEACHER PROOF CURRICULUM, CATERING TO THE TEST, AND MIND AS MACHINE

What I have been proposing is a profound respect for the cultural identity of students— a cultural identity that implies respect for the language of the other, the color of the other, the gender of the other, the class of the other. But these things take place in a social and historical context and not in pure air. These things take place in history.

—Paulo Freire, *Mentoring the Mentor* (1997, p. 308).

In the type of teacher education described here we begin to understand how naïve a facts, figures, and fragments approach to curriculum is when we are all in part constituted and positioned by our identities and identifications rich with opportunities for historical and contemporary self-study. What Freirian thought has to offer future and current educators is critical contextual awareness, that beliefs, values, and perspectives do not exist in a vacuum but in a mutual re-informing reciprocity between consciousness and practice. This is what Vygotsky (1978) termed zone of proximal development (p. 86), illuminating the role social interaction plays in thought and the importance of recognizing that learning does not happen in isolation but in social situations that involve exchanges between learners. Individuals are never their own beings; they are constructed by and construct perspectives on political beliefs, spiritual understandings, gender roles, racial definitions, and sexual identities.

A Freirian approach to teacher education illuminates who we are (critical consciousness) as well as whom we might want to become (social transformation). Such awareness assists educators in exceeding the present state of curriculum, recasting identities as current and future teachers in light of the ability to discern the forces that shape who we are and how we think. Freire's writings make the line between knowledge and cultural context less distinguishable as questions regarding teacher identities (who we are as educators) and identifications (what gets categorized as relevant knowledge) come together in deliberations over the proper role of schooling in a participatory democracy. As those who have seen their knowledge marked irrelevant and felt their social, economic, and cultural positions unchangeable there is the recasting of their paralysis that allows for movement, a "limiting situation they can transform" (Freire, 1970b, p. 33).

What Freire focuses on throughout his work involves freeing education from the constraints of the classical curriculum: a faculty psychology model that focuses on mental discipline. In this classical approach to education the mind was exercised as if it were a "muscle whose development depended upon simple but repeated exercises...Memorization and recitation, like repetitions of muscle motions in a gymnasium, were thought to 'pump up' the brain" (Pinar, Reynolds, Slattery & Taubman, 1995, p. 73). In contemporary teacher education programs inspired by Freire's work, such a take on intellect is considered reductionistic and incomplete, thwarting the responsibility teacher educators have to prepare preservice teachers to negotiate the complicated world we live in. Even though this responsibility to address complexity has been included, particularly in the form of multiculturalism, from federal reports to accreditation agencies,[2] a faculty psychology mindset remains the dominant prevailing force in teacher education. The near obsession with categorizing intellect and ranking human ability has left the world divided into a series of registers of ascending importance, a universe predicated upon authorizing dominant representations and de-legitimating those of various others and their cultural styles and intellects.[3] The important role of public education in engendering sustainable relationships between humans and the world has been eclipsed by the abstraction of curriculum and pedagogy within teacher preparation programs into universalized lockstep procedures, data-driven assessments, and decontextualized facts. This division that has been established between hard (seemingly neutral) and conjectural (seemingly ideologically-laden) knowledge has had a detrimental impact on what we teach future public school educators. This and other mechanical ways of thinking about teaching and learning counter the amazing potential critical consciousness has for liberating human existence from the weighty constraints of Cartesian-Newtonian dissection and classification. As teacher educators utilize Freirian thought, their students are reconnected to their place in the world, reinvigorating human thoughtfulness as individuals search out the natural affiliations between people and their surroundings.

By separating intellect from purpose, power, and context, prospective teachers who find their passion for teaching arises out of a love of children and youth, or a deep interest in nurturing the growth of the next generation, learn such ideas hold little weight in teacher education programs where the study of education has been removed from the people it purports to benefit. Similarly, future teachers who might eventually work in diverse communities will have few skills related to cultural problem detection.[4] Unable to recognize the implications of innumerable realities at play in a single classroom, there will be only attention to decontextual facts that often have little relevance to the lives of students. These normalizing tendencies of Cartesian-Newtonian dualism so prevalent in our society brought noted eco-cultural educator Wendell Berry (1990) to ask and then respond to the question, "what are people for?"

The ascendance of modern notions of progress and near absolute faith in scientific methods has challenged the role of culture. Historically in Western thought[5] such contextual ideas were less important than those that provided access to transcendent understanding or universal truths. In the process, knowledge that could be generalized and extracted from its context and made to stand on its own was elevated above its grounding and effectively diminished ways of knowing that were specific to various communities and ways of life. While the complexities of pre-modern, modern, and post-modern views (see Malewski, 2004 for an overview) are too numerous to explore here, there are some distinctions that are particularly relevant for teacher education. Beyond perspectives that illustrate the interrelationships between mind, body, and spirit, culturally specific knowledge can surface vastly different systems of meaning. Across the range of social classes, for example, there are often dramatically different understandings of time and space.

As Lareau (2003) points out in her study of culture, class, and family, middle class parents spend much of their time engaged in what she terms concerted cultivation. This is the search for programs, activities, and lessons intended to help their children develop talents and inclinations necessary to be socially and materially successful. In comparison to the intentional nurturing of conversational, leadership, and intellectual skills, working class parents engaged in what she termed the natural growth strategy. These children did not spend their time moving between planned activities, events, and lessons. Instead, the children of working class parents directed their energies toward child-initiated play and self-directed leisure time activities. With strict boundaries between their lives and the lives of the adult who care for them, working class children experienced more autonomy and flexibility than the children of middle class parents.

Her conclusions are particularly telling for the importance of culturally specific knowledge and teacher education. Families function in particular social structures that dramatically affect outlooks, lifestyles, and opportunities. Geographic location, available public resources, the conditions of local schools, economic and ethnic composition of nearby neighborhoods, and parents educational and professional background, all impact conceptions of time and space. As middle class parents engaged their children in extracurricular activities with the aim of cultivating certain forms of cultural knowledge, working class parents had different aspirations and, in communities of plagued with chronic unemployment, rather than engaging in extracurricular activities to build up a socially valuable repertoire of skills, children often found work within leisure activities as a way of developing purpose and direction (Kelley, 1998).[6] Categorical differences that give meaning to life can be located in culture.

Similarly, culturally specific knowledge can be looked at from the perspective of global inter-dependence and what can be learned from cross cultural comparison and contrast. The ways of thinking in many Andean peasant communities illuminates the manner in which Western knowledge differentiates between animate and inanimate systems (Apfel-Marglin, 1998). From their culturally specific way of looking at the world humans, animals, nature, and the universe exist in the inextricably interconnected arrangement of all living things. There is little differentiation between the mountains and human beings; all are thought to be living in symbiotic relationships. Freire brought these tensions between Western and non-Western concepts under examination when he wrote about his educational experiences with Brazilian peasants, finding in his efforts toward teaching them to read and write, he was also being transformed by the experience of learning new ways of thinking and being in the world (Freire, 1996, 1998; Freire & Macedo, 1987). In a Freirian approach the primary role of culturally specific knowledge and the study of the forces that emerge and give shape to teacher identities is central to teacher preparation (Gay, 2000, 2002; Ladson-Billings, 2005).

What Freirian thought challenges teacher educators to do is utilize cultural knowledge to move students and teachers from being disconnected, uninvolved bystanders of knowledge production toward engaged participants striving to understand the ways culture and power work to elevate some ways of knowing while denigrating others. With the ability to perceive social, political, and economic contradictions, teachers and students are able to reflect and act upon the world in order to transform it. Freire aspired to use literacy in the broadest sense of the term to bring critical consciousness to the disenfranchised so that self-empowered they could change the circumstances under which they lived. A significant portion of his work involved educating teachers to think about the significance and implications of identifying themselves as agents of cultural change (Freire, 1973). When teacher education programs fail to attend to culturally specific ways of knowing, what Williams (1961) defined as "a particular way of life which expresses certain meanings and values not only in art and learning but also in institutions and ordinary behavior" (p. 57), self-knowledge attributable to the diverse symbolic and material practices of students and teachers gets lost in what Kohn (2001) terms a "fetish" for "one size fits all education."

Villegas & Lucas (2002) pick up on these concerns over teacher identity, asserting that dissatisfaction with fragmented curriculums and scripted instruction is feeding a need for contextually specific and yet momentous re-envisioning of the purposes of public education and, therefore, teacher preparation. They employ the term "strand" to highlight the interconnection and shared purpose of the six qualities[7] they found gave coherence to cultural responsive (or specific) teacher education curriculums. The vision they propose is an effort to reposition knowledge within culture, place, and power by rethinking the role of teacher education. Efforts like this one and others (Edwards, Gilroy, & Hartley, 2002; Nieto, 2005; Zeichner, 2003) illustrate the problems with Cartesian-Newtonian thought in regards to the separation of knowledge from culture within teacher education. In this artificial binary the supposed real facts (universally applicable) are on one side and conjectural understandings (contextually relevant) on the other. With the overvaluation of disembodied information there is the equation of intellectual ability with the recitation of common truths that sidestep important questions regarding our ability to put education in the service of advancing the quality of life for all people.

What Freirian thought brings to our awareness involves recognition that all ways of knowing originate out of conjectures and particular worldviews, and overly rational thought can be particularly harmful without a prevailing ethical counterforce.[8] Implicitly attending to the problematic assumption that knowledge as it has been officially recognized in colleges and universities and public education is a social good, the assertion by Villegas and Lucas (2002) that we must "make issues of diversity central rather than peripheral" (p. 21) extends a Freirian-style critical consciousness in order to propose a series of basic premises for significant curricular change. In this and other emerging perspectives (Helfenbein, 2004) the gap between knowledge and culture is bridged and teacher identities and identifications are characterized by their raced, classed, gendered, placed, and sexed positions. In illustrating the problems with near exclusive reliance upon instrumental reason and empirical evidence, there are new possibilities for studying dominate-subjugate relationships and the implications of innumerable cultural styles and intellects for curricular understanding.

Attending to the insights of critical consciousness, teacher education positions bodies of knowledge and teacher and student identities in relation to everyday school activities through Freirian notions of praxis, defined as reflection upon the world so that appropriate action can be taken to transform its oppressive elements (Glass, 2001). This is curriculum and pedagogy without guarantees but with deep understanding that explicitly aims to achieve liberation via a politics of deconstruction that utilizes critical thinking to mark the origins of subjugation. Out of critically informed reflection for those disenfranchised, Freire (2000) posits "will come their engagement in the struggle for their liberation. And in the struggle their pedagogy will be made and remade" (p. 33).

Curriculum in this praxis-focused context relies upon the creative friction of critical intellection rubbing against teacher and student practices in and out of school. From this vantage point, the teacher is always an intellectual striving to develop patterns of reflection and action in their classroom centered upon examinations of culture, power, and identity, patterns that become the motor force through which learners feed their own ongoing need to critically analyze their sense of self as well as the world around them. With such an approach, knowledge is never for knowledge's sake but informs the ways we think and act in various curricular situations. Taking direction from Pinar's (1975) seminal work, critical consciousness wedded to praxis gives us a form of currere[9] that illuminates not only the individual experience of the public, but also how the public positions individual experience, and how actions might be required to change the relationships between the two.

It seems then that knowledge is not insular as might have been thought. Instead, it culturally positions just as it is culturally positioned, all enfolded in increasingly diverse and complex relationships where the more one examines identity and the world, the more linkages and patterns are brought to the surface for further exploration. These are the connections and histories that might at first seem disparate but under deeper analysis extend beyond traditional intellectual centers to reveal what gets produced between established nodes of thought. This is what Deleuze and Guattari (1987) point to as the translational possibilities of "rhizomatic epistemologies" that eclipse hierarchical thinking with lines of flight that dissolve intellectual power blocs.[10] Teachers who understand these new forms of rooting and routing knowledge employ the concept of splitting apart locations of authority to extend Freirian theorizing to rethink teaching and teacher identity. With these ideas at hand, educators can begin to grapple with what happens when the symbolic and material conditions under which knowledge is authorized and disseminated is transformed and new patterns of production and circulation allow us to reconceptualize who we are as teachers and learners, to expand the possibilities of becoming not-yet-known. Teacher preparation within this context involves de-territorializing and re-imagining the boundaries of educational knowledge.

WHATEVER IS OLD CAN BE NEW AGAIN:
RE-ENVISIONING FREIRIAN THOUGHT TO RE-THINK
CULTURE, POWER, AND KNOWLEDGE

*The consciousness of incompleteness in human beings leads us to involve
ourselves in a permanent process of search. It is precisely this constant search that gives
rise to hope. In truth, how can I possibly search without hope that I will find what I am
looking for. But this incompleteness as human beings also pushes us toward action
and thus makes us beings with options, beings who have the possibility of decisions,
beings what have the possibility of rupture, and finally beings who have
the possibility of being ethical.*

—Paulo Freire, *Mentoring the Mentor* (1997, p 312).

In the post-state[11] context of curriculum and teacher education what Freire
offers involves re-membering that public schools as state apparatuses are
sites of ideological struggle (Althusser, 1971). With the culture wars
between liberals and conservatives over what knowledge will be deemed
worthy enough to pass along to the next generation, educators are asked to
come to terms with a national identity predicated on the evisceration of
gender, race, class, and sexual differences. Critically conscious teacher educators declare that a legacy steeped in denying particular people their histories has a profound impact on teacher personas and thought deemed
important enough to teach. Our identities as educators and Americans do
not stand-alone as a sort of benign example of freedom. Instead, when
taken up by critical complex teacher educators, concerns over a national
identity and the discourse used to characterize current and historical
events are extended to debates over what makes up the school curriculum.
Understanding what Freire and Macedo (1995) meant when Freire
pointed out that "history represents a time of possibilities and not deter-
minism…[where the] struggle for freedom is possible when we insert ourselves in history so as to make ourselves equally possible" (p. 397) means
attending to the raced, gendered, and classed dimensions of a country
united and divided along the lines of various social group memberships.
The culture wars over how we will prepare future teachers, what will be
knowledge thought worthy enough to acknowledge in schools, and what
role public education will have in embracing a "pedagogy of the
oppressed" are also battles over what will constitute an American identity
and who the next generation will be (Pinar, 1993).

What Freire brings to teacher education involves knowledge and culture
brought into relationship with national identity and social group membership. White teachers cannot understand themselves without recognizing
that their cultural positioning has been informed by the other which gives
them a sense of self. Similarly, people of color cannot hope to understand

their symbolic and material self without a critical understanding of whiteness. Each of these identities are interrelated with each other and past and present political, economic, and social realties. As Frantz Fanon (1967) has pointed out in "every people in whose soul an inferiority complex has been created by the death and burial of its cultural originality" (p. 18) there is included in the oppressed as well as the ones oppressing the narratives of both.[12] The knowledge held by people different along race, class, gender, region, and sexual identity lines transverse and translate, giving form to both hybrid thoughts in some moments and reified boundaries in others. When teacher educators avoid examinations of the relational character of our cultural heritage, they deform the possibility of developing teachers more capable of attending to a varied and complex past that in very substantial ways matters to who we are in the present moment.

This need for re-formed, therapeutic education requires moving beyond multicultural competencies to address cultural unconsciousness and socially induced traumas. These are the ways of knowing that Britzman (1998) notes "constitutes normalcy as a conceptual order that refuses to imagine the very possibility of the other precisely because the production of otherness as an outside is central to its own self-recognition" (p. 82). That is, we must address attempts to teach difference through multiculturalism that aims to use the "truth of the excluded" (p. 86) to persuade those who are not open to diversity to transform their attitudes. Future teachers must be prepared for what they will experience with students who unwittingly pursue ignorance, resist alternative knowledge forms, and utilize knowledge of the cultural styles and intellects of the other to reaffirm their own centrality.

Against privileged identities that rely upon the erasure of the other to retain their form, a Freirian inspired teacher will engage dialogue and personalization to engender critical consciousness and thoughtful practice to break down oppressive divisions. These struggles by teacher educators to impart a willingness to shift identities and reconfigure social relations are not without risk of disappointments or invention of new forms of oppressive relations that must be taken under examination. This is the very real problem of ushering in repression under the guise of emancipatory strategies. Ellsworth (1989) illuminates these struggles when she and a group of her students employed the strategies of critical pedagogy in an attempt to challenge oppressive social structures. What she found was that putting into "practice the prescriptions offered in the literature" in regards to "student dialogues, and voice" that the results "were not only unhelpful" but actually worked against the conditions they were trying to create, exacerbating "eurocentrism, racism, sexism, classism, and 'banking education'" (p. 298). Far from overcoming oppression as she had hoped, the "rationalist assumptions" and failure to examine power in the classroom led to the discourses of critical pedagogy becoming the "vehicles of repression" (p. 298). Freirian oriented teachers view the failures of teaching to go as planned as moments through which educators might produce and learn new strategies.

Aware that education is much more unpredictable than transmission models imply, these "stuck places" (Lather, 1998) in the classroom where efforts at empowerment backfire and authorizing student voices lead to situations where learners experience further subjugation, illuminate the need for vastly different understandings of teaching. This is precisely the point of bringing critically informed Freirian orientations to bear upon teacher education: to position the moments where knowledge breaks down and thought refuses to move as prime opportunities for working toward teachable moments and self-transformations. Educators confronted again and again with instances where knowledge falls apart and curriculums leave them stranded seek passages within the unconceivable moments of teaching where directive partners and learners can gain insights from ruptures in cognition and logic. A post-state Freiran critical consciousness will require teachers who examine, reflect, and act upon the unthought that makes student and teacher identities and identifications possible.

Accordingly, the examination, reflection, and action process named here involves attending to who we are in light of social, political, and historical forces. These unsettling critical interrogations set in motion questions over what constitutes a teacher self. As the history of teacher representations, intellectual traditions, and school rituals are investigated, the appearance of an Enlightenment-style self that exists outside a cultural context begins to dissolve under the weight of seemingly disparate forces brought into relationship with our sense of who we are. The events of school become part of a larger puzzle regarding accounts of teaching and learning as they are examined through the study of experiences in and out of school.

As a Freirian inspired teacher education program prepares teachers to see reflection and action as inextricably linked, the false binary between fact and intuition begins to give way to more nuanced and textured understandings of curriculum and pedagogy. Out of critical consciousness linked with praxis, current and future teachers find the drive to produce and disseminate their own knowledge grounded in revealing the connecting elements of dominate-subordinate conceptual orders. When teachers see in themselves continuous reflection and action aimed at emancipatory forms of curriculum understanding, they can also locate the ability to reconceptualize their own identities in light of their examination of how they have been continuously culturally and materially positioned. Teachers prepared in these types of programs begin to see in bureaucratic curriculums the fabrication of knowledge from a distant location that is then imposed upon an unsuspecting student body without opportunities for deliberation over its meaning or participation in its construction.

If the conservative assertions of a value neutral curriculum continue to endure, such as those of the No Child Left Behind Act of 2001, then the emancipatory vision that Freire spent his life conceptualizing and practicing[13] will be in vain. For each generation of future teachers prepared under the auspices of teacher education programs that view students as products, teachers as vehicles for delivering information, classrooms as spaces of replication, and knowledge as uncontested, we retreat from educating a citizenry to maintain and advance a participatory public democracy where all people understand the importance of engaging in self-actualization, examining counter-discourses, and understanding the conditions of their own existence. As these teachers trained in our programs employ one-size-fits-all curricular theories, there will be a loss of ability to attend to difference, that in one culture paying attention for a Mexican-American girl means averting her eyes while in another for a European-American boy it means looking the teacher straight on. To the extent a teacher deems the former lazy and the latter engaged, unaware of the curricular and cultural implications, there is the potential for "subtractive schooling" (Valenzuela, 1999). That is, the perpetuation of the phenomenon where cultural outsiders experience successive decreases in self-esteem, belief that they are intelligent, and sense of possibility for their lives with every generation educated in the public schools of the United States.

In these everyday moments, where decisions are made without deep reflection because historical practices are believed to set the precedent for the way things should be done in the present, "white supremist capitalist patriarchical" (Hooks, 1995) ways of thinking and acting will be prevalent, white middle class heterosexual males will seem to naturally rise to the occasion, and historical identities involving privilege, denial, erasure, and subjugation will carry on largely unchanged. Repositioned from being civil servants to classroom managers, teachers trained in the technicist tradition will see themselves as little more than glorified floor supervisors in a factory where their responsibility is to ensure that students memorize and regurgitate facts. Following a Fordist model of production, teachers will find they exist outside of themselves and their lived experiences, personal dispositions, and concern for the next generation are no longer valued and, where it does not improve test scores, might even be disparaged. Teacher education programs engaging in reform efforts do not have to adopt reductionistic models; they can engage in standards of complexity (Kincheloe, 2001; Malewski, 2001), forms of principled consciousness raising that retain the key dimensions of a Freirian pedagogy, particularly critical consciousness and praxis.

There is hope in that teacher identities are never fixed and always retain the possibility of being reconceived in relation to counter-discourses, alternative forms of knowledge, and variances in ideological outlook. A Freirian teacher education program promotes unlearning through critical examination of our ideological assumptions. Course materials and field experiences in these culturally relevant programs attend to the development of critically aware professionals who help students and teachers decipher the ways in which changes in material distributions, symbolic processes, and mediated realities shape our thoughts and actions (Fraser, 2003). Detailed research into the economic, political, social, and historical dimensions of official knowledge (Apple, 1993) can bring students to a critical form of what Greene (1995) termed "wide-awakeness," a hyper sensitivity to the ways particular rituals, behaviors, interactions, and beliefs shape our orientation toward educational roles in schools and society and appropriate ways of thinking about curriculum.

CONCEPTUALIZING A FREIRIAN INSPIRED TEACHER EDUCATION PROGRAM: CRITICAL CONSCIOUSNESS AND PRAXIS AS GUIDEPOSTS FOR DEVELOPING TEACHERS-RESEARCHERS

The challenge is to never paternalistically enter into the world of the oppressed so as to save it from itself. The challenge is also to never want to romanticize the world of the oppressed so that, as a process of staying there, one keeps the oppressed chained to the conditions that have been romanticized so that the educator keeps his or her position of being needed by the oppressed, "serving the oppressed," or viewing him or herself as a romantic hero.

—Paulo Freire, *Mentoring the Mentor* (p. 307).

The very idea of a Freirian-driven teacher education program requires developing teacher-intellectuals who study their own identities as well as the ideas, beliefs, and histories of their students, parents, constituents, and communities. These inquisitive teachers refuse to see their positions as educators as simply a job, instead leading a life where they explore various answers to the question of what it means to experience the public sphere as well as engage in the study of the economic, social, and political forces that give shape to personal and public curriculums. Given the awareness they have of the various ways that power relations shape life experiences, culture, power, and language become key dimensions in the study of teaching and learning. Past traumas, a sense of rights, the capital accorded to particular vernaculars, family legacies, experiences with teachers as youth, interpretations of love, and ideas regarding what life pursuits are feasible are infused with questions of power.

Teachers accorded such insights are dangerous to bureaucrats threatening the imposition of national standards. They recognize the shortcomings of technocratic orthodoxies and standardized curriculums and are able to articulate cogent opinions on what public education officials and other teachers ought to do. They believe public education is fundamentally a civic arena in a democratic community. Not always looking external to their thoughts and deeds, these prospective and current teachers also critique and refine their own practices, seeking to better understand, on a personal level, their ways of knowing and interacting in the world. As Freirian educators, they consciously strive to blur the boundaries between knower and known, between learner and teacher, while owning their role as initiators and directive partners of educational experiences.

To access the way power feels (Boler, 1999) and operates (Britzman, 2000; Lather, 2004), teachers must retain reflection and action cycles as Freire described them while also grounding such processes in concerns over how power and culture get put to use. When curriculum is developed to serve the status quo, affirm end-state remedies, or transform the origins of inequalities, how are different interests being served in the process? As a prospective or practicing teacher, how am I complicit in the reproductive and transformative aspects of schooling? What are the current politics of curriculum at the school I (student) teach at? In each of these questions there is an implicit understanding that each educator positions him or herself in relation to different social forces just as the weight of an educator taking a position changes the dynamics of social forces. No curriculum, teaching style, or belief system is value free. There is only the truer sense of owning one's agenda and outlook on the world (Saukko, 2003); there is little in education that can be thought about as objective either in its initial form or the ways it gets put to use. Every pedagogical moment, curricular idea, and disseminated thought involves power relations.

Beyond simplistic notions of escaping or coveting power, the Freirian practitioner retains a commitment to the vocational process of humanization through social transformation and recognizes dehumanization as "a distortion of the vocation" (Freire, 2000, p. 28). In the process of enabling knowing subjects central to a Freirian orientation, being and thinking in the world is always shaped by each teacher's position in the web of reality. Easily taken as the whole of human existence, who we are as curricularists, pedagogues, and learners must always be scrutinized for how it is shaped by culture and power.

Freirian teacher preparation offers the ability to be self-directed. This is the human capacity for self-actualization and the ability to analyze and make meaning out of the continuously changing terms under which teachers and students live. Critically informed teacher preparation is not to be engaged by a privileged few; it is a right and responsibility of the citizenship of participatory democratic communities to demand transparency in regards to how knowledge produced, why particular educational theories are developed, and the ramifications of public policies that are implemented. As a basic foundation, awareness of the workings of power, culture, and identity and how they play out in school curriculum provide a framework upon which other dimensions of an intellectually rigorous teacher education program can be established. Through their leadership, notions of resource equity and symbolic difference are maintained as two key elements of programs that successfully prepare the next generation of public school educators—teacher identities centered on social justice. Given the tools to think critically about and take action to transform oppression, teachers who embrace a Freirian sense of agency have the tools to articulate passionate, cogent responses to the onslaught of technocratic rationality that has placed certainty, memorization, and preformed solutions in a heightened position above ambiance, creativity, and the search for answers that have yet to exist (West, 2004).

One of the reasons a Freirian orientation has been informative over decades is that while its aims are conceivable for each generation, they allow for transference of space and time without losing their ability to inform everyday practice under real, contextual circumstances. This is another cyclical process in Freirian thought that involves a double movement, that even as aims are established and pursued another dimension is taken up that illustrates the limitations of the pathways educators have chosen to take. Freiran informed educators do not move through an idea; these teachers dwell in its possibilities and through consciousness raising activities put intellect to work though reflection and practice. They recognize that with the passing of time and change in context the form of critical consciousness and praxis that will be taken up has to change, from slight modifications to fit the different cultural contexts they enter into to dramatic reconceptualizations when paradigm shifts[14] in thought have occurred. As the dimensions of time and space change, so do the pursuits undertaken. In this curricular orientation, the aims of teacher educators change from that of a typography of lesson plans and instructional strategies to analysis that takes place at the crossroads of various critical intellectual traditions, those of critical theory, experiential learning, phenomenology, critical race theory, hermeneutics, narrative inquiry, and post-structuralism. Out of these explorations, teachers develop a sense of the various lenses that can be used to develop more complex curricular understandings and more refined educative practices (Kincheloe, Slattery, & Steinberg, 2000).

Curricular understanding cannot be separated from educational experiences. Some scholars working in Freirian thought would go so far as to say that critically informed teacher education involves educational experiences translated into deeper meaning that then inform our actions (Connolly, 1981; Stokes, 1997). Freirian inspired educators are always threading post-structural notions of consciousness with experiential knowledge, giving consideration to who they are as producers of discourse and its relationship to their everyday practices in and out of schools. This culturally centered teacher education is driven by attempts to put curriculum in the service of humanizing education, improving relationships among people, and creating the conditions where teachers challenge the othering that occurs in identifying the self and, through new modes of being, enter into coalitions of synergetic learning that splinter binary logic.

In an era of conservative restoration, these actions take on a heightened political presence, requiring not simply newfound awareness but the ability to engage in praxis driven activities that are more than "reactionary countermoves" (Lyotard, 1984, p. 16) to the imposition of technocratic ways of thinking about teacher preparation and public life. The dimensions of public education that brought me to be involved in the enterprise had little to do with portfolio assessments, multicultural competencies, or replicating learning outcomes across sections; rather, what has been my motivation involves a rhetorical question that I use to begin and end every course I teach, "when the sun sets on your life, how will you know the world is a better place because of your role in it?" With this question in mind, teacher educators can engage in Freirian inspired knowledge production and dissemination that spurs continuous reconceptualization of curriculum and puts culture, identity, and power at the forefront of making meaning in our lives.

WHERE THE RUBBER HITS THE ROAD:
A DESCRIPTION OF FREIRIAN INSPIRED PROJECTS
IN TEACHER EDUCATION

During the past four years two faculty members have been involved in using Freirian thought to re-envision courses in Purdue University's Teacher Education Program. In particular, as part of a larger grant,[15] they have attempted to utilize Freirian themes of dialogue, personalization, and praxis to inform multiculturalism, career possibilities, social justice, technology, and field experiences. What follows is a description of some of the highlights from The Diversity and Technology Project, a Freirian approach to developing courses integrated with virtual field experiences as a means of blending theory with practice. These courses were possible thanks to relationships cultivated with teachers working in an inner city elementary school, populated by a majority of historically oppressed students in East Chicago, Indiana. Over the course of the Project, eight different sections of two courses were involved. These are some of the practices we engaged in over the last two years.

Each semester we began our courses with letter writing project where we prepared preservice teachers for a journey to an inner city school. The aim of the letter writing was to begin the process of breaking down, as well as address, the origins of stereotypes many preservice teachers have of inner city youth, particularly from predominantly low income, of color communities like those of East Chicago, Indiana. Accordingly, we paired up preservice teachers with students from the host school in attempts at developing mentoring relationships that, as described earlier, worked the hyphen. We emphasized cross cultural, cross translational learning that would sustain ongoing relationships between all learners involved, particularly as they interacted through two-way video conferencing during weeks where they did not physically visit the host school. Accordingly, for their first assignment, preservice teachers crafted letters to one of the students at the host school who was their assigned "buddy." The letter addressed the following five topics: a unique introduction of the preservice teacher, including professional and personal interests; memories of their own experiences as students at the grade level of the host students; the reason for the visit to the host school; and a question for the host student that would be answered in a response letter from the host student and during the first visit to the school. Along with the letters preservice teachers enclosed their photographs. All the letters were then sent prior to their first visit and, in turn, during most semesters, preservice teachers received a return letter with a picture of their buddy. Faculty built on these exchanges to introduce the concepts of power, identity, culture, and knowledge production.

After the letter exchanges, preservice teachers engaged in their first visit to the host school. Within the first two weeks of classes students gathered on a university bus and started the trek to East Chicago. With some key concepts of paramount importance to a Freirian approach to teacher education in mind, assignments on the bus trip were designed around rereading practices (Edgerton, 1996), an approach that required preservice teachers to move beyond classroom issues to examine the social, political, and economic dimensions that shape individual experiences of education. Accordingly, preservice teachers were required to keep journals as they traveled through various parts of the state, from more developed commercial centers along the highways to economically distressed rural and urban areas. While some of the questions were light hearted, such as finding some interesting landmarks, students were also asked to respond to the following questions: What does it seem people do for a living in the parts of the state you observed? Do you notice any differences in the upkeep of the public infrastructure (roads, buildings, offices)? How do you imagine people provide for themselves in terms of food, shelter, and clothing in the rural, suburban, and urban areas that you observed? How might cultural surroundings shape identity?

The aim of the writing was to encourage preservice teachers to position their perceptions, histories, and experiences within various cultural contexts, to reflect upon the role of culture in shaping individual thought and experience. By the time preservice teachers arrived at school, they had detailed records of their own thoughts on the implications of culture for community, identity, and knowledge production. Upon entering the school preservice teachers and host students gathered in the hallway with pictures in hand, attempting to locate their buddies and, once they were found, continued the dialogues they had started in their letters. The letters and dialogues, along with the observation described in what follows, were used to inform course papers that addressed comparison and contrast of culture, identity, and power in field experiences in two different settings.

Led by faculty members, preservice teachers were asked to observe the following aspects of the classroom and their relevance to culture, identity, and power: classroom management, the organization of lessons, pedagogical devices, the response of the students, and the use of bilingual instruction. Preservice teachers continued to journal in response to the following questions:

- Do the students behave in ways different from or similar to the ways in which the students behave at the other field experience in which you are currently involved?
- How did the students react to the concurrent use of Spanish and English?
- How does the teacher maintain control over the classroom while allowing for creative expression from students?
- Given what you observed, how can we talk about culture, identity, and power in the classroom?

Subsequent to the host teacher's instruction from the front of the classroom, the observation portion of the site visits ended, and the preservice teachers joined their buddies and assisted them with their individual assignments.

Through this experience the preservice teachers had an opportunity to explore the perceptions students have of the formal curriculum. The host teacher had stations arranged around the key subject areas. Host students were allotted a specific amount of time to work on lessons related to the subject-content area before moving to the next station. Preservice teachers would help students with mathematics, science, social studies, or writing and reading lessons and then rotate with the students when the teacher announced their time was up. After host students and preservice teachers rotated through every station, the teacher requested students take their assignments home and complete them or file them in their desks until the next opportunity to complete their individual work. After they engaged in individual instruction, the preservice teachers again wrote in their journals on the topic of official school curriculum. The preservice teachers were asked the following questions:

- How would you describe the official curriculum in each of the subject areas and the extent to which it was relevant to the life of the student?
- Given the pedagogy and curriculum of the host teacher, what hidden curriculum is taught to students?
- After you spent time helping students with their lessons, what—if anything—do you feel was missing from the curriculum?

After the preservice teachers engaged in observation and individual instruction, they accompanied the host students on a lunch outing to a nearby authentic Mexican restaurant. This element of the site visit had four aims: (a) to illustrate the immense role of cultural context in shaping perceptions; (b) to illustrate the responsibility teachers have for the well-being of their students, particularly on field trips and out-of-classroom activities, (c) to place preservice teachers in largely unfamiliar contexts where negotiations require them to rely upon the knowledge and Spanish speaking ability of their buddies; and (d) to provide host students an opportunity to display their own intellectual abilities, cultural awareness, and personal knowledge. The majority of students, in the East Chicago school, were bilingual and of Hispanic/Latino heritage, while few if any preservice teachers were either bilingual or racial and ethnic minorities. In the context of the Mexican restaurant, the host students had an opportunity to display their culturally specific expertise, including the pronunciations of Mexican dishes on the menu and descriptions of their ingredients. This reversal of authority provided an opportunity to question banking models of teaching and learning that assume teachers make deposits in students who have little worthy prior knowledge.

On the trip back to the university, faculty members led the preservice teachers in a discussion of the entire experience. Preservice teachers used their journal entries to write many of their course papers, some of them requiring them to use culture, identity, and power to critically analyze the four epistemological sites out of which curricular understanding occurred: personal knowledge, subject knowledge, social knowledge, and teacher knowledge. The aim of all the papers was to blur the boundaries between the knower and the known by mapping experiences from the site visit onto a typography that illustrates explicit, implicit, and null perspectives on curriculum (See Eisner, 1994; Gadotti 1994). The relationship between the three elements of the journals and the four elements of the papers helped guide the two way video conferencing or "virtual" field experiences that they engaged in throughout the rest of the term, in addition to visits to the school. The following is a brief description of three of the curricular and pedagogical approaches the two faculty members developed out of Freirian notions of dialogue, personalization, and praxis.

Lesson Plans as Dialogic

For preservice teachers, enacting curriculum over two-way video conferencing was interpreted as incorporating disciplinary and contextual knowledge with the personal knowledge of host students, all while mastering the use of and exploring the philosophical assumptions of technology. In one particular instance, preservice teachers engaged in a social studies lesson and found that the curriculum and instruction focusing on careers and jobs in society would need to be flexible enough to incorporate student perceptions and experiences. When preservice teachers held up pictures of a mailman to the video camera, showed a detailed picture of a post office on the document camera, and discussed the history of the postal service, they realized that host students did not conceptualize the mailman as a government employee. Instead, students remarked that their mail carrier was a friend of the family, sometimes invited in for a beverage, and frequently called by his or her first name. The preservice teachers rarely held such close relationships with postal employees. Their lesson, intended to engage the students in practical knowledge, grew into a dialogue that involved preservice teachers and students educating each other about their experiences with the mail service.

When preservice teachers went to the next part of their lesson and replaced the photo of the mailman with a convenience store owner and instructed students about how people consume household goods in an industrial society, including a discussion of consumer fetishism, one student looked troubled and quickly raised his hand. Attempting to engage student interests, his preservice teacher mentor called on him to speak. Preservice teachers found out that in the last year his uncle was shot while working as a cashier at a convenience store. Shocked by the openness of the student, the preservice teacher placed the microphone on mute and asked the faculty member in charge for help. The faculty member and preservice teacher together affirmed the student's statement by asking how his uncle was doing. After the faculty member established that the student's uncle had returned to health, this unexpected turn in the lesson plan was utilized as an opportunity to address oppression, privilege, safety, and violence, and the role of the police in providing security in a properly run democracy.

Book Drives as Praxis

As part of virtual field experiences, the curriculum was designed to provide preservice teachers with periodic opportunities to conduct debriefing sessions with the teacher without students present. Through these dialogues, many preservice teachers gained valuable insight into host students and their families that defied easy categorization and challenged preconceived notions of historically oppressed groups. During a 4th year connection to the East Chicago school, a host teacher described her experience organizing a field trip and the response she received when she sent a request home for chaperones; every parent but one expressed an interest in taking a day off work or rearranging their schedules so that they might assist in the field trip. Contrary to many stereotypes perservice teachers has that suggest low income Hispanics/Latinos and African Americans do not value education, the host teacher reported that there was a high regard for education and learning opportunities among the parents of the host students.

Through ongoing debriefing sessions with the host teacher, however, the preservice teachers learned that students often lacked opportunities many preservice teachers considered fundamental to their K–12 educational experiences. They noted in their journals that they were impressed by the school's physical facilities and wondered how an area noted for being economically impoverished was able to afford a relatively new school. They learned the building was recently renovated through an influx of funds from casinos operating within the district; however, because the funds were restricted, the school still lacked music, gym, and art teachers. In addition, the host teacher noted that other teachers remarked they had little time to involve students in these extracurricular activities given the lack of support and new state testing mandates.

Preservice teachers' notion of praxis was built out of challenging stereotypes in ways that provided opportunities to take well-thought-out action to assist students in reaching critical forms of awareness. Preservice teachers knew that, according to Freire, literacy was a key component of critical consciousness. Through debriefing sessions with the host teacher they learned of a project that would give students more control over their own learning. After talking with the teacher, the preservice teachers discovered that over the summer students often lost the progress they made on their reading skills, the result of a lack of age-appropriate books and magazines in their homes. In response, preservice teachers worked with parents of the host students to organize an ongoing book drive for the entire school. This book drive exemplifies one of the ways in which preservice teachers began linking the needs of students with their own actions as educators, tying ethical considerations and students as knowledgeable subjects to teacher practices. By working with communities in their own hometowns, the local university community, and the community surrounding the host school, over two terms parents of the host students and preservice teachers raised over 5,000 books. In addition, preservice teachers raised additional funds to buy "culturally specific" books aimed at exploring the subjugated histories of African Americans and Hispanics/Latinos.

Buddy System as Personalization

Once students recognized that it is not the title of teacher but what one does as a teacher that is most important in Freirian inspired teacher education, they were more open to the idea that they should approach the host students not as future teachers, but as directive partners who build a caring relationship where they share experiences learning with each other. Such an approach was not romanticized as it was taught to pre-service teachers. The two faculty emphasized that while personalization was to be interpreted as respecting knowledge across learners, in various situations, such as the walk from the school to the restaurant, the preservice teachers would have to watch their buddy carefully. What we focused on was the open-ended nature of learning, that prescribed roles often assumed that students had little insight to offer teachers and confine the possibilities for knowledge production. In place of this model, we asked preservice teachers to suspend their formal roles and engage with the students as if all of those in attendance had the aim of learning from various perceptions of public life, or what they shared in sociality. Interestingly, personalization often led to preservice teachers being surprised at the activities they had missed that were taking place in the community on the way to restaurant. One student pointed out that two buildings on a nearby street we had walked down had vastly different roles in the community: one was a social services center and the other was a known drug trafficking house. Letters, individual mentoring, informal identifiers, and personal responsibility were all important aspects of personalizing the educational process.

CONCLUSION

The Freiran approach utilized in the Diversity and Technology Project to help the two faculty involved reach their aims. Preservice teachers began to grasp that the overly rigid, formal approaches to teaching and learning where often inconsistent with the needs of students, particularly in situations where students has beliefs, values, and customs that were in direct opposition with those of dominant cultures that often inform public education. They began to appreciate the notions of critical consciousness and praxis and were able to draw these ideas into relationship with changes in their own beliefs and actions as future teachers. Preservice teachers also learned that most successful when they related disciplinary knowledge to students' personal lives and provided ample opportunities for them to discuss their own experiences spontaneously. A Freirian approach to virtual field experiences allowed students to shape the significance of each lesson plan and contribute to the knowledge created. Preservice teachers became cognizant of their own cultural values and their position on the web of reality.

A Freirian approach emphasized the process of coming to understand the significance of teaching, as well as the impact various social group identifications have on life experiences and interactions in education (see Malewski, Phillion & Lehman, 2005 for additional information). Gadamer (1979) used the metaphor of the horizon to describe the character of such interactions. Each preservice teacher had a horizon of understanding he described as "the range of vision that includes everything that can be seen from a particular vantage point" (p. 143). A Freirian inspired teacher education program help preservice teachers map their horizons, thus enabling them to understand the horizons of others. Through the dimensions of personalization, dialogue, and praxis, they began to integrate others' horizons into their instruction and observation. Through visits to schools combined with virtual field experiences, both informed by a Freirian understanding of pedagogy, a particular form of confrontation—one that troubles the prejudgments of preservice teachers—took place. Preservice teachers reported that, often for the first time, learning from those different in race, class, gender, and ethnicity engendered a critical encounter with the self. The approach described in this chapter assumed that only when preservice teachers moved beyond "curriculum as the deliverables" toward "curriculum as critical consciousness wedded with praxis" could they fully open themselves to the significance of the stories coming from those who were historically oppressed.

NOTES

1.   In contemporary schooling, the emphasis on specialized knowledge and preparing for state testing limits the ability of students to see connections between abstract ideas and their everyday practices. Students can, for exam-

ple, study economic facts but never examine the relationship between the cheapFrench fries they consume at lunch, the means of food production, and global capitalism, and its impact on standards of living around the world. A Freirian approach to teacher education emphasizes the study of realities that might at first seem unrelated but under deeper examination reveals the implicit connection between individual practices and broader social issues. See Apple (1996) *Cultural politics and education. New York: Teachers College Press* for an illustration of the ongoing relationship between politics, culture, and education, and, of course, American's love of cheap French fries.

2. See for example the National Council for the Accreditation of Teacher Education report (Rev. 2002), *Professional Standards for the Accreditation of Schools, Colleges, and Departments of Education*; Teacher Education Accreditation Council, *Goal: Public assurance that educators are competent, caring, and qualified*, Quality Principle I: Evidence of student learning; U.S. Department of Education Office of Postsecondary Education 2005 report, *The Secretary's Fourth Annual Report On Teacher Quality: A Highly Qualified Teacher In Every Classroom.*

3. I have never seen greater evidence of the "ranking of human ability" than the 1996 controversy over the Oakland, CA school board's resolution to recognize Ebonics as the "primary language of African American children" and take it into account in their Language Arts lessons. Nearly ten years ago, the backlash is just as informative today of prevailing efforts to de-legitimate attempts to recognize and accord respect to alternative ways of communicating and being in the world. For a sociolinguist's take on the issue, see John Rickford's essay, *The Ebonics controversy in my backyard: A sociolinguist's experiences and reflections* (retrieved on December 17, 2005 from http://www.stanford.edu/~rickford/papers/EbonicsInMyBackyard.html).

4. Problem detection is an increasingly important concept in an era where the symbolic and material dimensions of life are expanding and contracting at an increasing pace. This at the same time that teachers are feeling the "press" of reductionistic approaches to teaching and learning mandated by state and federal officials. The central idea is that we must teach students the ability to proactively search out problems, not as they have been defined by others, but through open-ended creative and critical investigations of discursive realities. See Kincheloe, J & Weil, D. (2001). *Standards and schooling In the United States: An encyclopedia.* Santa Barbara, CA: ABC-Clio.

5. I use this term even with the realization that a passing reference to Western thought fails to attend to the nuances of the concept and brings with it the risk of reducing a complicated idea to a few superficial dimensions. For interesting examples and histories of Western ideals in the curriculum field, see Reid, W. (1999). *Curriculum as institution and practice: Essays in the deliberative tradition.* Mahwah, NJ: Erlbaum and Schwab J., Westbury, I. & Wilkof, N. (1982). *Science, curriculum, and liberal education: Selected essays.* Chicago: University of Chicago Press.

6. This book offers a detailed explication of the problem of using general categories without particular regard to cultural contexts in academic scholarship. Academic categories are used help "make sense" of social phenomena in ways that can incite misunderstanding and violence. Kelley describes how middle class notions of work and leisure used to demonize the African

American urban underemployed and unemployed are problematic. In particular, he details how such categories fail to attend to how social policy and capitalism have left many inner city people without opportunities to make a living within neoliberal economic arrangements. As a consequence, many find meaning ("work") in what are thought of by a predominantly white middle class as leisure activities ("play").

7. The six qualities are as follows: 1) socioculturally conscious, 2) an affirming view of students from culturally diverse backgrounds, 3) commitment and skills to act as agents of change, 4) constructivist views of learning, 5) learning about students, and 6) culturally responsive teaching practices.

8. For an excellent example of how instrumental rationality has backfired and its relationship to concerns over the erasure of ethics, see the United Methodist News Service article (August 3, 2001), *Church agency blasts Philip Morris over "savings" claims*. (Retrieved December 17, 2005 from http://www.wfn .org/2001/08/msg00021.html)

9. Currere, as it has been used in curriculum scholarship, is the study of individual experiences with schooling as they have been reported by the individual. In this chapter, I expand this idea to be inclusive of not only reports on individual experiences, but also critical analysis of how various publics give shape to the character of personal histories.

10. The notion of post-structural power blocs is helpful for conceptualizing the ways power collects and dissolves making and remaking various educational centers that shape teacher education, public policy, and curriculum. Rather than suggest that there are static groups of elites that control dominant discourses, an approach that is entirely too simplistic, it might be more informative to think about the ways that thought collects around problem opportunities. That is, the way that power/knowledge informs discursive problem resolutions: knowledge of solutions that in shifting, changing forms collect on a problem once it surfaces in our public consciousness.

11. By post-state I mean the loss of the search for truth as a motivation for education, as evidenced in multiculturalism and constructivism movements where truths are multiple and contingent, alongside attempts to re-institutionalize truth as central to education through the recent imposition of standards and evaluation. In the mix of relative and concrete knowledge Freire's work acts as a reminder that contestations over how we know what we know should lead toward organization around principles of social justice and concern over ethical practice.

12. One reason to discuss Freire in a post-state involves the importance of revisiting or restudying his ideas as they changed over his lifetime. A common error in citing his thought involves a certain form of presentism that denies the evolution of his thinking after *Pedagogy of the Oppressed*. What might need to happen at this juncture in history is to move Freire's scholarship into more hybrid relationships with post-structuralism, queer theory etc.

13. Freire was not simply an educational theorist. From 1947–54 he was director of the Education Department and, from 1954–57, superintendent in Pernambuco State. After that he practiced as an educator in numerous ways, eventually becoming secretary of education in Sao Paulo from 1989–1991.

14. This is a loose reference to Kuhn's notion of a characteristically violent revolution in scientific thought where another replaces one conceptual world-

view. See Kuhn, T. (1996). *The structure of scientific revolution* (3rd ed.). Chicago: University of Chicago Press.

15.   Purdue University's 2000 PT3 implementation grant, entitled "P3T3: Purdue Program for Preparing Tomorrow's Teachers to use Technology," was launched at a fortuitous time to provide support for ongoing reforms of teacher education at the institution. In fall 1999, Purdue began to implement completely revamped teacher education programs, and the final courses in the new programs were put into place and the first group of students graduated in spring 2002. The P3T3 project played a pivotal role in bringing to fruition these substantial reform efforts.

REFERENCES

Althusser, L. (1971). Ideology and ideological state apparatuses: Notes toward an investigation. In L. Althusser (Ed.), *Lenin and philosophy and other essays*, (pp. 127–186). New York: Monthly Review Press.

Apffel-Marglin, F. (Ed.) (1998). *The spirit of regeneration: Andean culture confronting western notions of development.* London: Zed Books

Apple, M. (1993). *Official knowledge: Democratic education in a conservative age.* New York: Routledge.

Apple, M. (1996). *Cultural politics and education.* New York: Teachers College Press.

Berry, W. (1990). *What are people for?* New York: North Point Press.

Boler, M. (1999). *Feeling power: Emotions and education.* New York: Routledge.

Britzman, D. P. (1998). *Lost subjects, contested objects: Toward a psychoanalytic inquiry of learning.* Albany: State University of New York Press.

Britzman, D. P. (2000). Teacher education in the confusion of our times. *Journal of Teacher Education, 51*(3), 200–205.

Connolly, R. (1981). Freire, praxis, and education. In R. Mackie (Ed.), *Literacy and revolution: The pedagogy of Paulo Freire* (pp. 70–81). New York: Continuum.

Edgerton, S. H. (1996). *Translating the curriculum: Multiculturalism into cultural studies.* New York: Routledge.

Edwards, A., Gilroy, P., & Hartley, D. (2002). *Rethinking teacher education.* New York: Falmer Press.

Eisner, E. W. (1994). *Cognition and curriculum reconsidered.* New York: Teachers College Press.

Ellsworth, E. (1989). Why doesn't this feel empowering? Working through the repressive myths of critical pedagogy. *Harvard Educational Review, 59*(3), 297–324.

Fanon, F. (1967). *Black skin, white masks* (Charles Lam Markmann, Trans.). New York: Grove Press.

Fraser, N. (2003). *Redistribution or recognition?: A political-philosophical exchange.* London: Verso Press.

Freire, P. (1970a). *Cultural action for freedom.* Cambridge, MA: Harvard Educational Review and Center for the Study of Development and Social Change.

Freire, P. (1970b). *Pedagogy of the oppressed.* New York: Seabury Press.

Freire, P. (1973). *Extension or communication.* New York: The Seabury Press.

Freire, P. (1996). *Letters to Christina: Reflections on my life and work* (D. Macedo, Trans.). New York: Routledge.

Freire, P. (1997). *Mentoring the mentor: A critical dialogue with Paulo Freire.* New York: Peter Lang.

Freire, P. (1998). *Teachers as cultural workers: Letters to those who dare teach.* Boulder, CO: Westview Press.

Freire, P. (2000). *Pedagogy of the oppressed* (Myra Bergman Ramos, Trans.). New York: Continuum.

Freire, P. & Macedo, D. (1987). *Literacy: Reading the word and the world.* South Hadley, MA: Bergin & Garvey Publishers.

Freire, P. & Macedo, D. (1995). A dialogue: Culture, language, and race. *Harvard Educational Review, 65*(3), 377–402.

Gadamer, H. G. (1979). *Truth and method.* London: Sheed and Ward.

Gay, G. (2000). *Culturally responsive teaching: Theory, research, and practice.* New York: Teacher College Press.

Gay, G. (2002). Preparing for culturally responsive teaching. *Journal of Teacher Education, 53*(2), 106–116.

Glass, R. D. (2001). On Paulo Freire's philosophy of praxis and the foundations of liberation education. *Educational Researcher, 30*(1), 15–25.

Gadotti, M. (1994). *Reading Paulo Freire: His life and work.* New York: SUNY Press.

Greene, M. (1995). *Releasing the imagination: Essays on education, the arts, and social change.* San Francisco: Jossey Bass.

Helfenbein, R. (2004). A radical geography: Curriculum theory, performance, and landscape. *Journal of Curriculum Theorizing, 20*(3), 67–75.

Hooks, B. (1995). *Killing rage: Ending racism.* New York: Henry Holt Press.

Kelley, R. D. G. (1998). *Yo' mama's disfunktional!: Fighting the culture wars in urban America.* Boston: Beacon Press.

Kincheloe, J. (2001). Introduction. In J. Kincheloe & D. Weil (Eds.), *Standards and schooling in the United States: An encyclopedia* (Vol. 1–3, pp. 1–103). Santa Barbara, CA: ABC-Clio.

Kincheloe, J., Slattery, P. & Steinberg, S. (2000). *Contextualizing teaching: Introduction to education and educational foundations.* New York: Longman

Kincheloe, J. & Weil, D. (Eds.). (2001). *Standards and schooling in the United States: An encyclopedia* (Vols. 1–3). Santa Barbara, CA: ABC-Clio.

Kohn, A. (2001, June 10). One size fits all education doesn't work. *Boston Globe.*

Ladson-Billings, G. (2005). *Beyond the big house: African American educators on teacher education.* New York: Teacher College Press.

Lareau, A. (2003). *Unequal childhoods: Class, race, and family life.* Berkeley, CA: University of California Press.

Lather, P. (1998). Critical pedagogy and its complicities: A praxis of stuck places. *Educational Theory, 48*(4), 487–498.

Lather, P. (2004). This is your father's paradigm: Government intrusion and the case of qualitative research in education. *Qualitative Inquiry, 10*(1), 15–34.

Lyotard, J. F. (1984). *The postmodern condition: A report on knowledge.* Minneapolis: University of Minnesota Press.

Malewski, E. (2001). Administrative leadership and public consciousness: Discourse matters in the struggle for new standards. In J. Kincheloe & D. Weil

(Eds.) *Standards and schooling in the United States* (Vols. 1–3, pp. 105–124), Santa Barbara, CA: ABC-Clio.

Malewski, E. (2004). Organizational change in public education: From crucial to critical leadership. In J. L. Kincheloe & D. Weil (Eds.), *Critical thinking and learning: An encyclopedia for parents and teachers* (pp. 313–324). West point, CT: Greenwood Press.

Malewski, E., Phillion, J., & Lehman, J. (2005) A Freirian framework for technology based field experiences. *Contemporary Issues on Technology and Teacher Education: Special Issue on Intercultural Education and Educational Technology,* on-line journal (http://www.citejournal.org/).

Nieto, S. (2005). Schools for the new majority: The role of teacher education in hard times. *The New Educator, 1*(1), 27–43.

Pinar, W. (1975). "Currere": Toward a reconceptualization. In W. Pinar (Ed.), *Curriculum theorizing: The reconceptualists* (pp. 396–414). Berkeley: McCutchan Publishing Corporation.

Pinar, W. (1993). Notes on understanding curriculum as racial text. In C. McCarthy & C. Crichlow (Eds.), *Race, identity, and representation in education* (pp. 60–70). New York: Routledge.

Pinar, W., Reynolds, W., Slattery, P, & Taubman, P. (Eds.). (1995). *Understanding curriculum.* New York: Peter Lang.

Saukko, P. (2003). *Doing research in cultural studies.* New York: Sage.

Stokes, W. T. (1997). Progressive teacher education: Consciousness, identity, and knowledge. In P. Freire, J. W. Fraser, D. Macedo, T. McKinnon, & W. T. Stokes (Eds.), *Mentoring the mentor: A critical dialogue with Paulo Freire* (pp. 201–227). New York: Peter Lang.

Valenzuela, A. (1999). *Subtractive schooling. U.S. Mexican youth and the politics of caring.* Albany: State University of New York Press.

Villegas, A. M., & Lucas, T. (2002). Preparing culturally responsive teachers: Rethinking the curriculum. *Journal of Teacher Education, 53*(1), 22–32.

Vygotsky, L. S. (1978). *Mind and society: The development of higher mental processes.* Cambridge, MA: Harvard University Press.

West, C. (2004). *Democracy matters.* New York: Penguin Books

Williams, R. (1961). *The long revolution.* New York: Columbia University Press.

Zeichner, K. M. (2003). The adequacies and inadequacies of three current strategies to recruit, prepare, and retain the best teachers for all students. *Teacher College Record, 105*(3), 490–519.

CHAPTER 9

CHALLENGING PATRIOTISM AND NATIONALISM THROUGH TEACHER EDUCATION

The Implications of Preservice Teachers' Understandings of Human Rights

John P. Myers
University of Pittsburgh

ABSTRACT

This chapter explores the challenges to teaching human rights in secondary education by examining social studies preservice students' views about the nature of human rights and their place in the curriculum. Human rights education, which seeks to build a universal culture supportive of human rights, is considered in this chapter as a means to address the dominance of patriotism and nationalism in U.S. education (for example, see Kang, 2002).

Unsettling Beliefs: Teaching Theory to Teachers, pages 167–184
Copyright © 2008 by Information Age Publishing
All rights of reproduction in any form reserved.

167

The ideologies of patriotism and nationalism play more prominent roles in U.S. education (Nash, 2005), where schooling is disproportionately nationally-focused in comparison to other countries (Sir John Daniel, quoted in Perkins-Gough, Lindfors, & Ernst, 2002). Recent events, such as the Iraq War and September 11, have spurred calls from some conservative educators for a greater emphasis on schools for developing patriotism and unquestioned support for foreign policy (e.g. Ravitch, 2002). As well, traditional history teaching that focuses on the development of patriotic views of the past has recently been supported and heavily funded by the U.S. Congress.[1] While not all forms of patriotic education are ethnocentric, it remains a persistent danger (Fullinwider, 1996). These same developments have led other educators to question the role of patriotism and nationalism in education. Nash (2005), for example, suggested that a new form of patriotism is needed that includes pluralism and respect for diversity as major themes.

In a globalizing world, the role of the nation state and nationalism are changing. Globalization has produced greater interdependence among nations while at the same time creating or intensifying world problems that are beyond the scope of a single nation state to solve (Held, 2002). This situation has led scholars in various fields to assert that we have reached the "end of the nation state" as we know it (Ohmae, 1995). Two aspects of globalization—the global economy and human rights discourse—undermine the sovereignty of nation states, although for very different reasons. The global economy operates across national borders thereby weakening national governments' power to regulate the activities of multinational corporations. Human rights discourse challenges national sovereignty because it is based on the premise that rights are supranational and take precedence over national laws.

These two dimensions of globalization, however, have been treated quite differently in the U.S. educational system. On the one hand, there is growing belief that education should be linked with the global economy (e.g. Ashton & Green, 1996). Neoliberal reforms, which apply market mechanisms to schooling, view the primary function of schooling as preparing workers for the global economy (Torres, 2005). In this increasingly accepted model, schools are responsible for building "human" capital by training workers with the skills required for the global economy. The study of human rights, on the other hand, has been largely marginalized in the U.S. educational system. While state social studies curricula do not completely ignore human rights, they are not a major part of the curriculum (Stone, 2002).

In the following section, the social theories of nationalism and cosmopolitanism are discussed in light of the effect of globalization on the nation state. I introduce human rights discourse as one of the key elements of cosmopolitan thinking. Next, I describe the state of human rights education in the U.S. Finally, I present the data analysis from a case study of preservice teachers involving their views and understandings of human rights education.

NATIONALISM, COSMOPOLITANISM, AND SOCIAL THEORY

Nationalism

Nationalism, which refers to political movements that are trying to obtain state power, is a key element of modernist theory.[2] From this perspective, the modern nation state formed only under certain preconditions, including capitalism and a nationalist ideology. As a result of the modernization of society, peoples who previously held only local loyalties began to form national identities. As a social theory, then, nationalism adheres to the belief that social cooperation is premised on shared ethnicity, language, and culture. Anderson (1991) expressed the modernist viewpoint that nations were socially constructed for political and economic purposes in describing the nation as an "imagined political community":

> The nation is imagined as limited because even the largest of them encompassing perhaps a billion living human beings, has finite, if elastic boundaries, beyond which lie other nations. No nation imagines itself coterminous with mankind. The most messianic nationalists do not dream of a day when all the members of the human race will join their nation in the way that it was possible, in certain epochs, for, say, Christians to dream of a wholly Christian planet. (Anderson, 1991, p. 7)

Although nationalism is not itself inherently violent or repressive, much of the scholarly work on the topic has focused on its negative manifestations. One of the key problems of modernism has been the persistence of extreme forms of nationalism, which are at the root of much of the violence and oppression in the world today (Pfaff, 1993). In extremist forms, nationalism has led to xenophobia, racism and religious intolerance.

The sovereignty of the nation state, however, has been challenged by the processes of globalization, especially by the operation of global markets outside of the control of national governments (Torres, 2002). Kofi Annan, Secretary-General of the United Nations (UN), elaborated on this belief, discussing its implications for individual persons:

> State sovereignty, in its most basic sense, is being redefined...States are now widely understood to be instruments at the service of their peoples, and not

vice versa…individual sovereignty–by which I mean the fundamental freedom of each individual, enshrined in the Charter of the United Nations and subsequent international treaties–has been enhanced by a renewed and spreading consciousness of individual rights. (quoted in Doyle & Gardner, 2003, p. 1)

Delanty and O'Mahony (2002) have also examined the transformation of the nation state due to globalization. They assert that the weakening of the state under globalization has "decoupled" the nation from the state as well as citizenship from nationality. Under these conditions, they argue, nationalism has flourished in a variety of new forms, ranging from violent to transnational, that exist outside of the bounds of the nation state. These nationalist groups across the world are revolting against states in attempts to find their own means of political expression, which can be local, regional, and transnational.

By separating the nation and the state, globalization has created greater optimism for cosmopolitan thinking and the emergence of a cosmopolitan community (Held, 1995a). Cosmopolitan thinking in philosophy considers that all human beings belong to a single community bound by their membership in the human race. It has a long history that has been focused on opposition to the nation state and the kinds of separatist and ethnic nationalisms that accompany it, while reconciling the role of local identities and cultures (Held, 2002). It has also produced a significant literature on related concepts, especially on the emergence of global citizenship (Heater, 2002).

Cosmopolitanism

Cosmopolitanism and nationalism are not diametrically opposed because nations do not inherently require a state. Cosmopolitanism has taken a variety of expressions, ranging from calls for a world government to closer relations and thinking between groups and nations. The major opposition to cosmopolitanism comes from the principle of state sovereignty, which posits that states maintain supreme authority over their territory. State sovereignty conflicts with universal ideals such as world government or human rights, which imply an authority higher than the nation state. For example, the resistance to the United Nations and other international organizations by conservative religious and political groups is commonly due to the perceived threat to national sovereignty (Fullinwider, 1996).

Social Theory

The doctrine of universal human rights is the foundation of much of cosmopolitan thinking. Although there is not yet a social theory of human rights, it is a concept closely intertwined with theories of society (Baxi, 2002). Human rights principles are based on the premise that all human beings are born with the same rights. It does not rely on the power and sovereignty of any particular political community for its justification. Cosmopolitan thinkers conceive of a human rights framework as providing the moral and legal framework needed for global governance and politics (again, not necessarily a world government) as well as for a moral vision that emphasizes respect and celebrates differences in the world (for such a view, see Appiah [1993]).

One of the key justifications for human rights is the promotion of justice and the protection of groups from the dangers stemming from extreme nationalist ideologies, especially racism, chauvinism, religious intolerance, and ethnic cleansing (Andreopoulos, 1997). Human rights discourse addresses these issues from a universal perspective based on the belief that all human beings share a set of intrinsic rights and that our membership in the human race is more important, for the goals of justice, than our cultural identities. Human rights also have been posited as the moral compass to counteract the negative effects of market globalization, particularly the spread of a market ethos that promotes economic progress at the expense of human rights (Spring, 2004; Torres, 2002).

The concept of human rights is in the midst of the debate between cultural relativism and ethical universalism. The universal principle underlying many conceptualizations of human rights is the source of much of the controversy surrounding human rights. Cultural relativism, which is based on the premise that all experience is shaped by culture, is the main ethical position opposing human rights. In this respect, there are not any superior cultures, just differences between cultures, and each culture should only be judged according to its own values and norms. It differs from moral relativism, which denies the existence of universal moral absolutes for judging the behavior of people, because cultural relativism does not exclude the possibility of moral universals. Both of these relativisms have challenged the definition and legitimacy of human rights. As one human rights scholar pointed out:

> It is also argued that universal human rights are simply impossible because what counts as "human" and as rights belonging to humans, are context-bound and tradition-dependent. There is no transcultural fact or being that may be called "human" to which universal human rights may be attached. (Baxi, 2002, p. 97)

Ironically, while the basic premise of human rights is widely accepted, there is not a consensus over their substance and meaning. Held (1995b) captured this dilemma in reference to the United Nations World Conference on Human Rights in Vienna in 1993: "Human rights discourse may indicate aspirations for the entrenchment of liberties and entitlements across the global but it by no means reflects common agreement about rights questions" (Held, 1995b, p. 115). As well, the doctrine of human rights is criticized because it is believed to be hiding Western beliefs and values behind a veneer of universalism, referred to as "human rights imperialism" (Huntington, 1996). This criticism of the universality of human rights on relativist grounds (e.g. there cannot be human rights that are identical for all cultures) has led to the proposal of culturally-specific regional charters of human rights (e.g. the African Charter on Human and Peoples' Rights).

HUMAN RIGHTS EDUCATION IN U.S. SCHOOLING

Human rights education, along with other curricular topics containing universal themes, such as peace, environmental and global education approaches, has been met with particular resistance in the United States. Typically, opposition has come from conservatives who promote "blind patriotism" to the federal government and its foreign policy (see Cunningham, 1986). These groups discourage discourses that contain universal thinking and international cooperation, instead favoring a competitive view of the world in which nations contend for limited wealth and resources (Lamy, 1990).

One of the standard definitions of human rights education comes from the United Nations, which it developed for its Decade for Human Rights Education (1995–2004). In this definition, human rights education is identified as the "training, dissemination and information efforts aimed at the building of a universal culture of human rights through the imparting of knowledge and skills and the moulding of attitudes" (Office of the United Nations High Commissioner for Human Rights, 1996, p. 2). One key aspect of this definition is the emphasis on a "universal culture" of human rights, a broad concept which presupposes the alignment of some societal values across cultures and the need for a consensus about human rights within cultures (Baxi, 1997).

There are also diverse regional understandings of, and pedagogical approaches to, human rights education. Magendzo (2005), referring to human rights education in Latin America, makes the case that a critical approach is lacking in the field. He and his colleagues have worked to integrate critical pedagogy with human rights education. Their work has been part of efforts in Latin America to make human rights education a major component of preservice training in order to challenge authoritarian traditions and to raise consciousness about past and present rights violations in the region. They suggest three pedagogical emphases for a critical human rights education: a) the personal and collective memories of human rights violation; b) the teacher as a 'subject of rights'; and c) the promotion of personal liberation through pedagogy (Magendzo, 2005). This work explicitly draws on the Latin American tradition of popular education and Freirean concepts of education as a liberatory act (e.g. Freire, 1987).

Yet, in the U.S. human rights education has not become a significant part of the curriculum[3] (Stone, 2002). When human rights education has been adopted, it has been primarily nationally-oriented, in terms of focusing on national civil liberties and has neglected economic inequalities (Banks, 2002; Orend, 2004). However, this is not the case in other world regions. Human rights education has become a major aspect of national curricula in much of the world, particularly in Latin America (Cuellar, 2000). It has also received considerable attention from international organizations and nongovernmental organizations. UNESCO has been especially active in promoting human rights education.[4] The "World Plan of Action on Education for Human Rights and Democracy" expressed some of the thinking behind these efforts:

> Yet the last decade of the twentieth century is experiencing the recurrence of the most serious human rights violations, caused by the rise of nationalism, racism, xenophobia, sexism and religious intolerance…The rise of nationalism and intolerance mentioned above calls for special and anticipatory educational strategies aimed at preventing the outbreak of violent conflicts and the related human rights violations. Incremental changes can no longer be considered satisfactory. Education should aim to nurture democratic values, sustain impulses for democratization and promote societal transformation based upon human rights and democracy. (UNESCO, 1993)

The urgency for learning about human rights that is felt in much of the world is absent in the U.S., where nationalist and patriotic sentiments are dominant.

The concept of universalism is most clearly articulated in curricular areas that focus on topics such as peace, environmental, and human rights, which are largely absent from the social studies curriculum. Global education, an approach that is based on the interconnections between people and places across the world, has a history of opposition from conservatives who accuse it of undermining patriotism (Lamy, 1990). These critics contend that social studies education should socialize youth to support American values and institutions by teaching loyalty and patriotism, typically by education that uses the symbol of the flag and the Pledge of Allegiance

(Nash, 2005). The values underlying global education, such as peace and interdependence, are seen by these groups as "naïve world order views" (Tye & Tye, 1992, p. 63).

Nationalists believe that the "radical agenda" of some social studies professionals dissuades "not just a love of America and its guiding principles, but any interest in the fortunes of our nation in particular" (Hymowitz, 2002). In a diatribe against the "global-multicultural-diversity curricula" in the social studies, Saxe (2003) argued that any educational strategy other than unquestioned patriotism amounts to undermining the future of the nation and contradicts teachers' positions as public employees. Conservative religious groups have attacked the United Nations as the instigator of a conspiracy that would implement a new world order based on morally relativist beliefs. According to one such critic, the educational system's role in this conspiracy is to indoctrinate children to global spirituality:

> To match international as well as national goals, schools must train students to open their minds to new possibilities and to discard the old truths that block "progress" toward global oneness. In the name of tolerance, diversity and understanding, traditional beliefs are being quenched and more "inclusive" earth-centered beliefs are filling the vacuum. (Kjos, 1996)

Collective values such as peace, unity, ecological sustainability and interdependence are viewed as undermining local (e.g. parental) authority and traditional values, while stripping the nation of its identity and mission as a Christian nation.

One explanation for the lack of a strong human rights education movement and human rights culture in the U.S. is that it challenges the sovereignty of the federal government:

> It is primarily out of recognition of the power of human rights to challenge and change domestic policies and practices that the United States government, while championing human rights abroad, for many years and through all administrations, has resisted the application of human rights at home. It is out of the same recognition of this transformative power of human rights that a growing number of U.S. organizations and activists are using human rights to inform and even to infuse their work for social justice. (Cox & Thomas, 2004, p. 6)

The U.S. government has not been involved in the efforts of the United Nations in promoting human rights education. Nor did it officially participate in the United Nations Decade for Human Rights Education. Participation was particularly strong in countries from "developing" regions with histories of human rights violations, although Canada and Western European nations also chose to participate (Office of the High Commission for Human Rights, 2003).

The limited research that examines human rights education in the U.S. supports the conclusion that this topic has been largely excluded from the curriculum. For example, as of 2002, 40% of U.S. states included human rights education in the state curriculum although the depth and comprehensiveness varied, some are optional guidelines for the curriculum, and most use a knowledge transmission model that ignore learning behaviors and skills (Banks, 2002). This research also found that when human rights are present in the curriculum, they focus on human rights violations in other countries. As well, when human rights are mentioned in the curriculum, they typically are limited to civil and constitutional rights as well as national historical topics such as slavery and genocide (Orend, 2004). The concept of global human rights is rarely dealt with in depth, if at all, in terms of the international framework of treaties and covenants. This led one researcher to describe the national tendencies of human rights education in the U.S. as "inward-looking" (Orend, 2004).

RESULTS

This research focused on preservice students' views of human rights and their expectations for teaching about them. I was particularly interested in the ways that they planned to teach human rights as a specific curriculum topic as well as in the message that they would convey about them through their teaching. The students were also asked to consider teaching about human rights in light of the challenges of reconciling human rights with nationalism and patriotism.

If universal human rights are to ever become part of the secondary curriculum in the U.S., social studies teachers require a better understanding of them. In this course, human rights education was introduced as a single lesson in a preservice course entitled "Curriculum in Social Studies Education." I understood this lesson as laying the groundwork for the integration of critical approaches to human rights education in teacher education. While there was administrative support for addressing this topic in the course, there was not sufficient space to make it a major focus. In such a short time, my general goals were to introduce the students to basic principles of human rights, engage the major controversies over rights, and reflect on their role in social studies education.

Because universal human rights are rarely taught in the U.S. education system, I did not expect my students to have a very in depth understanding of the topic. A few had studied human rights as part of their undergraduate education and one student who majored in anthropology was familiar with the debate between universalism and relativism. I also expected apathy to be one of the challenges to teaching about human rights education. These students have not had direct experience with civil war or military dictatorships, such as is the case in many Latin American nations (Magendzo, 2005), and I was concerned that they would not be able to see the relevance to their lives and professional roles. However, because these students come from a liberal urban environment and had previously expressed sympathetic views in class, I did not expect major resistance to the introduction of human rights education.

The lesson introduced the students to the idea of human rights as an integral topic for organizing the social studies curriculum through reflecting on, discussing, and critiquing this topic. The lesson consisted of four parts:

1. Open discussion of the role of human rights in social studies education.
2. Focused dialogue on the readings in small groups with reports to the entire class.[5]
3. Classroom activities for human rights education in secondary education.
4. Analysis of the activities and the relationship between their pedagogy and content.

These activities took place during one 160-minute class. Although this is insufficient to prepare preservice students to be able to teach human rights in the future, it did provide them with an introduction to the field and knowledge of some basic activities.

The discussions revealed that the students' thinking about human rights focused on civil and political rights within the national context. Most of them conceived of human rights as arising from the Bill of Rights rather than from an international movement. For example, one student typified this view when asked which human rights should be part of the curriculum: "Nationally acknowledged rights because they are actually ones that nations promise to uphold." This is unsurprising, considering their previous education and the tenuousness of a global human rights culture in the U.S. Another student related civil and political rights to national prosperity: "Each is necessary in relation to the development of our country—political processes, our economy and industrialization." This student focused on the historical role of human rights within the United States as a supportive factor in national development rather than as an independent public good.

Four of the students recognized the lack of emphasis on social rights, explaining that the type of rights depends on the shared values in a given society. One student elaborated on why social rights are not supported in the U.S.:

> Other cultures across the world may not share the same economic, political or social values with people living in the U.S. The values that we have tend to be characteristic of a capitalist society and it is unrealistic and unfair to enforce a lot of what we call "human rights" on other countries because they do not follow a capitalist framework.

Another student also commented on the role of the economy in determining the types of rights that a society values:

> Competition-based societies like the U.S. are going to emphasize property rights because they make the economy work. Collectivist societies work on a state-driven economic model that emphasizes a different sort of rights. In effect, rights which do not serve to benefit the state are less important.

The students' explanation—that we emphasize economic and political values because we are capitalist—understands rights solely as the products of a given society, especially in terms of the needs of the economy, rather than as a means to protect citizens from the abuses of state power.

The data also indicated that the students view rights as primarily national in scope. Of the 22 participating students, 18 referred either directly or indirectly to the Bill of Rights when asked which rights should be taught in school. None of the students specifically mentioned international documents, such as the Universal Declaration of Human Rights (UDHR) or international conventions. The students' focus on civil and political rights over cultural and social rights (e.g. the right to food and to health care) is in accordance with the history of human rights in the U.S. For example, the U.S. government ratified the International Covenant on Civil and Political Rights but not the International Covenant on Economic, Social and Cultural Rights, which former President Carter signed on October 5, 1977 but still has not been ratified by the Senate. These covenants are two of the foundation documents of human rights law, which together with the UDHR are known as the International Bill of Human Rights (United Nations High Commissioner for Human Rights, 1999).

The students' national emphasis is significant because it tends to polarize national rights, which they saw as linked exclusively with the Bill of Rights and as consisting of mainly civil and political rights, with rights in other countries, which they tended to understand primarily in terms of places where rights violations occur. Only two students mentioned using examples of rights violations within the U.S. One of the students commented: "I feel that a greater emphasis should be placed on rights that are being denied here—civil, and, to an extent, political rights so that students can achieve a more full understanding of their role in society." Following Magendzo (2005), this finding suggests that most of the students did not recognize themselves (or their students) as subjects of human rights violations.

The data also revealed that students have some confusion over the distinction between national and international rights. Most of the students did not see any connection between national rights, which they equated with the Bill of Rights, and "international" rights, which they understood as referring to rights connected to the United Nations. These comments written by one of the students typified this view:

> I think that all rights that are protected by the government (i.e. Constitution) should be taught in schools. They are a part of our national identity and guaranteed to all students. Someday the students might need to know what rights they have.

This student did not make the connection that the U.S. signed the UDHR and has ratified some human rights conventions, thereby also guaranteeing these rights.[6] While the students were correct to distinguish between the Bill of Rights and international conventions, they are both safeguarded by the federal government. The students did not recognize this relationship, further polarizing the U.S. with the rest of the world in terms of human rights practices. Their national focus for human rights can also be attributed to their suspicions of the universality of human rights. In discussions and in the questionnaires, the students did not deny that there are rights common to all cultures but they were reluctant to assert their universality.

The students were at best suspicious of the universality of human rights, usually preferring to talk about rights in culturally relevant terms. While 13 of the 22 students acknowledged that some universal rights exist they avoided naming them and struggled to resolve this tension. The students who did mention specific universal rights included the rights to freedom from physical harm, to life, to dignity, to property, and to religious expression. Most often, however, students asserted that rights are unique to cultures. The following was a typical comment:

> Different beliefs and values in various cultures dictate which rights are deemed important and which are not even considered in a particular society. One society cannot, and should not, impose what they believe to be human rights onto other cultures because in effect they are destroying a part of that culture. I don't think that one person, or one nation, can be allowed to define human rights on a universal level.

Rights, for most of these students, are only as valuable as a culture deems them to be. In this regard, the students did not distinguish between "rights" and "beliefs" but saw them as equally adaptable and contingent.

Another barrier to teaching about human rights was that the students did not see where universal rights fit within the social studies curriculum. They believed that human rights in some form should be included in the curriculum but they struggled over where they fit and their relative importance in light of other curricular themes, such as national citizenship and multiculturalism. One student's comments typified this sentiment: "Looking at human rights as a broader idea concerning the world, I don't think there is place in the school curriculum because there is already so much that must be covered." Ultimately, these preservice students showed interest in human rights but were restrained by the official curriculum and their own beliefs, knowledge, and preconceptions of universal human rights.

CONCLUSIONS

This research explored the introduction of universal human rights in a social studies teacher education program as a means of addressing the dominance of patriotism and nationalism in U.S. education. The focus was on the ways that students understood the universal and national scales of human rights as well as their beliefs about its role in the social studies curriculum. For educators interested in introducing human rights in teacher education courses, this research raised two challenges.

First, most of the students believed that rights were defined within the national context. For these students, the legitimacy of human rights is derived primarily from their historical development in the U.S. They viewed rights narrowly in terms of the development of civil and political rights, particularly in terms of the Bill of Rights. Some of this opposition can be traced to a lack of knowledge of the U.S. government's role in the development of universal human rights and of the federal government's current participation in human rights covenants. Indeed, many of the students were uncertain about the role of universal human rights within the social studies curriculum, particularly in courses on U.S. history, rather than having any opposition to their curricular significance.

The second challenge is that most of the preservice students in this research did not identify with human rights, including the students that strongly supported and were interested in universal notions of human rights. Rather, they associated human rights with developing, undemocratic nations and, with the exception of two students, overlooked rights violations that occur within the U.S. Human rights violations, in this sense, are deplorable acts that happen to other people in usually distant places that are not associated with their daily lives. This is another reason that most of the students did not see a prominent role for universal human rights in the social studies curriculum. The characterization of human rights violations as being exclusive to "developing" nations signals a major challenge to the introduction of universal human rights in U.S. schooling. As long as rights violations are perceived to be other people's problems, it seems unlikely that universal human rights will be accepted as an important curricular topic within an educational system that does not value learning about the world. Thus, one key is the development of a broader understanding of human rights that pays attention to the interrelationship between rights in U.S. society with the rest of the world.

This research raises recommendations for educators working on the introduction of universal human rights in teacher education. First, greater knowledge of human rights and of the interpenetration of rights between national and global contexts are essential. A key aspect of this is the presentation of human rights as an unfinished dialogue by entering into the debates over the universality of rights and the ways that they have been challenged along cultural, ethnic, and religious lines. One strategy for starting this process is to introduce students to regional charters of human rights in comparative perspective, which will raise issues about the diverse cultural and regional interpretations of human rights.

There also is a need for future teachers to see the connection of human rights with their lives and with their students' lives. A major challenge then is to make preservice students, often from middle class, suburban backgrounds, conscious of the inequalities experienced by some social groups within the U.S. A starting place for preservice teachers could be analyzing the role of schools in the reproduction of social inequalities. A major focus of this would be on the study of urban schools and the experiences of students of color in these schools. This would provide a powerful connection with their education as a teacher and the broader social context. Doing this from a human rights perspective is significant, rather than from a strictly national understanding of inequalities, because it would provide the students with a framework that would help them to see inequalities, including educational inequalities, as part of broader patterns across the world and at the same time challenge narrow nationalist understandings of social studies education.

Personally, this research has provided me with insights into the way that I will teach human rights education in my social studies preservice courses. Many of the students were interested in the role of human rights in the social studies curriculum but do not have the knowledge to identify teaching opportunities for human rights within the official curriculum. This stemmed from their confusion about the relationship between national and universal rights. In my future teaching, I plan to do specific work on aligning human rights with the official curriculum to help the students that are interested in teaching human rights to integrate it knowledgeably in their courses.

Three practices seem particularly important for supporting these efforts: a) provide opportunities to study the history of human rights from national and universal perspectives, focusing on the relationship between these; b) identify with preservice students the possibilities in the official curriculum for the introduction of universal human rights, such as where existing topics on rights within national contexts can be linked with international movements and developments; and c) connect human rights education with community-based learning approaches that overcome the barriers between the classroom and students' lives. Such efforts in teacher education programs are a first, but much-needed, step in mediating the excessively nationalist discourse in U.S. education by connecting it with a half-century of efforts to make the world more peaceful and safe.

NOTES

1. For example, the Teaching American History Grant Program was established in 2001 by the U.S. Congress under the Elementary and Secondary Education Act. In 2006, $120 million dollars was appropriated to this program.

2. Other scholars of nationalism, sometimes referred to as "nationalists" or "primordialists," believe that nations are naturally occurring and have always existed. For them, therefore, it does not make sense to discuss the "birth of nations" but they focus instead on questions of how to define "nations" and how they developed from older cultural groups (e.g. "ethnie") (See Smith, A. (1998[1986]). *The ethnic origin of nations.* Oxford, UK: Blackwell Publishers.)

3. There exceptions to this in some states but this stands true in most cases. For an example of human rights education, see the "This Is My Home" curriculum in Minnesota (from http://www.hrusa.org/thisismyhome).

4. For example, see the "Recommendation Concerning Education for International Understanding, Co-operation and Peace and Education relating to Human Rights and Fundamental Freedoms" of 1974, the International Congress on the Teaching of Human Rights in 1978, the International Congress on Human Rights Teaching, Information and Documentation in 1987, and the "World Plan of Action on Education for Human Rights and Democracy" in 1993.

5. There were three primary readings:

    Banks, D. (2002). *Promises to keep: Results of the national survey of human rights education 2000.* Available at http://www.hrusa.org/education/PromisestoKeep.htm.

    Reardon, B. (1995). *Educating for dignity, learning about rights and responsibilities, a K–12 teaching resource.* Philadelphia and London: University of Pennsylvania Press.

Teeple, G. (2005). *The riddle of human rights.* Amherst, NY: Humanity Books.

6.   The UDHR, however, does not have the force of law but is considered customary international law.

REFERENCES

Anderson, B. (1991). *Imagined communities: Reflections on the origin and spread of nationalism.* New York: Verso.

Andreopoulos, G. J. (1997). Human rights education in the post-Cold War context. In G. J. Andreopoulos & R. P. Claude (Eds.), *Human rights education for the twenty-first century* (pp. 9–20). Philadelphia: University of Pennsylvania Press.

Appiah, K. A. (1993). Citizens of the world. In M. J. Gibney (Ed.), *Globalizing rights* (pp. 189–232). New York: Oxford University Press.

Ashton, D., & Green, F. (1996). *Education, training, and the global economy.* Brookfield, VT: Edward Elgar Publishing.

Banks, D. (2002). *Promises to keep: Results of the national survey of human rights education 2000.* Retrieved from http://www.hrusa.org/education/PromisestoKeep .htm

Baxi, U. (1997). Human rights education: The promise of the Third Millennium. In G. J. Andreopoulos & R. P. Claude (Eds.), *Human rights education for the twenty-first century* (pp. 142–154). Philadelphia, PA: University of Pennsylvania Press.

Baxi, U. (2002). *The future of human rights.* New Delhi: Oxford University Press.

Cox, L., & Thomas, D. Q. (Eds.). (2004). *Close to home: Case studies of human rights work in the United States.* New York: Ford Foundation.

Cuellar, R. (Ed.). (2000). *Experiencias de educación en derechos humanos en América Latina [Experiences of education in human rights in Latin America].* San José, Costa Rica: Instituto Interamericano de Derechos Humanos.

Cunningham, G. (1986). *Blowing the whistle on global education.* Washington D.C.: U.S. Department of Education.

Delanty, G., & O'Mahony, P. (2002). *Nationalism and social theory.* Thousand Oaks, CA: Sage.

Doyle, M. W., & Gardner, A.-M. (2003). Introduction: Human rights and international order. In J.-M. Coicaud, M. W. Doyle & A.-M. Gardner (Eds.), *The globalization of human rights* (pp. 1–19). Tokyo: United Nations University Press.

Freire, P. (1987). *A pedagogy for liberation: Dialogues on transforming education* South Hadley, MA: Bergin & Garvey

Fullinwider, R. K. (1996). Patriotic history. In R. K. Fullinwider (Ed.), *Public education in a multicultural society* (pp. 203–227). New York: Cambridge University Press.

Heater, D. (2002). *World citizenship: Cosmopolitan thinking and its opponents* New York: Continuum

Held, D. (1995a). *Democracy and the global order: from the modern state to cosmopolitan governance.* Cambridge: Polity Press.

Held, D. (1995b). Democracy and the new international order. In D. Archibugi & D. Held (Eds.), *Cosmopolitan democracy: An agenda for a new world order* (pp. 96–120). Cambridge, UK: Polity Press.

Held, D. (2002). The transformation of political community: rethinking democracy in the context of globalisation. In N. Dower & J. Williams (Eds.), *Global citizenship: a critical introduction* (pp. 92–100). New York: Routledge.

Huntington, S. P. (1996). *The clash of civilizations and the remaking of world order.* New York: Simon & Schuster.

Hymowitz, K. (2002). Anti-social studies. *Weekly Standard, 7*(33).

Kang, S.-W. (2002). Democracy and Human Rights Education in South Korea. *Comparative Education, 38*(3), 315–325.

Kjos, B. (1996). *Brave new schools.* Eugene, OR: Harvest House Publishers.

Lamy, S. (1990). Global education: a conflict of images. In K. Tye (Ed.), *Global education: from thought to action* (pp. 49–63). Alexandria, VA: ASCD.

Magendzo, A. (2005). Pedagogy of human rights education: A Latin American perspective. *Intercultural Education 16*(2), 137–143.

Nash, M. A. (2005). "How to be thankful for being free": Searching for a convergence of discourses on teaching patriotism, citizenship, and United States history. *Teachers College Record, 107*(1), 214–240.

Office of the High Commission for Human Rights. (2003). *Summary of national initiatives undertaken within the Decade for Human Rights Education (1995–2004).* Retrieved November 1, 2005, from http://www.unhchr.ch/html/menu6/1/initiatives.htm.

Office of the United Nations High Commissioner for Human Rights. (1996). *Plan of action for the United Nations Decade for Human Rights Education, 1995–2004.* New York: United Nations.

Ohmae, K. (1995). *The end of the nation state: the rise of regional economies.* New York: Free Press.

Orend, B. (2004). Human rights education: Form, content and controversy. *Encounters on Education, 5,* 61–80.

Perkins-Gough, D., Lindfors, S., & Ernst, D. (2002). A curriculum for peace: A conversation with Sir John Daniel. *Educational Leadership, 60*(2), 14–17.

Pfaff, W. (1993). *The wrath of nations: Civilization and the furies of nationalism* New York: Simon & Schuster.

Ravitch, D. (2002). September 11: Seven lessons for the schools. *Educational Leadership, 60*(2), 6–9.

Saxe, D. (2003). Patriotism versus multiculturalism in times of war. *Social Education, 67*(2), 107–109.

Spring, J. (2004). *How educational ideologies are shaping global society: Intergovernmental organizations, NGOs, and the decline of the nation-state.* Mahwah, NJ: Erlbaum.

Stone, A. (2002). Human rights education and public policy in the United States: Mapping the road ahead. *Human Rights Quarterly, 24,* 537–557.

Torres, C. A. (2002). Globalization, education, and citizenship: Solidarity versus markets? . *American Educational Research Journal, 39*(2), 363–378.

Torres, C. A. (2005). No Child Left Behind: A brainchild of neoliberalism and American politics. *New Politics, 10*(2).

Tye, B., & Tye, K. (1992). *Global education: a study of school change.* Albany, NY: State University of New York Press.

UNESCO. (1993). *World Plan of Action on Education for Human Rights and Democracy.* Montreal: UNESCO.

United Nations High Commissioner for Human Rights. (1999). *Fact sheet on "The International Bill of Human Rights."* Retrieved from http://www.unhchr.ch/html/menu6/2/fs2.htm.

CHAPTER 10

CRITICAL THINKING, SOCIAL JUSTICE, AND THE ROLE OF PHILOSOPHY

Kathy Hytten
Southern Illinois University

ABSTRACT

The goal of this chapter is to show the contemporary value of philosophy of education as part of a teacher education program that challenges high-stakes accountability schemes and contributes to the development of critical and reflective thinking about education. First, I provide an overview of what philosophers of education do and their role in helping to cultivate particular habits and dispositions toward inquiry. Second, I describe three philosophical dispositions that are especially valuable contributions to a curriculum for teacher education. Third, I translate these dispositions into some suggestions for educational practice.

Unsettling Beliefs: Teaching Theory to Teachers, pages 185–200
Copyright © 2008 by Information Age Publishing
All rights of reproduction in any form reserved.

CRITICAL THINKING, SOCIAL JUSTICE,
AND THE ROLE OF PHILOSOPHY

What does social justice mean? Recently I posed this question to my under-graduate teacher education students. I had hoped for a lively discussion and thought for sure my students would have plenty of insights on this issue. The question was clear and to the point, and the readings that they had done so far in the semester, along with a month's worth of class discussion, would seemingly easily allow them to not only define social justice, but also to talk thoughtfully about its relationship to both democracy and education. They had studied George Counts (1932) *Dare the Schools Build a New Social Order* and excerpts from John Dewey's (1985) *Democracy and Education.* They had also read Ann Diller's (1999) call for students to become philosophers of their own education, Bill Ayers (2001) comments on teaching as an ethical enterprise that should be grounded in core values, David Purpel's (1999) thoughts on the need for moral outrage in education, George Wood's (1998) ideas on how educators can help to cultivate the habits of responsible citizenship, Westheimer and Kahne's (1998) eloquent account of schooling for participatory democracy, Bill Bigelow's (1998) teaching strategies for getting students to understand the often deleterious human impact of globalization, and Apple and Beane's (1995) compelling descriptions of a variety of existing democratic schools. While none of these readings had explicitly defined social justice, it is an implicit and overriding theme throughout them. Yet, the responses I got from my students, at least the few who didn't give me blank stares, were vague and tentative. They suggested justice is the same as fairness, but then struggled to go much further in unpacking fairness and describing what it might look like in the social realm. While I was asking them to think deeply and critically, to make sense of broader theory, an all too familiar pattern emerged: they seemed to want me to tell them what to think and, more urgently, what to say on their upcoming paper on the topic. They were frustrated with ambiguity, impatient with the difficult work of uncovering assumptions and fundamental beliefs, and habituated to expect me to tell them what they need to say and do, ultimately in order to get a good grade. In short, while they may have been well "schooled," they were hardly well educated (see Kohl, 1994, p. 142).

Arguably, the current educational climate has exacerbated the problem of cultivating critical thinking in schools. High stakes accountability schemes, marked by a movement "back to the basics," increased use of standardized assessments, and an overemphasis on competitive achievement, have all complicated our efforts at helping students to become reflective and engaged learners. Moreover, they have also overshadowed the importance of teaching theory to teachers. The examples of negative outcomes abound. Sheldon and Biddle (1998) lucidly show how reform proposals built around standardized testing have all sorts of problematic consequences: a narrowed skill and drill curriculum, controlling pedagogies and teaching to tests, and perhaps most damaging, diminishment of student interest and motivation. While they accede that standardized curricula and assessment may raise "superficial performance," too often they also result in "an educational climate that alienates teachers from teaching and students from learning" (p. 166). Similarly, Kohn (1999) outlines the costs of the overemphasis on achievement that is characteristic of such practices as sorting and selecting in schools, competitive grading, academic contests, class ranks, and most notably, comparative norm referenced testing. He argues that students begin to see learning as a means to an end (e.g., a good grade or victory) rather than as something valuable in and of itself. At the same time, students lose interest in learning that doesn't provide external rewards, avoid challenges that are mentally taxing, and actually develop study habits that are antithetical to understanding (e.g., focusing solely on getting the right answer at the expense of understanding why the answer is right and seeing connections and implications of ideas). Meier's (2002) reflections on the standardization movement are equally telling. While she laments the shift in our conception of learning from using our minds well to succeeding on tests, she is just as concerned with the seeming reduction of teaching to following scripts and coaching materials put out by test producers, the removal of anything not related to tests from the curriculum (e.g., students interests and current events), and the increased drop-out rate of students in states that have adopted high stakes testing systems.

Certainly there are alternatives to such approaches to schooling which seem to dampen rather than awaken curiosity, interest and engagement. They exist at schools throughout the country, however few and far between they lie. Yet while powerful portraits of such schools exist in the literature (e.g., Apple & Beane 1995, Wood 1992, Meier 1995, Westheimer 1998), they tend to be marginal to mainstream educational discourse. They are seen as anomalous exceptions rather than visions for what could be if we were to foreground student "learning" instead of superficial measures of student "achievement." While more depictions of "schools that work" (Wood 1992) would be valuable, so too would a more articulate and compelling theoretical grounding that can complement these portraits, as well as bring together some of the shared features of schools that challenge the problematic corollaries to high stakes accountability schemes. Here I think philosophers of education can be particularly useful. Philosophy plays an important role in thinking about education, despite the fact that connections among philosophy and education are often troubled and tenuous. Historically, pre-service and practicing teachers studied philosophy of education, however, in many places this is no longer the case, as the overall presence and influence of foundations programs (of which philosophy is typically a part) on campuses seem to be waning. Thus it seems useful to revisit the question of what philosophy can contribute to our thinking about education. It is also timely in light of the fact that philosophy of education as a field is in transition, and educational philosophers themselves have been reconsidering their roles and impact, for example, as witnessed in the summer 2002 special issue of *Educational Theory* devoted to the "dilemma of relevance." In this essay, I make a case for the contemporary value of philosophy of education, particularly in contributing to the development of critical and reflective thinking about education, and in helping prospective teachers to see the value of theory. First, I provide an overview of what philosophers of education do and their role in helping to cultivate particular habits of mind and dispositions toward inquiry. Second, I describe three philosophical dispositions that are especially valuable contributions to a curriculum for teacher education that responds to the drive for high stakes accountability. Third, I translate these dispositions into some suggestions for educational practice.

Philosophy of Education

There are a variety of reasons why philosophy of education, and even more broadly, the teaching of theory, is not more central and/or integral in teacher education programs. Primary among these are a misperception of what philosophy is all about, coupled with negative experiences and associations that students often have with the idea of philosophy in general. When I begin to talk about philosophy with my students, I notice how, for many, their attitude, demeanor, and even posture, tends to change. They associate philosophy with abstract and exclusionary jargon, problems with no answers, and questions of no meaningful relevance. They recall experiences of being made to feel stupid in philosophy classes. They see philosophers dwelling unproductively in the realm of ideas and utopian visions, when what they need and want are practical insights and strategies that they can apply in their everyday lives as teachers. These problems are worsened when they perceive philosophers as arrogant (however unintended it may be), especially when they implicitly and explicitly claim that what they do to is more important or more valuable than other approaches to thinking and understanding the world, rather than one tool among many. Overcoming these barriers is essential to making a case for how philosophy can be a valuable resource in challenging educational reforms that are antithetical to engaged and critical teaching and learning.

A related problem faced by philosophers of education is a lack of agreement about the contours of their work and the most useful role they can play in education. This problem is shared in the broader discipline. Siegel (2002) notes that "'what is philosophy?' is itself one of philosophy's perennial questions; there is no clearly correct, widely agreed upon, or uncontroversial characterization of the field" (p. 277). Historical approaches to teaching philosophy of education have ranged from exposing students to the ideas of "great" thinkers (e.g., Plato, Rousseau, Dewey), to ensuring that they know the differences between philosophical schools (e.g., idealism, realism, existentialism, pragmatism) and can trace their educational implications, to introducing them to classic philosophic questions in the educational realm (e.g., what is the nature of learning, how can we distinguish between education and indoctrination). While all these approaches may be interesting and important, especially to those who wish to specialize in this discipline, I think there is a more modest, yet more useful and relevant role that philosophy can play, particularly in teacher education. At its heart, philosophy involves asking fundamental questions, uncovering assumptions, making arguments, and exploring alternatives. All of these activities help students to think more clearly, deeply, and reflectively about their practice. Ultimately, what may be most valuable about philosophy is the contribution it can make in helping students to draw upon these critical thinking skills in order to develop particular habits and dispositions toward inquiry.

There are a number of possible habits and dispositions that we, as philosophers, but also as students, teachers and thinkers, can bring to inquiry. For example, we might be genuinely committed to finding answers to questions that we have asked, and that matter to us. In such cases, we bring passion to learning; we are engaged, earnest and enthusiastic. John Dewey (1933/1998) might say that we are "whole-hearted." We have all had this experience at some point in our lives, where we have been consumed by something of interest to us, whether it is building a clubhouse, learning to cook, finishing a crossword puzzle, mastering a second language, or making it to the final stages of a computer game. This is not to say all are equally valuable learning experiences, but that we bring certain habits of mind and behavior to activities that matter to us, for example, determination, patience, openness, and experimentation. Alternatively, we may approach learning rather passively. When teaching is predominated by lectures, textbooks and worksheets, and what is rewarded is how well we absorb information passed on to us, we have a tendency to become passive and even apathetic. We may worry about what is on an upcoming test, or about our grades, or even work diligently to memorize information, but we don't often become absorbed in what we are doing to the point where we are open to the possibility of becoming different people because of what we are learning. Of course, there are many positions between these extremes of engaged learning and passive routine, yet considering the extremes is useful in helping us to think through the kinds of habits we want to encourage in students.

Talking about habits and dispositions towards learning, Diller (1999) argues that we should help students to become philosophers of their own education. By this, she means that we should teach them to become "mindful" learners; people "who know how to make education their own" (p. 2). She argues that three particular capacities can best help us to do this. These capacities can easily be framed as habits of inquiry, also. The first two of these involve learning to look at things from different perspectives, notably, from a distance and from alternative angles. When we look at things from a distance, we are less likely to by myopic, and better able to see a big picture. Think for example of trying to cross a busy multi-laned street. From ground level, it is difficult to see the gaps in oncoming traffic that simultaneously are very easy to see peering down from the comfort of a high-rise apartment balcony. Finding different angles to view situations from has a similar effect. Sometimes we feel stuck between two difficult choices when a third option we haven't considered opens up new possibilities. For example, I may feel that I need to drop out of school because I can't pay all my bills, seeing bankruptcy or getting a full time job as my only options, when my academic advisor points me to the possibility of a paid internship that can keep me in school and address my financial concerns. Similarly, as teachers we may feel isolated in our classrooms and not get enough distance from our own everyday practices to see other possibilities for helping students to engage disciplinary content and ideas. Learning to look at things from a distance and from different angles both entail the disposition of "open-mindedness." They require that we habitually ask different questions, seek out viewpoints that we may not have considered, and hypothesize about alternatives. Dewey (1933/1998) suggests that the disposition of open-mindedness "includes an active desire to listen to more sides than one; to give heed to facts from whatever source they come; to give full attention to alternative possibilities; [and] to recognize the possibility of error even in the beliefs that are dearest to us" (p. 30).

Diller's third suggestion for becoming a more thoughtful learner is consistent with Dewey's vision of open-mindedness. She calls for us to be open to startling revelations of our own ignorance, and to be humble enough to use these experiences to expand our understanding of the world around us. Drawing from Plato's metaphor of the torpedo fish, Diller refers to this as the capacity to be torpefied. In order to unpack this metaphor it helps to know that a torpedo fish is similar to an electric ray, a creature that when stepped on can jar a person with such strength as to knock them off their feet. Similarly, a torpefying learning experience is one that mentally knocks us over; it involves "the shock of suddenly realizing we do not know what we thought we knew" (p. 1). Diller likens this to experiencing a kind of awe and astonishment at new insights; a revelatory "aha" moment. For example, I used to move through the world as a white person presuming that I should be colorblind and that I should treat all people the same. When I started to study diversity issues more deeply, I was torpefied by the realization that the stance of colorblindness can be very racist, especially when coming from someone in a dominant cultural position (see, for example, Thompson 1999). Without being in the habit of questioning even my most fundamental beliefs about the world, and assuming that they may change, I would not have been able to see race issues in a new light and would probably still be extolling the virtues of colorblindness. This is not to say, however, that this was an easy or quick process. Ultimately, the point here is that such habits and dispositions as whole-heartedness, seeking out multiple perspectives, and being open to fundamental changes in our worldviews and consciousnesses are integral to thinking critically. These are the very types of habits that philosophers of education engage in and, therefore, are also well positioned to help teacher education students to develop. They are also the kind of habits of mind and learning we often say we want students to cultivate.

Rethinking philosophy of education involves clarifying what it is that philosophers do, in part so as to demystify philosophy itself. The habits that philosophers bring to inquiry are habits that are valuable for all critical thinkers. Contrary to how those of us who do philosophy sometimes position it as an esoteric and highly specialized pursuit, we are all capable of engaging in philosophical and theoretical thinking. In fact, many of us regularly philosophize without realizing that is what we are doing. When we ask questions about assumptions, describe relationships among ideas, raise counterpoints, analyze language, unpack taken-for-granteds, create arguments, connect disparate viewpoints, provide critical commentary on ideas, propose hypothetical experiments, disrupt commonsense, render givens as contingent, clarify logic, dig beneath the layers of experience, and offer alternative possibilities, we are doing philosophy. We can engage in these pursuits randomly and haphazardly, or thoughtfully and systematically. Which of these paths we take depends in large part both on how well we understand the process of critical thinking itself and on how well we have developed productive habits of inquiry. While ideally students should learn these habits quite early in their educational careers (e.g., grade school), it is never too late to unlearn bad habits and to develop better ones. Developing and strengthening good habits of inquiry is particularly important for teacher education students, as they will consciously and unconsciously pass these habits on to their students.

Critical and Reflective Thinking

Perhaps the most useful role philosophy can play in teacher education is to help students to develop the habits of inquiry that allow them to be critical and reflective thinkers. It is only when they develop these habits that they are in a position to challenge educational reforms that hurt rather than enhance teaching and learning. Most students and teachers that I interact with know deep down that teaching practices that are premised on increased standardization, frequent testing, and ever more information acquisition are seriously problematic. Yet they struggle to articulate the kinds of thoughtful and well-developed counter arguments that can challenge these high stakes accountability practices. Moreover, they begin to see such practices as inevitable and start adapting to them, as opposed to "creatively maladjusting" in the ways that Kohl (1994) so eloquently describes. Kohl argues that educators should resist and subvert education practices that result in passive learning, that don't attend to student needs, that assume the current structure of schooling works for all kids, that foreground predictability and regularity, and that reduce learning to getting right answers as opposed to asking provocative questions. He sees such maladjustment not as "a rejection of public education, but an affirmation of its possibilities" (p. 134). This type of maladjustment is part and parcel of a critical and reflective approach to inquiry. In teacher education, there are similarly problematic habits to which philosophers agree that students should maladjust: taking ideas and teaching strategies for granted, rushing to quell doubt and ambiguity, and quickly and shortsightedly latching on to proposed educational reforms and solutions. Alternatively, we can frame each of these aforementioned habits in positive ways. Among the most important habits that students of education can develop, three stand out for their potential to usher in a vision of schooling that transcends high stakes accountability. First, we should teach students to uncover, analyze, question and critique fundamental assumptions. Second, we should teach ways in which to productively deal with uncertainty. Third, we should help students to seek out and propose alternatives to the status quo.

Uncovering and questioning fundamental assumptions, conventions, taken-for-granteds, and dogma are "philosophy's strongest traditions" (Bredo 2002, p. 267). While what it means to unpack assumptions may seem obvious, it is worth briefly revisiting, as it as at the heart of what philosophers do. Philosophers aim to make explicit the conceptual structures and ideologies, the theories, that condition our thinking, especially in light of the fact that most of us don't even realize that we have such structures in our heads. Yet as Hooks (2000) compellingly writes, "everything we do in life is rooted in theory. Whether we consciously explore the reason we have a particular perspective or take a particular action there is also an underlying system shaping thought and practice" (p. 19). Likewise, Bowers (2001) shows how primary socialization, at home and school, leads to the development of particular linguistic and ideological frameworks that can limit our ability to see other alternatives. For example, he claims the predominant pedagogical practices and metaphors of schooling are premised upon problematic, and unarticulated, notions about the nature of progress, the autonomy of individuals, and the anthropocentrism of the world. By asking questions about these assumptions, and studying alternative assumptions, we can make explicit the core beliefs that guide our actions, and more consciously uphold those that we think should guide our actions.

An important part of philosophy's role in education is helping students to analyze the fundamental assumptions that guide their practice. We can best do this through a pedagogy that is premised on questions, that disrupts commonsense, and that consciously aims to stimulate curiosity. In the drive to get teacher education students to absorb learning theories, develop lesson plans, cultivate classroom management strategies, and master their discipline, we rarely afford them opportunities to reflect deeply and broadly on their practice, for example, to ask about the ultimate purposes of schooling in a democracy, the social and moral responsibilities of teachers, the relationship between education and social reform, the knowledge of most worth, and the consequences and impact of different teaching strategies. While a philosophy of education class is one place to do this, it is even more important that this kind of questioning is pervasive throughout the curriculum, in all classes and in a larger guiding vision for teacher education programs. A pedagogy of questions is a pedagogy that affirms students as agents in the world and that heightens their engagement with ideas. It is grounded in a particular vision of curiosity, one that Freire (1998) describes as essential to humanization: "curiosity as restless questioning, as movement toward the revelation of something hidden, as a question verbalized or not, as search for clarity, as a moment of attention, suggestion, and vigilance, constitutes an integral part of the phenomenon of being alive" (pp. 37–38).

The predispositions to be curious about ideas, to ask deep questions about assumptions, and to care about why we do things are all part of a philosophic way of being in the world. So too is being disenchanted with the status quo. Were teachers to assume this way of being, students might be more engaged in learning, less likely to put up with rote skill and drill classrooms, and better able to resist educational practices that turn them into numbers and test scores. The core questions that students are habituated to ask in Meier's (1995) Central Park East High School provide a powerful example of both mindful learning and a philosophic disposition toward the world. "They are: the question of evidence, or 'How do we know what we know?'; the question of viewpoint in all its multiplicity, or 'Who's speaking?'; the search for connections and patterns, or 'What causes what?'; supposition, or 'How might things have been different?'; and finally, why any of it matters, or 'Who cares?'" (p. 50). Students can learn to ask these types of questions in any of their classes, and thus bring more reflective habits to learning both in and outside of the classroom.

A second, less widely talked about habit that philosophers can help students to develop is the kind of critical patience necessary to dwell productively with doubt and uncertainty. Clearly all the questions listed above are complicated, and not surprisingly, answers are invariably diverse and complex. As I found when trying to get my students to explore the meaning of social justice, we have too often habituated students to be impatient with perplexity. We tend to ask students to come up the "right" answer to questions, as opposed to helping them deal with the fact that there may be no right answers, and instead only more or less persuasive possibilities. In part, this quest for certainty is due to the desire to control learning, and is a consequence of fearing that our authority as teachers will be undermined if we don't present ourselves as experts in the classroom. Yet as Diller (1999) and Lather (1998) remind us, there is power in stuck places. Only when we are uncertain, or confronted with a challenge, do we really think critically, for it is moments of stuckness that disrupt routines and commonsense, and call upon us to look at things differently. Dewey (1933/1998) writes that "thinking is inquiry, investigation, turning over, probing or delving into, so as to find something new or to see what is already known in a different light. In short, it is questioning" (p. 265). We don't undertake this kind of questioning unless we deeply confront our own beliefs, and allow ourselves to be confused, and even seemingly lost.

In making a case for the doubt as providing previously unforeseen opportunities to learn, Burbules (2000) illustrates how the experience of getting lost on the world wide web, while arguably frustrating, also exposes us to new ideas, insights and prospective connections. He claims that we need to learn to see that getting lost isn't always a bad thing, as "there is no way to remain open to the possibility of happening upon something new if one is not prepared to accept getting lost" (p. 181). Helping our students to develop the disposition to see opportunity in uncertainty, and potential in doubt, not only serves to increase their engagement in learning, it also stimulates their curiosity and creativity. "Curiosity and interest, which are essential to learning, grow out of and depend on feelings of doubt and puzzlement; they do not threaten interest, but can enhance it. Something that does not puzzle us isn't interesting" (Burbules 2000, p. 182). Habituating students to doubt is integral to critical and reflective thinking, and is important in order to challenge the shortsighted press to be always "right." Postman (1995) echoes this idea in proposing that we get rid of textbooks in teaching, as they tend to simply present us with the results of inquiry, often as packaged and immutable truths, which not only make learning seem dogmatic and trivial, but also distances students from the process of inquiry. He laments that in the standardized teaching and learning that is quintessentially represented in textbooks, "there is no sense of the frailty or ambiguity of human judgment, no hint of the possibilities of error. Knowledge is presented as a commodity to be acquired, never as a human struggle to understand, to overcome falsity, or to stumble toward the truth" (p. 116).

Teaching students to see opportunity in perplexity, however, is not the same as creating cynical skeptics who see no value in past ideas, and/or who also feel they must continually reinvent the metaphoric wheels of knowledge. Rather, a healthy form of skepticism generates the interest and engagement that is necessary to uncover and analyze assumptions. Patience and reflectiveness are equally important, although unfortunately both are all too uncommon in our high pace, high intensity, information gluttonous society. A third habit is an important complement to patience with uncertainty; however, and this is a disposition to search for alternatives to the status quo, and to imagine different futures. In looking at ideas and practices from multiple perspectives and angles, and seeking out other possibilities—however marginalized or hidden they may be—philosophers help to create hope. Burbules (2002a) maintains that "the balancing of hope and doubt is, in my view, intrinsic to the educational endeavor—and it is philosophers who can help sustain this dual vision of hopefulness and skepticism" (p. 353). One consequence of the press to cover ever more content in classrooms is that students are given few opportunities to speculate about alternative visions for schooling, education, and the future. I often ask my students early on in the semester to describe their own philosophies of education, imagining, for example, how we should provide learning opportunities in an ideal world. Sadly, the majority simply recreate the present structure of schooling that we have now, with perhaps a few modifications such as adding a subject or two, or lowering class sizes. The difficulty they have is because they have been so infrequently asked to think about what could be, and instead have been required to absorb and reproduce what is. Similarly, after reading Freire's (2000) *Pedagogy of the Oppressed*, I ask them to design an emancipatory educational experience, reiterating numerous times that they should not feel beholden to any taken-for-granteds about schooling. Yet commonly they begin with assumptions that they tend to feel are inviolable: 50 minute classes, 20–30 same age students, standard subjects, etc. It takes unlearning bad habits to get them to question these practices that seem so essential to the meaning of schooling, and to develop the practice of scrutinizing that which appears at first glance to be inevitable. Here a philosophical disposition to imagine possibilities, supported by examples and depictions of schooling built around different visions, can help students to think outside of the boxes they/we have created. This disposition balances critique and optimism, and ideally results in an open-minded and engaged approach to ideas. This is certainly a different depiction of the role of philosophy than many people assume. In the light of this vision, we see that "society needs philosophers not because it needs somebody to prove things to them, but because it needs people whose role it is to think differently, to stand outside of convention and consider alternatives that, however outlandish, enlarge the scope of human possibility" (Burbules 2002b, p. 11).

An important part of imagining alternatives and learning to question our own beliefs is seeking out viewpoints that are not part of the dominant or mainstream discourse. Along with this it is equally important to learn to listen to, and collaborate with, others in this pursuit, including community activists, elders, and "experts" whose home is outside of the often narrow confines of the academy. A useful example to illustrate the important effort this requires involves considering how we teach students of education about multiculturalism. While there is a large body of material on this subject, the bulk of it comes from a rather narrow ideological perspective—one that sees diversity in celebratory and power evasive ways: expanding the canon, learning about the traditions and values of minority groups, and honoring the achievements of non-whites. The ultimate ends seem to be helping white teachers to deal better with their minority students and to accommodate them better in the classroom. Yet these approaches are typically premised upon unquestioned assumptions about the meaning of pluralism, equity, justice and democracy. Richardson and Villenas (2000) powerfully show how dominant approaches to multiculturalism "dance with whiteness" in relying on categories and worldviews unique to white, Eurocentric, capitalist nations. At the same time, these approaches ignore the knowledge systems and philosophies of the historically colonized: indigenous peoples, Latinos, African Americans, etc. Philosophers can help students to develop the habit of finding and exploring these nondominant alternatives, particularly as they are critical in learning to be more self reflexive about one's assumptions and practices. Margonis' (1999) habits with respect to this issue provide a compelling model. He writes, that "the philosophy which most excites me offers substantive alternatives to the dominant ways of thinking about our society and our lives. Without knowing which philosophies will lead to a more just society, I am continually looking for worldviews which offer alternative visions of truth and reality; of the individual's relation to the group and world; and of fair economic, political, and social institutions" (pp. 17–18).

Theory into Practice

As I have argued throughout this essay, philosophers of education can play a valuable role in helping to shape attitudes, habits and dispositions toward inquiry, especially among prospective teachers. Cultivating the habits of unpacking fundamental assumptions, seeing possibilities in uncertainty, and seeking out alternative perspectives in teacher education is one tool we have available to us in stemming what appears to be a relentless pursuit towards high stakes accountability schemes that so clearly are antithetical to engaged teaching and learning. There are multiple possibilities for bringing philosophical dispositions into teacher education. What we might do with graduate students in an advanced philosophy of education class obviously differs from the role philosophy plays in pre-service teacher education. That is, a present day curricula for philosophy of education depends heavily on audience. In my own work at a large, public, Midwestern university, I rarely teach students who want to specialize in philosophy of education. In fact, I rarely teach students who have any interest in philosophy of education at all. Yet when I can help students to move beyond their initial leeriness toward philosophy in general, they are able, at least to some degree, to ask different kinds of questions and to develop and/or refine some useful habits that can inform their ways of being both in the classroom and in the world. They are also better able to see and defend the theories that go behind the educational practices they are most drawn to.

There are any number of content topics that can generate deep and reflective critical thinking. Stengel (2002) begins thinking about these through questioning "what do both educators and philosophers care about?" Critical thinking is one potential candidate. Moral understanding is another. Aesthetic expression might be a possibility. Social responsibility seems a likely choice" (p. 288). All of these are valuable options, and in fact, there is no specific content material that best helps students to develop the kinds of philosophical habits and dispositions I have talked about throughout this essay. A critical process of learning, and the asking of different kinds of questions, can be applied to almost any thematic content. For example, we can ask of any educational practice that we engage in what ultimate purposes it serves, what vision of education it is premised upon, what knowledge of most worth it assumes, and what consequences it has for students. Yet we still obviously must make choices about the issues and themes that will guide our pedagogical decision making. In designing the one required foundations course for teacher education students at my university, I have found that three broad, yet interrelated, topical areas work well in getting students to think more deeply about the habits they bring to learning, while also helping them to explore the connections between school and society, which is the ultimate goal of the course. These themes revolve around issues of democracy, diversity, and social justice. In conclusion, I will very briefly outline how we might address these topics so as to begin to cultivate the kinds of critical and reflective thinking I have been arguing are so important. This is not to provide a model, but rather one vision of possibility, one image of the questions upon which a philosophically-grounded curriculum for teacher education might be premised.

The issue I frame this course around is the relationship between education and democracy. We can all agree that we in the US live in a society that claims to be democratic. Moreover, one important role of schooling (if not the most important role) is to help students to develop the skills, abilities, and habits, of both heart and mind as Wood (1992) would say, needed to function as citizens, and to make democratic living possible. Beginning from these assumptions, we explore a number of questions. How can we define democracy? Where do our society and our schools fall short of democratic ideals? If not to further a vision of democracy and democratic citizenship, what other fundamental purposes should schools serve in society? What differences exist between procedural and participatory notions of democracy? What educational practices, structures, and curricula best foster the habits of democratic citizenship? How do we conceptualize ideas of responsibility and the common good as they relate to our visions of democracy? Here we also move into questions about diversity. How can democracies balance the will of the majority while also respecting the voice and the rights of minorities? What role should schools play in fostering equality of opportunity? What is the relationship between culture, power, and privilege? What moral and educational responsibilities do people from the dominant culture have in the face of diversity? What might culturally relevant teaching and learning look like? What beliefs should guide our vision of multicultural education?

It may be obvious that the issue of social justice is implicit in most of these questions. According to Oakes & Lipton (2003) a social justice perspective looks at the underlying values and politics that pervade education; attends deeply to inequalities associated with race, class, gender, sexuality, and language; and begins with critical questions about how educational practices and conventional wisdom came to be, who benefits from them, and how we create more empowering alternatives (p. xiv). In many ways, this type of curriculum directly parallels an approach that fosters the philosophic habits and dispositions I have outlined in this essay. Talking about social justice brings us full circle to my opening narrative about the difficulties my students had even making sense of this concept. After much initial struggle and resistance, and then, pointing to passages in the readings, prodding students to ask more questions, and helping them to dig deeper, they were able to begin to outline some characteristics of social justice, for example: goods and services should be equitably distributed, people effected by a decision should have a say in it, everyone should have opportunities available to help develop their potential, people shouldn't be used as objects for others benefit, and people shouldn't have "more" if it directly causes the suffering of those who have "less." More important than these characteristics, however, is that they were practicing the process of thinking critically: uncovering their assumptions, dealing with their frustration, and imagining alternative possibilities. While I would like to say that they have gotten really good at this, and that they now naturally bring these habits to the current topics we are discussing, and to their other learning experiences, that would be a bit naïve. But, we have to start somewhere.

REFERENCES

Apple, M., & Beane, J. (Ed.) (1995). *Democratic schools.* Alexandria, VA: Association for Supervision and Curriculum Development.

Ayers, W. (2001). *To teach: The journey of a teacher* (2nd ed.). New York: Teachers College Press.

Bigelow, B. (1998). The human lives behind the labels: The global sweatshop, Nike, and the race to the bottom. In W. Ayers, J. Hunt & T. Quinn (Eds.), *Teaching for social justice* (pp. 21–38). New York: Teachers College Press.

Bowers, C. A. (2001). *Educating for eco-justice and community.* Athens: University of Georgia Press.

Bredo, E. (2002). How can philosophy of education be both viable and good? *Educational Theory, 52*(3), 263–271.

Burbules, N. (2000). Aporias, webs, and passages: Doubt as an opportunity to learn. *Curriculum Inquiry, 30*(2), 171–187.

Burbules, N. (2002a). The dilemma of philosophy of education: "Relevance" or critique? Part Two. *Educational Theory, 52*(3), 349–357.

Burbules, N. (2002b). 2001: A philosophical odyssey. In Rice, S. (Ed.), *Philosophy of education, 2001* (pp. 1–14). Urbana, IL: Philosophy of Education Society.

Counts, G. (1932). *Dare the schools build a new social order?* Carbondale: Southern Illinois University Press.

Dewey, J. (1933/1998). *How we think.* New York: Houghton Mifflin Company.

Dewey, J. (1985). *John Dewey: The middle works, 1899–1924, volume 9.* Carbondale: Southern Illinois University Press.

Diller, A. (1999). Facing the torpedo fish: Becoming a philosopher of one's own education. In Tozer, S. (Ed.), *Philosophy of education, 1998* (pp. 1–9). Urbana, IL: Philosophy of Education Society.

Freire, P. (1998). *Pedagogy of freedom: Ethics, democracy and civic courage.* Lanham, MD: Rowman & Littlefield Publishers, Inc.

Freire, P. (2000). *Pedagogy of the oppressed.* New York: Continuum.

Hooks, B. (2000). *Feminism is for everybody: Passionate politics.* Cambridge, MA: South End Press.

Kohl, H. (1994). *"I won't learn from you" and other thoughts on creative maladjustment.* New York: The New Press.

Kohn, A. (1999). *The schools our children deserve: Moving beyond traditional classrooms and "tougher standards"*. Boston: Houghton Mifflin Company.

Lather, P. (1998). Critical pedagogy and its complicities: A praxis of stuck places. *Educational Theory, 48*(4), 487–497.

Margonis, F. (1999). Searching for alternatives. In Tozer, S. (Ed.), *Philosophy of education, 1998* (pp. 17–19). Urbana, IL: Philosophy of Education Society.

Meier, D. (1995). *The power of their ideas: Lessons for America from a small school in Harlem*. Boston: Beacon Press.

Meier, D. (2002). Standardization and standards. *Phi Delta Kappan, 84*(3), 190–198.

Oakes, J., & Lipton, M. (2003). *Teaching to change the world* (2nd ed.). Boston: McGraw Hill.

Postman, N. (1995). *The end of education: Redefining the value of school*. New York: Alfred A. Knopf.

Purpel, D. (1999). *Moral outrage in education*. New York: Peter Lang.

Richardson, T., & Villenas, S. (2000). "Other" encounters: Dances with whiteness in multicultural education. *Educational Theory, 50*(2), 255–273.

Sheldon, K., & Biddle, B. (1998). Standards, accountability, and school reform: Perils and pitfalls. *Teachers College Record, 100*(1), 164–180.

Siegel, H. (2002). Philosophy of education and the Deweyan legacy. *Educational Theory, 52*(3), 273–280.

Stengel, B. (2002). Cause for worry or agenda for action? *Educational Theory, 52*(3), 281–290.

Thompson, A. (1999). Colortalk: Whiteness and *off white*. *Educational Studies, 30*(2), 141–160.

Westheimer, J. (1998). *Among school teachers: Community, autonomy, and ideology in teacher's work*. New York: Teachers College Press.

Westheimer, J., & Kahne, J. (1998). Education for action: Preparing youth for participatory democracy. In W. Ayers, J. Hunt, & T. Quinn (Eds.), *Teaching for social justice* (pp. 1–20). New York: Teachers College Press.

Wood, G. (1992). *Schools that work: America's most innovative public education programs*. New York: Penguin/Plume Books.

Wood, G. (1998). *A time to learn*. New York: Penguin Putnam Inc.

CHAPTER 11

BEYOND UTOPIANISM AND PESSIMISM

Teaching "Prophetic Pragmatism's" Tragic Sense

Kip Kline
Lewis University

ABSTRACT

This chapter asserts the need for a tragic sense in education. The metaphors that dominate educational rhetoric are too often naively optimistic, utopian, and bereft of a confrontation with tragic circumstances such as the large numbers of students in classrooms that, despite their best efforts, teachers will not be able to reach or the fact that many students will not, for various reasons, be able to learn all we hope they might. Yet, adopting a sense of the tragic in education, if it is to have meliorative potential, must emphasize human agency and allow for some form of hope. This chapter locates such a tragic sense and discusses the teaching of this theory to preservice teachers.

Unsettling Beliefs: Teaching Theory to Teachers, pages 201–213
Copyright © 2008 by Information Age Publishing
All rights of reproduction in any form reserved.

201

INTRODUCTION

I love children. I want to work with children.

There is much anecdotal evidence that these are among the most popular responses of preservice teachers to any question regarding their motivation for studying education. Students of mine who have used these clichés are taken aback when I suggest to them, in response, that opening a day-care or running a private babysitting service would afford them the opportunity to work with children with much less external constraint than a career in teaching. While the desire to work with children may be a necessary condition for a successful teacher, the naïveté that lies behind the cliché is quite often an adumbration of a real ignorance of the more tragic circumstances of education. Those of us who teach preservice teachers, it seems, often find ourselves wanting to temper the idealism of our students by introducing them to the lamentable aspects of a career in education and yet we also want them to retain their exuberance for teaching. Put another way, we are caught between the Scylla of encouraging the maintenance of utopian impulses and the Charybdis of promoting pessimism about the educative process.

If those of us who teach preservice teachers are to avoid pessimism and utopianism, we must find a "third way," that neither succumbs to the threat of tragic circumstances in education and leads to cynicism nor clings to pie-in-the-sky visions of Hollywood-style teachers who somehow manage to dodge all the obstacles en route to transforming groups of children. This third way, then, will have to acknowledge tragic circumstances but simultaneously hold a belief in and commitment to human agency. It will have to allow us to take the notion "I want to work with children" and, as John Dewey (1999) encouraged us to do in "My Pedagogic Creed," neither humor nor suppress it. In short, we must develop a tragic sense of education that goes beyond pessimism and utopianism.

The following is a consideration of ideas about the tragic sense applied to education, an examination of a notion of the tragic that goes beyond pessimism and utopianism, and some reflection about my attempts to teach such a tragic sense of education to preservice teachers. I first discuss Nicholas Burbules's (1990) tragic sense of education, locating its problems and then consider Cornel West's (1989) sense of the tragic found in his particular brand of neopragmatism, "prophetic pragmatism," as a corrective. Further, I explore the applicability of prophetic pragmatism's tragic sense to education and discuss my experiences teaching it to undergraduates.

BURBULES AND WEST: TWO NOTIONS OF THE TRAGIC

American education has long been strongly associated with progress. While it might be fair to say this connection has been beneficial, it has also contributed to a deficiency in the discourse regarding the tragic circumstances that affect the educational endeavor. Adopting a sense of the tragic for education takes a courageous and necessary step toward complicating the "education equals progress" motif and in so doing steers clear of the kind of naïve utopianism that ultimately leads to disillusion. Of course, there are competing notions of the tragic; the best fit for educators is one that maintains a kind of hope while acknowledging the real and unavoidable tragic pitfalls in the educative process. This is certainly a delicate path to navigate, but it amounts to a compulsory task for educators at all levels, including those who teach preservice teachers. We are in danger of falling into disillusionment, burnout, and ineffectiveness if we refuse to confront the tragic and cling to a pie-in-the-sky optimism; yet in the absence of a driving sense of real hope it is difficult to imagine a good reason to devote our lives to the process of teaching and learning.

According to Nicholas Burbules (1990), educators are faced with a dilemma. It seems necessary that we hope for our efforts to result in the betterment of individuals and society, yet only the most naïve of us can retain our optimism as experience reveals the difficulty of effecting significant change. Of course, exchanging a naïve utopianism for a pessimistic fatalism is no way around the dilemma either; so, Burbules offers the tragic sense as a means to navigate between them.

Burbules's (1990) conception of the tragic seems inadequate in that it severely limits the possibilities of the tragic sense as an ameliorative agent in the face of difficulties in education. While he offers criticism of both pessimism and utopianism, he seems to be much more concerned with the avoidance of the latter. He does mention hope, though it is mostly a gesture. He certainly wants to say that education is unequivocally a Sisyphean endeavor.

Burbules's (1990) treatment of the tragic sense of education does offer liberation from quantifiable standards and generates an appropriate call for solidarity, but it fails to provide the real hope that might sustain us in the face of the dilemma. Cornel West's (1999) prophetic pragmatism provides ameliorative meat for the bones of Burbules's conception of the tragic. West's is primarily a political project that, using Emersonian sensibilities, "understands the…(pragmatist) swerve from epistemology…not as wholesale rejection of philosophy, but rather as a reconception of philosophy as a form of cultural criticism" (p. 168). One part of prophetic pragmatism is a distinctive conception of the tragic. West makes clear that "tragic" is a multivalent term. However, West's sense of the tragic is derived from the modern context, in which tragedy is "bound to the idea of human agency" (p. 165). Further and most salient, while Burbules's sense of the tragic seems to navigate between pessimism and utopianism, West's denies both "Sisyphean pessimism and utopian perfectionism" (p. 167). In their stead, prophetic pragmatism offers the possibility of incremental human progress in the face of the impossibility of human utopia. In this way, West's sense of the tragic supplies the hope of human agency that is lacking in Burbules's notion. Prophetic pragmatism is "...a kind of romanticism in that it holds many experiences of evil to be neither inevitable nor necessary, but rather the results of human agency, that is, choices and actions" (p. 166). West's treatment of the tragic implies that if our educative efforts are often doomed to miss the mark it is, at least in part, because we have constructed them that way. Applying the tragic sense found in prophetic pragmatism to education surely would mean to temper what West calls "utopian impulses" but to remain hopeful about and committed to human possibilities, albeit without a guarantee of success. In this way, prophetic pragmatism offers what Burbules does not in his conception of the tragic, that is to say, an emphasis on human agency and possibility that can sustain us in our efforts.

Here, I consider West's (1999) sense of the tragic as the linchpin of the convergence of prophetic pragmatism and education. Further, I find West's idea of the prophetic thinker (clearly central to his particular brand of pragmatism) to be an indispensable notion when applying prophetic pragmatism's tragic sense to education.

TRACING THE ROOTS OF THE TRAGIC IN PROPHETIC PRAGMATISM

The sense of the tragic in prophetic pragmatism is meticulously nuanced. Again, it begins with the assertion that "tragic" is a term with many meanings. For prophetic pragmatism, the idea of tragedy is set apart from the Greek notion in which "the action of ruling families generates pity and terror in the audience" and is rather tethered to "a society that shares collective experience of common metaphysical and social meanings" (West, 1989, p. 227). Prophetic pragmatism's sense of the tragic emanates from what West calls the modern context of tragedy "...in which ordinary individuals struggle against meaninglessness and nothingness" within "a fragmented society with collapsing metaphysical meanings" (p. 227). This adaptation of tragedy to the modern context provides the criterion by which prophetic pragmatism accepts or rejects the sense of the tragic found in the various thinkers in American pragmatism.

Though West (1989) begins his genealogy of pragmatism with a celebration of Ralph Waldo Emerson, he is critical of Emersonian pragmatism's optimistic theodicy. West admits that Emerson did have a sense of
the tragic, but "the way he formulated the relation of human powers and
fate, human agency and circumstances, human will and constraints made it
difficult for him...to maintain a delicate balance between excessive optimism and exorbitant pessimism regarding human capacities" (West, 1989,
p. 226). West argues that only "the early (Sidney) Hook and (Reinhold)
Niebuhr—their work in the early thirties—maintain the desirable balance"
(p. 226). This balance is important for West since without it there is no way
to confront what he calls "the complex relations between tragedy and revolution, tradition and progress" (pp. 226–227). Prophetic pragmatism recognizes historical human atrocities and brutalities as well as "present-day
barbarities." In fact, it is this recognition that requires of prophetic pragmatism a conception of the tragic. It must not avoid these facts of the
human condition. Yet, the conception of the tragic for the prophetic pragmatist is rooted in the modern context of tragedy, and for West this means
not only the context of a fragmented society with collapsing metaphysical
meanings, but also, and "more pointedly, the notion of the 'tragic' is
bound to the idea of human agency, be the agent a person of rank or a
retainer, a prince or a pauper" (p. 227).

Here the sense of the tragic found in prophetic pragmatism becomes
profoundly attractive. It is both critical of Emersonian theodicy and yet
gives primacy to the agency of all persons. West (1989) claims that the Reinhold Niebuhr of the 1930s best exemplifies this complex sense of the tragic:

> Niebuhr's struggle with liberal Protestantism...forced him to remain on the
> tightrope between Promethean romanticism and Augustinian pessimism. In
> fact, Niebuhr never succumbs to either, nor does he ever cease to promote
> incessant human agency and will against limits and circumstances. (p. 228)

Thus, it is primarily from the early Niebuhr that prophetic pragmatism
derives its sense of the tragic. What makes West's treatment of the Niebu-
hrian "strenuous mood" (and consequently the prophetic pragmatist conception of the tragic) attractive is that it is unwilling to sidestep real and
unavoidable human atrocities, some of which are admittedly not trans-
formable; while at the same time maintaining "utopian impulses" through
an unfettered belief in the agency of all persons. West (1989) anticipates
that this may make his sense of the tragic seem a bit schizophrenic—a
Sisyphean outlook in which human resistance to evil fails on the one hand,
and the promotion of a quest for utopia on the other. However, West
claims that "prophetic pragmatism denies Sisyphean pessimism *and* utopian perfectionism, offering in their stead the possibility of human

progress and the human impossibility of paradise" (p. 229). This is a subtle but profound movement away from a navigation between excessive pessimism and a pie-in-the-sky utopianism to a kind of paradigmatic shift that includes replacing the polar ideas with a singular conception of the evil in the world; an appreciable portion of which might be ameliorated through human agency, precisely because it is a product of human agency.

Prophetic pragmatism is a form of tragic thought in that it confronts candidly individual and collective experiences of evil in individuals and institutions—with little expectation of ridding the world of all evil (p. 228).

A HOPEFUL CORRECTIVE TO NICHOLAS BURBULES'S SENSE OF THE TRAGIC

When juxtaposed with West's (1989) sense of the tragic, Burbules's (1990) seems less committed to human agency, less convinced of possibility and hope, and more concerned with the dangers of utopian impulses. Burbules begins with the Greek context and employs the tragic protagonist and the perspective of the audience as locus of his conception of the tragic:

> It is in the spectator's point of view that the tragic sense reveals itself, and an essential element in our response, says, Hans-Georg Gadamer, is the realization that this is how it is "in life; it is not just pity for the protagonist that affects us, but a kind of self-knowledge in which we recognize our situation as well. (p. 470)

Thus, Burbules (1990) concludes that all of us, like the tragic protagonist, operate under circumstances of incomplete information and that we always run the risk of ignorantly working toward ends that are self-defeating. It is telling that Burbules begins building his conception of the tragic with the spectator. It suggests that he relies on fate as the source of evil. This point is further evidenced by Burbules's (1990) use of the Bernard Williams (1981) concept of "moral luck."

> A second factor that should make us modest about our utopias is what Bernard Williams calls "moral luck": "One's history as an agent is a web in which anything that is the product of the will is surrounded and held up and partly formed by things that are not. (Burbules, 1990, p. 473)

It is clear that Burbules is placing an emphasis on the "things that are not" (products of the will) and that utopian impulses must be abated because of this concept of "moral luck"; a concept Burbules uses to suggest that fate plays a much more significant role than human agency in matters of evil in the world.

Burbules tempers the pessimism that results from the spectator observing the tragic protagonist with Herbert Muller's (1957) idea of tragedy "going all the way through" the worst of human possibilities to "display the most splendid possibilities of the human spirit" whereby it "earns an honorable peace" (p. 25). This idea leads Burbules to claim that maintaining this tragic sense is an admission of "the inherent difficulties and uncertainties of our efforts" that bears the fruit of inspiring solidarity and "persistent and conscientious effort" while being realistic about "the worth of what we are trying to accomplish" (p. 471).

Prophetic pragmatism agrees that we work with incomplete information and that there is existential benefit from tragedy that "goes all the way through." Yet, in the end, it claims we can hope for more than just increased solidarity and an honorable peace while maintaining the tragic sense. We can hope for real ameliorative progress, even in the face of evils since some of those evils are the result of human construction. Put another way, instead of rooting the sense of the tragic in the passive *spectator* of events caused by uncontrollable fate, West begins his sense of the tragic with the concept of the *participant* in events of which we are the partial cause.

It is clear from "The Tragic Sense of Education" that Burbules (1990) is much more concerned with "the dangers of utopianism" than he is of excessive pessimism in educational endeavors. Repeatedly he warns us that our "inspirational metaphors" are naïve and promise more than can be delivered; that every battle won is another battle lost in education, that a stride made for one child usually results in two steps back for another. It does not take an educator long to encounter colleagues who have fallen into the trap Burbules warns us about. Certainly we have all come into contact with the naïve, slogan-toting teacher who greatly underestimates the obstacles in the way of educative efforts. All too often, this leads to disillusionment and eventually burnout or a complacent acceptance of the status quo. In other instances this naïveté results in a hyper-affective approach to the classroom that can undermine real educative efforts and contribute to anti-intellectualism in the profession. However, it seems that what Burbules is offering as a correction to this naïve optimism may tend toward overcompensation. His sense of the tragic so emphasizes the avoidance of utopianism that he runs the risk of falling victim to Paulo Freire's (2000) idea of "semi-intransitive consciousness" in which a failure to imagine better possibilities results from a preoccupation on survival. (Burbules does mention this concept of Freire's, but only as evidence that some writers on education do encourage utopian impulses. He does not defend such a practice). Again, prophetic pragmatism's emphasis on human agency is what is needed to balance Burbules's conception of the tragic. Without such an emphasis Burbules is left with jettisoning utopian impulses, proclaiming education to be a Sisyphean endeavor, and an emphasis on the role of fate at the expense of the role of human agency in matters of evil in the world as they intersect with the educative process.

While Burbules's conception of the tragic sense stands in some contrast to that of prophetic pragmatism, he does consult the pragmatist tradition as he builds his case. William James, Sidney Hook, John Dewey, and Richard Rorty all figure in a section of Burbules's (1990) "The Tragic Sense of Education" that is primarily dedicated to the pragmatist idea of uncertainty. Here Burbules talks about "the quest for certainty" that Dewey (1929) described; the idea that uncertainty, for many, is undesirable and therefore Burbules claims, "most people grasp at the nearest plausible rationale rather than struggle with their doubt" (p. 476). Burbules (1990) concludes that the quest for certainty is "hostile to the process of education, in which uncertainty and doubt are inevitable" (p. 476). With this much, prophetic pragmatism agrees. However, the conclusions, once again, fall short of giving hope for ameliorative progress. The prophetic pragmatist avoids the "quest for certainty," which leads to an open-ended future and an unfinished history that, combined with the primacy of human agency, yields a hope that Burbules's "moderation and tolerable trade-offs" do not.

CONCLUSIONS FOR EDUCATION

In "The Tragic Sense of Education" Burbules (1990) makes observations about the process of education, the efforts of educators, and the prospects for success and/or results. He acknowledges that aiding in the reconstruction of worldviews is part and parcel of a good education. But he is sure that teachers can, at best, only make a limited contribution to this process:

> The educational process is imperfect and incomplete. We interact with students for a relatively short time in their lives; in that time, we are often more effective at tearing down their preconceptions than we are at enabling them to reconstruct something more complete. When the process is unfinished, as it usually is, how then do we argue that it is all for the best, having robbed students of something dear to them and given them so little in return? (p. 474)

Of course the process is incomplete, but that does not necessarily eliminate the possibility of real, albeit incremental, progress toward salubrious reconstructions of worldviews at particular moments in the process. Furthermore, for the prophetic pragmatist, the most salient part of the process is exactly what Burbules admits educators can do. At the Coalition of Essential Schools' Fall Forum in 2000, Cornel West (2000a) remarked that he hoped, in his address to the constituents, he would say something that unnerved or unsettled them:

Very much like the experience that we want with each and every one of our students for them to recognize that, if only for a second, their worldview rests on pudding. That kind of existential vertigo, that kind of tragic qualm that goes hand in hand with the best kind of education.

Admittedly this is kind of "unhousing" as West likes to call it, presents the particular difficulty of avoiding leaving our students in a freefall once we have led them into "existential vertigo." Therefore, we must navigate this unsettling delicately and meticulously. Anecdotal accounts of West's own way of being in the classroom suggest that he does not simply pull the rug out from under students' worldviews in order that they might learn from the tough love of the fall. Indeed, this unnerving must be executed with great care if it is to be a part of the process of a healthy worldview examination and reconstruction. So, the metaphor West uses is telling. A world view that "rests on pudding" does have some sort of footing, albeit a rather unstable support at best. So, the idea is to expose students to realities that challenge their unquestioned assumptions. The point is that the kind of unsettling that goes along with the best kind of education need not leave students with "so little" as Burbules suggests. On the contrary, it offers the necessary conditions for students to examine their assumptions in a safe environment, in fact, to have their worldviews challenged through the process of being led into existential vertigo.

This existential vertigo is part and parcel of what Neil Postman and Charles Weingartner (1969) had in mind when they conceived of teaching as a subversive activity. The first chapter of their book suggests the linchpin of good education is developing persons who might contribute to "counter-cyclical" or "anti-entropic" forces; to do so these persons must develop an internal "crap detector" (p. 3). Of course, this development hinges on the unsettling and unnerving that West knows is an important component of educative efforts. Put another way, part of the process is aiming the "crap detector" inwardly, if one is to develop counter-cyclical sensibilities.

In order to assert a similar point to that of Postman and Weingartner (1969), West (2000a) is fond of fusing Socrates and Malcolm X; from Socrates we get "the unexamined life is not worth living," but from Malcolm X we are cautioned that the examined life is terribly painful and leaves us vulnerable. This has clear implications for teaching.

> Good teaching is all about unsettling perspectives and unstiffening prejudices and allowing persons to be emancipated and liberated from whatever parochial cocoon they find themselves in at the moment. Each and every one of us is always linked to some parochial cocoon; we are never free. It is a perennial process that takes courage. (West, 2000a, p. 44)

It is clear that West believes teachers can effect significant change by guiding this kind of unsettling and by encouraging students to liberate themselves from their parochial assumptions. However, Burbules (1990) seems to be convinced that the impact of teachers on students is more modest. He asserts that for the majority of students "we (teachers) can do little" and that we are resigned to "taking solace from the few students we feel a sense of rapport with, even as we recognize the vast majority for whom we have little or no lasting effect" (p. 475). From where do these conclusions about the effect of teachers on students come? His particular experiences as an educator notwithstanding, clearly there are other teachers who could provide anecdotal evidence to the contrary.

Teacher as Prophetic Thinker

Though the above is evidence that Cornel West has spoken to audiences explicitly about education, he has not applied the broader idea of the tragic sense in prophetic pragmatism to education in direct ways. It seems that the best entrée into this connection, especially when it comes to introducing preservice teachers to prophetic pragmatism's tragic sense is to examine West's notion of "prophetic thought" and then consider the notion of "teacher as prophetic thinker." This approach not only invites a deeper examination of the tragic sense in prophetic pragmatism, but also fuses theory and practice as students of education consider the theoretical notion of prophetic thought in light of actual teacher practices.

There are four basic components to "prophetic thought" as Cornel West (1993) conceives of it. The first, discernment, refers to a nuanced sense of history, one that eschews "pure traditions or pristine heritages" in favor of a "deep analytical grasp of the present in light of the past" that recognizes every culture as a result of "the weaving of antecedent cultures." West uses jazz as an example of such a quilting of cultural artifacts from different traditions; European instruments with New World African rhythmic and harmonic sensibilities. This discernment is the basis for moving beyond Eurocentrism and multiculturalism.

> . . . multiculturalism and eurocentrism are for me not analytical categories, they are categories to be analyzed with a nuanced historical sense, and also a subtle social analysis. By subtle social analysis, I mean powerful descriptions and persuasive explanations of wealth and status and prestige. (West, 1993)

So, discernment provides a way of tracking who is "bearing the social cost" at particular historical moments. Clearly this is one of the ways in which West confronts tragic circumstances. In my experience teaching prophetic thought to preservice teachers, I have found it important to stress the nuances of "discernment." The idea that all cultures are the result of the weaving of antecedent cultures and the notion of tracking those that bear the social cost at various points in history are indispensable points of emphasis that help develop a more sophisticated understanding of West's "discernment" as opposed to a more clichéd understanding such as "we must learn from history in order not to repeat it," or something like that.

Connection, the second component, focuses on human empathy, or "never losing sight of the humanity of others." This "profoundly moral moment" of attempting to understand the plight of others is another essential part of gaining the prophetic perspective. West (1993) draws the idea of connection from the essay "On a Certain Blindness in Human Beings" in which William James (1903) was critical of the lack of empathetic identification with the Filipinos during the U.S. occupation of the Philippines. Instead of seeing the humanity of the Filipinos, West says that James claimed "many of his fellow citizens (did not) empathetically identify (with them)...but rather cast them as pictures and portraits" (p. 5). Not only is this empathetic human connection an important component of prophetic thought, it is another way of meeting tragic circumstances "head on."

When teaching "connection," I find that the emphasis must be on the profundity of the "moment." Students sometimes conflate this deeper idea of West's with a kind of pedestrian sympathy. Generally speaking (though this does not apply to all of them), preservice teachers have not had the sorts of experiences that have exposed them to the kind of tragic circumstances in education that they will eventually face as they enter the classroom and the mantra "I want to work with children" has not been made problematic by the kind of real and deep human problems that confront the educational process. Therefore, I find it necessary to respectfully challenge students' ideas about empathy through thought experiments based on real classroom situations that I have experienced or that other educators have experienced. Again, considering the idea of the will to see and embrace humanity in all its guises attains a more sophisticated understanding of "connection."

The third component is tracking hypocrisy, a process that is both external and internal as it seeks to accentuate the gap between rhetoric and reality while maintaining a self-critical posture as well. West acknowledges the courage of this task that points out the human hypocrisy of others and is open to reciprocal criticism. Tracking hypocrisy is another way of examining the role of human agency in tragic circumstances as the self-critical component forces us to situate ourselves within the hypocrisy we point out. "We are often complicit with the very thing we are criticizing" (West, 1993, p. 6).

Tracking hypocrisy is a two-tiered commitment of courage and this is the way I teach undergraduates to understand this component of prophetic thought. The first tier of courage is the one in which we have the will to, first, do the work of tracking hypocrisy, not just of individuals, but institutions. This "work" means the willful acquisition of relevant knowledge. For classroom teachers, that takes a variety of forms, but I try to give my students ideas about how easy it is to fall into the trap of disinterest due to the amount of work it takes to attain the kind of knowledge that is the prerequisite for tracking hypocrisy in educational institutions. The work, then, must be followed by the courage to act on the hypocrisy that is revealed. The second tier, perhaps the more difficult one, is locating ourselves within the hypocrisy we are tracking. West (1993) makes it clear that tracking hypocrisy must have a self-critical component if it is to be an effective part of prophetic thought. Undergraduate students of education typically recognize the level of maturity and commitment that is required for locating oneself in the hypocrisy being tracked.

Finally, the fourth component is hope. Here West (1993) makes a distinction. Hope is not to be conflated with optimism. He recognizes that we are "world-weary" and that we may have "misanthropic skeletons hanging in our closet," but we face them by reminding ourselves that history is incomplete and the future is open-ended. Optimism is not an option for West. The evidence does not suggest we have reason to be optimistic. Thus, West steers clear of any naïve utopianism. Yet, with an emphasis on human agency, West suggests that the evidence that does not yield a reason for optimism can be changed. He admits that there is something audacious about this hope, yet, without it, "all you have is sophisticated analyses. Ironic reflection" (p. 6). The prophetic pragmatist brand of hope, of the four components of prophetic thought, most explicitly begins to uncover the sense of the tragic in West's program. Equal emphasis on tragic circumstances and human agency yield a notion of hope that looks human atrocities in their face and maintains itself because of the open-endedness of history and ameliorative agential power. West refers to this as a "blues hope," or a "blood-stained, tear soaked hope," and even an "earned hope." Though a majority of the preservice teachers I have taught have not had the experiences that can yield such an earned hope that is distinct from optimism, they most certainly will be confronted with such experiences when they deal with the tragic parts of the educational process. Again, thought experiments can help preservice teachers begin to imagine circumstances they had previously not imagined in schools and in their particular future classroom.

Consider the teacher as a prophetic thinker. Certainly this educator conceives of teaching as a subversive activity as she deliberately reveals the gap between rhetoric and reality. She is able to confront human tragedy with a nuanced sense of history. She emphasizes human agency and human connection. She clings to an audacious sense of hope. It is not a kind of cheap optimism that she embraces, buoyed fragilely by worn-out apothegms. It is a hope that is rooted in the idea that, in spite of the evidence to the contrary, we can, because of a belief in human agency, "look beyond the evidence and create new evidence" (West, 2000b, p. 44). These are the ways in which my classes approach the idea of the tragic sense in prophetic pragmatism as applied to education. Students have responded well to the task of wrapping their minds around sophisticated theory and applying it to the practice of teaching.

Avoiding naïveté and an overestimation of our powers, creating solidarity and maintaining conscientious effort are all worthy pursuits. They are also quite congruent with prophetic pragmatism's sense of the tragic and West's concept of the prophetic thinker. But prophetic pragmatism adds the primacy of human agency and an audacious sense of hope that yield ameliorative power. West (2000b, p. 44) calls himself a "prisoner of hope"— an apt description for a teacher.

REFERENCES

Burbules, N. C. (1990). The tragic sense of education. *Teachers College Record, 91*(4), 469–479.

Dewey, J. (1929). *The quest for certainty: A study of the relation of feelings and action.* New York: Capricorn Books.

Dewey, J. (1999). "My Pedagogic Creed" in R. Reed & T. Johnson (Eds.), *Philosophical documents in education* (pp. 92–100). New York: Longman.

Freire, P. (2000). *Pedagogy of the oppressed,* New York: Continuum.

Muller, H. J. (1957). *The uses of the past: Profiles of former societies.* New York: Oxford University Press.

Postman, N., & Weingartner, C. (1969). *Teaching as a subversive activity.* New York: Delacorte.

West, C. (1989). *The American evasion of philosophy: A genealogy of pragmatism.* Madsion: University of Wisconsin Press.

West, C. (1993). *Prophetic thought in postmodern times: Beyond eurocentrism and multiculturalism,* (Vol.1). Monroe, ME: Common Courage Press.

West, C. (1999). *The Cornel West Reader.* New York: Civitas.

West, C. (2000a). "Cornel West's Opening Remarks," Coalition of Essential Schools Fall Forum, 2000. Retrieved from http://www.essentialschools.org/pub/ces _docs/fforum/2000/speeches/west_00.html.

West, C. (2000b). A grand tradition of struggle. *English Journal, 89*(6), 39–44.

Williams, B. (1981). *Moral luck: Philosophical papers, 1973–1980.* New York: Cambridge University Press.

CHAPTER 12

CRYING OUT WITHOUT VOICE

The Silence of Teachers

Richard Conley
North Carolina State University

ABSTRACT

This chapter explores the need for entry-level teachers to engage in an active form of teacher participation when joining a new school. It draws the distinction between collegial participation and collaborative participation, the latter form involving full dialogue and reflection. The methodology develops from Albert Bandura's (2001) *Social Cognitive Theory* but explores a little-researched phenomenon, high-performing teachers exiting high-performing schools.

*Conspicuous by their absence from the literature of research on teaching
are the voices of teachers, the questions and problems they pose, the frameworks
they use to interpret and improve their practice, and the ways they define
and understand their work lives.*

—Lytle & Cochran-Smith (1990, p. 83)

Unsettling Beliefs: Teaching Theory to Teachers, pages 215–243
Copyright © 2008 by Information Age Publishing
All rights of reproduction in any form reserved.

INTRODUCTION

Why would a quality instructor leave a high-performing public school to teach in another high-performing public school in the same district? Since entering the school system in 1993, approximately 50% of the teaching populations of three of my previous schools (all three recognized as Schools of Excellence by the state) have departed. In fact, by the five year mark, almost 50% had departed, most to other schools, some to retirement (Wake County Public School System, 2005). If half the teachers were departing after five years from quality schools to migrate to other schools, the problem was clear that the schools were losing personnel to other schools at a high rate, considerably higher for middle schools. This exodus of qualified personnel, many of them, excellent, poses a significant problem for the district and especially the individual school since replacement procedures require time, labor, and expertise to find a suitable teacher in a competitive arena. It is time to listen to the voices of those who are entrusted to teach for their voices have been neglected too long now and our public school educational system cannot stand to "lose" our best teachers, even to other schools.

I have spoken to many teachers over the years and they have a uniform chant, a lack of validation in the decision-making process either at the team or administrative level. Understanding the ramifications of losing so many teachers who potentially stabilize school climates and organizations due to their experience and familiarity with the organization, I believed it essential to talk to teachers who had recently transferred or "migrated." Further understanding that each school has a particular school climate, I found it problematic that three high-performing middle schools lost so much personnel at such an accelerated rate (averaging from 15 to 20% annually), an average of 10 to 14 teachers a year (Wake County Public School System, 2005). The state middle school turnover rate was almost double the overall turnover rate, including high-performing schools designated as Schools of Excellence where 90% or more of their student population scored at or above grade level on end of year standardized tests (NC Department of Public Instruction).

I had worked in four middle schools (one twice) and certainly the school climate and personnel were different yet migration rates were still high. Consequently it was important to understand the organizational design and features of a high-performing school to observe the daily routine, expectations, and protocol. This entailed actually talking to and interviewing teachers at all grade levels and content areas who had recently migrated. Schools are institutions governed by rules, policies, legislation, and mandates sent from legislative branches, government agencies, and the boards of education. Therefore, understanding how organizational features affect teachers' perceptions and attitudes proved to be a central research pursuit. Once I had researched these concerns, my fieldwork helped me understand the organizational flow of information and operations at the school level better and I was able to frame the phenomenon of teacher migration more competently. Upon completion of the initial research, a recurrent theme emerged—the teacher voice and how it fit into their existing organization. Too often, decisions were made by administrators; the process did not validate or empower the teachers themselves, resulting in dissatisfaction and lower organizational efficacy. Teachers remained enclaves in their own classroom and disconnected from the overall school culture. Their voices were not heard consistently. It was time to spend some time and talk with teachers directly about the overlooked problem of teacher migration.

Background

After 12 years in the public school system as teacher, assistant principal, and principal, I decided to conduct a case study of a high-performing middle school in the district in an effort to shed light on the central question of the effect of school climate on teachers' perceptions. My observations provided me with an organizational vantage point from "inside the building" during my time as a site-based educator. Conducting research in these same buildings as social science researcher twelve years later provided a rare viewpoint. The dual perspective afforded me an insight into what I lived in the school—the praxis, versus what I studied in the university, the theory. My efforts to elucidate the problem through greater understanding of the teachers and their decisions to leave schools engaged the belief that praxis and theory are not mutually exclusive; actually, it is quite the opposite. Praxis and theory are necessary complements in a high-functioning organization that thrives on both, albeit in different proportions. The voices of some of our top educators resonated clearly with me in all three roles: as a teacher, I had beginning experiences to talk about from my past; as an assistant principal, I had overseen formal observations and observed instruction on a daily basis; as a principal, I had interacted with all the teachers in the building and learned much about consensus, politics, and organizational design.

After completing the research, I analyzed the data and drew several conclusions. One of the conclusions I reached pointed to the recurrent theme of a lack of real voice on the part of the teachers. A second conclusion I reached was that beginning teachers cross a large divide between teacher education programs in the university and the immediate classroom requirements. However they will remain in their assigned school for the most part through the, the first three years, or the "survival" period. After that period, if they do not find their ideals challenged and validated by the administration or other instructors, many will migrate. Frank, a National Board Certified teacher, elaborates:

> By the time teachers put in three or four years in, they're ready to spread their wings and assert themselves in a professional environment. If they're in a building and the administration doesn't teach people to work with dissent and value it, those teachers are going to leave out of frustration. Accomplished teachers will also leave and I think if you look at the migration pattern you see that lots of teachers in that central part of their teaching career, four to seven years in, are the ones leaving. They're past the survival mode and are approaching the professional part of their career.

Many beginning teachers are not adequately prepared for the transition from college to the classroom. Instead, they depend on experienced educators to show them the way and serve as moral support during this novice period. Let us call this designated period the three year period, and teachers finding themselves within this period are referred to as Initially Licensed Teachers or ILTs (North Carolina Department of Public Instruction, 2005). Likewise, many public schools themselves are not prepared to thoroughly acculturate these beginning teachers through an ongoing process outside of the mentor program required by the district.

Thus, in this chapter I will explore the voices of teachers yearning for a sense of continuous growth and how public schools and the university can forge more effective programs together to support that growth and strengthen identity-building. The purpose of this chapter is to introduce some central concerns and problems of teachers from an organizational point of view in an effort to enhance our understanding of why teachers depart high-performing schools. The experiences of beginning teachers often have a lasting effect on their attitudes at a particular school. Some of these experiences need to be examined, including the transition from their teacher education programs in the university to the school organization itself. Beginning teachers hear "two voices" speaking at the same time but the fainter one, that of their preservice teacher education, wanes in the distance and loses its authenticity and force in the immediacy of the moment.

Teacher turnover rates, whether through attrition or migration, create staffing problems for the school organization. This turnover becomes influenced by the "character and conditions of the organizations within which employees work" (Ingersoll, 2001 p. 3). While much research has focused on teacher attrition rates (Boe & Gilford, 1992, Grissmer & Kirby, 1997, Ingersoll, 2000, Murnane, Singer, Willett, Kemple & Olsen, 1991,

Price, 1989), less has been carried out for teacher migration, particularly looking at organizational characteristics and conditions (Ingersoll, 2001).

Methods

Understanding that all teachers work in unique school climates, I interviewed and listened to the voices of my fellow educators. At times during the chapter, I will quote the words of the interviewees and identify them with pseudonyms. All of the staff members interviewed work at a high-performing middle school designated as The Professional Learning School (TPLS). Pseudonyms will be used to respect the confidentiality of these teachers. TPLS located in the southeast United States, is a traditional middle school on a 10 month calendar with a 6th–8th grade configuration and slightly fewer than 900 students in enrollment. TPLS is in the middle of its second year and is a Professional Learning Community school (DuFour & Eaker, 1998). Thirteen interviews were conducted along with field notes compiled for more than thirty meetings and extensive Blackboard discussions and list forums (Conley, 2006). The range of teacher experience extended from first year teachers to teachers with twenty-seven years of experience. I interviewed teachers from all three grade levels, two principals, two assistant principals, an academically gifted program supervisor, and a president of the parent teacher association who was a former mathematics teacher. All interviews were recorded and the participants were provided with a CD of each interview along with a written transcription of the original text.

An emergent theme from the interviews is that many teachers, both new and experienced, are departing from their settings to establish roots in new ones. They are stifled by the complacency of administrators zealously following district mandates or expressing only token gestures in matters of true curriculum and instructional reform. Teachers, whose voices are not heard, will either stay in a quality school, only to teach in autonomous fashion, or depart to another school where they believe administrators will validate their insight. Many do not choose to leave the profession after the first three years since they want to establish a niche and are not in a position move on so quickly based on a perceived lower status. After three years, though, they are likely to migrate and this is highly problematic for school systems who must replace, train, and acculturate new educators to their existing school climates.

The other concern is how to strengthen organizational ties between the university and the specific school organization so that not only beginning teachers are monitored and supported through their early years but also other more experienced teachers looking for new ideas and research findings. Increased visible presence of the university professors on the public school site along with context-specific student internships in varied situated learning roles could foster a mutual trust between higher education and public schools who seem to be constantly searching for a successful means to bridge the gap between the two organizations.

Context

My research came at an opportune time since I was able to gain entry into a new middle school in its second year of operations. All one hundred staff members had migrated (except five or six beginning teachers), many from high-performing schools. Another advantage of the setting was the innovative organizational design of the school which was different than any I had experienced as an educator. The school was self-designated a *Professional Learning Community*, a relatively recent designation and model fashioned after Richard DuFour's model (DuFour & Eaker, 1998). The district had researched the model for years and decided that the collaborative and collective inquiry features of the model fit the middle school model well. TPLS was the first of twenty-seven schools in the district to actually make the necessary organizational and leadership changes to move forward with the new design.

In an effort to improve school improvement and enhance student achievement, a professional learning community "provides a process for stakeholders to engage collaboratively in dialogue" (Huffman & Jacobson, 2003). Due to the inherent weaknesses of the top-down administrative leadership, one of which is a "lack of commitment by the faculty" (DuFour & Eaker, 1998, p. 240), the facilitative style becomes more effective. Teachers collaborate constantly, almost to the point where tension was visible earlier in the year in TPLS regarding time management issues:

> We dealt with another situation on the 6th grade and there was some very heated debate about meeting times. I, again thought we're going to have a civil war here, PLC (Professional Learning Community) vs. PLC. And I'm not 100% of why we've been able to break through it with common ground. (Anthony)

DuFour and Eaker (1998) state that "what separates a learning community from an ordinary school is its collective commitment to guiding principles that articulate what the people in the school believe and what they seek to create" (p. 25). Therefore I was able to gather research from a high-performing school of a fully-migrated staff and also gain entry to the inner structure and workings of a innovative, collaborative model supported by school reformers such as Richard DuFour (DuFour & Eaker, 1998) and Michael Fullan (1993). The staff members I interviewed consisted of teachers at all three grade levels, two principals, assistant principals, academically gifted coordinator, and the parent/teacher association president. TPLS, a professional learning community, turned out to be a selling point for the incoming teachers who appeared quite excited about working in a school that featured common planning time, longer planning period, collaborative teams with no designated team leader, and collective accountability. Here is some of the feedback of those interviewed regarding the transition to a more empowered learning setting:

Anthony, an eight year teacher, pointed out that his transition from a high-performing traditional school to a professional learning community school entailed full team collaboration. He pointed out that, "As I come to TPLS and I've been thrown into this team collaboration, that everything is a collaboration; where, in my previous school, nothing was collaboration. It's been an interesting transition because we have to meet about everything." Frank, a 12 year teacher, concurred with Anthony regarding more collaboration with a professional learning community model and added that teachers receive more exposure to varied instructional practices.

Carol, a first year teacher, cited some of the specific advantages of working in a professional learning community model school by pointing to "common assessments" among the teachers. She said that she "can walk down to a teacher's room and she can sit down with me and give me suggestions." This type of peer support is essential for all teachers but particularly beginning teachers like Carol.

The traditional middle school teaming design essentially groups grade levels of students on four teacher teams of approximately 125 students each. Beginning teachers rarely choose what team they will be placed on nor would it matter since they most likely do not know the personnel anyway. A senior or more experienced teacher is generally chosen to be the team leader while beginning teachers learn to defer to experience and status. I have seen many teachers, both young and old, choose not to confront fellow team members regarding questionable decisions made on the team. If a professional and collaborative structure were in place, not headed by arbitrarily appointed team leaders,, these issues would not exist. Yet they do and the residual effects of silence become a decision in itself, a bad decision, since it silences the newcomer's voice. They choose not to fight the battle, particularly as the newest addition to the profession. The dominance of more experienced teachers or teachers as leaders on the teams represents power and power misused in overt or subtle ways becomes a question of control. This implies that in a power structure where one teacher has more dominance over others to make major decisions, the effect often predisposes the teacher towards a stubbornness—a resistance to anything or anyone that threatens the status quo.

The term "voice" will under gird the chapter theme and it is essential that the reader understand my semantic use of the word. The term, voice, is never to be implied in an isolated manner, from a solitary individual. Rather the use of voice in the school setting seeks other voices constantly through socialization. Therefore voice, socialization, and formal socialization or organizational theory will underlie the chapter argument.

ORGANIZATIONAL EFFICACY: THE THEORY OF HOW TEACHERS BECOME AN INTEGRAL PART OF A HIGH-PERFORMING TEAM

Teachers need to feel empowered and competent in order to promote their sense of self-efficacy. In 1977, Albert Bandura developed a social cognitive theory that viewed individuals as 'self-organizing, proactive, and self-regulating rather than reactive and shaped by external events' (Pajares, 2002, p. 116). From the theory, Bandura went on to examine self-efficacy beliefs, individual beliefs in capabilities of performing specific tasks (Bandura, 1977). He discovered that the first years of teaching were crucial to a teacher's sense of self-efficacy since efficacy may be most "malleable early in learning" (Woolfolk Hoy, 2000, p. 2). Beginning teachers walk into a building and onto a team in most middle school organizations. Not fully knowing what to expect, the experience of socialization may be "comparatively intense" (Etzioni, 1975, p. 246). This phenomenon is heightened just before and shortly after the teachers become part of the school (Woolfolk Hoy, 2000). Beginning teachers exhibit a professional vulnerability in the initial stages of teacher entry as their sense of teaching efficacy is in question, their belief in their ability to perform the task of teaching. While teaching efficacy increases during the preservice years, it declines during the student teaching phase (Hoy & Woolfolk, 1990; Spector, 1990). Therefore, beginning teachers may be susceptible to the level of support provided by other teachers or administrators in the initial stages of teaching. Teacher efficacy displays a resistance to change once it has become established (Woolfolk Hoy, 2000). Thus early experiences set the tone for teachers' beliefs in their personal capabilities as effective teachers.

Carl, the principal of TPLS, elaborates on providing support for teachers with the Professional Learning Community model, particularly beginning teachers:

> Any instructional change is going to take place with the teachers. I think, that, in my conversations with teachers, what they've said is it's very, very pow-

erful because you have this sharing of ideas. DuFour calls it the "intellectual capital" (Schmoker, 1999, p. 19). You can pull on all the experiences of teachers, the best of everybody to draw from and that should directly impact the students. That's the key component. I think the team is important, for example, when you bring new people into the organization, especially if you bring in novice teachers. To be able to bring novice teachers into a team, the support they are provided, the expertise they have sitting across the desk from them, is invaluable. I know that in the county there are mentor programs but I would wager that the type of support the novice teacher gets here because of the collaborative culture, far exceeds anything you'd get with the county. So the team is where the greatest changes take place.

Carl's "teaming" is not the traditional middle school team of four teachers with a team leader. The teams in TPLS are larger groups of teachers placed by grade level and smaller groups within the one large group, by content area. When asked if a team leader was necessary in the professional learning community model, he replied:

I'm not sure. I don't know. Team leaders have always been, in my experience, kind of a position that's very ambiguous because it's always difficult to determine what their role is, how much power do they have. The one key component to a team leader is communication. That's what it basically boiled down to and it's pretty much what it is here. They really don't have any more power than anyone else but in traditional schools it might be difficult because if you've had team leaders for years, they thought of themselves as "number one among equals." But here we don't really recognize team leaders. We have a grade level representative who is a conduit for communication but as far as having any more power or influence, I don't see it.

The concept of *organizational efficacy* or *collective efficacy* is an important indicator of how well an organization believes it can develop as a whole. The teachers I spoke with seemed quite confident of their teacher efficacy and competence in the classroom but perceptions of organizational and group competence determine how high-performing a school truly is (Bandura, 1986). For instance, several of the teachers interviewed migrated from a "high-performing school" and believed themselves to be strong teachers in the classroom. However, their belief that the organization as a whole was efficiently run or directed towards addressing student and teacher needs was put in question. In fact, the very definition of what constitutes a high-performing school was redefined. Here is Ellen, a teacher who migrated with 27 years of experience, responding to the question, "Is it possible to have a high-performing school with weak leadership?":

Well, it depends on what you mean by high-performing schools. If you have a middle school that draws on a population with highly educated parents and highly motivated students and that's your basic population...you're going to look good on paper. But if you mean that everyone is high-performing...all students, teachers, administrators, janitorial staff, etc., I would say "No." And eventually that would be reflected in the paper's scores.

Organizational efficacy appears quite high at TPLS, in only its second year. As I walk around the building, sit in on meetings, and talk to the various staff members, a general confidence and enthusiasm is generated. The staff believe themselves capable of setting high goals and finding the motivation to pursue them effectively. Collaboration and empowerment of teachers are essential components to pursue this level of efficacy.

WHAT IS VOICE?

My use of the word, "voice", in the title phrase, "Crying Out Without Voice," proceeds from the Bakhtin school of thought regarding language and consciousness. Mikhail Bakhtin, a Soviet literary scholar, semiotician, and philosopher, experimented with language use and its relationship to psychological processes. Bakhtin posited that voices always exist in a social setting and that each person's voice anticipates another person's. Voices do not exist in isolation in dialogical thinking (Bakhtin, 1981). Surveying the social arena that beginning middle school teachers step into allows us to examine the implications of the teacher's "voice" in a team context. The very basis of beginning teachers' survival depends on the collegial exchange of language and ideas among other teachers. The very basis of beginning teachers' growth, however, depends on the critical exchange of language and ideas among other teachers.

The term "voice" is a much-used term but does it imply mere participation? Verbalization? Representation on a committee? Giving presentations? Sharing information and best practices? It is possible that we think we are lending strong ears to beginning teachers' voices but in fact are not making a significant difference to their growth and belief system. Allen (2004) elaborates the distinction clearly by citing four different types of voices, only one of which leads to veritable transformational change. Allen explains that teachers are often given the following voices: voting voice, advisory voice, delegated voice, and dialogical voice. It is only with the dialogical voice that teachers make major decisions and become part of a high level of collegial networks. The commitment level and risk level for teachers are higher with a dialogical voice since it is the only voice with transformational power. The dialogical voice, the one that is primarily missing in present public school education, is the most essential one for transformation and richer educational experiences. A central question for the dialogical voice is "What will be the impact on others when information is implemented?" (Arnett, 1992, p. 9). Furthermore, the dialogical voice posits two or more people in dialogue processing information yet reflecting on the political, social, and pedagogical implications of their decision. The Brazilian educator, Paolo Freire, believed that to "speak a true word is to meaningfully change the world" (Young & Arrigo, 1999, p. 86). However the concept of reflection and follow-through is vital for the experience. Without reflection, the vitalized learning experience is lost. One of the 6th grade teachers interviewed, Anthony, supported this assertion:

> There are things that even we can do better. One of the things we need to do more is reflection and assessment. As that data comes in, kind of reflecting on what we've done well, and what we need improvement on. If we're going to make it better as a whole school, we need to focus and look at some things on our own PLC (Professional Learning Community group).

In the dialogic sense, the truly transformative sense, teachers' voices are rarely heard and if heard, not taken seriously for the major organizational and curricular changes made (Holmes Group, 1990). Beginning teachers often exit the teaching profession due to their lack of influence in decision-making (Ingersoll, 2001). At the middle school level, the problem is more pronounced since middle school design is of a teaming nature, generally consisting of 2–4 team members, and a consensus is required for major decisions. However, the team leader's voice is more dominant and beginning teachers defer out of respect and avoidance of conflict. A team, by definition, hearkens all voices, integral components of a unified entity responsible for the education of 60–150 students. Suffice to say that if every voice on the team is not "heard", the team's cohesiveness and agenda is imbalanced and valuable input is lost. An ineffective school organization only hurts its most valuable recipients, its children. Every decision made at every public school level must be for the improvement and enhancement of a youngster's educational support. Ellen, a veteran teacher of twenty-seven years, explains why she left her previous school:

> I was frustrated at my former school. I felt that tiny procedures were most important there. I thought the kids were not considered first. And I saw a lot of inequities and I saw poor leadership.

The inefficacy of not listening to and validating the voice of beginning teachers undermines the school's ability to provide coherence, strength, and direction as an organization. Carol, a first year teacher who graduated from a well-known school in the area, praised her teacher education experience in general, but was critical about her validation as a preservice teacher:

One professor was really nice but I almost felt she never really got to know us. She was busy and I never knew whether that was true or not. I felt that maybe she was fake or something. I mean, she got my name wrong 1 ∫ years into the program.

Carol's group of preservice teachers totaled thirty. Ultimately this disconnect, or incongruity affects the preservice students in an adverse manner and can happen in the teacher education setting or at their beginning school. Relationship-building is an integral part of collaborative school cultures. Public school education can never be about "convenience" or an "easier workload." Educators come into the lives of young students who do not get a second chance. Once the damage of ineffective teachers or poor decision-making is done, it is often irreparable.

The Problematic Voice: Teacher Migration

I once worked as an assistant principal with a first year Social Studies' teacher whom we will call Barbara. She was on a four teacher team in a traditional middle school. Barbara was young, dynamic, filled with enthusiasm and had a plethora of exciting ideas. Her students loved her and fed off of her energy. Her classes were exciting, challenging, fun, and deeply insightful. Students were constantly engaged in some higher order activity followed by appropriate reflection and feedback. This was a truly gifted teacher. She stayed for a few years and left that "high-performing" middle school to transfer or migrate to another traditional middle school with more economic and social challenges and lower standardized test scores. Why? For several years this young, dynamic teacher had collaborated on a team where her real voice was not heard but rather her "echo", meaning that her zest, exciting practices, and idealism were tolerated in a collegial manner but not truly validated. Even at the higher level of administration, the direction and vision needed by the teacher was lacking or not clearly defined. This was evident by her feeling 'stuck' on a team for four years where she got along with the other three team members who were all experienced teachers, but did not always embrace her more progressive ideas. The principal was aware of this and decided to keep her on the team for "balance" since Barbara was a young teacher and the other team members were older, with experience. Barbara, talking about her previous high-performing school:

I felt that the school was always about initiatives before they could decide if the current schedule/initiative worked. Being innovative is wonderful, but in many ways it can wear out a staff—especially when the staff never has a vote in the decision-making.

This is a classic case of a teacher crying out "without voice." Barbara finally left, not primarily for the lack of voice but it proved to be a key reason.

Anthony was another teacher who left a high-performing school after seven years to transfer or migrate to another high-performing school in the same area. He made constant references to the lack of true collaboration at the team level for lessons and instructional practices. He was intrigued by the notion of another middle school just two miles away that had just finished its first year modeled on Richard DuFour's *Professional Learning Community* (DuFour & Eaker, 1998), based on content area collaboration and collective inquiry. Many such situations abound of teachers leaving "high-performing" schools to go to other schools, to "migrate" to other schools. A principal of a high-performing school recently told me that she has lost about 80 teachers over a period of six years, an average of 12 teachers lost a year and of those 80, only about six left for retirement reasons. This particular middle school consistently has some of the highest test scores in the county yet teachers still choose to depart when their voices were not "heard."

One out of five beginning teachers leaves the classroom after three years. Younger teachers leave at higher rates than older teachers. The highest turnover is in the fields of special education, mathematics, and science (Ingersoll, 2001). Of those beginning teachers, those who are dissatisfied with student discipline and the school environment are more likely to migrate or leave the profession (Boser, 2000). The 20% turnover representing the exodus rate of beginning teachers is dramatically higher than those in other occupations and suffices to say that such a high turnover rate occurring in the private sector among major corporations would financially and organizationally challenge and eventually undermine the company's viability. In effect, the system would lose money on their investment, the most valuable investment of all, its human resources.

The Preservice Voice

Preservice teachers in teacher education programs are dependent upon instructors to teach them the essentials of curriculum, instruction, pedagogy, methodology and other key features of the world the beginning teacher will call "work." The understanding is that the preservice teacher walks away from the program several years after entry with the rudimentary skills and insight to help start them out in a real classroom with real middle school students. However, research supports that as teachers become more experienced as teachers, they tend not to value this research to the same degree (Gore & Gitlin, 2004). This is largely because, as beginning teachers acquire more experience in the classroom, much of what they learn is on the job, seeking advice from other teachers and administrators. The actual interaction with the students on a consistent basis is often an abrupt entry into the demands of teaching. Mere exposure to the extreme limitations of one cooperating teacher over a few months is not an encompassing experience (McPherson, 2000). How much of the practical day to day classroom management, team verbal exchanges, instructional practices, and knowledge of district and legal guidelines are based on needs not anticipated or focused on in traditional teacher education programs?

A teacher who stands in front of 25 to 30 middle school students, five times a day to teach the same class, knows that there is a significant gap between academic research and classroom practicality. For instance, each student has a face, name, and personality along with specific developmental skills, needs, and desires. At the academic research level, these students remain faceless, nameless, and devoid of personality. Certainly, it is supremely naïve to believe that academic research and teacher education programs can provide a comprehensive agenda that will accurately simulate the plight of the teacher. Nevertheless, the immediate contact and personal context of the classroom setting must be simulated as much as possible. Beginning teachers have practical problems and immediate contexts to take care of. Some examples are the major personality and group differences seen from one class to another. What works for the first period class is totally irrelevant and ineffective for the more challenging sixth period class. What do beginning teachers do with the stubborn and disruptive student who persists with inappropriate behavior? How do beginning teachers understand the details of IEP (Individualized Education Plans) and how do they differentiate instruction for the special programs' child? What effective combinations of differentiation must be employed to account for the heterogeneity of 125 students on a team? Each class is entirely unique and unpredictable. It is this decontextualization and unpredictability that academic research of teacher education programs does not engage at the same level. Beginning teachers in a classroom crisis will look to transfer the theory of university research to their decision making but time does not allow for it. The concrete-specific nature of the situation requires an immediacy and utility not seen in remote teacher education programs. So now the "louder voice" of the teacher educator is faint and barely an echo while beginning teachers shout loudly for help. It is not enough to equip preservice teachers with the requisite methodological skills and learning theory. The induction period must place them in supportive roles while engaging in direct contact with prospective students. The plethora of problem-solving situations that take place routinely in the school setting must be integrated into the teacher education program. Knowledge of organizational dynamics and efficacy is crucial to greater understanding on the part of the beginning teacher. Socialization and its many nuances are also essential to better understand the dynamics of team collaboration and interaction.

Beginning teachers need to see academic researchers and teacher educators in their classrooms helping them with the myriad learning situations to model and share expertise. The perception is that once the beginning teacher has graduated, they are "on their own" which can be terribly daunting. Emotional ties and sound rapport are established between preservice teachers and their teacher educators. The bridges that remain between the university mentor and the public school classroom need to be extended to behind the first year of mentorship. After all, if the effort to support professional growth is an ongoing process and in-service teachers are considered beginning teachers for the first three years, why would the support diminish between the university and public school after the first year? I question the assumption that second and third year teachers need less pedagogical and moral support than first year teachers. It is often the second and third year teachers who still struggle and question their teaching status. Not always receiving it from a receptive administration, these teachers are ripe for teacher migration.

Some beginning teachers in their first year share their thoughts at a high-performing school:

- I almost felt like I wasn't prepared for teaching. I don't know if that's typical of a college. You're not really prepared until you jump into it. We spent an entire semester planning one lesson plan, then the next semester we planned lessons almost every day. So I didn't know why we weren't taught to, not just write a good lesson plan, but also be efficient about it rather than analyze every little word. (Carol)
- (on her cooperating teacher)—I didn't get along with my cooperating teacher. She didn't like me in the classroom and the kids liked me a lot. If my teacher was doing something I knew wasn't right, I couldn't go to her. (Carol)
- Every time I turn around there's paperwork for something. My program didn't really cover a lot of students with special needs, IEPs (Individualized Education Plans), those sort of things I was never introduced to until I was here. There should be some sort of course in undergraduate where they talk about those things, some of those documents used. (Danielle)

Notwithstanding the many close ties established between preservice teachers and their teacher education mentors, the systemic divide between these mentors and university researchers and teachers is significant. The predominance of the term "achievement gap" among student test scores has become so popularized that the problem of the immense gap between the theory of higher education and practice of the real classroom remains subordinated to a secondary position. The qualitative differences between teachers in the same building become subsumed to the more imperious needs of the state legislation and state board of education. This is another gap that seems to be getting far less attention than the "achievement gap." At the public school level, within the immediacy of the "teaching moment", theory is virtually not practical. Teachers plan lessons and coordinate goals with their peers but they teach on their feet. Once the preservice teacher becomes an in-service teacher, the legitimate ties and responsibilities of the teacher educator become slowly dissolved. Perhaps the collegial and familiar ties established by the teacher and teacher educator remain and they see one another on occasion but the in-service teacher is virtually on their own. The professional relationship between the two is not a balanced one since the hierarchical status of the two places the teacher educator at the top of the hierarchy and any research "sharing" is generally not reciprocal either during the preservice and certainly after that time period (Lingard & Blackmore, 1998).

Gore & Gitlin (2004) speculate that the "socializing impact of the workplace for in-service teachers erases the perceived value of educational research" (p. 38). The primary source of moral and management support comes from fellow teachers who share the "immediacy" of the teaching experience (Gore & Gitlin, 2004). Carol, a first year teacher, talks about advice received from experienced teachers:

> All the time, like interims, how to handle parents, lesson plans, students with issues, how to handle counselors, what to expect in interviews, and peer observations. They come in…I actually have to meet a teacher tomorrow who did a peer observation with me and she's supposed to give me suggestions on things I can improve on, any type of constructive criticism.

The other first year teacher, Danielle, added:

> When I first came here, everyone was so willing to help and they understood what it was like. And I think the one piece of advice from several teachers is 'Take time for yourself.' If you don't take that personal time, you'll go crazy and get burned out. I think your professional life is better when you also have a personal life away from it.

Even a skilled administrator cannot truly empathize with beginning teacher's plight since the administrator is removed from the classroom and "spread thin" with discipline referrals, facility, and supervisory assignments. The direct transfer or application of skills acquired by preservice teachers in the university pales as the general context of university theory fades before the specific context of the classroom. How can we correct this disparity and imbalance of the teacher educator/student relationship during the preservice stages and throughout the early years of in-service time? Bonds between the university and public school should never be dissolved. If we understand that continuity, coherence, and stability are three central features of a high-performing organization, we must ensure that this triad is expansive enough to link preschool, elementary school, middle school, high school, and the university.

"Time" and "reflection"—Anthony, the 6th grade teacher, used these two words in conversation with me the other day while discussing the next step for his high-performing school. The grade level teachers in TPLS now have common planning time of ninety minutes daily. However, with planning, grading, PLC meetings, IEP conferences, fieldtrips, assemblies, and parent/teacher conferences, the teachers are actually working with far fewer than ninety minutes. Little time, in fact, remains to carry out group and individual reflective practices that question and assess instructional practices. The teachers are now being asked to generate ample data to assess student academic performance, disaggregate it, and interpret it to further identify problem areas and implement learning objectives. Teachers in general, are not taught how to disaggregate data and analyze the results. This is a skill that the district requires and is assigning site-based teams to attend workshops, and then train the staff over a period of time. Disaggregating data and analyzing results are time and labor intensive. Those 90 minutes diminish further.

It is clear to me and others that more time and focus needs to be spent in the public schools themselves by the academicians (Sachs & Groundwater-Smith, 1999). Academicians consequently become theorist/practitioners and support the immediacy of classroom teaching. If beginning teachers are not going to transfer the pedagogical, curricular, and instructional skills to the classroom on any prolonged basis, what is the purpose of the divide? It is inefficient and a wasted effort of time and human resources. Working side by side on a collaborative project to gather practical and theoretical insights would create a "relational analysis" (Gore & Gitlin, 2004, p. 54). This analysis would dramatically assist in understanding pedagogical practices from diverse viewpoints. What we are looking at is a unique way to alter the organizational power structure and relationship-building between the new in-service teachers and their university educators. Essentially we are beckoning more latitudinal communication between the theoretic and praxis elements, opening up new "spaces of freedom" (Foucault, 1988).

Each new school represents a particular "fit," based on demographics, school leadership, and school climate yet, preservice teachers are prepared more for exclusive methods and foundations courses in teacher education. Beginning teachers lack familiarity with organizational and cultural differences that place them in an emotionally and psychologically challenging setting. This "lack of fit" (Haritos, 2004) between beginning teachers' needs and goals and the demands of the learning environment may result in frustration, alienation, and teacher migration or attrition. Once beginning teachers, already without "voice", are assigned to their schools based on availability, they may feel overwhelmed upon initial interactions with students and new personnel (Kagan, 1992; Virta, 2002). A greater understanding of the school as an organization is imperative for preservice teachers. Those who lack this information, which are the majority of the prospects, encounter difficulty on site adjusting and adapting to organizational changes (Kuzmic, 1994).

A clear example of placing a teacher in an unfamiliar role due to an organizational change is Anthony being asked to compact his 6th grade social studies yearly curriculum into two semester classes with no formal training:

> My professional life has grown each year and I've done a better job each year with the exception of last year where I felt like I professionally didn't do as well. Part of it was going from a year long course to a semester course and never had taught a semester course. Teaching it all in the course of a year to teaching it all in the course of a semester was something that I had a tough time with.

When asked if he received any staff development or personal training regarding the change, Anthony stated:

> No, nothing at all. They gave me more time during the day, 90 minutes but you still had all the external things that took me out of the class...the pictures, the fire drills. I had 90 minutes but I didn't get the same amount of time I had the year before. I didn't feel like I did a great job for those students. It was a decent year but it was my one negative.

Anthony transferred the following year. The school organization and leadership decided to make significant organizational and structural changes to the curriculum and expected the teacher to simply adjust. Notwithstanding the absence of staff development for the young teacher, his equal absence of organizational knowledge left him in his words 'out there' to make the necessary curriculum and instructional changes on his own. His command and degree of networking and intercommunication between key personnel and himself regarding the potential dilemma would have provided him with more moral support and collaborative adjustments.

Highly motivated teachers or whom Fullan (2003) refers to as "positive deviant teachers," are valuable resources to help disseminate best practices and motivate others. They can be used both on and off campus but must create links with other schools and teachers to effect real change in the system. These teachers are teachers who may not be official district mentors yet are dynamic and can have a very positive influence on beginning teachers. More differences among teachers are found classroom-to-classroom in the same building than between schools (Fullan, 2003). This disparity makes a school organization less effective as coherence and continuity of the school mission and goals may be compromised. One of the big advantages of the professional learning community and effective use of these "positive deviant teachers" is that it confronts this dilemma and due to the constant collaboration and consensus, reduces the variation dramatically.

Socialization and Organization: Two Unheard Voices

Beginning teachers enter a teacher education program as preservice candidates with certain predispositions regarding the world. These are based on perceptions of experiences involving family, friends, acquaintances, and sometimes strangers who have a fortuitous impact on their lives. When they enter the teacher education program, they are not walking into the program devoid of personal experiences and previous value statements. In fact, that understanding is often missed or neglected as the prospective teachers are deemed lacking in experience, thus needy recipients of professional knowledge and skills. These prior personal experiences of preservice teachers accompany them and may exert more influence than the teacher education program itself (Su, 1992). This raises questions about the socialization value of the teacher education programs as they presently exist regarding values, beliefs, and attitudes of the preservice teachers who enter them. Su (1992) continues to assert that even after becoming preservice teachers, they continue to "frequently refer to the continuing influence of their own public school education as a strong, early socializing agent" (p. 325). Preservice teachers focus on developing expertise in content areas and delivery and lack the greater understanding of how an organization functions in a social context. They walk into a team structure, a "baptism by fire."

Limited attention is given in teacher education programs to socialization and organizational issues themselves (Ginsburg & Clift, 1990). These two components greet the new teachers, sometimes rather abruptly. Not understanding the school as an organizational institution with its accompanying design, structure, and dynamics, beginning teachers are vulnerable to internal problems that arise and how to handle them. The teachers also tend to look for "solutions" to these problems in the students or teachers themselves instead of understanding the networking and social dynamics that focus on the processes. For instance, one of the biggest and most frustrating challenges for beginning teachers is the student behavior component. Not understanding the behavioral or psychological antecedents of misbehavior such as power, control, lack of recognition, and desire for belonging, beginning teachers can be heard to say that the problem is "out of control" or that the students are "impossible" or "totally disrespectful." The problems than becomes localized to individual, then collective groups of students instead of understanding that many children misbehave because of organizational and structural policies in place at the school. These may include the number of bells, transition time from one class to another, lack of staff supervision, teacher avoidance of rapport with the students, etc. These need to be addressed and questioned in a constructive manner. Negativity can run rampant in an unhealthy school climate when the perception is that the problem is not being addressed properly. Socialization is an ongoing and dynamic process (Waugaman, 1994), not a one-time training program. Preservice teachers must be prepared in this area and organizational dynamics to better confront and understand how an effective system functions.

Becoming Social Within a Team: The Existing Voice of Power

What prepares beginning teachers for the socialization setting? Besides understanding the multiple learning strategies and modes of students, curriculum and instructional methods, and educational philosophies, preservice teachers are not fully prepared for the interplay of power and control that takes place in a team setting. This is due to the power inherent in the team leader position, a power that carries weight with decision-making. One notable instance of this was when an experienced team leader submitted discipline referrals for her younger protégé to me as the assistant principal. Generally, when a student misbehaves in a class and the infraction is of a more serious nature, the teacher of the class submits a discipline referral form with their name on it. In this case, the team leader wrote down the teacher's name and her name. It was difficult to determine whose class the student was in. I asked the team leader if she would please allow her teammates to submit their own referrals and she became upset and adamant in her refusal to comply. She said that she was 'representing' her team. In fact, she was usurping the younger teacher's authority and autonomy. The younger teacher mentioned to me that it 'wasn't worth the battle.' Instances such as these are carried out often in middle school team settings. It is better to avoid possible confrontation and withdraw than exacerbate team harmony.

In most cases, a more senior teacher will be designated as the team leader and beginning teachers defer, at first out of respect, then to avoid confrontation. This psychological posturing diminishes the opportunity for beginning teachers to lend a voice and subsequent input to strengthen the team and business runs on autopilot. Valuable opportunities are lost to collaborate and create dynamic learning environments for students. Traditional middle school team structures set up uneven power constructs that can intimidate new teachers. The structure becomes a hierarchy with top-down information flow instead of a facilitative infrastructure where all voices are heard. TPLS, working with the professional learning community model, forgoes team leaders, substituting a rotating system of all teachers in the group. The idea seems to be working effectively and all teachers have a voice.

Another area of concern for the preservice teacher is being assigned to only one cooperating teacher. The success of the student is largely dependent upon the chemistry between the cooperating teacher and the student. Should the cooperating teacher be less "cooperative" than the student needs, the experience is a negative one. The overall experience, meant, in theory, to be a broadening, expansive one, often turns out to be a bitter, intimidating one. Here are the thoughts of two first year teachers in TPLS:

> I didn't get along with my cooperating teacher. She didn't like me in the classroom and the kids liked me a lot. I'm a nonconfrontational person but she created issues so I struggled a lot (Carol).

Carol ended up seeking advice from her friend's cooperating teacher who was a "lot more professional." Danielle, another first year teacher, added:

> It was a bit rocky. I did my student teaching with a teacher who was teaching for thirty-two years and she had certain things in place....not that I came in and challenged them but I also had ideas of my own. It was hard to be creative in that atmosphere.

My experience in the public school system is that these preservice teachers would benefit much more concretely from undergoing a more situated learning internship than being assigned to one cooperating teacher. The situated learning internship would assign them to one school but in different roles over a period of time. For instance, a six month internship would involve rotating for one month among core classes, technology and media personnel, special programs, administration, elective classes, and the parent and business community. In this manner, the preservice teacher would become exposed to and familiar with key departments and features of how a public school operates and functions from a more comprehensive, realistic view. This would allow their entry into the school to be less fraught with unknowns. Danielle, reflecting:

> My program didn't really cover a lot of students with special needs, IEPs (Individualized Education Plans), those sorts of things I was never introduced to until I was here. There should be some sort of course in undergraduate where they talk about these things, some of those documents used.

Beginning teachers are assigned to a middle school team with a dozen or so special education students. Each one of the students has an IEP and IEP meetings are conducted throughout the year with the parent attending. These teachers know virtually nothing about the legalities and district requisites that are part of the protocol in those meetings. That places the beginning teachers in an extremely awkward situation since a violation or error in practice in the classroom or during the meeting can possibly lead to a lawsuit.

Beginning teachers enter a dual world, a balance of navigating through social civilities and showing politeness towards older team members at the same time they seek to lend a unique voice to the team. If the power distribution among the team members is not symbiotic and balanced, beginning teachers recede and isolate themselves. Understanding that no team is perfectly "balanced," beginning teachers in the professional learning community are part of a larger grade level group who meet regularly and everyone's voice is heard. No one teacher is assigned or delegated as the information vehicle or spokesperson unless the entire group feels comfortable with the decision. The outer appearance of beginning teachers on a traditional team may seem normal, with the customary greetings, smiles, and pleasantries but inside the frustration mounts. This sense of isolation and pretense of professional contact may lead to teacher attrition or turnover (Collins, 1999; Luft, 1992/1993). In public schools we "choose our battles" and the invested power and dominance of key figures in the school building have constructed their voice over years of seniority. A coalition of more senior educators can stifle and increasingly pose almost insurmountable walls for beginning teachers. Granted, cases abound with responsible experienced teachers serving as excellent role models and mentors to beginning teachers. However, my experience has shown that the pervasive negativity and power of control exhibited by key figures in the organization has a damaging effect. Beginning teachers, by lieu of their relative inexperience in the school setting, withdraw silently. Administrators are often reluctant to confront these key figures who may have a commanding voice in the community and throughout the school. Consequently, an issue is minimized or diverted unless it causes a true threat to the school's mission and value system.

THE BALANCE BETWEEN THE COLLABORATIVE VOICE AND THE AUTONOMOUS VOICE

Professional Learning Communities and Future Challenges

Professional Learning Communities present themselves as largely collaborative by design. DuFour refers to the foundation as "a group of collaborative teams that share a common purpose" (1998, p. 26). As I have attended all the PLC (Professional Learning Community) weekly meetings at the 6th grade level, I have noticed a recurrent theme among the twelve teachers when they are assembled; concern for greater time management. TPLS is a high-performing school with a very popular principal and many excellent teachers who "migrated" to the school to have an opportunity to work in a quality educational setting and share collaborative practices.

The reality of teacher autonomy and teacher collaboration is now emerging as several teachers are feeling frustrated that they have to attend so many meetings and talk about noninstructional issues. Tom, a 6th grade science and math teacher said it was like 'listening to twelve different opinions.' The demands on the teachers' time in the collaborative setting are starting to become greater after a highly successful year last year of learning how to work together. Fullan (1993) warned of this potential dilemma when he wrote of the "uncritical conformity to the group, unthinking acceptance of the latest solution, suppression of individual dissent" (p. 34). What I am observing presently is the mounting frustration of teachers understanding the importance of planning with co teachers but not willing to join the larger groups for diminished productivity sessions. Conflict and tension with fellow teachers in the same grade level leads to emotional withdrawal and a dispassionate participation. So as to avoid a direct confrontation, teachers concede by either remaining silent or discreetly voicing their concern to a trusted peer. How can beginning teachers balance teacher collaboration with individual autonomy? Now, the added concern of a data-driven curriculum and organization in the second year is of mounting concern because teachers just do not have the time. That is a recurring theme. Let us look a bit deeper at the concept of teacher collaboration.

In theory, collaboration at the public school level is promising and encouraging. Anytime teachers can get together to share their practices and expertise, students will benefit. As long as the process is democratic and all have a voice, the process can be successful. In practice, however, teachers are not conditioned, trained, or prepared for collaborative work. Britzman (1986) refers to teachers' autonomy as "invisible walls" created by the "culture of teaching." These "invisible walls" ensure privacy and autonomy and much collaboration only invites noninstructional conferences involving parent/teacher conferences, Individualized Education Plan meetings, field trips, awards assemblies, fundraisers, etc. Initial steps towards collaboration bring updates on teachers' progress and pacing within the curriculum with no serious time for reflection on why they are teaching what they are teaching. Teachers are not trained to collaborate and the profession has been a highly individualistic endeavor. Frank, with thirteen years experience, says:

> Most teachers are uncomfortable working with other teachers. It's probably the most difficult part about our work here because we've never done it before...learning to make concessions, to listen to other peoples' viewpoints, being willing to question things that we've done forever. A teacher's work is very personal to them, close to their hearts, investing in themselves completely. And when you can close your door and do that completely, you're like the master hero of the universe and to open that up to other people for scrutiny is incredibly difficult. And in most middle schools there's no opportunity, no time, and no instruction on how to do it. Even if you wanted to do it, it would be so uncomfortable that you would back away from it real quick.

An apparent inherent irony of the collaborative, collegial, and democratic model is that schools become more political (Blase & Blasé, 1999) and the socialization of its members vie for control which is ultimately power. The proposed dismembering of the traditional four teacher team now enters a sociopolitical arena when entire grade levels are involved. Granted, breakout groups of three or four teachers in the same content areas can still maintain coherence, direction, and effectiveness for there are far fewer personalities to contend with. However, the larger the group, the more difficult it appears to conduct an effective and time-costly meeting of mutual trust and knowledge-building. Beginning teachers are constructing an "identity" and opportunities must be granted to "hear their stories" to further develop that identity (Harris, 1995). Problems surface when other staff members (except assigned mentors) do not afford them the time to listen and internalize their experiences (Rogers & Babinski, 1999).

Social processes and problems are fluid in this social world, not static or fixed. Most preservice programs do not adequately address the "peer socialization processes in schools" (Feiman-Nemser, 2001). If a school endeavors to foster a truly 'collaborative' organization, it becomes a community and thus should invite preservice teachers into that community (Rosenholtz, 1989). Teachers taught to teach in professional "isolation" find collaborative practices challenging and often difficult. Two kinds of cultures have been traditionally awaiting teachers' entry into the school building: *cultures of individualization* with relative teaching isolation and occasional sharing with peers (Little, 1990) and *balkanized cultures* where teachers work in self-contained groups, often according to content areas

(Hargreaves, 1994). Competition generally takes place between the varied groups for resources. The very nature of the two aforementioned cultures serves as organizational barriers to veritable professional relationships among teachers. Preservice teachers trained for "professional isolation" (Avila de Lima, 2003, p. 216), devoid of socialization and collaborative skills, are teachers destined for frustration and teacher migration and possible exodus from the profession itself.

THE VOICE OF THE FUTURE

One of the biggest challenges for collaborative ventures such as the Professional Learning Community models in the future will be how to balance the autonomy and creative nature of the teacher as individual with the openness and collaborative nature of working with peers.

My observations of teachers in TPLS are promising, observing productive and enthusiastic dialogues regarding planning and lesson plans. What I have not seen yet are an extended dialogue into the reflective practices regarding curricular choices and educational philosophy. The school is working towards this goal and the teachers are aware of it; but, only time will allow for it and time is limited to little more than four hundred minutes during the school day. Further research on the evolution of the school over the next three years would reveal more about the professional learning community.

My eight years as a public school administrator affords me a retrospective and panoramic view of the evolution of beginning teachers and the demands placed upon them by federal, state, and local governments. Added to these demands are the formidable tasks of quality lesson plan preparation, classroom management, differentiated learning situations, and parental interaction. In the midst of this compilation of specialized and excessive responsibilities, professional educators and policy analysts call for collaborative designs to foster and enhance closer and more cohesive networks of professional peers. These proposals are admirable and are working in schools all over the country. However, without the understanding that beginning teachers' experiences are embedded in a socialized matrix, involving status, language, power, and organizational dynamics, beginning teachers are lost.

Hargreaves (1997) cites the uncertainty whether teachers will truly be able to work collaboratively in the "post-modern age" or become "deprofessionalized" due to the excessive demands nonexistent twenty years earlier (p. 86). The very nature of learning for both students and teachers is changing dramatically so it is not simply a question of more demands but rather more demands and adaptation to new manners of learning (American National Commission on Teaching, 1996). This is in the midst of a high-stakes testing environment.

The very nature of teaching beckons change because the very nature of learning is also changing. Without sound learning, there is no sound teaching. As educators, we often tend to associate learning with students and teaching with teachers. The successful schools of the future will erase these psychological paradigms and true teachers will never stop learning. That is a voice that we all must hear, a voice ringing clear into the hopeful future.

In conclusion, I cite Danielle, a first year teacher at TPLS, who, when asked if she wanted to share some final thoughts with me during an interview, said:

> When I was going over these questions, I realized that I'm seven weeks into being a real teacher so it was very helpful as a professional to have me reflect on these questions. I realized that having taken time to sit down and think about these things was really helpful to me.

Let us all listen to the voices of our best teachers. If they do not find their voice in education, they will look for it elsewhere. It is time for us to listen.

REFERENCES

Allen, L. (2004). From votes to dialogues: Clarifying the role of teachers' voices in school renewal. *Phi Delta Kappan, 86*(4), 318–321.

The American National Commission on Teaching. (1996). *Report on the National Commission on Teaching and America's future, what matters most: Teaching for America's future, 1996*, p. 13. New York: National Commission on Teaching & America's Future.

Arnett, R. (1992). *Dialogic education: Conversation about ideas and between persons.* Carbondale: Southern Illinois University Press

Avila de Lima, J. (2003). Trained for isolation: The impact of departmental cultures on student teachers' views and practices of collaboration. *Journal of Education for Teaching, 29*(3), 197–217.

Bakhtin, M. M. (1981). *The dialogic imagination.* Austin: University of Texas Press.

Bandura, A. (1977). Self-efficacy: Toward a unifying theory of behavioral change. *Psychological Review, 84,* 191–215.

Bandura, A. (1986). *The social foundations of thought & action.* Englewood Cliffs: Prentice-Hall.

Bandura, A. (1997). *Self-efficacy: The exercise of control.* New York: W. H. Freeman.

Bandura, A. (2001). Social cognitive theory: An agentive perspective. *Annual Review of Psychology, 52,* 1–26.

Blasé, J., & Blasé, T. (1999). Principals' instructional leadership and teacher development: teachers' perspectives. *Educational Administration Quarterly, 35*(3), 349–378.

Boe, E., & Gilford, D. (Eds). (1992). *Teacher supply, demand, and quality: Policy issues, models and databases.* Washington DC: National Academy Press.

Boser, U. (2000). A picture of the teacher pipeline: Baccalaureate and beyond. *Education Week Supplement, Quality Counts 2000: Who should teach? XIX* (18), 17.

Britzman, D. P. (1986). Cultural myths in the making of a teacher: Biography and social structure in teacher education. *Harvard Educational Review, 54*(4), 442–456.

Collins, T. (1999). *Attracting and retaining teachers in rural areas* (Report No. EDO-RC–7). Charleston, WV: ERIC Clearinghouse on Rural Education and Small Schools. (ERIC Document Reproduction Service No. ED438152).

Conley, R. (2006). *Teacher migration from high-performing middle schools: A case study.* North Carolina State University, Raleigh, N.C. www.lib.ncsu.edu/theses/available/etd-03062006-105250.

DuFour, R., & Eaker, R. (1998). *Professional learning communities at work: Best practices for enhancing student achievement.* Bloomington, IN: National Educational Service.

Etzioni, A.. (1975). *Comparative analysis of complex organizations.* New York: Free Press of Glencoe.

Feiman-Nemser, S. (2001). From preparation to practice: Designing a continuum to strengthen and sustain teaching, *Teachers College Record, 103*(6), 1013–1055.

Foucault, M. (1988). Truth, power, self: An interview with Michel Foucault. In L. H. Martin, H. Gutman & P. H. Hutton (Eds). *Technologies of the self: a seminar with Michel Foucault* (pp. 16–49). Amherst: University of Massachusetts Press.

Fullan, M. (1993). *Change forces: Probing the depths of educational reform.* London: Falmer Press.

Fullan, M. (2003). Change agent: An interview with Michael Fullan. *Journal of Staff Development, 24*(1), 55–58.

Ginsburg, M. B., & Clift, R. T. (1990). The hidden curriculum of preservice teacher education. In W. R. Houston (Ed.). *Handbook of research on teacher education* (450–465). New York: Macmillan.

Gore, J. M., & Gitlin, A. D. (2004). (Re)visioning the academic–teacher divide: Power and knowledge in the educational community. *Teachers and Teaching: Theory and practice. 10*(1), 35–58.

Grissmer, D., & Kirby, S.N. (1997). Teacher turnover and teacher quality. *Teachers College Record, 99*, 45–56.

Hargreaves, A. (1994). Changing work cultures of teaching. In F. Crowther, B. Caldwell, J. Chapman, G. Lakomski, & D. Ogilvie, (Eds.), *The workplace in education: Australian perspectives—First Yearbook of the Australian Council for Educational Administration* (pp. 39–51). Sydney: Edward Arnold.

Hargreaves, A. (1997). The four ages of professionalism and professional learning. *Unicorn, 23*(2), 86–114.

Haritos, C. (2004). Understanding teaching through the minds of teacher candidates: A curious blend of realism and idealism. *Teaching and Teacher Education, 20*(6), 637–654.

Harris, D. L. (1995). *Composing a life as a teacher: The role of conversation and community in teachers' formation of their identities as professionals.* Unpublished doctoral dissertation, Michigan State University. UMI Dissertation Abstracts, UMI Number: 9605874.

Holmes Group (1990). *Tomorrow's schools. A report of the Holme's Group.* East Lansing, MI: Author.

Hoy, W. K., & Woolfolk, A.E. (1990). Socialization of student teachers. *American Educational Research Journal, 27,* 279–300.

Huffman, J., & Jacobson, A. (2003). Perceptions of professional learning communities. *Leadership in Education, 6*(3), 239.

Ingersoll, R. (2001). Teacher turnover, teacher shortages, and the organization of schools. *Teaching Quality Policy Briefs, 3,* 1–7.

Ingersoll, R. M. (2002). The teacher shortage: A case of wrong diagnosis and wrong prescription. *NASSP Bulletin, 86*(631), 16–30.

Kagan, D. M., (1992). Professional growth among preservice and beginning teachers. *Review of Educational Research, 62,* 129–169.

Kuzmic, J., (1994). A beginning teacher's search for meaning: Teacher socialization, organizational literacy, and empowerment. *Teacher and Teacher Education 10*(1), 15–27.

Lingard, B., & Blackmore, J. (1998) *Education, Challenges for the Social Sciences and Australia* (Vol. 1, pp. 101–112). Canberra: Academy of the Social Sciences in Australia.

Little, J. W. (1990) The persistence of privacy: Autonomy and initiative in teachers' professional relations, *Teachers College Record, 91*(4), 509–536.

Luft, V. (1992–93). Teacher recruitment and retention practices in rural school districts. *The Rural Educator 14*(2), 20–24.

Lytle, S., & Cochran-Smith, M. (1990). Learning from teacher research: A working typology. *Teachers College Record, 92,* 83–103.

McPherson, S. (2000). *From practicum to practice: Two beginning teachers' perceptions of the quality of their preservice preparation.* Unpublished master's thesis. Queen's University Faculty of Education, Kingston, Ontario.

Murnane, R. J., Singer, J. D., Willett, J. B., Kemple, J. J., & Olsen, R. J. (1991). *Who will teach? Policies that matter.* Cambridge, MA: Harvard University Press.

North Carolina Department of Public Instruction (2005). School Report Cards.

Pajares, F. (2002). Gender and perceived self-efficacy in self-regulated learning. *Theory Into Practice, 41*(2), 116–125.

Price, J. (1989). The impact of turnover on the organization. *Work and Occupations, 16,* 461–473.

Rosenholtz, S. (1989). *Teachers' Workplace: The Social Organization of Schools* (New York, Teachers College Record).

Sachs, J., & Groundwater-Smith, S. (1999). The changing landscape of teacher education in Australia, *Teaching and Teacher Education, 15*(2), 215–227.

Schmoker, M. J. (1999). *Results: The key to continuous improvement, 2nd ed.* Alexandria, VA: Association for Supervision and Curriculum Development.

Spector, J. E. (1990, April). *Efficacy for teaching in preservice teachers.* Paper presented at the annual meeting of the American Educational Research Association, Boston, MA.

Su, J. Z. X. (1992). Sources of influence in preservice teacher socialization. *Journal of Education for Teaching, 18*(3), 239–258.

Virta, A. (2002). Becoming a history teacher: Observations on the beliefs and growth of student teachers. *Teaching and Teacher Education*, 687–698.

Wake County Public School System (2005). Department of Evaluation and Research.

Waugaman, W. R. (1994). Professionalization and socialization in interprofessional collaboration. In R. M. Casto, & M. C. Julia (Eds.), *Interprofessional care and collaborative practice* (pp. 71–94). Belmont, CA: Brooks/Cole.

Woolfolk Hoy, A. (2000). *Changes in teacher efficacy during the early years of teaching.* Paper presented at the annual meeting of the American Educational Research Association, New Orleans, April 28, 2000.

Young, T. R., & Arrigo, B. A. (1999). *The dictionary of critical social sciences.* Boulder, CO: Westview Press.

CHAPTER 13

TEACHING THEORY AS "OTHER" TO WHITE URBAN PRACTITIONERS

Mining and Priming Freirean Critical Pedagogy in Resistant Bodies

Sherick A. Hughes
University of Maryland

ABSTRACT

This chapter addresses two primary questions: How did I decide to equip my body for meeting the student body at the intersection of racialization, conscientiousness, and resistance? How did I attempt to teach social theory to predominantly white, able-bodied practitioners in a manner that is critical of their own sub-conscientious participation in the detrimental forms of "othering" that permeate pre-K–16 settings? I offer an approach to mining and priming a Freire-based critical pedagogy in order to help my students and me (a) locate social theory in our daily experiences of privilege and oppression as grade school teachers, administrators, and teacher educators (b) to read the privilege and oppression of our worlds into the words of social theory, (c) to position social theory in action as "theorizing," which void of prac-

Unsettling Beliefs: Teaching Theory to Teachers, pages 245–271
Copyright © 2008 by Information Age Publishing

tice is rendered "off-base" at best, and (d) to position practitioners' work as "practicing," which if completely void of theorizing might be rendered sloppy, short-sighted, and wrought with preventable educational errors. To conclude, I make final remarks that summarize my "findings," [which are not intended to be exhaustive], but to be transferable while naming, organizing, and summarizing what I am learning about teaching theory to practitioners as "other."

PROLOGUE

It seems that no matter how much some of my students and I attempt to critically and conscientiously resist it, "the body" in our graduate classroom of predominantly white able-bodied urban grade school practitioners "is no longer *an object in the world...*it is our *point of view on the world,* the place where the spirit takes on a certain physical and historical situation" (Merleau-Ponty, 1964, p. 5, italics in original). By the time I reached my second semester at the university, I had already amassed a couple of graduate student whistleblowers among the theory class of practitioners. One such student of color, Karma (note: pseudonyms are used throughout the chapter to protect all students' anonymity) followed me to my office one evening during that Spring semester of 2004 near midterm to lament:

> you should've seen how they [several of her White classmates with whom I was having the most difficulty engaging], looked at each other and looked at you and looked back at each other, after you turned your back to the classroom. They were whispering something and acting like they were surprised and had a problem with learning from a Black male professor ever since the first day of class... I noticed also that when you give us handouts/rubrics and explained them, some of them still want to do what they've always done and they disrespect your assignments in a way that is not so for other professors, White professors; no, when White professors give out rubrics with little explanation, I might hear them complain after class, but they don't do that *questioning your credibility thing* and disrespect to the White professors in the classes I have with them... It's not fair to you...

Another student of color, Paula (a pseudonym) from the same course section emailed me after White graduate students "acted out" and resisted the class-elected facilitator (another student of color) as well as the peer-critique assignment I left for the class, while I was away presenting at AERA2004.

> During my college experience, I have only had a total of three Black instructors. Each one of you has experienced the wrath of "White privilege." I wasn't aware of what it was until I took your class. My first Black instructor at a com-

munity college was traumatized, questioned at every turn about his knowledge and teaching methods by the white students. He, a few weeks into the
semester, quit.

My second Black instructor, also at that college, was a female who taught psychology. The white students tormented her each and every day, once again
questioning her knowledge about the subject, the way she spoke, and the way
she pronounced words. She received such bad evaluations that she also
resigned, but only after she had a nervous breakdown. It appears to me that
because of the mental thoughts held by these students, they felt that as White
students, they were not receiving the education they were entitled to because
the instructor was Black.

I don't know if I'm getting out of your class what you are intending for me to
get, but I do have a different understanding of the issue than I did when I
first entered. There is no doubt that racism is here to stay. The faces of it
change, and at times it becomes more subtle and covert, but the purpose of it
is still to dominate and control. I don't feel that what happened to the other
instructors will happen to you, but as a Black person, it hurts me to think that
someone can just hurt someone for no other reason other than they are of a
different "race." I hope I haven't overstepped my bounds in what I have
shared with you, but it was on my heart to do so, just so you would know that
someone else knows what it's really all about.

As my former students of color describe above, the moment I step into a
graduate classroom of white, able-bodied grade school practitioners, I feel
marked pejoratively as "other" by some students. It is an "othering" based
upon the first glimpse of me that is socially constructed and devolving
"from measurement against an unnamed, absent [physical] standard"
(Laubscher & Powell, 2003, p. 8). I also identify myself as "other" in this
pedagogical situation. Thus, it is also imperative to explore relationships
between white graduate students' communicative behavior directed toward
me as other, my self-identification as "other," and the how negotiation of
"self and other" vs. "self as other" plays out in a social theory course of
white, urban grade-school practitioners.

INTRODUCTION

Helfenbein and Diem (2006) propose that some distinct and specific differences arise when contrasting approaches to "effectively" teaching theory
to stereotypic full-time graduate students of education versus "effectively"
teaching theory to a graduate student audience of currently practicing novice and veteran teachers and administrators. I conceptualize a measurement of effectiveness here by thinking through "the degree to which
students by the end of the semester can demonstrate an ability to compre-

hend, analyze, apply, synthesize, and evaluate (adapted from Bloom's Taxonomy) educational theorizing (Noblit, 1999) as lived "practitioner" experience. Noblit (1999), creator of the meta-ethnography, equates social theory to pottery, it cracks, it breaks down, only to be "watered" and replaced by an innovative version of it to explain a new time. Noblit (1999) is not arguing against the idea of generative knowledge. He is arguing against grand theories. For Noblit, theory is not fact, but historicism, another explanation of lived experiences told in its own relative present time, about the past for the future. It is in this light, that I view my predecessors, and my own autoethnography with any working transferable knowledge and theorizing that arises from it. Two of my social theory-based courses attempt to engage graduate students in dialectical discussions and critical demonstrations of social theorizing coupled with practicing (i.e., critical praxis) to minimize educational privileges and oppression in urban preK–16 education.

I adopted an approach to mine and prime Freirean critical pedagogy in order to help my students and me (a) locate social theory in our daily experiences of privilege and oppression as grade school teachers, administrators, and teacher educators (b) to read the privilege and oppression of our worlds into the words of social theory, (c) to position social theory in action as "theorizing," which void of practice is rendered "off-base" at best, and (d) to position practitioners' work as "practicing," which if completely void of theorizing might be rendered sloppy, short-sighted, and wrought with preventable educational errors. With such a foundation for critical praxis, it is my hope that my students and I might create together better approaches to curriculum, unit, and lesson planning that reflects the type of teacher and administrative leadership inherent in Freirean critical pedagogy. As I attempt to teach social theory in this setting in this way, I am learning to be better prepared for failure yet, to survive and to engage again a successful struggle for hope. Each day of the semester a predominantly white and able student body is there awaiting my body to learn and teach together at the risky intersection of racialization, conscientiousness, and resistance. This chapter presents my plight to engage my student body at that intersection as "other." It addresses two primary questions: How did I decide to equip my body for meeting the student body at the intersection of racialization, conscientiousness, and resistance? How did I attempt to teach social theory to predominantly white, able-bodied practitioners in a manner that is critical of their own sub-conscientious participation in the detrimental forms of "othering" that permeate pre-K–16 settings?

In the remaining portions of this text, main points are organized in the following manner. First, I describe the Freirean critical pedagogical framework used to theorize and synthesize my ideas. I begin this part of the chapter by revisiting the subtitle of this chapter, which serves as a metaphor for a significant portion of my claims, before delving into the particularities of the autoethnographic qualitative method employed here. Next, my positionality and reflexive purview is made more explicit followed by demographic details of the setting of the social theory-based courses examined here. Then, I offer narratives illustrating several white student bodies' practitioner experiences of social theory and the two variant categorical forms of resistance that I engaged along with them. I demonstrate how I began mining and priming Freirean pedagogical strategies and the promise and challenges of implementing these strategies in my course to address such resistance. To conclude, I make final remarks that summarize my "findings," [which are not intended to be exhaustive], but to be transferable while naming, organizing, and summarizing what I am learning about teaching theory to practitioners as "other." In essence, this chapter employs a particular theoretical framework and qualitative method that might better account for blemishes in my pre-K–16 research, teaching, and service that surface upon a deeper examination of my pedagogy as a physically identifiable Black American "other."

THEORETICAL FRAMEWORK

Freirean Critical Pedagogy: Mining and Priming

If anyone understood the life challenges and triumphs of educational mining and priming was educator Paulo Freire, who writes "my condition didn't allow me to have an education. Experience showed me once again the relationship between social class and knowledge" (1974, p. 5). Freire is well known for his critique of the what he perceived as a banking model in education, where teachers learn to put knowledge in students, and created a notion of teaching as mining where first and foremost the teachers responsibility is to pull knowledge out—to build upon the knowledge students bring to the pedagogical situation (Freire, 1974, p. 76). The term "primer" is used commonly in the titles of textbooks and it is seemingly intended to reflect motives of putting something into students' minds. It is also common for the term "primer" to conjure the phrase "priming the pump." I remember priming the pump at my grandmother's house. Without indoor plumping until the 1980s and the grandchild of a slave, her family had to mine for water. Once the mining was complete and the water pump was in place, the family used water collected from a previous day's rain to "prime the pump." Priming the pump involved the combination of using the body to pour rain water into the top of the pump and moving vigorously the handle of the pump up and down to build air pressure into the pump in order to draw water out. After enough priming with the previously collected water, the pump draws out water well beyond the quantity and quality of that which was used for primer that day. It is my intention to use Freirean critical pedagogy for the purposes of mining and priming in this way—both putting in the collected substance of education and drawing out the yet unseen educational substance within students. This dual mining and priming approach attempts to push students to take ownership of critical pedagogy and to adapt and modify it to enhance their school leadership roles, and to fill their particular space in ways that neither Freire nor I might have imagined or have been able to accomplish in the same way in "their" space.

The esteemed Freire spent a lifetime advocating for Brazilian peasants, and from this experience he developed theories for conscientious thought and action in pedagogy or "critical consciousness" (a process known in Portuguese as *conscientização*). Freirean critical pedagogy involves dialectical conversations between teachers and students, where the teacher listens to understand what knowledge students already bring to the subject based on their personal learning experiences of the world. Through this approach, in 1962, his critical literacy groups taught 300 peasants to read and write in just 45 days (Gadotti, 1994, p. 15). In less than ten years, Freire was exiled from Brazil, not for teaching peasants literacy skills, per se, but for teaching peasants how to read their worlds of oppression so that they might liberate themselves. In the 1980s, he was welcomed home to national acclaim in Brazil.

The late Brazilian educator is responsible for much of the way critical pedagogy is considered today (Wink, 1990, p. 90). This form of critical pedagogy as implemented with marginalized groups influences my own work, including my doctoral dissertation and book titled *Black Hands in the Biscuits Not in the Classrooms: Unveiling Hope in a Struggle for Brown's Promise.* Educational researchers cannot agree upon one critical pedagogical form, nor should we do so in my opinion. Hence, I label the particular theoretical mining and priming I pursue when teaching theory to practitioners, a Freirean Critical Pedagogical approach. The reason I engage a mining and priming of Freire and an adaptation of his work is because we represent two separate realities. Freire launched his critical pedagogical teams to educate Brazilian peasants; what I call critical pedagogy for his people. I launch critical pedagogical adaptations to enhance the learning situation as a Black tenure track professor with predominantly white grade school practitioners. In short, Freire to a larger degree launched his work with a like ethnic group and I am doing it as an ethnic "other" The particular Freirean theorizing that was applied in my classroom and to this chapter draws from two of his works: (a) *Pedagogy of Hope*, and (b) speech on *Teaching and Learning* transcribed by Joan Wink (2005, pp. 85–90).

In *Pedagogy of Hope,* Freire explains pedagogy of hope and struggle as necessary concomitant forces toward an education strong in social justice, where the adequately educated can transcend social oppression, hopefully without reproducing it. In arguing that hope is a fundamental human need, Friere warns us against separating hope from action. Freire tied all of this specifically to education, in ways I find my student practitioners and I did as we tackled social theorizing. He depicts the union of hope and struggle:

> The idea that hope alone will transform the world…is an excellent route to hopelessness, pessimism, and fatalism. The attempt to do without hope, in the struggle to improve the world, as if that struggle could be reduced to calculated acts alone, or a purely scientific approach, is a frivolous illusion…. without a minimum of hope, we cannot so much as start the struggle. But without the struggle, hope…dissipates, loses its bearing, and turns into hopelessness. One of the tasks of the serious progressive educator, through a serious, correct, political analysis, is to unveil opportunities for hope, no matter what the obstacles may be. (Freire, 1994, p. 8–10)

Like Freire, I want my social theory course to further the process of unveiling educative opportunities for educational hope. My focus speaks particularly to school practitioners and myself. The narratives of this chapter continue to breathe hope today as they trace changes and continuities in the struggle for adequate educational opportunities through a balance of theory and practice.

In his 1993 speech in Southern California on teaching and learning, Freire first stressed that "There is no possibility for teaching without learning. As well as, there is no possibility for learning without teaching" (Wink, 2005, p. 85). After reading this transcription and coupling it with my previous background in Freirean theorizing, I moved beyond understanding pedagogy as the one dimensional art of teaching. Freire's work again, helped me to understand the complexities of our educational settings as multi-dimensional. I now find pedagogy and more specifically critical pedagogy as *the critical art and social science of teaching and learning*—(a) of *sculpting* model units and lessons for all students in attempts to prepare them for survival and self-sufficiency as they graduate from one stage of education in life to the next, (b) of *scaffolding* to *paint* a heightened portrait for all students in attempts to help them reach their highest potential, and (c) of conscientious *performance* with a collage of emotion-evoking and best-practice-content-based instruction methods in attempts to engage an education that instills a critical temper. This critical temper of pedagogy can allow students to recognize and alleviate oppression of self and others while balancing life with the thoughts and actions that breathe hope. There are essentially seven requirements of "progressive teachers" detailed in Freire's

1993 speech. I take these seven requirements quite seriously as I construct and conduct my graduate social theory-based courses each semester.

1. Teachers need to be humble…It is necessary for the progressive teacher to be humble precisely because of the impossibility of separating teaching from learning. If the teacher is not humble, the teacher does not respect the students. It is as if the students have nothing to do in the process of learning but just to listen patiently to the voice of the teacher. This is precisely the totalitarian teacher. The totalitarians do not need to be humble (Wink, 2005, p. 86). Wink (2005) also notes Freire modeling this theme when his young grandson was being ignored in the company of adults, including Maxine Greene, "Every time you ignore a person's question, you dehumanize him" (p. 92).

2. Another condition [requirement] of [progressive] teachers is that they recognized that we are always becoming, because we never just are. We are always becoming…when students come to us, [we need to realize] that they already know many things…it is assumed that the only place for us to know is only in school. We assume that the knowledge of the streets is not important. To think this is a terrible mistake. When kids come to school, they are already able to read the reality. Before reading the words, kids already read the world. (Wink, 2005, p. 86).

3. By teaching, I learn how to teach. It is fantastic that there exists the possibility for me to know much better what it means to be a teacher, precisely because I am teaching (Wink, 2005, p. 87). The teacher grows by teaching the object to be grasped by the students. If the students don't grasp the object with their bare hands, the students only memorize description, but they don't *know* the object. Knowing is not a question of memorization…Knowing is something different. It is kind of an adventure. Knowing is a reinvention of the object being known. It is a recreation. It is a mutual process of teaching and learning. The more the teacher refuses to learn with the students, the less the teacher teaches (Wink, 2005, p. 87).

4. When I say bureaucratic [in this context], I am talking about a teacher's mind becoming bureaucratized. These are people who do exactly what they were told…even when there are structures of society which work to bureaucratize the minds, there is always a possibility for us to be saved…my friends, please don't allow yourselves to fall into the trap of bureaucratization of the mind. React against it so that you may continue to be human. (Wink, 2005, p. 88).

5. Look, we organize the schedule, and when we finish the organization of the schedule, we become less than the schedule….Look,

don't think I am against principles, against discipline, against order. Without these things, we have nothing. However, we are greater than the time, which we organize. If we don't do that, we become machines. Please don't do that (Wink, 2005, p. 89).

6. ...there is no possibility for greater achievement without taking risks. The more we, as teachers, do this [bureaucratization of the mind actions], the less our students are free to risk. Without freedom, you cannot risk. When you are not free, you have to risk in order to get freedom. Teaching is not [like] spending a weekend on a tropical beach. It is to be committed to the process of teaching, the adventure, and to the students (Wink, 2005, p. 89).

7. We have to bear witness for students...how is it possible for me to speak about risk if students discover that I never risked....Education is, above all, testimony. If we are not able to give testimony of our action, of our love, we cannot help the students to be themselves (Wink, 2005, p. 89).

QUALITATIVE METHODS

Autoethnography

Similar to Laubscher and Powell (2003), this chapter employs the particular techniques of critical reflexive autoethnography. A quarter of a century ago, Hayano (1979) spoke to the potentialities of autoethnography. He actually describes autoethnography's capacity to create an alternative venue for marginalized voices. Reed-Danahay (1997) describes autoethnography as enlisting "a rewriting of the self and the social" (p. 4). The questions of my chapter lend themselves more to the autoethnographic techniques, precisely because of the qualitative genre's capacity to engage first person voice, and to embrace the conflict of writing against oneself as I find myself entrenched in the complications of my position of teacher as "other." Lastly, I might also begin to think of autoethnography as pedagogy (e.g., Dalton, 2003; Banks & Banks, 2000) in and of itself; as an innovative teaching and learning tool for gathering information and guiding critical praxis.

Data, Interpretation, and Analysis

Data in this chapter are in the form of narratives from the four students (one white male and three white females) that I felt built the most challenging barriers initially limiting my abilities to reach them with social theory in the ways that I intended. Narratives from a fifth white student (a white female) are presented to illustrate the possibilities of engaging peer-leadership from student practitioners with more "pre-requisite" abilities in social theory. The students were enrolled in one of two of the social theory-based courses I teach—Sociological Foundations of Education (SFE) and Intergroup/Intercultural Education (IIE). Moreover, all narratives here are drawn from my professional journal notes, students' assigned after class comments (ACCs), students' term papers, and random emails from students representing one section of SFE course (Spring, 2005) and one section of the IIE course (Fall, 2004). Thus, an attempt was made to triangulate sources (i.e., data includes narratives of a white male and females; narratives from the SFE and IIE courses; and narratives from me—one voice of evidence that speaks from a targeted, non-white "other's" perspective. This triangulation effort was employed with hopes that it could expose and sift through contradictions en route to an empirical space where more robust and defensible claims are made. Student narratives were then organized according to how they emerged and merged as themes reflecting student resistance and Freirean pedagogy. Themes were considered in relation to the resistance categories of Pare (1994) and Hughes (2005a), as well as Freire's *Pedagogy of Hope* and the seven requirements of "progressive teachers" detailed in his 1993 speech. These procedures help me to organize and theorize attempts at mining and priming Freirean pedagogy in my social theory course of practitioners.

I understand my work itself as a social construction of events leading me to speak in the present about the past for the future (Dr. George Noblit, J. R. Neikirk Professor of Education, UNC-Chapel Hill, 2002, personal communication). Finally, there are two other key issues for which to account in my telling of this story: (a) the constructions of my participants (students' constructions) and, (b) my appropriation of their constructions in my efforts to make them transfer to readers (writing what students shared with me, but organizing it while heavily considering reader diversity). With this information in mind, I set out to offer you as accurate of an account as I can contemplate.

WHO I AM—POSITIONAL AND REFLEXIVE PURVIEW

"You don't look like a professor," I am sometimes told. My body does not match the traditional older white-haired male authority figurine with verbal and nonverbal communicative behaviors that most of my white graduate students have come to expect and to respect. I am a dark brown, 5'10", 248-pound former high school three-sport varsity athlete, and former college Rugby player. I have broad shoulders and a medium able-bodied build that one might expect of a former athlete who still maintains a brisk walking, occasional jogging, and weightlifting routine. I have most visible traditional Northwest African facial features, hair color and texture, and skin color. It is not unusual for me to wear a two-piece suit, button-down shirt and tie the first day. Sometimes my head is bald, sometimes an inch thick, or at times, I have a fade (similar to the crew cut, but with a smoother "faded-looking" hair transition from the thicker hair on the top of the head to the thinner hair of the side of the head and side burns.

I am a product of post-*Brown* Southern schooling. I attended three predominantly white institutions in pursuit of the professoriate. Along the way, I taught as a Teacher's Aid in urban and rural grade schools. I am not a licensed teacher however most white practitioners give me some credence due to the fact that I have successfully taught grade-school students within the last five years. I am a Black man rooted in a working poor class background in NE Albemarle who became more academically, socially, and economically mobile through formal and informal education in ways that most of my counterparts did not. I am a first generation college student who grew up approximately six miles from the Bartlett Plantation where my family was enslaved only four generations ago. Today, I am a tenure track professor at a large Research Intensive, predominantly white university in the Midwest. I am also founder and President of an educational non-profit organization named G3, inc., which slates me as an administrator supervising 6 graduate-level teachers who work with me as Graduate Associates (GAs) to create, advocate, and implement Personal Education Plans for youth and families of the foster care system.

My Courses

There are two graduate student courses in which I enlist practitioners to engage social theory: Intergroup/Intercultural Education and Sociological Foundations of Education. Both courses emphasize multiculturalism and race. White graduate students from both courses offer narratives evidence of the claims and arguments I pursue in this chapter.

Course Description #1 Intergroup/Intercultural Education

This course involves the evolving role of intergroup and intercultural education in the U.S., including the historical and contemporary relationship of schooling and "race" to educational outcomes. In this course, we examine racialized groups of people and the strength of intergroup/intercultural loyalties and divisiveness among and within these groups in the U.S.; thus, to some degree we are interrogating ourselves. While learning about "others" and how to teach "others," we will also engage self-critique and learn how to be critical of "othering." (See Kevin K. Kumashiro (April, 2001, *Ed. Researcher*). This course tends to enroll approximately 20–25 graduate students per semester. Most of those graduate students are matriculating as the MA level.

Course Description #2 Sociological Foundations of Education

This course involves a critical examination of the socio-cultural foundations of schooling in the United States, including purposes of schooling in a multicultural society and the resulting nature of teacher work. It is an exploration of the uses of the sociology of education in the study and practice of education. The course is organized so that as students learn key concepts and theories, they will also use them to analyze, critique, and construct educational lesson plans and simulate instruction. The key premise is that education (and all social life) is a socially constructed endeavor. This perspective has many practical ramifications but we limit ourselves to those involving knowledge, power, social class, gender, race and schooling. This course also tends to enroll 20–25 graduate students per semester with the bulk of them being Master's level students.

MY STUDENT BODIES OF RESISTANCE

Most of the students of Sociological Foundations of Education largely identify as and harbor the somatic characteristics of the U.S. ethnic group that tends to be associated with the word white and female, although both courses posted unusual numbers of white males (approximately 1/5 of the classroom) at the time of this study. They also identify themselves and are identified as "practitioners" in a large public university in the state of Ohio. In the state of Ohio, the law requires teachers to begin their graduate level credit hours within the first two years of teaching, and it also requires them to accrue at least 30 credit hours of graduate work by the end of their fifth year of teaching. Irrespective of one's support or aversion to this law, its consequences undoubtedly contribute to classroom climates replete with a mixture of student actions that I perceive as one of three types of resistance, all encompassing some degree of ignorance.

In my educational life, ignorance has played the role of a sort of social cancer, eating away at my black male, lifelong learning body and seemingly eating away at the part of my white student body controls both symptoms of denial and/or guilt. When the social carcinogenic nature of ignorance enters the bodies of my graduate classroom, it appears to connect to at least the two variant forms of resistance narratives synthesized by Hughes (2005a) (a) Benign Resistance, (e.g., inquisitive, tired, and/or frustrated yet open to new ideas, experiences, challenges, and counter-evidence) and

(b) Malignant Resistance (e.g., harsh, negative, or angry resistance to new ideas, experiences, challenges, and counter-evidence; an effort to become more firmly entrenched in some piece of "knowledge" that has long be taken-for-granted as "Truth"). Hughes' (2005b) work in this chapter is linked to five accompanying resistance behaviors characterized by Pare (1994). By categorizing and locating the type of resistance students bring into the course, I am afforded more signs for how to address their needs allowing us to work together to begin preventing and treating the social cancer that accompanies it. These identified forms of resistance should be contemplated neither as stepwise nor as self-sufficient, but just as I find them to exist: as two volatile expressions that may be identified when ignorance and resistance manifest together in my graduate theory class of practitioners. For instructional and clarification purposes, the illustrative resistance narratives below are placed within Freirean and Resistance theoretical frameworks. These narratives of struggle are not exhaustive, but they do represent *archetypal* cases of both Benign and Malignant Resistance narratives through the lenses one or more white urban practitioners in my social theory-based courses. Ultimately, the resistance portion of this chapter is followed by my attempts to mine and prime Freirean Critical Pedagogy of Hope and Progressive Teaching by modeling them.

WHITE PRACTITIONER BODIES OF RESISTANCE

I have made some progress with changing students' attitudes with this method, but I battle consistent themes of resistance and work against them, all the things students are willing to see in "others" but not in themselves as detrimental to educating children. I believe strongly that a chapter with a theoretical framework of resistance theory rather than Freirean Critical Pedagogy would make it imperative for me to consider also my own bodily resistance in relation to the student bodies of resistance. Therefore, it is not within the scope of this chapter to go deeply into resistance theory. However, I do find it necessary and appropriate to name and describe briefly the work of the contemporary resistance theorist that drove me to adopt the categorization that I chose in order to grasp the varying types of resistance I perceived from my white graduate student practitioners. Pare (1994) posits five patterns of resistance behaviors emerging from her ethnographic study of resistance and attendance in adult basic education courses: (a) withdrawal behaviors, (b) awareness behaviors, (c) challenging behaviors, (d) assertion behaviors, and (e) solidarity behaviors (p. 40). A student exhibiting the withdrawal behavior "avoids the dominant situation," altogether [by physically leaving or silence] while the student expressing the awareness behavior might "verbalize an understanding of dominance" (Pare, 1994, p. 40). Challenging behaviors are "confrontive, which challenges the dominant situation (i.e., me as the Black "other" professor)," while assertion behaviors "can be assertive of a marginalized identity. Finally, a student exhibiting solidarity behaviors might become "expressive of subordinated solidarities against dominance" (Pare, 1994, p. 40).

In Pare's (1994) study, the marginalized identities that enlist resistance are based upon "the political identities related to race, ethnicity, class, gender, and geography" (p. 40). The twist in the plot of this chapter that differs from Pare (1994) is that the white body is in an unusual position where it finds itself in the space of a legitimated "other" (whether they like it or not), legitimized by their predominantly white institution. Narratives of the white student body presented below provide further evidence of this claim. Each emergent theme is written in quotation marks and accompanied by one of the behavioral patterns found in Pare's (1994) ethnography. The tone of the narrative is noted as malignant or benign to describe to readers the nonverbal cues and body language that I observed when the theme was communicate at least two or more times. I have also noted the pseudo-initials of graduate urban practitioners who communicated narratives relating to one or more themes of struggle near the beginning and middle of the course. Following the thematic narratives of struggle, additional narratives from the same students are highlighted. Those narratives represent a correspondence and transformation of initial narratives of struggle into end-of-course narratives of hope.

Emergent Themes and Behavioral Patterns From White Body-Related Narratives of Struggle

"Silence as Power-White Body" Withdrawal Behaviors
- "I had my hand raised earlier and you didn't pick me, so I'm just not going to talk again"—"KM" (Malignant Resistance)
- "Everything is about being politically correct now, I don't want to offend anyone, so I just don't say anything and I don't ask any questions"—"SD" (Malignant Resistance)

"Intimidated, Anxious, and Guilty-White Body" Awareness Behaviors
- "You and some of my classmates use all the big theory words, and I have to translate them or get past them to see how this class fits with my teaching needs" —"KM" (Benign Resistance)
- "The thing that I really have had a difficult time with is I never fully recognized my feeling of guilt for being white"—"NM" (Benign Resistance)

"Colorblind—White Body" Challenging Behaviors
- "There were 3 or 4 blacks at my school and they were fine, everyone liked them, there were no racial tensions, so I don't understand what you're saying."—"KM" (Malignant Resistance)
- "I don't see how this theory stuff applies to my [all White, middle class] school...and to the subjects I teach..."—"DD" (Malignant Resistance)

"White Body in Denial" Assertion Behaviors
- "I feel that race is not really a big issue in my life"—"NM" (Malignant Resistance)
- "I had few different 'races' in my school...my close male friend was Black and he dated White girls and it was accepted."—"KM" (Malignant Resistance)
- "To be fair [to the kids], there is one way to focus on special education intervention in early childhood"—"SD" (Malignant Resistance)

"White Body Support Group" Solidarity Behaviors
- Student A: "I came with _____ because she was too anxious [to meet with you alone] and she's embarrassed..." (Benign Resistance)
- Student B: "...Yeah, the class is moving way to fast for me. I'm just lost. I don't get the theories and I've never had a class like this before...I didn't feel right contacting you about it, but I don't want to fail, what can I do?" —"DD" (Benign Resistance)

Resistance is not to be ignored or underestimated. Pare (1994) contends that not only should instructors "expect and recognize resistance...but also they should encourage the more conscious and verbal types of resistance" (p. 108). She explains that her ethnography suggests that a sort of critical conscientious resistance should be encouraged because it is "socially just, contributes to an improved learning context, student retention, and [overall] institutional success" (Pare, 1994, p. 108). After considering Pare's work, I began to contemplate student attrition for my courses, but it is a rare problem, likely because the two social theory-based courses that I teach are part of the graduate core course requirements. However, in retrospect the students who leave my section for another section, or who leave the course altogether for that semester may attend the first day or first couple of class days, but most often without saying a word. Therefore, I might begin to consider "retention" in the mental sense as well. Will white students retain the information and stay with the course mentally, if I find constructive ways to manage the individualized types of resistance they express? This question is an important one as we consider one final piece of Pare's (1994) work. I have adapted her concluding claims below (my modifications are bracketed). It should not be surprising if mental and physical retention increases in my social theory classroom of graduate-level white urban practitioners when:

- [my white] students [and I] feel that [our white and black bodies] are accepted and welcomed into the classroom;
- the classroom seems more receptive to all kinds of [white] student [body] and [black professorial body] input, even to what appears to be negative input;
- [white] student [body] and black [professorial body] resistance is encouraged to be more overt; and
- [my white students and I] focus (a) [critically and conscientiously] on homogeneity, (b) [critically and conscientiously upon] dominant culture and control, and (c) [critically and conscientiously on both the theoretical and practical connections of] diversity, democracy, and marginalized discourses" (p. 108).

Although, I find Pare's (1994) work to be transferable, neither Pare (1994), nor Freire (1994), nor Wink (2005), nor Merleau-Ponty (1964), nor Laubscher and Powell (2003) can speak from my unique border brokering perspective. The dark-brown, black American male body that I take to class represents one of the least, if not *the* least protected segments of the U.S. population. It is a body that must address the resistance of a predominantly white and female American body, representing arguably, the most protected and least oppressed group in the world. Now, with the detailed narratives of struggle and the particularities of my plight mind, let us move to considering the counter-narratives of hope that emerged from my autoethnographic journey.

FREIREAN MINING AND PRIMING BY A BLACK "OTHER" AND WHITE BODY-RELATED NARRATIVES OF HOPE

In retrospect, it seems that my background in Freirean Critical Pedagogy drove many of the educational tools I employed to counter the resistance I perceived. It was interesting for me to find concrete evidence to back this claim. When I considered my actions, in relation to Freire's requirements for progressive teachers, it seems that I must have engaged my mining and priming techniques on a sub-conscious level. It was not until I began writing this chapter that I began to compare and contrast the narratives and emergent themes against a Freirean theoretical backdrop. Below, I present (a) thematic narratives of hope emergent from my white graduate student practitioners, and (b) illustrate the relationship of their emergent narratives to my attempts at mining and priming Freirean pedagogy as a progressive "other" teacher. I understand my work here as unfinished, but as a commencement. Indeed, the most promising strategies and possibilities arising from my social theory course of white practitioners involve an evolving project and not a static one.

Humility in Teaching and Learning Theory

I started designing a syllabus that included at least one historical and one contemporary theorist for each assigned reading period. This construction enlists the students to make connections of theorists for example: Marx & Engels (1848) and Shujaa (1994); Mannheim (1936) and Minh Ha (1989); Weber (1918) and Bourdieu (1977); Bowers (1984) and Gramsci (1926); Foucault (1976) and Weeks (1991); Du Bois (1903) and Lorde (1979); McIntosh (1989) and Rousseau (1762); Scott (1990) and Lande (1977); Berger and Luckmann (1966) and Giroux (1983, 1996); Noblit (1999) and Giddens (1979); and finally Freire (1974, 1994), Wink (2005), and Hughes (2005b). These pairings are not intended to be static. They are dynamic and changing pairings forcing me to re-read the theorists and the re-theorize, thereby reconsidering my own taken-for-granted knowledge about a given historical theorists' connection with the present and vice versa. I am often humbled by the responses and new synthesis of ideas generative by my students and me as we approach the end of a semester. I am also humbled by the wealth of knowledge brought to theory courses by what I label "senior" students—defined by students who showed more "senior" prerequisite abilities with the subject matter content of a given historical theorist's connection, and representing formal and/or informal educational settings. Hence, from my purview, a "senior student" is not necessarily "senior" by traditional university standards. Early on, I began enlisting, embracing, and cultivating senior leadership in my social theory classroom.

White Student Body Sample Narratives of Hope

White Female Urban Practitioner, SFE Class Group Leader, "ES," April 30, 2005

I have tried to be a general source of knowledge and perspective for my group members and I hope I have done them some sort of service in my actions. Although, I am not physically involved in our group presentation, I believe I have been a sort of "background source" giving them a "legs" up on the other groups…For that, I am proud, because I have had class with "KM" before and know that they care about their education.

White Female Urban Practitioner, "SD," April 13, 2005

Discussions from this course have made me realize how 'one sided' I can be when focusing on writing outcomes and intervention strategies to help children (0–3) who qualify for early intervention services....Pierre Bourdieu's work was practical, focused on everyday life, as he wrote about key terms such as Habitus. Bourdieu say Habitus as the "key to reproduction because it is what actually generates the regular practices that make up social life. It is the product of social conditioning and so links actual behavior to class structure'...It challenges our 'free will.' Habitus will steer the way you behave or respond to the world. How can I assume that the children I see on a daily basis have had the same opportunity or exposure to an educational environment (i.e., toys, books, language, adequate resources) similar to the Habitus I was raised in?

White Female Urban Practitioner, "SD," May 2, 2005

"The challenge can be overwhelming to the teacher who must consider whether to modify the classroom environment, the classroom equipment and materials, the activities, or the expectations he or she has of the child....Bourdieu's habitus...and Shujaa's ideas, guide, and the social construction of these thinker have given [much] to the world. I, too, have been educated and challenged through readings and classroom discussions this semester to look beyond the boundaries I have built and engage myself in the celebration of human life beyond acceptance and tolerance...A person's habitus can steer the way they behave or respond to the world. To become an effective teacher, I must distinguish my knowledge base that lies within the blending of content and pedagogy.

White Female Urban Practitioner, "KM," December 12, 2004

Once the obstacles are acknowledge, only then, can these obstacles be overcome (McIntosh, 1989). I do not think of myself as a racist, however, I have not, as a teacher, been aware of the difficulties that other ethnic groups may face. As I stated before, awareness of the problem is half the battle. Teachers have a dual responsibility after the acknowledgement as occurred. The dual task consists of recognition of social relations as well as beginning social change and emancipation.

Reading the World versus Reading the Words

I also use a Freire's reading the world approach to teach social theory. During this process, I ask questions and try to learn something about their daily lives as practitioners. The idea is not to "get to personal" but to understand their struggles, frustrations, and the socially relevant differences between them and me, between their lived experiences and mine. This social construction of our experiences are then critiqued and applied through real classroom case studies as much and as often as time permits. I also use an instrument for monitoring the type of resistance I perceive on an individual basis through written and verbal after class comments (ACCs) where students may (a) write a detailed question(s) about something said in class, (b) comment on something that was said in class that challenged them to rethink their position, or (c) comment on something said in which they disagreed, but still challenged them to consider another viable alternative.

White Student Body Sample Narratives of Hope

White Female Urban Practitioner, SFE Class Group Leader, "ES," April 30, 2005

I appreciate your comments, as I usually do! I also appreciate your knowing me as a student. I believe that knowing your students and "how they work" is an important part of teaching and I think that you school a complete understanding of this.

White Female Urban Practitioner, "DD," May 4, 2005

The lesson plan [I observed and critiqued], I believe, was slightly [but not fully] attentive in the area of diversity....Within the Mathematically Speaking category of the lesson plan on page 3, its states that, "students will learn to use mathematics to make sense of their world." Diversity also comes into play here because regardless of identifying, multicultural, and unique aspects of the individual, they will most likely learn the skill that are needed in this particular lesson and use them in ways appropriate to their own environment and according to their own ways of living [of knowing].

White Female Urban Practitioner, "SD," May 2, 2005

It's the capacity of the teacher to transform content knowledge I possess into forms that are pedagogically powerful. Using the ability and background presented by my students to adapt variations in planning and preparation, classroom environment, and instruction could mean stepping outside my habitus.

White Male Urban Practitioner, "NM," December, 2004

I'm not one who talks very much in class, but I was always listening and absorbing. Through ACCs I've turned in and you have handed back, I have gained an immense understanding of myself. You helped me to recognize and understand white privilege. That is not to say that I now fully understand white privilege, but I am much more aware.

Practicing and Theorizing as Knowing versus Memorizing Theory and Rote Methods to Teach

I began course preparation by designing more (a) Type II (i.e., "performance task's...learners are asked to do or perform to demonstrate knowledge or skills" (Haney, 2005, p. 3); and (b) Type III assessment-based assignments (i.e., "long-term events or extended student projects. They involve student investigation of topics over extended periods of time, encourage student creativity, and offers students some choice and decision-making about the content and process related to their project" (Haney, 2005, p. 3). Type II assessments come in the form of student presentations, debates, posters, etc. My students engage Type III assessments via the lesson/unit planning-trial—implementation—revision mechanisms that stretch throughout an entire semester (Haney, 2005, p. 3).

White Student Body Sample Narratives of Hope

White Female Urban Practitioner, "KM," December 12, 2004

I learned the most from my project and will share my findings with other [white urban] teachers so they may see where they need to make changes as well. I hope to continue working at the urban public school where I am now employed and I hope to use my new-found knowledge to do a better job.

White Female Urban Practitioner, "DD," March, 2005

I believe that this lesson plan is attentive in about 75% of all criteria. However, the modifications I made for the lesson [via social theorizing] have increased the attentiveness greatly. I feel that it will be very effective and useful in the classroom setting, but should also be carefully examined that it directly meets the standards and needs of a particular classroom. Obviously aspects of this lesson may be modified accordingly. Children with more sever disabilities may struggle with some of the activities within this lesson. Modifications and adaptations can be made as appropriate.

Bureaucratization of the Mind: Saving Ourselves

At midterm, students had progressed, but none felt organized around a set of mechanisms to guide class discussions. In light of this discover, I decided to replace the initial "stage" setup for the course with a set of guiding principles to engage discussion through a Snauwaert & Hughes (2004) three moral resources of peace include: (a) knowledge (e.g., through revisionist history, breadth and depth of knowledge and experiences with the "other"), (b) reasonableness (being open to new ideas, experiences, challenges, and counter-evidence), and (c) empathy (the highest form of human validation, its living vicariously in someone else's struggle or hopes).

White Student Body Sample Narratives of Hope

White Female Urban Practitioner, "SD," December 12, 2004

In the future I will do a lot more listening and will try to use what I have learned to make myself a better teacher and a better person.

White Male Urban Practitioner, "NM," December, 2004

I must admit going into the first day of class I thought that this would be just another class. I felt that 'race' was not really a big issue in my life. I have black and Hispanic friends and teach in a predominantly black school, therefore I thought I knew how to 'deal' with the issue of 'race.' As I learned in the very first class, boy was I wrong. The very first class hit me very hard, and I told everyone I knew about the class, literally. I have always felt uncomfortable around other 'races' because I felt that they didn't like me because of my being white. I never addressed this issue before this class. You have helped me in ways unexplainable.

Bureaucratization of the Mind: A Syllabus Schedule Isn't Greater Than the Course

During the first day of my inaugural section of SFE, I realized that 95% of my students were not only practitioners, but at the Master's level. Some of them tried to "tough it out," but few had the pre-requisite courses that would have allowed them to comprehend the readings at my original pace. I thought that my initial revision would be enough to catch up everyone, yet I soon realized that I must continue revising the syllabus on the spot when necessary to ensure more students could participate in the demonstrations I expect.

White Student Body Sample Narratives of Hope

White Female Urban Practitioner, "DS," March, 2005

Thank you for taking the time to adjust the syllabus and to review the theorist. It really helped me. I think I am finally getting the connection of the importance of theory in practice.

Understanding the Challenges and Promises of Freedom and Risk

It is a risk to create student groups and to mix them according to diversity in ethnicity, SES, gender, and sexual orientation. I find, however, that by creating diverse group opportunities (e.g., at least one practitioner and one underrepresented minority in each group) I increase opportunities for hybrid peer learning and support. I also began assigning detailed individual roles for group members where everyone, including underrepresented group members could now fulfill roles of legitimate authority, thereby offering an additional space for open dialogue and resistance.

White Student Body Sample Narratives of Hope

White Female Urban Practitioner, "KM," December 12, 2004

I would like to say that I am not resistant to change [Scott, 1990], but I guess that I just did not know how to change or where to start. My classmates [group members] helped me with this element. There were talking, all I had to do was listen…and make an attempt to comprehend the changes I need to make in my own thinking….White teachers need to explore deeper and think more reflectively in order to understand the reality of a racial problem in our schools. First, teachers need to recognize, and acknowledge the reality of ethnic diversity, before we can understand how to approach and tack the difficulties that arise from the lack of knowledge about variations of thinking and lifestyles (McIntosh, 1989).

Education is Testimony

When teaching social theory irrespective of the audience, it is almost unfathomable to pursue the course without appropriating personal accounts of my own teaching and learning experiences as other. I'm strict to keep my testimony pertinent most of the time; however, I also began my inaugural year of teaching theory to practitioners by finding spaces for humor (Richman, AERA 2005 personal communication). Through testimony, I also present real and current cases so, students have an opportunity to see me engage [even if virtually] successful praxis with pre-K–16 students. I try to offer concrete evidence of my current work with grade school students in foster care through G3, Inc., the educational 501(c)(3) nonprofit agency that I founded and for which I serve as the President.

White Student Body Sample Narratives of Hope

White Female Urban Practitioner, "SD," December 12, 2004

I loved hearing the presentations made by others and I would have liked to have more time to get into more detail with many questions in my head still unanswered.

White Male Urban Practitioner, "NM," December, 2004

I find myself often times reflecting on things said, and stories shared in class, truthfully. This class is now winding down, but my understanding and recognizing the issue of "race" is just beginning. I now feel more comfortable being white and feel better about me. At the same time, I feel more comfortable dealing with my students and seeing things from the "other side of the fence." Again, I am not claiming to be magically "healed" or having figured everything out. However, with your help, I have grown in ways I didn't know were possible. Thank you for your time, knowledge, and efforts. Surely this is class I will not forget.

CLOSING REMARKS

Laubscher and Powell (2003) write, "the body...is not to be considered a mere anatomical vessel that houses a separable Cartesian mind, but is integrally connected to its surroundings and the fundamental place from which the world is made meaningful" (p. 8). My experiences of the body when implementing a social theory course to practitioners is risky and it can be quite lonely. Often, I feel little validation of the particularities of those experiences from the White faculty body that espouses social justice. Typical replies of "I get some of that too," suggests that they don't get it at all. One retired emeritus, white male faculty member from my department did seem to really "get it" and he spoke of the embodied "other" unexpectedly at AESA 2005:

> I've spoken with Sherick briefly over the last couple of years, but on several occasions about the type of experiences he shared today; and he's told me about the type of [Freirean] teaching strategies he uses. It finally dawned on me recently that although I teach similar courses and subject matter to many of the same students, I get some quite different results during the process. I'm a passivist, a socialist, a radical-independent, and some other things...but most of the [white] students don't know this about me nor do they question it. I guess I get to hide behind this old, white haired, white man's shell to protect me [my body] from the degree and kind of criticism he receives from our students.

That retired white professor was an audience member, and still a clear leader in my department. The AESA 2005 panel was replete with faculty members and graduate students from our department. The audience included other seasoned social justice educators, including the chair of my department, and recognized scholars from Eastern Michigan University and the University of Illinois at Chicago. I thanked him for sharing his thoughts publicly and for validating the particularities that separate his experiences teacher theory to white practitioners from my experiences. I also suggested that such validation was crucial to fulfilling any social justice education mission and imperative for the retention of faculty of color are predominantly white departments, colleges, and universities. In his, albeit resistant, body I am finding an example of the type of leadership that might emerge from the Freirean critical pedagogical mining and priming that I take into my predominantly white, able-bodied graduate educational settings. I am finding that one route to take my students and me toward this realization devolves from Freirean critical pedagogy. It is not intended to be a cookie-cutter model, but it does offer some transferable strategies for me to engage a kind of teaching and learning as "other" that renders my social theory classroom a space for critical praxis, and as a space for the mind and body to experience self-reflexive critical thinking. Social theory through Sociological Foundations of Education and Intergroup/Intercultural Education courses can indeed, become (a) spaces to invite practitioners to feel the utility of theorizing while practicing and (b) to invite theorists to feel how practicing gives theorizing its utility in pre-K thru 16 settings (Mannheim, 1936).

As a tenure track professor of Education in the academy, I am finding a more detailed description of the shared body that my students and I bring to our transactions at the crossroads of racialization, conscientiousness, and resistance. It is the body of a binary; of a two-colored Siamese twin thinking and acting out a paradox of education—forever learning, yet forever ignorant. It is a body of carcinogens, rendered benign or malignant by the relationship between me as "other" and my white graduate student practitioners. It is the body of an agent: ethnic and resistant; living, learning, struggling, and hoping. I agree with Foucault's allusion that all critical conscientiousness of "othering," all of the time is a dangerous and sure route to be perceived as mad or insane by most people within my sphere of influence. Therefore, to engage a sustainable Freirean pedagogical leadership approach in predominantly Black and Latino urban grade schools, white teachers and administrators might spend their time reading their worlds into the information from a graduate social theory course. More specifically, they might use class time discussions, and assignments to reconsider how to (a) survive the daily life of practicing in the current "othering" of schooling, (b) begin theorizing and finding occasions to position oneself outside of that structure, (c) begin rethinking taken-for-granted knowledge about the "other," (d) begin understanding self as "other," and (e) begin the lifelong process of being critical of "othering" (Kumashiro, 2001).

If and when, during this period of reconsideration, my students and I acquire or renew critical conscientiousness in our own lives; I am learning that we mustn't be complacent or haphazard with its usage, lest we risk missing too often emancipatory educational opportunities. When my students and I bring social baggage to our pre-K–16 teaching and learning settings on our bodies, we also risk missing opportunities to see how the liberation of the *white* side of a pedagogical body is tied to the liberation of its *black* side; its inside, to its outside.

It is a social baggage that renders us forever ignorant, to some extent in our attempts to resist everything from change to corrupt leadership. In essence, I have attempted with this chapter to offer a pedagogy of theorizing (Giroux, 1996), and practicing from a target's perspective. I hope sincerely that my plight might offer some transferable information to readers seeking alternatives to optimize the teaching and learning of social theory with practitioners wherever you find yourselves doing so as an "other."

REFERENCES

Banks, S. P., & Banks, A. (2000). The critical life: Autoethnography as pedagogy. *Communication Education, 49,* 233–238

Berger P. L., & Luckmann, T. (1966). *The social construction of reality: A treatise in the sociology of knowledge.* Garden City, NY: Anchor Books.

Bourdieu P. (1977). *Outline of a theory of practice.* Cambridge: Cambridge University Press.

Bowers, C.A. (1984). *The promise of theory.* New York. Teachers College Press.

Dalton, M. (2003) Media studies and emancipatory praxis: An autoethnographic essay on critical pedagogy. *Journal of Film and Video,* 55(2–3), 88–97.

Du Bois, W. E. B. (1903). *The soul's of Black folks.* Chicago: A. C. McClurg.

Ellis, C., & Bochner, A. (2000). Autoethnography, personal narrative, reflexivity: Researcher as subject. In N. Denzin & Y. Lincoln (Eds.), *Handbook of qualitative research* (pp. 733–768). Thousand Oaks, CA: Sage

Foucault, M. (1976). *The history of sexuality, Vol. 1: An introduction* (pp. 92–102). New York, NY: Vintage Books.

Freire, P. (1974). *Pedagogy of the oppressed.* New York: Seabury.

Freire, P. (1994) *Pedagogy of hope: Reliving pedagogy of the oppressed,* New York: Continuum.

Gadotti, M. (1994) *Reading Paulo Freire. His life and work.* New York: SUNY Press.

Giddens A. (1979), *Central problems in social theory,* Los Angeles: University of California press.

Giroux, H. A. (1983) Theories of reproduction and resistance in the new sociology of education: A critical analysis," *Harvard Educational Review*, 53(3), 257–293.

Giroux, H. A. (1996). *Counternarratives: Cultural studies and critical pedagogies in post-modern spaces*. New York: Routledge.

Gramsci, A. (1926) *Intellectuals and hegemony. Prison Notebooks*. New York: International.

Haney, J. (2005). Assessing student Success. *EXCITE*, 3(2), 1–6.

Hayano, D. M. (1979). Auto-ethnography: Paradigms, problems, and prospects. *Human Organization*, 38(1), 99–104.

Helfenbein, R., & Diem, J. (Eds). (in press). *Unsettling beliefs: Teaching social theory to teachers*. Charlotte, NC: Information Age.

Hughes, S. A. (2005a). *Teaching theory as other against othering: A critical pedagogical approach*. In R. Helfenbein, S. Hughes, B. Hatt-Echeverria, & J. Diem, Symposium, Unsettling Beliefs: Teaching Social Theory to Teachers. American Educational Studies Association Conference. Charlottesville, VA, (November, 2005).

Hughes, S. A. (2005b). Some canaries left behind?: Evaluating a state-endorsed lesson plan database and its social construction of who and what counts. *International Journal of Inclusive Education*, 9(2), 105–138.

Kumashiro, K. K. (2001) "Posts" perspectives on anti-oppressive education in social studies, english, mathematics, and science classrooms. *Educational Researcher*, 30(3), 3–12.

Lande, C. H. (1977). Introduction: The dyadic basis of clientalism. In S. W. Schmidt et al. (Eds.), *Friends, Followers, and Factions: A Reader in Political Clientelism* (pp. xiii–xxxvii). Berkeley: University of California Press.

Laubscher, L., & Powell, S. (2003). Skinning the drum: Teaching about diversity as "other." *Harvard Educational Review*, Summer, 203–247

Lorde, A. (1979, 1984). The master's tools will never dismantle the master's house. In *Sister Outside: Essays and Speeches*. Freedom, CA: Crossing Press.

McIntosh, P. (1989). White privilege: Unpacking the invisible knapsack. *Peace and Freedom*. July/August, 10–12.

Mannheim, K. (1936) *Ideology and Utopia: An introduction to the sociology of knowledge* (Trans., L. Wirth & E. Shils., 1968). New York: Harcourt, Brace & World.

Marx, K., & Engels, F. (1848/1978). Manifesto of the Communist Party. In R. C. Tucker, (Ed.), *The Marx-Engels reader* (2nd ed., pp. 473–479). New York: W.W. Norton.

Merleau-Ponty, M. (J. M. Edie, trans.) (1964). *The primacy of perception: And other essays on phenomenological psychology, the philosophy of art, history and politics*. Evanston, IL: Northwestern University Press.

Minh-Ha, T. T. (1989). *Woman, native, other: Writing postcoloniality and feminism*. Bloomington: Indiana University Press.

Noblit, G. W. (1999). *Particularities: Collected essays on ethnography and education*. New York: Peter Lang.

Pare, A. L. (1994). *Attending to resistance: An ethnographic study of resistance and attendance in an adult basic education classroom*. Thesis. University of British Columbia. Retrieved December 3, 2005, from http://www.nald.ca/fulltext/attendng/PAREV3.pdf

Reed-Danahay, D. E. (1997). Introduction. In D. E. Reed-Danahy (Ed.), *Auto/ethnography: Rewriting the self and the social* (pp. 1–19). New York: Oxford University Press.

Rousseau, J.-J. (1762/1987). *The social contract or principles of political right.* (M. Cranston, trans.) New York: Penguin.

Scott, J. C. (1990) *Domination and the arts of resistance: Hidden transcripts.* New Haven, CT: Yale University Press.

Shujaa, M. J. (1994). *Too much schooling, too little education: A paradox of Black life in White societies.* Trenton, NJ: Africa World Press.

Snauwaert, D. & Hughes, S. A. (2004). *The central place of* Brown *in the field of social foundations of education.* Paper presented at the American Educational Studies Association Conference, November, 2004, Kansas City, MO.

Weber, M. (1918). Bureaucracy. In H. Gerth & C. Wright Mills, (Eds. & trans.), *From Max Weber* (pp. 196–198, 224–230). New York: Oxford University Press.

Weeks, J. (1991). *Against nature: Essays on history, sexuality, and identity.* (pp. 79–85). London: Rivers Oram Press.

Wink, J. (2005). *Critical pedagogy: Notes from the real world.* New York: Pearson.

CHAPTER 14

SOCIAL JUSTICE ACTIVIST TEACHING IN THE UNIVERSITY CLASSROOM

Silvia Cristina Bettez
University of North Carolina at Greensboro

ABSTRACT

This chapter focuses on one area of potential activism within academia—teaching to promote social justice. It is a reflection on my teaching experience, both inside and outside of the academy, as well as an assessment of the literature on teaching for social justice. In the conscious examination of how my work as an instructor of social foundations and multicultural education engenders social change, I have identified seven skills, practices, and dispositions of activist social justice education. These components are not meant to be all-inclusive or definitive. Rather, I hope to inspire critical discussions about activist social justice teaching in hopes of promoting, among educators, a more conscious connection between politics and practice.

One of the questions that most compels me as a teacher, and teacher educator, is what it means to teach for social justice. Having worked in community and teacher education for many years, I am always in search of new content that inspires students and strategies that help them to develop

Unsettling Beliefs: Teaching Theory to Teachers, pages 273–296
Copyright © 2008 by Information Age Publishing

more thoughtful habits of being in the world. As I do this work, I think about (and live) the emotional challenges of participating in social justice activism: the disruption of our worldviews, the demands on our energies, and the struggle of building supportive communities. Assessing the literature on this topic, as well as reflecting on my own experiences, I realized that there are a number of habits, skills, and dispositions that social justice educators talk about as important, though I have not seen any place where these are brought together. Drawing from both my experiences and the literature on activist social justice teaching, this essay is a compilation of the lessons I have learned from social justice practice and activist teaching. It is my hope that this may be a useful resource for educators who are drawn to foregrounding social justice issues in their work and that it may inspire more discussion on this topic.

One night while beginning to work on this chapter, I was home alone sitting at my computer when, at about 10 pm, I heard a strange noise. At first I thought it was my cat, Bailey, but as I entered the living room to investigate the noise I heard someone turning my doorknob. A wave of fear swept over me as I tried to remember if I had locked the door. Glancing at the deadbolt, I realized thankfully that I had locked it. Approaching the door cautiously, I looked out of the peephole to find a man standing there that I didn't recognize. I stood there silent. He knocked. I ignored it. He knocked again, this time more loudly. Thinking that maybe he was confused and had the wrong apartment, I answered, calling out, "who is it?" He responded, in a low, deep voice, "It's the killer." In the firmest tone I could muster, I said, "you need to leave!" Angrily, he replied, "why don't I take my penis out then?" My legs literally started to shake underneath me as I thought, "this guy came to sexually assault me." I shakily went to the other room, grabbed my phone, and called the police. The man remained standing outside my door for several more minutes but left before the police arrived 15 minutes later. I made a report and have not heard anything since.

This event changed the direction of my thinking on the topic of activist, social justice teaching and forced me to reconsider my own experiences as a community activist and scholar, as well as how I imagine my work in the future. I had two strong, personal, juxtaposed reactions. First, I was struck by the feeling that all this work I do—writing, reading, and thinking about social justice—doesn't seem to mean much when placed in direct contrast to the threat of being raped. I have no idea if this man stalked me. For several weeks I lived in constant fear that he might return, causing me to change my daily patterns, sleep at a friend's house, and consequently get behind on my work. Second, in my less anxious moments, I wondered, "How can I use this experience to inform my work and politics as a scholar?" These two reactions reflect the tensions of balancing and integrating activist and academic work, a challenge faced by all of us who aim to do social justice work in the academy. While intellectually I saw ways to integrate this experience into my scholarly life and practice, it also renewed in me a longing to return to more community based social justice work. Writing through these tensions helps me to see that in some ways the dichotomy between activist and academic work is artificial. Teaching that consciously foregrounds and promotes social justice is always a form of activist work. Learning from others' experiences of teaching and learning can help us become better activist teachers.

Before returning to graduate school, I worked as a community educator to prevent domestic violence and sexual assault. I often worked with the Latino/a community, homeless women, and other underserved populations. In that capacity, it was easy to see and name the direct connections between my values and my work to effect social change. Yet I have been hesitant to stay in the academy as I fear that academic work will consume my energies and distract me from my desire to engage in community work with people of color—work that seems much more tangible and meaningful. I worry that each job I take in the academy moves me further from community work outside the academy. Within activist communities, academia is often posed as existing outside of or in opposition to the "real" community work that directly promotes equity. At the same time, rarely do people discuss activism within institutions of higher education.

Since entering graduate school, my sense of purpose as a person committed to the promotion of social justice has been continually challenged. This recent frightening incident made me question, once again, whether or not what I do truly makes a difference in promoting equity and if the university system is the best place for me to accomplish my work and reach my goals. Though I still have doubts, I have remained in the academy, and writing this chapter has helped to remind me of the ways that writing, research, and college-level teaching can be forms of political activism. The key to framing scholarly work as activist is to consciously ask the question: *How might my work bring about social or political change?* This chapter focuses on one area of potential activism within academia—teaching to promote social justice. It is a reflection on my experience as well as an assessment of the literature on teaching for social justice. In preparation for this essay, I reread essays I had previously written and looked through the books and articles that have most moved and inspired me as a teacher and scholar, and, in the spirit of qualitative research, I extracted recurring themes. In addition, I thought critically about my work as a teacher—both as a community educator and as a university-level instructor of social foundations and multicultural education—and asked myself, "What makes my work activist?" and "How do I work to promote social justice in the classroom?"

I take my definition of social justice from Bell (1997) who writes, "social justice includes a vision of society in which the distribution of resources is equitable and all members are physically and psychologically safe and secure" (p. 3). Equitable is a key term here. Equity does not always mean equal. Equal implies sameness; equity implies justice. Because we live in a society that has a history of great injustice in which people have had widely varying access to opportunities based on their social grouping, creating equity today does not always mean treating everyone the same. In the preface to the book *Teaching for Diversity and Social Justice*, the authors write, "our goal in social justice education is to enable students to become conscious of their operating world view and to be able to examine critically alternative ways of understanding the world and social relations" (1997, p. xvii). My vision of social justice education aligns with that statement, though I would add that social justice teaching should inspire students to *act* upon their new understandings in ways that deconstruct power imbalances and promote equity. This is where activism applies. Educators who consciously work toward that goal are engaging in activist teaching, and activist teaching inspires activism—meaning direct *action* arising from critical consciousness.

Discussions about social justice education often focus on the need to combine theory and practice. They commonly reference Freire's (2003) concept of praxis, that is, "reflection and action upon the world in order to transform it" (p. 51). Praxis has been established as a core component of activist education, yet it is important that we engage in ongoing dialogue about how to execute praxis, especially since it seems many of us are better at calling for praxis than engaging in it. In the conscious effort to think through how my work in the classroom might bring about social change, I have identified seven skills, practices, and dispositions of activist social justice education. These components are not meant to be all-inclusive or definitive. Rather, I hope to engender critical discussions about activist teaching in hopes of promoting a more conscious connection between politics and practice. The list includes:

1. Promoting a mind/body connection
2. Conducting artful facilitation that promotes critical thinking
3. Engaging in explicit discussions of power, privilege, and oppression
4. Maintaining compassion for students
5. Believing that change toward social justice is possible
6. Exercising self-care
7. Building critical communities

In the rest of this chapter, I unpack each of these components, look at how they relate to social justice education for pre-service teachers, relate them to examples from my own teaching practice, and offer some specific strategies for how we can best cultivate these in our own teaching practice and in our work with prospective teachers.

PROMOTING A MIND/BODY CONNECTION

Activist teaching encourages people to use their personal experiences and ways of knowing and encourages an understanding that all knowledge is situated. Situating knowledge requires a conscious connection between mind and body, yet too often these are kept separate in education. In her essay *Whiteness and the Politics of Location* Raka Shome (1999) states, "...the whole of academia and the Western cultural thinking that drives it encourages such a mind/body split in a scholar" (p. 125). Western academia promotes the false idea that research and teaching are connected only to the power of the mind. However, as Shome states, "nonwhite instructors under 'white eyes' find that they are unable to succumb to this ideology of the mind/body split" (p. 125), especially as their non-white bodies position them differently in the eyes of their students. Echoing Shome, bell hooks states, "as a black woman, I have always been acutely aware of the presence of my body in those [academic] settings" (1994, p. 135). I too have always been aware of my body as a teacher. When I taught HIV/STD prevention to Latino men in a county jail, I was acutely aware of my body as a light-skinned mixed Latina woman. As a teacher of multicultural education for college students who are predominately white I wonder how my students perceive me—as white, Latina, as both? On the first day of classes, I always identify myself to my students as the daughter of a Latina mother and white father. In a class made up of all white students, as I share experiences related to race, I know that I am "other" as I feel their gaze.

However, I address the importance of mind/body connection in the classroom, not only because as a Latina teaching white students I have no other choice, but also because I believe that emphasizing a mind/body connection in academia is a form of activism. hooks states, "Once we start talking in the classroom about the body and about how we live in our bodies, we're automatically challenging the way power has orchestrated itself in that particular institutionalized space" (p. 137). Promoting social justice is in large part about creating meaningful connections across lines of difference. However, in order for those connections to be made, the differences between people must be acknowledged. Naming is powerful; to name our experiences and identities allows us to forge genuine connections and to consciously break through otherwise invisible borders.

Historically schools in the US were created, in part, to bring together diverse people to participate in a "common shared identity" (Feinberg, 1998, p. 3). This "common identity" was based on dominant white, middle-class, patriarchal, Western values. Thus one of the goals of the US education system was to teach people how to become more like the dominant culture. Students of color were expected to assimilate by disengaging from their bodies and cultural ways of being. Several social justice movements— including civil rights, feminist movements, and multicultural education— have challenged the lack of equity implicit in the ideology to promote "a common identity." This challenge has contributed to an increased understanding by many of the need to recognize and encourage the multiplicity of strengths that diverse peoples bring to classrooms and the benefits of encouraging people to maintain their cultures.

Culture is based upon many factors including race, class, gender, and sexuality. Acknowledging culture necessitates that we recognize the connections between mind and body, that we all speak from some social positionality that is meaningful. hooks states, "the erasure of the body encourages us to think that we are listening to neutral, objective facts, facts that are not particular to who is sharing the information" (p. 139). She writes about "engaged pedagogy" which draws upon Thich Nhat Hanh's philosophy of engaged Buddhism, claiming that "whereas Freire was primarily concerned with the mind, Thich Nhat Hanh offered a way of thinking about pedagogy which emphasized wholeness, a union of mind, body and spirit" (p. 14). As both a student and a teacher, I have found that assignments that invite the writer to explicitly relate theory and practices to personal experience help forge that connection between mind and body.

My favorite assignment to encourage this mind/body connection is short weekly reflection papers. As a graduate student I took a course titled, *Teaching Race, Teaching Gender* in which we were required to write weekly papers that incorporated both clear, coherent theoretical arguments *and* personal connections to the readings and concepts. The professor challenged us to engage personally with the material and the writing while maintaining academic rigor. Looking back on those writings, I find that the depth of my work increased as I was encouraged to connect mind and body. As a teacher, I now assign weekly reflection papers with pre-service teachers in which they are encouraged to share personal experiences that occur inside or outside the classroom that relate to the reading and course content. I encourage them to connect theory, with practice, with personal meaning. Recently a student of mine, Emma, wrote about an experience on spring break in which she was at a community pool conversing with a bilingual child who spoke to Emma in English while intermittently speaking to her grandmother in Spanish. In her reflection paper, Emma states:

Seeing this impacted the ideas taught us about the complexity of ESL students. For example, what if in a classroom this little girl was condemned for using her Spanish? The next time she came to visit her grandmother she may not have wanted to speak in Spanish.

Although I had shared a very similar story with the class about my bilingual cousin, it was not until this student was able to reflect on her own experience that she fully understood the possible negative consequences of a teacher devaluing a student's native language in the classroom. This is one of many examples in which encouraging personal connections has led to increased understanding of theory and practice.

Once the connections between the mind and body are acknowledged, it is easy to see how emotion plays an important role in the classroom. In schools and universities, emotion has been traditionally viewed as an impediment to more advanced rationalist thinking. Addressing emotion in the classroom may feel threatening to instructors who are then required to deal with whole people, rather than portions of people's minds, which carries the messy complexities that come with being human. Validating emotion in the classroom has the potential to shift power dynamics as white women and people of color, often culturally more emotive than white men, may be more willing to contribute to classroom discussions. Requiring students to remove emotion from the classroom and their scholarship is antithetical to activist teaching.

Activist teaching requires that teachers recognize and acknowledge the lived experience of their students. This requires acknowledging the connections between mind, body, and spirit. Activist teaching encourages situated voice and knowledge rather than an abstract disembodied voice. It is only through acknowledging how knowledge is situated that we can deconstruct the underlying operations of power and strive for greater equity.

CONDUCTING ARTFUL FACILITATION THAT PROMOTES CRITICAL THINKING

Paulo Freire argues that the key to transformative pedagogy is dialogue. In place of banking education, where information is deposited by a teacher into a student, Freire (2003) advocates for problem-posing education which begins "with the posing of the problems of human beings in their relations with the world" (p. 79). True dialogue requires critical thinking in which participants name, reflect, and act on the world (Wink, 2000). Dialogue-centered teaching requires artful facilitation and carefully crafted questions.

Ira Shor similarly argues that "empowering education" must be student-centered and participatory. Shor (1992) explains that participation is "the most important place to begin" to engage students because in traditional classrooms student involvement is low and it takes involvement and action "to gain knowledge and develop intelligence" (p. 17). Teaching in a participatory classroom requires patience and sharing power. This contrasts significantly with traditional ideas of teaching in which the teacher lectures and is expected to be in control of the classroom at all times. Like Freire, Shor advocates for problem-posing education. Problem-posing education encourages students to speak from their experience and to make critical connections among ideas and experiences. It is also a "situated model of learning" in which the teacher "situates learning in the themes, knowledge, cultures, conditions, and idioms of students" (Shor, 1992, p. 44). Student-centered classrooms in which teachers employ problem-posing education require educators to be willing to venture into unplanned territory. Creating specific questions and problems can help lead discussions into somewhat planned arenas. However, encouraging students to speak from experience means that unexpected discussions will arise. Often those discussions have the greatest potential to expand students' worldviews and understandings of operations of power. Thus, helping students navigate this unplanned territory through further problem posing questions then becomes the instructor's goal and challenge.

bell hooks' writing concurs with Shor's ideology. hooks emphasizes the importance of allowing students the space to share "confessional narrative" and participate in "digressive discussions." She notes that many professors who are critical of such teaching are so because "they lack the skill needed to facilitate dialogue" (1992, p. 151). Educators who do not have strong facilitation skills may be fearful of losing too much control in the classroom if they center students' knowledge and experience. However, creating a student-centered classroom requires the instructor to significantly relinquish power and authoritarian control. The key, for the instructor, is to reenter the dialogue to help contextualize student stories and to help maintain a balance of student voices such that institutional power imbalances are not being reified by students with each other. This can occur, for example, if white students and/or male students dominate discussions. With increased student participation, artful facilitation is imperative in order to effectively manage the content, conflict, and emotions that invariably arise in any meaningful classroom engagements.

Although students should be encouraged to speak from experience, it is equally important to disabuse people of the idea that they must possess previous personal connections in order to critically engage with material. For example, one need not be a person of color to respond to writings about the experience of a person of color. Critical thinking requires engagement; it is important to avoid developing an atmosphere where certain people are assigned authority over a topic because of who they are perceived to represent while others remain silent. Text, in the form of course materials, is the commonality that can provide all students an entryway into classroom discussions. Everyone has both the right and responsibility to respond to the text. Thus, it is important to carefully choose materials—whether those are theoretical articles, narratives, or media texts—that will inspire critical thinking and trouble dominant world views.

There are various ways to approach facilitation, and each person needs to develop her or his own style of facilitation. hooks reminds us that facilitating dialogue requires cutting off students who dominate conversations and challenging students to relate their experiences to the academic subject matter. She writes that "at times I need to interrupt students and say, 'That's interesting, but how does that relate to the novel we're reading?'" (p. 151). Artful facilitation requires learning how to interrupt people in respectful ways that allows for the continuation of dialogue. It also requires learning how to ask questions that can allow anyone to participate, and to open spaces for all to do so.

There are a few techniques that I have found to be effective in facilitating dialogue in a student-centered classroom. First, one way to promote dialogue is to create questions to pose to the audience to cover the points you wish to make. Instead of lecturing on a topic, I often design an outline and create questions to raise the main points of what I hope to cover so that student voices take center stage. Assigned reading means that all students (should) have some knowledge related to every topic discussed in class. Students, however, have varying needs and abilities when it comes to processing and articulating their knowledge. One way to create an atmosphere in which all students can participate is to pose questions at the beginning of class and allot time for students to craft written answers. This technique allows all students to participate and simultaneously provides students who might need it, such as non-native English speakers, some extra time to formulate their thoughts. Their written responses can serve as the basis for discussion throughout the class.

Second, instructors can consciously use body language and movement to engage students. Feminist professor Jyl Lynn Felman (2001) writes about performative teaching in the university classroom in her book *Never a Dull Moment*. Felman describes performance in the classroom as a reciprocal exchange between actor and audience, teacher and student in which students are "supporting actors." In the stage of the classroom, everything matters including dress, movement, classroom arrangement, and dialogue. Felman admits that performative teaching is "exhausting yet exhilarating" (p. 15). It requires constant attention, energy, and accountability to engage your audience. bell hooks (1994) also argues that "teaching is a performative act...meant to serve as a catalyst that calls everyone to become more and more engaged, to become active participants in learning" (p. 11). As a community educator I often used movement, classroom space, and voice tone to engage audiences; performative teaching is widely used and accepted in that context. In contrast, the university classroom is often mired in rules of propriety that require people to squelch ways of being that might be perceived as disquieting to traditional (white, middle-class, patriarchal, Western) norms. Performative teaching disrupts traditional teaching norms and can be used to engage students to actively participate in their learning. Even simple acts such as rearranging a classroom into a circle or U-shape can increase dialogue. Although initially intimidating, utilizing my skills as a performative teacher in the university classroom has assisted me in creating an atmosphere of learning that is challenging yet fun. Students comment on, and respond to, my clear passion for teaching. There are many possibilities in performative education but it takes practice, technique, and risk.

Third, related to performative teaching, I try to involve my students in movement, facilitation, and creative activities. This can be accomplished through student presentations, small group exercises, and the use of arts-based pedagogy. Too often learning in the classroom takes a didactic form. Many creative lesson plans can be employed in the classroom that center student voices and promote dialogue. One key element of artful facilitation is fostering an atmosphere of active listening. Students can learn to practice active listening skills, including non-verbal skills, through creative paired listening exercises (for explicit descriptions of active training techniques see Silberman, 1998). To engage students in active learning teachers can also utilize arts-based techniques in the classroom. Augosto Boal's (1992) Theatre of the Oppressed techniques utilize drama to involve students as not only spectators but "spect-actors" with the goal of creating scenes that assist participants in gaining a deeper understanding of issues related to social justice. Many arts-based instruction resources, such as works by Boal and anthologies about arts-based teaching like *Passion and Pedagogy* (2002), are available for teachers to assist in developing creative, artful facilitation techniques.

Fourth, I make an effort to pay attention to the nuances of discourses to help recognize when discursive tactics are being used to relinquish responsibility. In the article, "Engaging whiteness: How racial power gets reified in education" Hytten and Warren (2003) describe the appeals to disabling discourses that white students make to "get off the hook" from engaging in the work of understanding white privilege. There is a fine line between enabling and disabling ways of engaging privilege. In teaching pre-service teachers, I found that they often inadvertently appealed to strategies for talking about diversity that they assumed were open and critical, but actually reproduced white privilege. Artful facilitation requires recognizing when students are evading engagement with social justice issues and working to shift the discussion such that students are maintaining critical engagement.

There are a plethora of possibilities for engaging in artful facilitation. These are just a few suggestions of techniques I employ in my teaching. Promoting critical thinking requires students to be engaged and active in classroom discussions. It means asking challenging questions, encouraging students to connect personal experience with academic material, teaching students how to be active listeners, and fostering an understanding of alternative ways of viewing the world. Employing facilitation skills that promote critical thinking is a key component of activist education.

ENGAGING IN EXPLICIT DISCUSSIONS OF POWER, PRIVILEGE, AND OPPRESSION

In order to teach to promote social justice, there must be explicit discussions of power, privilege, and oppression (Johnson, 2001). There is contention among educators regarding this point. I have engaged in conversations with instructors/professors who claim to teach social justice but do not engage in explicit discussions of power; they argue that they don't want to "scare" or "alienate" students. Instead of talking about oppression, they would rather discuss "diversity" without naming hierarchies. Education that does not address issues of privilege and oppression is not transformative education. Avoiding issues of power and inequity allows students to continue to believe prevalent myths such as "we all have equal opportunities" or "if someone works hard enough they can be anything they want to be" or "everything people have, they earned." It is important to contextualize issues in ways that promote an understanding of the impacts of institutionalized forms of racism, sexism, classism, and heterosexism.

Teaching social foundations in a way that promotes social justice requires an examination of the culture of schools, both historically and currently. Historicizing the culture of schools helps to reveal institutional injustices and oppressions that disproportionately affect socially marginalized peoples (see Anderson, 1988; Tyack, 2003; Willinsky 1998; Adams, Bell, & Griffin, 1997). In addition, students should be provided with an understating of what Patricia Hill Collins (2000) calls the "matrix of oppression", that is, an understanding of the ways in which oppressions intersect. There are several resources that exist to aid in engaging in explicit discussions of privilege and oppression. Peggy McIntosh's (2000) article on white privilege and male privilege, originally written in 1988, has been reprinted in many places and is still one of the most widely used read-ings to discuss privilege. McIntosh defines privilege in terms of "unearned assets" about which people were "meant to remain oblivious." One of the most helpful aspects of her definition is that it explains why people are typ-ically unaware of their privilege. Naming and revealing privilege through classroom discussions makes people accountable and requires us to think about what we will do with our new knowledge; activist teaching challenges people to reflect and act on ways to lessen privilege and promote equity.

In our efforts to teach teachers how to promote equity in their class-rooms, we need to also make conscious efforts to minimize power inequi-ties in the university classroom. There is a large body of research about the ways in which the "culture of schools" reflect white, middle class ways of being (Hinchey, 2004; McLaren, 2003). As a result of the ways in which dominant culture is reflected in institutional school practices, white people and middle class students are often encouraged to claim space in the class-room while students of color and students of working class backgrounds learn to relinquish space. This happens in a variety of nuanced ways. First, white, middle class students often enter with the "cultural capital" (Bour-dieu, 1986) to know how to behave in a way that will be rewarded by main-stream teachers (Nieto, 1999). Second, mainstream teachers often use a "deficit perspective" in trying to understand students of color and their families (Delgado-Gaitan, 1992; Flores, Cousin, & Diaz, 1991; Ladson-Bill-ings, 1994; Nieto, 1999). This deficit perspective leads to devaluing stu-dents' ways of being such they would be less likely to participate. Heterosexism writ large creates an atmosphere in which many gay and les-bian students fear coming out in the classroom which impedes their ability to claim voice and speak from experience. In the all-women pre-service ele-mentary education classes I have taught, often the white middle class women's voices predominated in the classroom, especially at the beginning of the semester. In weekly reflection papers, the few students of color and working-class students in the course would privately share personal thoughts about classroom texts that diverged from their peers and would share opinions of dissent or frustration with racist and classist statements made by classmates. As an instructor I had to consciously work to encour-age marginalized students to voice their opinions in class and create exer-cises that allowed for anonymous voice in the classroom (Bettez, forthcoming). Explicitly naming oppression in the classroom assisted in creating entryways for underprivileged students to contribute their experi-ences in ways that could be validated.

The most useful text I have found to explain oppression is Allan Johnson's book *Privilege, Power, and Difference* (2001), which provides a theo-retical model for thinking about systems of privilege. Johnson argues that we must incorporate words such as sexism and racism into discussions of difference stating that, "we have to reclaim these lost and discredited words so that we can use them to name and make sense of the truth of what's going on" (p. 13). With pre-service teachers, it is imperative that we move beyond decontextualized discussions of race, class, and gender to highly contextualized discussions of racism, sexism, classism and other forms of oppression. It is through these explicit discussions that pre-service teachers may gain the greatest understandings of the experiences of their marginalized students.

In order to expect pre-service teachers to engage in such discussions, we must provide them with the tools and vocabulary they need to address these complex issues (in addition to Johnson's book, another helpful text is Lynn Weber's 2001 book *Understanding Race, Class, Gender, and Sexuality: A Conceptual Framework*). Once students gain theoretical and conceptual frameworks, it is important to augment the meaning of those frameworks with personal narratives about the intersectionality of race, class, and gender (see Andersen & Collins, 2001; Rothenberg, 2001; Fiske-Rusciano & Cyrus, 2004; Tea, 2003). Reading personal narratives often helps pre-service teachers to subsequently relate the theories they learn to their observations in the classrooms in which they student teach. Furthermore, personal stories help remind pre-service teachers that the actions they take can have a direct impact on individual students' lives implicating them to take responsibility to consciously counteract imbalances of power and privilege.

There are a variety of ways to approach teaching about privilege, power, and oppression. In my work I have found that the key to engendering personal transformation among pre-service teachers is to make the discussions of oppression explicit, provide students with vocabulary and a framework to discuss social justice issues, and contextualize theoretical issues with personal stories. Discussions of race, class, gender, and sexuality should address issues of racism, classism, sexism, and heterosexism. Pre-service teachers who acquire contextualized knowledge on the various manifestations of oppression—internalized, institutional, social, and individual—are better equipped to understand and respond to the complexity of their students' lives.

MAINTAINING COMPASSION FOR STUDENTS

The need to have compassion for students when teaching for social justice may seem too obvious to warrant mentioning, but I recognize my own need for constant reminders and assume that others might need them as well. In her essay, "Teaching for Hope: The Ethics of Shattering World Views" Megan Boler (2003) describes her struggles as a teacher of social foundations. Boler says that privileged students would often prefer not to think critically about issues of race, class, gender, and sexuality. Students frequently find their worldviews being challenged, leading them to become angry and defensive in response to being asked to engage in analyses of power and oppression. Teaching about social justice in many cases is what Boler calls a "pedagogy of discomfort." In response to this pedagogy, Boler argues that, "a particular compassion might be required for those who feel their 'self' is being annihilated and who are angrily protesting because they need something to replace what I am threatening to take away" (p. 126). Compassion, Boler explains, requires that one show responsibility and willingness to be there for another's suffering.

In my experience of teaching, I've watched students genuinely struggle when experiencing a pedagogy of discomfort. The struggle often leads to resistance, but eventually the resistance frequently leads to breakthroughs of new understanding and subsequent action. For example, in a multicultural education course I taught (with a co-teacher) for pre-service teachers, we had many discussions about the use of Black Vernacular English in the classroom. As we taught about the importance of validating students' home languages; we had one student who continually resisted, stating that she believed all students needed to be taught "proper" English and that she would not tolerate any other ways of speaking in her classroom as an elementary school teacher. We shared months of dialogue through reflection papers, in which she expressed anger and frustration. In her final paper she wrote:

> My belief from the beginning of the semester that students should use my language instead of their own slowly transformed over the course of the semester....My future classroom will be accepting of different types of language while continually teaching American Mainstream English in formal writing and discussion.

In great detail she described the process of her transformation, making reference to specific texts and dialogues that furthered her thinking.

Boler and hooks appeal to Buddhist teachings in an effort to understand and explain the role of feelings in the classroom. Boler foregrounds the writing of Buddhist psychologist Mark Epstein whose dialectical model of emotions helps explain and understand that, "the angry resistance of those who feel threatened in our classrooms is also a complex cry for recognition and care" (p. 120). As previously mentioned, bell hooks (1994) often evokes the writings of Buddhist Thich Nhat Hanh who "speaks of the teacher as healer" (p. 14). Buddhist Sharon Salzberg provides some guidance on how to enact compassion. Salzberg states that "kindness is compassion in action" (p. 5). She defines kindness towards others as an effort to pay attention to others and truly be present with them. Thus one of the ways we can give compassion to our students is to take the time to listen to them, hear them, pay attention to them, and recognize the ways they may be hurting.

I also experience discomfort as I listen to students' hurtful comments which sometimes evoke anger; however, the more I teach, the more I realize that holding onto my anger is not beneficial to either me or my students. Last semester, halfway through teaching a social foundations/ multicultural education course, I read Boler's article. As a result of her writing about compassion, I made an increasingly conscious effort to display acts of kindness to my students. As I enacted increasing compassion, I found students' resistance begin to dissipate which increased my empathy and allowed for greater room for growth for both my students and myself. Compassion and kindness can be demonstrated in everyday acts such as posing questions when grading papers rather than focusing on what students "did wrong"; creating spaces where voices of dissent are validated; making a concerted effort to reach out to students; creating opportunities for students to share stories and ask questions; and taking the time to ask students how they are doing, especially when there is some indication that a student is struggling with something. Taking the time to display kindness to students, true heartfelt kindness, can increase students' self-efficacy. Salzberg states:

> If ability is not a preordained, limited commodity, then our potential to grow, to understand, to love, to connect is significantly nourished by what we believe about ourselves. This is one of the great fruits of the kindness we receive from others—it supports our sense of being someone deserving of love, someone who can in turn accomplish something…(p. 10)

As teachers, we can enact compassion through displays of kindness which can assist our students in moving through their fear and trust in their ability to cope in the face of challenges to their worldviews.

Another tactic that has increased my empathy and compassion toward resistant students is recognizing the depth of what it means for them to examine alternative ways of viewing the world. As their worldviews shift, so do their relationships to friends and family. As students learn more about how oppression operates often they begin to see for the first time how, not only they, but also their parents, friends, and other family members, benefit from privilege and act in racist, sexist, and classist ways. Choosing to change their personal behaviors and perhaps to challenge others' oppressive behaviors for many of them means creating conflict and/or distance from people they love. These actions carry real pain. Recognizing that pain, and the difficulty of the choices students need to make as they acquire new knowledge about privilege, power, and oppression, assists me in being patient and compassionate with my students.

At the same time, there is a delicate balance between compassion and critique. Extending kindness to others, "doesn't mean that we become complacent or passive about naming wrongdoing as wrong or about seeking change, sometimes forcefully, with our whole heart" (Salzberg, p. 40). Maintaining a commitment to activist teaching means that we must teach in ways that challenge students to critically examine their worldviews. Social justice education requires that we learn to challenge and critique in ways that are compassionate.

BELIEVING THAT CHANGE TOWARD SOCIAL JUSTICE IS POSSIBLE

bell hooks argues that, "To educate as the practice of freedom is a way of teaching that anyone can learn" (p. 13). Educators must believe that anyone can learn and a "professor must genuinely *value* everyone's presence" (p. 8). Philosophical and scientific teachings spanning many years tell us that change is constant. The challenge is to create change that increases social justice. Johnson argues that "the greatest barrier to change is that dominant groups don't see the trouble as *their* trouble, which means they don't feel obliged to do something about it" (p. 140). If we believe Johnson's statement then there is hope in education because educators can help dominant groups to recognize that the trouble of privilege and oppression is everyone's problem and therefore everyone's responsibility. Johnson explains that "participating is all it takes to involve us" (p. 141) in society's troubles and it doesn't mean that we are bad people or that we're doing anything wrong. The flip side is that participating is "all it takes to give us the potential to be a part of the solution, for when we see how we're connected to the problem, we can also see how we can make a difference by choosing differently as we participate in making systems happen" (Johnson, 2001, p. 141). If we recognize that we can count on change, then we can believe social systems will indeed change as a result of our participation in them.

This belief that we can effect change on social systems as individuals must be transmitted to our students. As I describe the frustrations of teaching privileged, resistant students about issues of power and oppression, people sometimes ask me why I do this work. I do this work because I truly believe in the power of transformative education. I recognize that the frustration I feel, although it stems from a very different place, is the same as the frustration that my students feel. If either of us give up then there is no hope. I have to believe that what I do has the power to make change toward the promotion of equity. Similarly students have to believe that they have the power to make conscious change in their lives and that what they do to promote equity makes a difference. As teachers we can work to help students recognize and utilize their power to effect change.

One way to motivate students is to instill in them what Boler describes as "critical hope." Critical hope "recognizes that we live within systems of inequality in which privilege, such as white and male privilege, comes at the expense of the freedom of others" (p. 128). Critical hope entails a responsibility to choose "habits of being" (hooks) that promote justice. Clear explanations of what is lost and what is gained in doing social justice work might be needed in order to promote a sense of hope to those who are experiencing suffering as their worldviews are challenged (Boler, 2003, p. 130). We can also remind students that we don't have to deal with everything. Johnson's advice is: "Think small, humble, and doable rather than large, heroic, and impossible" (p. 167). In those difficult moments as teachers when it feels like what we are doing isn't making a difference, we must remind ourselves that change takes time but it is always possible. In addition, we need to pass that message along to our students and work to promote a sense of critical hope.

EXERCISING SELF-CARE

There is a high level of emotion involved in working for social justice. hooks, Boler, and even Freire (in his discussions of the need for love and humility) all write about the emotion involved in doing social justice work. However, there are relatively few writings that emphasize the need for those of us teaching to promote social justice to exercise self care. I would argue that activist work requires self-care of the mind, body, and spirit. In academia we are often best at promoting care of the intellectual mind; however, this is done sometimes at the expense of emotional, physical, and spiritual health. Teaching students to promote justice at the expense of their own health is antithetical to the goals of promoting social justice. Because a core component of social justice is promoting *well-being* (recall Bell's definition of social justice as including people who are "physically and psychologically safe and secure"), any time we are not taking care of ourselves we are working against our cause. Furthermore, we cannot be fully present for others if we do not take care of ourselves.

Professors can model to students that this work can be accomplished in a way that maintains health and sanity. This is not easy in academia; the institutional structure often requires more than full-time attendance to the job and the work is never done. The demands are at times increased for professors of color who, in addition to other work, are often asked to sit on committees or be involved in activities related to or representing people of color (Cleveland, 2004; TuSmith & Reddy, 2002). However, although the institutional structure of academia often prohibits self-care, there are those who do successfully care for themselves in mind, body, and spirit. Some of the ways that professors have modeled to me that they exercise self-care include playing music (two of my favorite professors regularly play instruments), describing the responsibilities they fulfill with their families, and discussing the benefits of exercise in their lives.

Since we all have varying needs, wants, and desires, each individual must personally determine what self-care means in her or his life. There are a variety of ways to care for self. One way is through balance and exercise. I do my best to exercise regularly. Sometimes I combine exercise with work, such as reading on the elliptical machine, but often I allow myself to enjoy the pleasure of letting my body take precedence over my mind, indulging in a variety of activities. I dance whenever possible—bellydance, salsa, cumbia, merenge, and hip hop. I have taken many years of martial arts and have found that training to be both relaxing and invigorating at the same time. Martial arts classes force me to free my mind from all my worries as I concentrate on sparring, katas, or whatever task at hand that requires me to be fully present in the moment. Furthermore, learning particularly difficult forms or defending myself against formidable opponents reminds me that I have the potential to overcome great obstacles. Many friends and mentors of mine practice yoga, describing similar benefits. One trick I have learned to help maintain time to exercise is to schedule it in my calendar like an appointment so that when people inquire about my free time I can honestly say that during those times I am not available.

A second way to exercise self-care is to be responsible to and spend time with friends and family. The nature of being an academic is that the work never ends. Effective teaching requires planning, providing students with detailed feedback on their work, and mentoring, all of which take time. It is easy to work non-stop and consequently work through meals, evade responsibilities at home, and skip out on leisure events with friends and family. Living out social justice politics means that we should also strive to fulfill our responsibilities towards our friends and family, whatever those may be. I have found that the time I spend nurturing relationships with friends and family ultimately help me in my work because they serve as my support system. It has been important for me to cultivate relationships both with people who help me leave work behind and people who support me in my academic work. The night the man tried to come into my apartment, after calling the police, I immediately called a longtime activist, Latina friend who was able to support me emotionally and also understand the depth of my subsequent conflict of feeling disconnected from the community service work I formerly did. After listening to my story, she reminded me of the importance of my work and what it means for me to be claiming space as a Latina in the academy. Her support aided me in following through on writing this piece.

Third, maintaining energy for activist teaching can be aided by spending time doing other things you love. The work of a scholar in many ways is sedentary and solitary. For some people it is important to counteract that by spending quality time outdoors. One of my mentors takes time every week to do something outdoors: hiking, kayaking, running. For others, quiet time is needed. In the past two years I have allowed myself the indulgence of reading for pleasure. I give myself time to read novels because I enjoy them, but I find that the stories I read enhance my life and activate my imagination. Those of us committed to the promotion of equity will often find that many of our leisure activities intersect with our social justice goals. For example, I joined a book club so that I can fulfill my desire to counteract the solitary work of research and enjoy time with a group of people; however, the book club has a focus on international women which allows me to gain a greater understanding of people who are different from me which enhances my work. I am also involved in community work with Spanish-speaking Latinas.

A fourth way to practice self-care is to ask for support from mentors and colleagues, something I will address further in the next section. In many ways self-care is very individualized beyond the basics of food and shelter because we have personalized needs and desires. Some of us feel rejuvenated when we have quality alone time while others of us are most energized by spending time with others. As activist teachers, we need to identify what activities we can engage in that make us feel happy and healthy and make a concerted effort to care for ourselves in the best ways possible. We also need to encourage self-care in our students. Self-care should nourish our mind, body, and spirit. To do this requires finding ways to take care of ourselves and others in ways that strengthen, rather than counteract, our politics.

BUILDING CRITICAL COMMUNITIES

Working as a scholar and a teacher in many ways is lonely work. Research and writing is most often conducted in isolation. Even when such work is collaborative, there are several components that may be conducted individually. Although I personally have had the benefit of co-teaching many classes, most teachers work by themselves. Teachers interact with students, but the act of preparing for teaching is usually a solitary process. Western culture promotes individualism and many of us believe that we must strive to take care of ourselves and accomplish work on our own. Contrary to the ideology of individualism and competition, I think that a key component of effective activist social justice teaching is creating strong support networks and encouraging our students to do the same. One way to do this is to build critical communities. These communities can be made up of scholars and teachers, but can also be composed of friends and family.

By community I am referring to two or more people who share common interests. I use the term "critical" in the way that it is used to define "critical pedagogy" such that people, name, reflect, and act on the world. Wink (2000) defines critical as "seeing beyond" and says, "it means looking within and without and seeing more deeply the complexities of teaching and learning" (p. 29). Thus, critical communities in this context refers to the gathering of two or more people who—through critically conscious dialogue and sharing—support each other and further each other's critical thinking.

Critical communities can be formal or informal. Formal critical communities include reading or writing groups about the topic of teaching, mentor relationships, collaborative teaching, and work groups such as a group of people coming together to collectively present on activist teaching at a conference. Informal critical communities include interactions such as conversations between colleagues in a community office, discussions about teaching in the hallways, and chats over coffee about teaching. Informal critical communities always have the potential to become more formal. For example, informal conversations about teaching practices between colleagues may turn into a panel presentation at a conference, a workshop at schools, and/or a community project.

A friend of mine recently reminded me that it is a skill to seek support and build community. Some of us have the capacity to build community with relatively little effort while others struggle to create community. Women's studies scholars can serve as models on building community. In the 1970s women of color began to engage in informal critical conversations about the missing voices of women of color in women's studies texts and classrooms. Those conversations resulted in the 1983 publication of one of the most widely known foundational texts in women's studies, *This Bridge Called My Back*. In the introduction to *A Gathering of Spirit*, Beth Brant (1984) describes how the book grew out of a conversation in the living room of then editors of the feminist journal *Sinister Wisdom* Michelle Cliff and Adrienne Rich, when they discussed the need to have an issue devoted to the writing of Indian women. Cliff and Rich purposefully engaged Brant in the conversation to ask her to edit the issue. There are a few cues to building community that we can take from those examples: let passion be a guiding force, utilize anger to motivate action, and seek out people who are experiencing similar struggles. Like Cliff and Rich, activist teachers should seek out connections with individuals who may bring a perspective on something identified as personally lacking. For example, a teacher might actively seek out conversations with people trained in Theatre of the Oppressed (1992) techniques to learn how to incorporate Boal activities in the classroom.

One way I have been able to build critical communities is through informal interactions with people at conferences. Conferences provide a venue for finding people with common interests. I have also built critical communities with some friends who are not in academia. Not everyone is interested in the details of the work I do, but there are some people in my life outside of my field with whom I exchange stories about work. Often times I have found that my friends who are not involved in academia can provide critical insights and suggestions that improve my teaching practice. Building critical community not only means that we need to seek out individuals to engage with but also means that we need to respond to others' needs for engagement. Each time we extend ourselves to share ideas and resources, we are creating critical communities.

There are many people currently engaging in forms of activist teaching to promote social justice. We can seek each other out and engage in conversations to garner support and improve our practice as we gain knowledge from each other on various ways to practice engaged pedagogy. Mentors can connect graduate students with alumni who have similar interests and college instructors can assist pre-service teachers in locating other teachers who actively strive to promote equity in the classroom. We need to support each other as colleagues and we need to teach our students to support each other as they embark upon this work. Building critical communities is an effective way to create support for the difficult work of social justice teaching.

CONCLUSION

There is a part of me that will always long to be involved in direct social service activist community work. The dichotomy that is posed between academia and activism nags at me such that when incidents happen to shake me—encountering a man trying to break into my house—I reassess my academic position and goals. I value community education and hope to find creative ways to maintain a connection to that work through teaching, research, and service. However, as I've watched my students in university classrooms change and grow, I recognize that as their consciousness is raised, the lives of the marginalized children in their current and future classrooms may be positively affected. The belief that my students can and will effect positive change in the lives of others is what compels me to continue this work in the face of challenges; teaching, no matter where it happens is a political act, and all political work to end oppression matters.

Social foundations of education is a ripe field for the enactment of activist social justice teaching, as it has recently shifted to center identity politics and deals with the philosophy, history, sociology, and anthropology of education (Noblit & Hatt-Echeverria, 2003). In this chapter I have tackled the question, "How do we teach to promote social justice?" through the identification of seven components of social justice activist teaching that I have garnered from experience and from listening to and reading about the experiences of others. These seven skills and practices serve as a starting point for further dialogue about how teaching at the university-level can be activist and transformative. Although I hope the seven components I detail in this chapter resonate with readers, what I wish for most is to inspire critical reflection and detailed discussions about the nature and components of social justice activist teaching. It is through reflection and dialogue that we may improve our practice and deepen our accountability to how we enact our politics in the classroom.

REFERENCES

Adams, M., Bell, L. A., & Griffin, P. (Eds.). (1997). *Teaching for diversity and social justice.* New York & London: Routledge.

Andersen, M. L., & Collins, P. H. (Eds.). (2001). *Race, class, and gender: An anthology* (4th ed.). Belmont, CA: Wadsworth.

Anderson, J. D. (1988). *The education of blacks in the south, 1860–1935.* Chapel Hill: The University of North Carolina Press.

Bell, L. A. (1997). Theoretical foundations for social justice education. In M. Adams, L.A. Bell & P. Griffin (Eds.), *Teaching for diversity and social justice* (pp. 3–15). New York: Routledge.

Bettez, S. C. (forthcoming). Teaching white students about white privilege. In T. Austin (Ed.), *"I treat everyone the same..." a resource book for exploring the influence of racism in education—Building antiracist allies in teacher education.*

Boal, A. (1992). *Games for actors and non-actors* (A. Jackson, Trans.). New York: Routledge.

Boler, M. (2003). Teaching for hope: The ethics of shattering world views. In D. Liston & J. Garrison (Eds.), *Teaching, learning, and loving: Reclaiming passion in educational practice* (pp. 117–131). New York: Routledge.

Brant, B. (Ed.). (1984). *A gathering of spirit.* Ithaca, New York: Firebrand Books.

Cleveland, D. (Ed.). (2004). *A long way to go: Conversations about race by African American faculty and graduate students.* New York: Peter Lang.

Collins, P. H. (2000). *Black feminist thought: Knowledge, consciousness, and the politics of empowerment* (Revised tenth anniversary ed.). New York: Routledge.

Delgado-Gaitan, C. (1992). School matters in the Mexican-American home. *American Educational Research Journal, 29,* 495–513.

Felman, J. L. (2001). *Never a dull moment: Teaching and the art of performance: Feminism takes center stage.* New York: Routledge.

Feinberg, W. (1998). *Common schools/uncommon identities: National unity and cultural difference.* New Haven, CT: Yale University Press.

Fiske-Rusciano, R., & Cyrus, V. (Eds.). (2004). *Experiencing race, class, and gender in the United States* (4th ed.). Mountain View, CA: Mayfield Publishing Company.

Flores, B., Cousin, P. T., & Diaz, E. (1991). Critiquing and tranforming the deficit myths about learning and culture. *Language Arts, 68*(5), 369–379.

Freire, P. (2003). *Pedagogy of the oppressed* (30th Anniversary ed.). New York: Continuum.

Hinchey, P. (2004). *Becoming a critical educator: Defining a classroom identity, designing a critical pedagogy.* New York: Counterpoints.

hooks, b. (1994). *Teaching to transgress: Education as the practice of freedom.* New York: Routledge.

Hytten, K., & Warren, J. (2003). Engaging whiteness: How racial power gets reified in education. *Qualitative Studies in Education, 16*(1), 65–89.

Johnson, A. G. (2001). *Privilege, power, and difference.* Boston: McGraw Hill.

Ladson-Billlings, G. (1994). *The dreamkeepers: Succesful teachers of African American children.* San Francisco: Jossey-Bass Publishers.

McIntosh, P. (2000). White privilege and male privilege. In M. L. Andersen & P. H. Collins (Eds.), *Race, class, and gender: An anthology* (pp. 95–105). Belmont, CA: Wadsworth.

McLaren, P. (2003). Life in schools: An introduction to critical pedagogy in the foundations of education. (4th ed). Boston: Allyn & Bacon.

Mirochnik, E., & Sherman, D. C. (2002). *Passion and pedagogy: Relation, creation, and transformation in teaching.* New York: Peter Lang.

Moraga, C., & Anzaldúa, G. (Eds.). (1983). *This Bridge Called my Back: Writings by Radical Women of Color* (2nd ed.). New York: Kitchen Table Women of Color Press.

Nieto, S. (1999). *The light in their eyes: Creating multicultural learning communities.* New York: Teachers College Press.

Noblit, G., & Hatt-Echeverria, B. (2003). *The future of educational studies.* New York: Peter Lang.

Rothenberg, P. S. (Ed.). (2001). *Race, class, and gender in the United States: An integrated study* (5th ed.). New York: Worth Publishers.

Salzberg, S. (2005). *The force of kindness.* Boulder: Sounds True.

Silberman, M. (1998). *Active training: A handbook of techniques, designs, case examples, and tips* (2nd ed.). San Francisco: Jossey-Bass/Pfeiffer.

Shome, R. (1999). Whiteness and the politics of location: Postcolonial reflections. In T. K. Nakayama & J. N. martin (Eds.), *Whiteness: The communication of social identity* (pp. 107–128). Tousand Oaks, CA: SAGE Publications.

Shor, I. (1992). *Empowering education: Critical teaching for social change.* Chicago: The University of Chicago Press.

Tea, M. (Ed.). (2003). *Without a net: The female experience of growing up working class.* Emeryville, CA: Seal Press.

TuSmith, B., & Reddy, M. T. (Eds.). (2002). *Race in the college classroom: pedagogy and politics.* New Jersey: Rutgers University Press.

Tyack, D. (2003). *Seeking common ground: Public schools in a diverse society.* Cambridge: Harvard University Press.

Weber, L. (2001). *Understanding race, class, gender, and sexuality: A conceptual framework.* Boston: McGraw Hill.

Willinsky, J. (1998). *Learning to divide the world: Education at empire's end.* Minneapolis: University of Minnesota Press.

Wink, J. (2000). *Critical pedagogy: Notes from the real world.* New York: Longman.

ABOUT THE CONTRIBUTORS

Silvia Cristina Bettez is an assistant professor in the Department of Educational Leadership and Cultural Foundations at the University of North Carolina at Greensboro. She wrote her essay while completing her doctoral work at the Univeristy of North Carolina at Chapel Hill. Her areas of interest include intersections of race, class, gender, and sexuality; critical multicultural education; qualitative methods; and feminist pedagogy. Before returning to graduate school, she worked for several years as a community educator and activist. She may be reached at scbettez@uncg.edu.

William R. Black is an assistant professor in the Department of Educational Leadership and Policy Studies at University of South Florida. He pursued Latin American studies degrees at the undergraduate and Masters levels, and has worked with legal rights organizations that served immigrant communities in Florida and Texas. Subsequently, he became a bilingual elementary teacher, an elementary school administrator, and a graduate student again as he completed his doctoral studies in Educational Administration at The University of Texas at Austin. He may be reached at WBlack@coedu.usf.edu.

Richard Conley received his PhD in Educational Leadership and Policy Studies from North Carolina State University. He was formerly an assistant principal and principal at several high-performing middle schools. His research interests include organizational efficacy, cultural cognition, and global education. He is widely traveled, having spent six years in the U.S. Merchant Marines and has studied overseas. He may be reached at reconley@comcast.net.

Matthew Ezzell is a doctoral student in sociology at the University of North Carolina at Chapel Hill. His research interests are in the reproduction of

Unsettling Beliefs: Teaching Theory to Teachers, pages 297–300
Copyright © 2008 by Information Age Publishing
All rights of reproduction in any form reserved.

and resistance to race/class/gender inequality, feminism and feminist activism, and anti-violence education. He has been active in anti-violence movements since 1998 and worked as a full-time community educator and advocate in the rape crisis movement before beginning graduate school. He may be reached at matt.ezzell@gmail.com.

William Gaudelli is an associate professor of social studies and education in the Department of Arts and Humanities at Teachers College, Columbia University. His research interests include global education, building democratic classrooms, reading visual texts, and teacher development. He received a doctorate in social studies education from Rutgers University in 2000 and subsequently taught social studies education at the University of Central Florida in Orlando. His secondary teaching experience includes a decade at Hunterdon Central Regional High School in Flemington, New Jersey where he taught world studies, anthropology, multicultural studies, and U.S. history. He has published a variety of pieces in scholarly journals, including *Teaching Education, Teacher Education Quarterly, Society and Culture,* and the *American Journal of Psychology,* along with a book, *World Class: Teaching and Learning in Global Times* (Erlbaum, 2003) which explores the intersection of theory and practice in global classrooms. He can be reached at gaudelli@tc.edu.

Beth Hatt is an assistant professor of educational administration and foundations at Illinois State University where she teaches research methods and social foundations of education. She received her Ph.D. from the University of North Carolina at Chapel Hill. Working against inequities in education, her research focuses on the educational histories of youth offenders and smartness as a cultural construct in schools. She may be reached at bhattec@ilstu.edu.

Rob Helfenbein is an assistant professor of teacher education at Indiana University–Purdue University Indianapolis, adjunct faculty in the Department of Geography, and a researcher in the Center for Urban and Multicultural Education in the School of Education. A former middle and high school social studies teacher, he offers courses in Middle School Methods, Teaching Secondary Social Studies, Education and American Context, and graduate level courses in Social Foundations of Education and Curriculum Theory.

Sherick A. Hughes is an assistant professor of Curriculum and Instruction at the University of Maryland. He pursued studies of race, class, gender, and education policy at the BA, MA, MPA, and Ph.D. levels. He was conferred a doctoral degree from the Culture, Curriculum, and Change program at The University of North Carolina at Chapel Hill. He has worked extensively in the pre-K–16 arena for and with Black, White, and Latino students and their adult stakeholders in both rural and urban educational settings. At the time he began writing the chapter for this book, he was an assistant professor at the University of Toledo. Dr. Hughes finds that meeting the daily challenges of resistance in teaching social theory to his students hinges upon his ability to connect his theoretical and practical experiences to theirs. He may be reached at shughes@alumni.unc.edu.

Kathy Hytten is an Associate Professor in the Department of Educational Administration and Higher Education at Southern Illinois University, Carbondale. She received her undergraduate degree in philosophy and religion from Colgate University and her PhD in social foundations of education, specializing in educational philosophy, from the University of North Carolina at Chapel Hill. She currently teaches graduate and undergraduate courses in philosophy of education, sociology of education, cultural diversity, social justice and globalization studies. In her research, she aims to make theoretically abstract ideas useful, accessible, and meaningful. Toward that end, she has published essays on pragmatism, cultural studies, whiteness theory, and education for social justice. She may be reached at khytten@siu.edu.

Kip Kline recently completed his PhD in Philosophy of Education at Indiana University with a dissertation titled, *Represent!: Hip-Hop and the Self-Aesthetic Relation.* He also recently became assistant professor of education leadership and foundations at Lewis University in the Chicago area. He teaches courses in philosophy of education, multicultural education, and qualitative research. In addition to pursuing the confluence of urban youth culture, philosophy, and education, his research interests include American pragmatism, radical hermeneutics and spirituality, and popular culture. He may be reached at klinech@lewisu.edu.

Erik Malewski is an assistant professor of curriculum studies at Purdue University. He is interested in scholarship involving critical theory, cultural studies, and post-structuralism as they inform the reconceptualization of curriculum and the social contexts of education. His most recent work has focused on technology and multiculturalism within teacher education, suicide, curriculum and public policy, and the internationalization of teacher education through study abroad. He is currently working on an edited book addressing intergenerational conversations on the state of the field of curriculum studies.

John P. Myers received his PhD from the University of Toronto in Curriculum, Teaching and Learning with a specialization in Comparative, International and Development Education. His research interests include cross-cultural approaches to citizenship education, social studies teachers' political activism, global and human rights education, and the implications of globalization for social education. He may be reached at myersjp@pitt.edu.

Robert Pleasants recently completed his doctoral degree in the Culture, Curriculum and Change Program in the School of Education at the University of North Carolina at Chapel Hill. His research interests are in teaching feminism, men's relationship to feminism, and anti-violence education. He is a former high school teacher and has facilitated high school anti-violence programs since 2001. He may be reached at bpleas@email.unc.edu.

Avner Segall is an associate professor in the Department of Teacher Education at Michigan State University. He holds an undergraduate degree in History from the Tel Aviv University, Israel and a PhD in Curriculum and Instruction from the University of British Columbia, Canada. In his chapter, he uses his experiences as a teacher educator of social studies student teachers, to explore the role of critical theory in their learning. Specifically, and looking back at the evolution of his own teaching, he uses Henry Giroux's distinction between a "pedagogy of theory" and a "pedagogy of theorizing" to illustrate the challenges that using "theory" alone poses in the educative process of learning to become a critical social studies educator. Theory alone, as a pedagogical approach, he argues, allows—indeed, invites if not encourages—student teachers to disengage from the implication of theory in actual realities of their schools/classroom and from theorizing and implication those, and their own roles in them, in the lived experiences of teaching and learning. He may be reached at avner@msu.edu